RELEASED

COMMODITY CONFLICT

Commodity Conflict

THE POLITICAL ECONOMY OF INTERNATIONAL COMMODITY NEGOTIATIONS

L. N. RANGARAJAN

CORNELL UNIVERSITY PRESS
ITHACA, NEW YORK

First published 1978 by Cornell University Press.

International Standard Book Number 0-8014-1154-8

Library of Congress Catalog Card Number 77-4625

Printed in Great Britain

CONTENTS

'Ye have eaten up the vineyard; the spoil of the poor is in your houses.'

Isaiah 3 : 14

'Chakramekam na vartate.' (One wheel does not move the chariot of progress.')

The Arthasastra of Kautilya

'A peace is of the nature of a conquest.
For then both parties nobly are subdued
And neither party loser.'

Henry IV, Part II, Act IV, Scene 2

PREFACE

I am indebted to many organisations and individuals for help in writing this book. The Government of India permitted me sabbatical leave for a year and a half; I am particularly grateful to Jagat Mehta for his constant encouragement, in both his official and personal capacities. The Ford Foundation, in New York and New Delhi, was generous and prompt in providing financial support; my special thanks to Peter Ruof and Vijay Pande. Needless to say, neither the Government of India nor the Ford Foundation are in any way responsible for the views and opinions expressed in this book.

The preliminary draft was written at the Center for International Affairs, Harvard University, and the manuscript finalised at the Institute of Development Studies at the University of Sussex, Brighton, England. My thanks to all those in the two institutions who made my stay both enjoyable and fruitful.

My early attempts at studying commodity conflicts were encouraged by Dharma Kumar and Prashanta Pattanaik of the Delhi School of Economics. The first draft was read with painstaking thoroughness and commented on perceptively by Benjamin Brown, Hugh Corbet, Jorge Dominguez, Angus Hone, Stephen Krasner, Joseph Nye, Richard Perkins and Raymond Vernon. I have benefited from discussions with Gerard Curzon, Carlos Fortin, Reginald Green, J.P. Hayes, David Henderson, K.B. Lall, M.G. Mathur, Bagicha Minhas, Karti Sandilya and Hans Singer. Whether they agreed with me or not, officials of FAO and UNCTAD shared their experience and knowledge without reservation; my thanks, in particular, to Indrajit Chadha, Bernard Chidzero, Anthony Leeks, Richard Perkins and Al Viton. If I list all names alphabetically and do not single out any for special mention, it is only because there is no way of· ranking in order kindness and friendship.

If this book is at all readable, it is due to my wife's constant admonition to eschew gobbledegook; her enthusiasm was as unflagging as her patience was inexhaustible. I am specially grateful to Zamir Ansari and Hugh Corbet for help in getting this book published.

I am grateful to Eva Morvay and Darshan Singh for assistance in typing the draft and the final text.

My debt to so many is proof that any merit this book has is due to them; the faults are entirely mine.

New Delhi, 12 April 1977   L.N. Rangarajan

ABBREVIATIONS

'77'	Group of '77' (developing countries)
AASM	Associated African States and Madagascar
ACP	African, Caribbean and Pacific (Lomé Convention)
ASEAN	Association of South East Asian Nations
BET	Basic export tonnage
CAP	Common Agricultural Policy of the EEC
CIEC	Conference on International Economic Co-operation
c.i.f.	Cost, insurance, freight
CIPEC	Council of Copper Exporting Countries
CSA	Commonwealth Sugar Agreement
DAC	Development Assistance Committee (of the OECD)
DC	Developed countries
EEC	European Economic Community
ESCAP	Economic and Social Commission for Asia and the Pacific (of the UN)
FAC	Food Aid Convention
FAO	Food and Agriculture Organisation
FEDECAME	Federation of Central American Coffee Exporting Countries
f.o.b.	Free on board
GATT	General Agreement on Tariffs and Trade
GSP	General Scheme of Preferences (Generalised System of Preferences)
IACO	Inter-African Coffee Organisation
IBA	International Bauxite Association
IBRD	International Bank for Reconstruction and Development (World Bank)
ICICA	Interim Co-ordinating Committee on International Commodity Agreements
IEA	International Energy Agency
IMF	International Monetary Fund
ITO	International Trade Organisation
LDC	Less-developed country
LME	London Metal Exchange
LTA	Long-term Textile Agreement
MCA	Monetary Compensation Amount (of the CAP)

Abbreviations

MFA	Multi-Fibre Agreement
mfn	Most favoured nation
MTN	Multilateral Trade Negotiations
NIEO	New International Economic Order
NOEDEC	Non-oil exporting developing countries
OAMCAF	Organisation of coffee producers of Africa and Malagasy
OEEC	Organisation for European Economic Cooperation
OECD	Organisation for Economic Cooperation and Development
OPEC	Organisation of Petroleum Exporting Countries
SDR	Special drawing rights
SITC	Standard International Trade Classification
SMR	Standard Malaysian Rubber
u.a.	Unit of account (EEC)
UNCTAD	United Nations Conference on Trade and Development
UNIDO	United Nations Industrial Development Organisation
UPEB	Union of Banana Exporting Countries
WTC	Wheat Trade Convention

1 THE ARENA OF CONFLICT

> During the last six years every part of the world's economy has been subjected to the most strains and stresses and none more so than that part which covers the production and marketing of foodstuffs and raw materials.
>
> J.W.F. Rowe, *Markets and Men*

During the first half of the 1970s, the world economy has been buffeted by the collapse of the international monetary system, the quadrupling of oil prices, the boom in commodity prices in 1973 and 1974 and by unprecedented inflation, followed by a recession, in almost all major industrialised countries. In this unstable world economic situation, instability has been most marked in trade in primary commodities – foodstuffs, fibres and minerals. Though it was written in 1936, J.W.F. Rowe's pioneering book on the regulation of international commodity trade also began with an almost identical sentiment.[1] Forty years later, the position still remains the same.

Schemes to regulate or control international trade in primary commodities have a history much longer than these 40 years. In 1863, European sugar producers held the first of many conferences to regulate trade in sugar, which was then characterised by cut-throat competition, dumping and 'bounties' (export subsidies). It took them 38 years of negotiations before an agreement could be reached. The Brussels Convention prohibiting dumping and abolishing all direct and indirect bounties was concluded in 1901 and came into force two years later – on 1 September 1903. Though the gap of 40 years between the beginning of negotiations and the coming into force of an agreement meant that sugar production and trade had changed much, the instrument at least put a stop, for some 15 years, to export subsidies. Control schemes were attempted for a few more commodities after the First World War. Sugar, wheat, coffee, tin and rubber – the commodities that are in the forefront of discussions today were also the focus of attention then. Rowe's book was a result of studying these control schemes and those tried out during the Great Depression. By 1939, the schemes had operated in two quite different circumstances – times of scarcity and periods of excess supply over demand.

The Second World War brought an abrupt end to all agreements negotiated in the 1930s. Since 1945, there have been almost continuous negotiations to regulate the trade in one or the other of the major commodities. In this period, the number of commodities considered fit for regulation has expanded from the original five or six to 18; the list is constantly being added to. Most of the studies on commodities nowadays take into account 36 commodities or commodity groups.

Just as the number of commodities under negotiation has increased, so has the number of participants. Before the Second World War, a few European countries could speak not only for themselves but also for their vast colonies. The British and Dutch Governments could negotiate between themselves the regulation of supplies of tea, tin and rubber, knowing that they could control the production and trade policies of all the major producers — undivided India, Ceylon, the Federated Malay States and Dutch East Indies. The rapid increase, due to decolonisation, in the number of independent participants has added to the complexity of conflicts. A concomitant effect of the decolonisation process has been the emergence of a sharp cleavage between the rich and the poor nations of this world. Commodity conflicts have thus become a part of the overall conflict of interests between the developed industrialised nations (the 'North') and the less industrialised exporters of raw materials (the developing 'South'). This division was superimposed on another that had emerged, after the war, between the free market economies of the West and the centrally planned socialist economies of the East. Today's world is divided, like Gaul, into three parts, each with its own ideology, motivation and perception of the other two groups.

Politics and Economics

Commodity trade does not take place in a watertight compartment of its own; it is a part of total international trade in primary commodities and manufactures and, in turn, an integral part of the international economic, monetary and political system. The aim of this book is to analyse commodity conflicts in the context of the prevailing economic order and political environment. Why involve politics in a purely economic activity? Bergsten, Keohane and Nye answer this as follows:

> The political order strongly affects national decisions about economic goals and the leeway given to transnational actors. It is appropriate, therefore, to begin with an analysis of the impact of world politics on the international economic order rather than, as is too often done, introducing politics merely as a constraint on the attainment

of independently determined economic goals.[2]

The framework adopted in this book is based on the one suggested by these three authors. The main argument is that there is a symbiotic relationship between the international economic system and the international political system, each affecting the other. 'The behaviour of Governments on economic issues will be affected by their political calculations, which will in turn be determined by the structure of world politics.' At the same time, the political steps of governments are also based on their economic interests and capabilities. In other words, the perceived national interest of any government is part economic and part political.

The following examples illustrate the linking of different issues by governments for negotiating purposes. In 1971, for instance, the United States linked trade and monetary negotiations together for the sake of getting a better monetary agreement, and there were also references to the need to attain a trade surplus to permit the United States to maintain its worldwide political and military position. At about the same time, the United States linked the reversion of Okinawa to Japan to Japanese agreement to limit its textile exports to the United States; and US troop levels in Germany have for 15 years been linked, at least implicitly, to German willingness to offset the costs of these troops to the US balance of payments. The Arab oil producers' actions on behalf of their political goals of a favourable Middle East settlement have often been almost indistinguishable from their economic goals of increasing revenue from their petroleum resources. Within the European Common Market, complex linkages and trade-offs between issues are commonplace'.

The inter-relationship between politics and economics is not confined only to the formation of the attitudes of governments to negotiations on specific issues. It also affects the very rules by which the international economic system operates. Diaz-Alejandro points out that markets are:

creatures of social and political systems, not mechanisms arising spontaneously and inevitably out of economic necessity. Which markets are allowed to operate and how, which are encouraged and which are repressed — these are political decisions, both nationally and internationally. . . Power, whether military or corporate, abhors an uncontrolled and truly competitive market. It would be an extraordinary world in which asymmetries in military and economic power were not reflected in asymmetries in economic relations.[3]

An economic order devised by a few countries, in the light of their own perceptions of their economic and political self-interest, cannot but be asymmetric in its operation. The distribution of the gains from the operations of such a system cannot automatically be assumed to be fair to all participants; fairness and equitability have to be demonstrated. The point of this statement

> is *not* to argue that the asymmetries in international economic order will inevitably lead to losses for LDCs [less developed countries]. The argument implies that whether or not they gain, or how much they gain, and how much of the burdens of adjustment they are likely to bear, has been of secondary importance to those responsible for setting or changing the rules of the game.

The International Economic System after the Second World War

Most of the countries of the world, with the exception of the centrally planned economies, form part of the international economic order constructed by the industrialised nations, under the hegemonic guidance of the United States. Hegemony is used here in the sense of the precise definition given by Bergsten and co-authors. A hegemonic system is one

> in which one state is able and willing to determine and maintain the essential rules by which relations among states are governed. The hegemonical state not only can abrogate existing rules or prevent the adoption of rules it opposes but can also play the dominant role in constructing new rules. A distinguishing characteristic of a hegemonical system, therefore, is that the preponderant state has both positive and negative power.[4]

Well before the end of the Second World War, serious thought had been given, particularly in the United States and the United Kingdom, to the nature of the economic system that should follow the end of the war. It was inevitable that the recent history of the Depression and the War should have moulded this thinking. The three main motivations that inspired the creators of the order were the fear of unemployment, the belief in the market mechanism as the most efficient means of allocating resources and the need for resource transfers for post-war reconstruction, particularly in Europe. The ground rules of the system were designed to meet these three objectives. It was also planned to have three institutions to oversee the operations of these ground rules. Of these, only two — the International Monetary Fund (IMF) and the World Bank — emerged in the form originally conceived. Stability of exchange rates and transfer of resources for post-war reconstruction were thus assured, at least for a couple of decades.

The third organisation, designed to deal with trade, had a more chequered history. The Conference on Trade and Employment, held in Havana in 1948, agreed on the creation of an International Trade Organisation (ITO). However, the ITO did not come into being because the then President of the United States decided, for fear of defeat, not to submit the treaty concluded at Havana to the US Senate for ratification. In spite of this scuttling of its own idea by the hegemonic power, the principles written into the Havana Charter were not abandoned. While the fate of the ITO was in doubt, a part of the Charter was activated, as a stop-gap measure, in the form of the General Agreement on Tariffs and Trade (GATT). The creation and survival of GATT is due to the fact that it contained the essential provisions to (i) prevent the export of unemployment and (ii) promote more competitive trade by reduction of tariffs on industrial goods. A legal framework was thus established for regulating trade in manufactures; but there were neither ground rules nor an institution for regulating commodity trade.

The commodity agreement part of the Havana Charter also had a kind of existence in the form of the Interim Co-ordinating Committee on International Commodity Agreements (ICICA), a body which, despite the 'Interim' of its title, had a life of 15 years. It was eventually absorbed into the United Nations Conference on Trade and Development (UNCTAD). In the 16 years between the Havana Conference and the first UNCTAD Conference in Geneva in 1964, many changes had taken place both in the structure of commodity trade and in the perceptions of the increasing number of participating governments.

The integration of the economies of Western Europe and the growth of agricultural protection in the European Economic Community (EEC), the growth of multinational corporations and their increasing control over the production and marketing of some commodities, the increasing dependence of Western Europe and Japan on imports of raw materials for their prosperity, political tensions and hostilities which promoted significant changes in the production patterns of some commodities, the changing power balance in the international economic system reflected in prolonged monetary instability — these are a few of the major influences which have affected commodity markets and complicated all international attempts to regulate them. The complexity was increased by the fact that all negotiations took place in an environment of growing divergence between the rich and poor nations.

Changing Attitudes to Commodity Agreements

Even though the Havana Charter was not ratified, the attitudes of the industrialised countries, particularly those of the hegemonic power, towards regulating commodity trade are best seen only in that document. The principles contained in the Charter (extracts from which are reproduced in Appendix 1) can be summarised as follows. Control of production or trade is to be resorted to only in exceptional circumstances, such as burdensome surpluses or serious unemployment. Prices can be regulated only to moderate pronounced fluctuations. Market forces must be allowed to operate with the maximum possible freedom. There must be absolute equality of power between the producing and consuming members in commodity agreements, though the burdens of regulation are to be born only by the exporting countries. To this set of principles actually written into the Charter, one must add the tacit agreement among the industrialised nations that GATT would concern itself only with trade in manufactured goods and that protectionism in the agricultural sector would be condoned. To a very large extent, the attitudes of most developed countries to regulation of commodity trade still conform to this philosophy.

For a variety of political and economic reasons, a commodity boom occurred at the time of the Korean War. From that high point, the prices of primary commodities not only continued to decline steadily but were often subjected to violent gyrations. On the other hand, throughout the latter half of the 1950s and the 1960s, trade in industrial goods expanded at a fast pace. The less industrialised poor countries, being unable to share in the growing world trade in manufactures, bore the brunt of the instability and reduction in commodity prices. These two factors highlighted the importance of foreign exchange earnings from the export of commodities for implementing the development plans of the poor countries. International commodity agreements were conceived of as one way of stabilising export earnings and, additionally, of providing a mechanism for increasing the transfer of resources from the developed to the developing countries. The Recommendation of the First UNCTAD Conference specifies the 'basic objective' of international commodity agreements as 'stimulating a dynamic and steady growth. . .so as to provide [the developing countries] with expanding resources for their economic and social development'.[5] Thus, the development objective was not only added to the other aims of commodity agreements but, in fact, became the most important one from the point of view of developing countries. The Havana Conference was a 'Trade and Employment' conference; the 1964 UNCTAD Conference was a 'Trade and Development' conference. Notwithstanding this change in emphasis, the immediate years after UNCTAD I did not witness any great progress in concluding more agreements. Accepting that equitable trading was a necessary ingredient of development in no way helped the resolution of commodity conflicts.

The lack of progress was mainly due to a fundamental difference over the purpose of commodity agreements. Since the early 1960s, every commodity negotiation has had to contend with the conflict between the stability objective preferred by the developed countries and the objective of additional transfer of resources sought by the developing. Seeing that the former had created for themselves an Organisation for Economic Co-operation and Development (OECD), the developing countries banded themselves together as the Group of '77'. The '77'|'s disappointment at the lack of progress in the commodity trade sector was expressed at their ministerial meeting in Algiers in March 1967, held preparatory to the second UNCTAD Conference. The Charter of Algiers listed 18 different commodities and commodity groups as requiring international action; it also revived the pre-war concept of co-operative action among producers to 'defend and improve their terms of trade'. The idea that producers alone could act as a group ran directly counter to the principle of the Havana Charter of equality of power between producers and consumers. Since the developed countries still subscribed to the Havana Charter philosophy, the second UNCTAD, held in New Delhi in 1968, failed to agree on this technique. However, the Conference did recommend an action programme for each of the 18 commodities, indicating for some, such as cocoa, even a time-bound programme. The Conference also considered a variety of proposals on the mechanisms to be used to deal with commodity trade problems under various headings – buffer stocks, access to markets and pricing policy.

This plethora of draft resolutions created the impression that, by 1968, the international community had succeeded in (i) identifying the specific commodities for which international agreements were possible and (ii) devising an appropriate mix of techniques for regulating each one. The degree of elaboration that UNCTAD II indulged in was not warranted by the history of commodity arrangements before 1968, nor was progress any more rapid after it. In reporting to the third UNCTAD Conference at Santiago in 1972, the Secretary-General had to acknowledge 'the general lack of progress' giving, as one of the reasons, 'the lack of political will' of interested governments. The virtual stalemate in commodity negotiations for over a decade resulted in the poor countries becoming more and more frustrated.

A consequence of the increasing frustration was the questioning, by the developing countries, of the legitimacy of the economic system itself. Economic negotiations could no longer remain on the 'low road'; they became a part of the 'high road' of political negotiations. As Bergsten and co-authors observe:

> In some systems at some times, the levels of structure and process are relatively well insulated from one another. Basic institutions and practices are accepted as legitimate by all major parties. Economic activity in these systems may involve very little direct political intervention. On the international level, only minor and infrequent attention may be paid to economic affairs by government officials. At other times, however, the rules of the game themselves are called into question by major participants. The system becomes politicised as controversy increases.

At this moment of maximum frustration occurred the dramatic quadrupling of the price of petroleum, brought about purely by producer action. Here was a genuine shock; that anathema of free marketeers, an association of producing countries alone, not only acted cohesively to increase prices and restrict supplies, but the rest of the world, rich or poor, developed or developing, was visibly powerless to do anything about it. This demonstration of power had its effect on both sets of countries. OPEC's success prompted a fear in the rich countries that similar action might well be repeated in other commodities, particularly basic industrial raw materials. The change in attitude in the developed countries towards supplies from the less developed countries has been described by Diaz-Alejandro thus:

> LDC export pessimists, and those in DCs [developed countries] who delight in convincing poor countries of their alleged economic impotence, not long ago used to argue that imports from LDCs were of marginal importance to the rich, and their purchase was presented almost as an act of DC altruism. This altruism, of course, could be

terminated if LDCs were naughty; witness the elimination of imports of Cuban sugar into the United States during the early 1960s and the boycott of Iranian oil in the 1950s. Hypotheses regarding the importance of cheap raw materials and primary products from the South for the prosperity of the North were brushed aside during the late 1950s and 1960s by pointing to the small percentages of those imports in gross national products. Arguments about supply reliability were also deemed mistaken or naive: it was all a matter of price, it was noted. Only frantic radicals or Third World types could be expected to take seriously the notion that Northern foreign policies had anything at all to do with assuring those countries with cheap and reliable supplies of primary products from the South. Events in commodity markets during 1972 and 1973, particularly the oil situation, have shaken these DC perceptions. Indeed, among some DC observers, attitudes on these matters have gone from indifference or contempt to a somewhat paranoid hysteria.[6]

The poor countries, on the other hand, felt a vicarious sense of triumph at the success of a few of their fellow-members at beating the system; with this came the hope that the producers of other commodities could emulate OPEC and better their lot.

Both the hysteria of the rich and the hope of the poor were proved later to be unfounded. The immediate effect of hysteria meeting resurgent hope was the spirit of confrontation, visibly demonstrated at the Sixth Special Session of the United Nations General Assembly. At this Session, in September 1974, the developing countries called for a revolutionary change in the international economic system. The demand for a 'New International Economic Order' (NIEO) was both incomprehensible and unacceptable to the rich nations, who for long had benefited under a system devised exclusively by them. The external environment in late 1974, when the world was beset simultaneously with monetary instability and high energy prices, was also not conducive to constructive negotiation. While the spirit of confrontation lasted, both developed and developing countries tried to marshal their respective forces. The industrialised nations formed an association of rich importers of oil – the International Energy Agency – deliberately excluding the numerous poor countries who were also importers of oil and, in fact, suffered far more from high energy prices. The developing countries, for their part, convened a Conference on Raw Materials, in Dakar in February 1975, from which the rich producers of primary products were excluded. The Dakar Declaration summarises the perception of the developing countries on the inequality and asymmetry of the international economic system; relevant extracts are reproduced in Appendix 2. The contrast between the Havana Charter and the Dakar Declaration is glaring.

The spirit of confrontation gradually gave way to a realisation in many, though not all, countries that a constructive dialogue was preferable to talking at cross purposes. One of the initiatives to commence a dialogue was the calling, by the President of France, of a Conference on International Economic Co-operation (CIEC). The CIEC was convened with the hope that by reducing the number of participants to a selected list of industrialised nations, oil producers and non-oil exporting developing countries, depoliticisation of the issues would be possible. It was also hoped that, by discussing all aspects of the international economic system, the inter-relationship between trade, energy, monetary and development questions could be effectively recognised. Of the four Commissions established by the CIEC, one was concerned solely with commodity trade (excluding oil). The Seventh Special Session of the UN General Assembly, a year after the Sixth one, also began on a more constructive note.

Beginning a dialogue only implies that negotiations on substantive issues can commence; it does not guarantee the success of the negotiations. The forums of negotiations have now shifted to GATT and UNCTAD. The position at the beginning of 1976 was that the Multilateral Trade Negotiations (MTN) and the fourth UNCTAD Conference at Nairobi would tackle constructively at least some of the problems that beset commodity trade. By early 1977, the MTN was still in its early stages; the state of progress of negotiations at UNCTAD IV and immediately thereafter is reviewed in detail in Chapter 13. The CIEC was stalled, first waiting for UNCTAD IV and then waiting for the American presidential elections.

The evolution of the attitudes of governments to commodity negotiations shows that commodity conflicts can be analysed only in the context of the international economic system as a whole. Apart from the many structural links between commodity trade and the other parts of the system, every government is influenced in its attitude to negotiations by its perception of the fairness of the system itself. Those who feel that it operates unfairly negotiate every instrument with a view to improving equity; others have different priorities.

Vulnerability and Dependence

In the developed countries, the fear of inflation is as potent a motivating factor today as fear of unemployment was in 1945. In the poor countries, the main perception is one of vulnerability, based on the perceived inequity of the system and the frustrations arising from their inability to change it. Apart from the OPEC countries after 1974, the rest of the poor countries have had little voice in determining how the international monetary system is managed; exchange rates may be fixed, floating or managed, may crawl or even wriggle like a snake, but all this is beyond their control. Until recently, many have found themselves powerless to control the multinational corporations' exploitation of their natural resources. Their earnings from commodity exports are unpredictable. In any case, their export commodities buy less and less, caught between declining commodity prices on the one hand and inflation in the price of manufactures on the other. Their markets have shrunk as agricultural protectionism, under the guise of regional integration, has expanded inexorably. They do not even have a voice on the transportation of their export products to the consuming markets. There have been few compensating factors; aid has steadily declined as the debt burden has increased. Few of the targets laid down in the grandiose documents of the First and Second Development Decades have been met. If the poor countries try to industrialise, they find new barriers erected against their manufactures; so-called General Schemes of Preferences bristle with exceptions and safeguards. On top of all this, the high cost of imports of food, fertiliser and fuel threaten to undo the development that has already taken place. No wonder they feel threatened and frustrated.

This is not to argue that there has been no development in the poor countries in the last 30 years. Nor is it implied that all their misfortunes are solely the result of the international economic system. Developing countries have made progress. Their agricultural production in general, and food production in particular, has risen as fast as in the industrialised countries. If their per capita production has not kept pace, this is only the result of falling death rates and rising population. Industrial production in the developing world has, at times, grown even faster than in the developed countries; technology has been transferred; foreign aid has made a contribution to development; and food aid and sales have promoted economic stability. If, in spite of this progress, developing countries feel frustrated, it is because they perceive the international economic system as one which distributes the gains from trade unfairly. The system is seen as asymmetric and one which makes them increasingly peripheral to it. Out of this perceived asymmetry and peripherality arise theories of *dependencia,* exploitation and neo-colonialism.

It is necessary to note that there could be two kinds of dependence. The closely integrated economies of the rich nations also make them increasingly dependent on each other. This integral interdependence increases the range of possible trade-offs between them. Hence it tends to equalise the bargaining power among the participants; none is reduced to a peripheral status. In fact, it could be argued that even the decline in bargaining power of the hegemonic state, the United States, was partly voluntary for the sake of greater political solidarity. Interdependence between the rich nations has thus made them more sensitive to each other. The peripheral dependence of the poor countries is of a different kind. Because they are peripheral, the rich countries can be, and often are, *insensitive* to the problem of the poor.

Efficiency and the Free Market

Whether the distribution of gains from commodity trade is asymmetric or not depends on the eye of the beholder. Perception of asymmetry involves a subjective determination of what is equitable and how important it should be in relation to other objectives, such as improving the efficiency of production and trade. Since an equitable system need not necessarily be the most efficient, conflicts over objectives also arise. A view strongly held in the developed countries is that a competitive market is the most efficient way of allocating resources. Are markets really free? Is free trade really apolitical in its effects? How deeply are governments committed to improving efficiency in the world as a whole?

In the overall systematic context, these questions are answered in the following quotations:

As is evident from all but a narrow economic perspective, free trade in fact is not neutral in its political effects. It is no surprise that countries achieving a dominant competitive position internationally, e.g. Great Britain in the latter part of the last century and the United States from the 1930s to the 1960s, favoured free trade. Increased trade enables such countries to strengthen their security position not only by accelerating their rate of income growth but also by creating dependency relationships on the part of other countries through trade and investment ties. . . It is actually possible for free trade to lead to immiserization for a particular country.[7]

Protection to Northern farmers has taken precedence during peace time over commitments to trade liberalization.[8]

If one examines the preferences of nation states as revealed through their actions rather than their pronouncements, economic efficiency does not appear to be highly regarded. The list of illustrations of this point seems endless. . . Indeed, if it were not for a longer-term historical perspective, one could argue that desire for economic efficiency is of secondary concern to nation states.[9] The list given by Krause and Nye to illustrate this point only goes to show that the subordination of efficiency to other welfare goals is a characteristic common to all governments — developed, developing or centrally planned.

Commodity Conflicts and Collective Economic Security

The arena of commodity conflicts is not the idealised free market beloved of some economists but the real, inefficient world, full of frustrated nations. As in the case of the other parts of the system, in commodity negotiations too it is not possible to separate the economic and political strands. The debate on whether commodity agreements should stabilise the market or improve the export earnings of developing countries is couched in economic terminology but is essentially ideological in character. The relationship between multinational corporations and host governments is often seen in the metropolitan countries as an economic one, while it is primarily a political matter in the developing host countries. Strategic considerations which make the United States decide that it will promote the conclusion of a Coffee Agreement but not join the first four Tin Agreements are purely political; but the US also joins the Wheat Agreements for valid economic reasons. Historical association of a political nature often determines commodity policy; the Commonwealth Sugar Agreement, the Yaoundé and Lomé Conventions are examples of European countries deciding which particular set of developing countries will benefit. Very little in international commodity trade is non-political; the buying of sugar is political; so is the selling of wheat.

Like every multilateral negotiation, commodity negotiations also involve conflicts of interest, co-operation among different participants and even unsuspected collusions. The bargaining power of the participants varies enormously. Just because OPEC has demonstrated success in a unique commodity, the inherent political and economic complexities in other commodities have not disappeared. The bulk of this book is therefore devoted to an analysis of the complexity of international commodity *markets* and international commodity *negotiations,* in an attempt to deduce the salient reasons for past failures and to indicate the lines of a possible new approach.

Chapter 2 is a brief survey of the tortuous history of negotiations in individual commodities. Chapter 3 is a factual presentation, inevitably statistical, of the structure of commodity trade – the characteristics of different commodities, the share of developed and developing countries and the export or import dependence of different countries on different commodities. The ideological conflict between the objectives of promoting stability and increasing the transfer of resources and the value which governments attach to efficiency are the main subjects of Chapter 4. Chapter 5 is an analysis of conflicts among exporting countries and Chapter 6 of conflicts between exporters and importers. This is devoted primarily to the problem of access in importing countries. A distinction has been made above between commodity markets and commodity negotiations for the reason that the success or failure of any inter-governmental agreement is determined by what actually happens in the market place; Chapter 7 therefore discusses the nature of commodity markets and the factors which affect the prices of commodities. While governments and traders may assume a certain predictability in the beahviour of commodities, the unexpected often happens; Chapter 8 is a discussion of unforeseen events – Acts of God such as droughts and frost, man-made intervention such as wars and hostilities, commodity booms and the impact of changes in the other parts of the system.

The resolution of commodity conflicts has necessarily to be by economic techniques; but politics affects the choice of techniques and the willingness to implement them faithfully. Chapter 9 evaluates the effectiveness of the various techniques of regulation; while many of them are well-known ones usually associated with commodity agreements, some others, not directly related to regulation of trade, are also considered. The widening of the range of techniques is necessary because the commonly used mechanisms are found to be inadequate to deal with the range of problems encountered. As the efficient implementation of the techniques depends on the observance of the rules of the game by all participants, this chapter also discusses discipline, enforceability and penalties.

In Chapter 10, the political strands that are interwoven in commodity conflicts are described separately. Such political influences are not always to the detriment of successful negotiation; historical associations, strategic considerations and regional affinities are thus examined for their constructive role in resolving conflicts. The amalgam of economic and political motivations is usually lumped together under the vague term 'political will'. The lack of the so-called 'will' is often blamed for failures in negotiations. Chapter 11 seeks to identify the constituents of political will and to derive therefrom the nature of the bargaining power of different states in the present international economic system. Chapter 12 draws together the ideological, political and economic factors and, as an aid to conflict resolution, identifies those that promote and those that inhibit international co-operation.

Since commodity conflicts, like other conflicts, cannot be wished away, a basic assumption in this book is that the root causes of conflicts are real, persistent and potent. A reduction of conflict by negotiation can only be justified on the grounds that it increases the welfare of all participants and that no one is seen to have gained an advantage perceived by others as unfair. Krause and Nye have defined this as collective economic security.

Broadly defined, *collective economic security* means governments' acceptance of international surveillance of their domestic and foreign economic policies, of criticism of the effects of their policies on the economic security of other countries, and of various forms of international presence in the operation of markets.[10]

The last chapter of this book is addressed to the aim of improving the collective economic security of all states in the specific area of commodity trade. The proposal made therein is for the negotiation of a *framework* Agreement on Commodity Trade. It is, in effect, an attempt to evolve a set of rules for the commodity trade game – a task to which the developed countries, who have devised rules for all other sectors of the international economy, have consciously not addressed themselves. The beneficiaries of freedom of action for themselves have naturally no desire to restrict their freedom. However, it is this author's firm belief that collective economic security cannot be improved in a system which makes a large number of participants feel vulnerable and frustrated.

Perspectives

It is necessary to add a few words at this point about the perspective from which the analysis in this book is attempted. First, the problems of commodity regulation are viewed together on the basis of the similarity of conflicts in all the major commodities – 35 in all. The traditional method of analysis has been to detail the history of negotiations in a single commodity (coffee, tin, wheat or whatever), thereby ignoring or taking for granted ideological and systemic perceptions. In this book, the history of past commodity negotiations has been used — neither chronologically nor commodity-by-commodity — but as an example illustrating, where appropriate, conflicts arising from similar causes.

The author of this book is from the Third World — indeed, the Fourth, i.e. the non-oil exporting developing countries — and makes no bones about seeing the world divided into three groups — the developed the developing and the centrally planned. Notwithstanding the progress that has been made by the developing countries, this author is led to the inescapable conclusions that the world is becoming increasingly divided into autarkic regions and that the developing countries are being constantly pushed to the periphery of the system. It is not necessary to bring in moral arguments to prove that the international economic system, as it operates now, contains many elements of inequity. But it is *not* alleged that this is due to any preconceived or premeditated plan by the rich countries deliberately to impoverish the poor. Where insensitivity or neglect can provide an explanation, attribution of premeditation is a superfluous luxury.

The basic theme running through all arguments in this book is that the increasingly autarkic and centrifugal international economic trading and monetary system is not a healthy development. This book is not addressed to those who disagree with this judgement and see nothing wrong in a world divided into three parts. There is nothing illogical in their believing that a three-part world can not only survive but that parts of it can prosper. Equally, it is not illogical to believe, as this author does, that such a system would be fundamentally unhealthy and that the resulting political system would be unduly unstable. If the oft-proclaimed interdependence and smallness of this world are to be taken at face value, the asymmetry of the effects of the system and the increasing vulnerability of the developing countries are negative factors which need corrective action.

It is obvious that no new theory of imperialism or dependency is propounded here. In fact, there is no adherence to any of the standard theories of inter-state relations. If the role of governments is stressed, it is because the subject of this book is negotiations and only governments negotiate the rules of the system. On the other hand, the role of non-state actors, particularly the market, has been emphasised throughout. If the virtues of a free market are questioned, it is because the real world is not a free market. There is little that is totally black or completely white in the real world. The rich countries are not automatically assumed to be all sinners and the poor pure as the driven snow. Wherever positive aspects are found, these have been noted; equally, shortcomings, where they abound, are pinpointed. In short, in the words of Jefferson, the perspective is 'not to find out new principles, or new arguments, never before thought of, not merely to say things which had never been said before; but to place before mankind the common sense of the subject, and to justify ourselves in the independent stand we are compelled to take'.

Notes

1. J.W.F. Rowe, *Markets and Men* (Cambridge University Press, Cambridge, 1936).
2. C. Fred Bergsten, Robert O. Keohane and Joseph S. Nye, 'International Economics and International Politics: A Framework for Analysis', *International Organization*, 29, 1975, pp.3-36. Unless otherwise specified, further quotations in this chapter are from this article.
3. This and the quotation following in the same paragraph are from: Carlos F. Diaz-Alejandro, 'North-South Relations', *International Organization*, 29, 1975, pp.213-41.
4. There is an important qualification attached to this definition: 'Possession of dominant rule-making power does not necessarily imply control over every political process taking place within those rules.'
5. 'Objectives and Principles of International Commodity Agreements', Annex A.II.1, Final Act, UNCTAD I, Geneva, 1964.
6. Diaz-Alejandro, 'North-South Relations', pp.00.
7. Robert E. Baldwin and David A. Kay, 'International Trade', *International Organization*, 29, 1975, pp.99-131.
8. Diaz-Alejandro, 'North-South Relations'.
9. Lawrence B. Krause and Joseph S. Nye, 'Economic Organization', *International Organization*, 29, 1975, pp.323-42.
10. Krause and Nye, 'Economic Organisation'.

2 MORE DISAGREEMENTS THAN AGREEMENTS

> Commerce, which ought naturally to be, among nations, as
> among individuals, a bond of union and friendship, has become
> the most fertile source of discord and animosity.
>
> Adam Smith, *The Wealth of Nations*

The number of primary commodities whose marketing has been the
subject of international attention is about 35.[1] These are: grains
(wheat, rice and maize); tropical beverages (coffee, tea, cocoa); sugar;
meat, particularly beef; oilseeds, oils and fats and oilseed cake; bananas
and citrus fruit; wine; tobacco; pepper; fibres (cotton, wool, jute, sisal
etc.); natural rubber; forest products, particularly wood and wood
products and shellac; oil (petroleum crude); minerals (bauxite, iron ore,
manganese ore, mica, rock phosphate); non-ferrous metals (aluminium,
copper, lead, nickel, tin, tungsten and zinc). These include all commodities for which formal agreements or informal arrangements have been
concluded in the past, those in which producers have attempted to
co-ordinate their policies, those for which some international forum
has been set up, even if the stage of informal arrangement has not been
reached, and, finally, those for which international action has been
recommended by a group of countries, though no such action has so
far materialised. The list corresponds to the one used by the World
Bank in its studies on price trends and terms of trade.[2] All commodities which are significant in the export earnings of developing countries
are in the list, which covers, as a whole, about four fifths, by value, of
exports of all primary commodities. It includes tropical products as
well as those from the temperate zone, in which both developed and
developing countries have substantial interest. While some, such as
timber, coffee or copper, are exported in large volumes, others, rubber
or mica for instance, have special problems of competition from
synthetic substitutes.

Almost all the 35 commodities, and a few others, such as dairy
products and mercury, have been the subject of attention in a wide
range of international forums. A detailed exposition of all the attempts
made to conclude an agreement and a blow-by-blow account of the
actual implementation of the few that have become operational would
fill many volumes. For example, *Tin: The Working of a Commodity*

Agreement, by William Fox, who was for 15 years the Secretary of the International Tin Council, is an illuminating survey of the politics and economics of an agreement in a single commodity.[3]

The negotiating steps leading to agreements and their working are described in articles in almost every issue of the *Journal of World Trade Law.*[4] The purpose of this chapter is not to retrace all the steps in all the commodities but to survey the past history with a view to deriving some conclusions on the rate of success in negotiations. In how many commodities have agreements been negotiated, how long does it take to do so and, once negotiated, how long do they survive? The history of commodity negotiations in the period between the First and Second World Wars is first briefly described. The forums for commodity negotiations that have grown up since the end of the Second World War and the negotiations in the important commodities since 1945 are then described in somewhat greater detail. The conclusions that can be drawn from past experience are then considered in relation to the conventional wisdom on the causes of failure in commodity negotiations.

Pre-Second World War Agreements

In Chapter 1, sugar negotiations were traced back to 1863. After sugar, the commodity with the longest history of international regulation is tin. In 1921, the then Federated Malay States and the Netherlands East Indies created the 'Bandoeng Pool' of tin stocks in order to remove excess supplies of the metal from the market to be sold later when prices had stabilised. Regulation of rubber dates back to 1922 and that of copper to 1926. In his first (1936) book, Rowe did not make a distinction between international attempts to regulate trade in a commodity and attempts by a single country to influence the market. Hence, *Markets and Men* included an evaluation of national regulatory policies such as the US Farm Fund and the Canadian Wheat Pools of the 1920s. Two such attempts by countries described today as 'developing' are worth noting. As early as 1907, the state of Sao Paulo in Brazil started to experiment with 'valorisation schemes' to bring about a balance between periodic surpluses and shortages – i.e. to even out production cycles. Gradually control of production and trade was assumed by the federal government so that, by 1921, regulation of the coffee market had become a permanent feature of Brazilian policy. Another attempt by a major producer to regulate the market was Cuba's policy of restricting its own supplies of sugar to prop up the market. This policy failed because 'it was, so to speak, a case of Cuba against the world, and a world in which every country was determined to be self-sufficient in the matter of sugar supplies'.[5]

All the agreements of the 1920s were negotiated and operated in conditions of relative world prosperity. The Great Depression, which affected all aspects of the international economy, had its destabilising effect on commodity trade as well. Having experimented with international regulation, it was natural for governments to try to mitigate these effects by co-operative action in the major commodities — copper, rubber, sugar, tea, tin and wheat. The Depression accelerated the collapse of the ailing sugar market which Cuba had vainly tried to support; by the mid-1930s the price of sugar had dropped to half a penny a pound. Attempts by Cuba to get other exporters to join in regulating supplies meant, as usual, many tortuous negotiations before the Chadbourne Scheme was signed in 1931. This was an agreement among the trade associations of the eight main exporting countries — five European producers, Cuba, Java and Peru — and provided for the restriction of exports and the gradual disposal of surplus stocks over a period of five years. It was a miserable failure mainly because production expanded in the non-member areas, particularly the British Empire, the United States and the Philippines. Finally, in 1937, an International Sugar Agreement was negotiated; during its three-year life, market prices never reached the minimum contemplated in it and so it broke down in 1940. Like sugar, the price of wheat also collapsed in 1930. Wheat-exporting countries met in London that year to consider the possibility of export quotas; but an international agreement was only signed in August 1933, between nine exporting and thirteen importing countries with balanced obligations on each side. For about a year, the agreement helped to stabilise prices, but then it too broke down.

The Bandoeng tin Pool was liquidated profitably in 1923 and 1924 and for five years there was no regulation of the market. The effects of the Depression prompted a short-lived attempt, in 1929, at control by the tin companies, who formed a Tin Producers Association. The realisation that only governmental action could be successful led to the negotiation of the First International Tin Agreement in 1931. Altogether there were four agreements between 1931 and 1946 and all of them operated reasonably successfully. Twice the agreements experimented with a buffer stock mechanism, which was later to become the central feature of all post-Second World War Tin Agreements. There were two reasons for the success of the Tin Agreements; first, almost all the exporters were members, and second, they were backed by two metropolitan powers, the United Kingdom and the Netherlands. The same two reasons were also responsible for the successful implementation of the early Rubber Agreements, though they can only be regarded as successful, however, in relation to their limited objectives. Being agreements only among producers, control of supplies in both tin and rubber was used for the benefit of producers but at the cost of consuming countries. The copper agreement was a limited one between producers, not governments, in Chile, Peru, Rhodesia and the Belgian Congo; producers in the United States voluntarily agreed to restrain their exports without actually participating; on the other hand, Canada, a major exporter, stayed out. The International Tea Agreement in 1933, which ran until 1955, was the only international agreement on tea that there has ever been. Since the market was almost wholly shared between India and Ceylon, both of which were, for most of the period, colonies of the largest importer, it was relatively easy to operate the agreement without conflict.

This brief summary does scant justice to the complexities of commodity negotiations in the inter-war period, which was notable for substantial changes in the pattern of world production in many commodities. Detailed accounts of the negotiation and operation of all these agreements can be found in Rowe's second book, *Primary Commodities in International Trade,* in the studies published by the Food Research Institute of Stanford University and in a set of articles on the wheat agreements in the *International Journal of Agricultural Affairs.*[6] Some lessons of the inter-war experience in commodity regulation are relevant to today's conditions. Excess supply was a problem then as it often is in some commodities now; likewise, production cycles are a permanent feature of some commodities. Unilateral attempts to regulate the market fail if the rest of the world goes on increasing production. The history of sugar production in Europe since the Second World War shows that the policy of achieving self-sufficiency by protectionist policies has not changed much in this century. There was much less opposition to 'cartelisation' in those days; most of the agreements were between exporting countries, some even between companies or associations of producers. Even so, exporters were not always able to agree among themselves. It was easier to do so when the producers were controlled by one or two metropolitan powers. The inter-war agreements exhibited other common symptoms of failure — insufficient coverage of the market, inadequate policing of control provisions and inability of the mechanisms to deal with shortages as well as surpluses.

Forums for Commodity Negotiation

According to the strict standards of the Havana Charter, an international commodity agreement must be an international treaty, with producer/exporters and consumer/importers as members, having as its aim the control or regulation of trade in a primary commodity by means of specific economic provisions and administered by an autonomous body in which the two groups have equal power. Any international arrangement that does not satisfy *all* the above criteria cannot be called a commodity Agreement, with a capital 'A'. By this definition, there have been agreements in only five commodities in the period since 1945 — coffee, cocoa, sugar, tin and wheat. As will be seen later, the fact of conforming to the Havana Charter criteria does not guarantee that such agreements are more effective in regulating trade than other less formal arrangements. If the definition of workable agreements is widened to include informal arrangements, then three more can be added to the list — tea, hard fibres and the group jute, kenaf and allied fibres. There are a few more, somewhat obscure, working arrangements. Under GATT, there is a Skim Milk Powder Arrangement to which a Protocol relating to butter fat has been added. A Gentlemen's Agreement on whole milk powder operates under OECD auspices. Until recently, the International Sultana Producers Agreement operated a minimum export price scheme.

In international negotiating structure, a Study Group usually precedes the commencement of actual negotiations. Such a group studies the problems of trade in a particular commodity until a broad consensus is reached on the need for regulation and the techniques applicable. Some groups may continue to exist for years without ever agreeing to begin negotiations. The International Study Groups for Rubber, formed in 1944, and for Lead and Zinc, formed in 1958, are two examples. There are ten Inter-Governmental groups under the Food and Agriculture Organisation (FAO), of which the one on rice has produced some guidelines on trade and that on bananas is discussing the possibility of an agreement. The other eight continue their studies. Ad hoc consultations are a stage prior even to the constitution of a Study Group; two such have been organised by the FAO for pepper and tobacco.

This does not exhaust the list of international forums engaged in examining the problems of commodity trade. The possibility of stabilising world cotton prices by an international agreement has been discussed twice and rejected both times by the International Cotton Advisory Committee. An International Wool Study Group was formed in 1974 under the auspices of the Commonwealth Secretariat. The UNCTAD Permanent Group on Synthetics and Substitutes has examined the special problems of this type of competition for rubber, hides and skins, lauric oils, shellac and mica. After the success of OPEC it has to be conceded that arrangements consisting solely of producer-exporters could also be an effective method, though not in a manner acceptable to consumer-importers, of regulating supplies, controlling production and maintaining or increasing prices. There are a number of such associations, though few can hope to emulate OPEC's success; the best known mineral producers' associations are CIPEC, the Council of Copper Exporting Countries, and the International Bauxite Association (IBA). The Association of Natural Rubber Producing Countries, though a less tightly organised regional (South-East Asian) group, has a membership that covers over 90 per cent of world exports and is discussing a price stabilisation scheme. Three other producer organisations have a much smaller coverage of the market and correspondingly little control over it.

UPEB is a union of only five banana exporting countries whose bargaining power, according to the UNCTAD Secretariat, will be severely limited unless it is internationalised. An Association of Iron Ore Producers has been talked about since 1969, but, as recently constituted, the membership does not include some major exporting countries. It is, therefore, mainly a consultative body and does not contemplate any regulatory function. The International Association of Mercury Producers, formed in 1974, has not succeeded in maintaining the price level. The International Wool Secretariat is an example of a producers' organisation primarily devoted to promoting the marketing of the product. Tungsten has two consultative bodies — the Primary Tungsten Association and an UNCTAD Committee on Tungsten. Limited producer groupings of a regional character also exist, either independently or as pressure groups within broader agreements. Examples of the former are the Asian Pepper and Coconut Communities, both constituted under the aegis of ESCAP, the Economic and Social Commission for Asia and the Pacific. Regional pressure groups within an Agreement are found particularly in coffee in the form of FEDECAME, a group of Latin American producers (though the two largest, Brazil and Colombia, are not members) and IACO, the Inter-African Coffee Organisation, which, in turn, includes OAMCAF, a group of Francophone coffee producing African countries.

Table 2.1 summarises the international consultative machinery that currently exists for the various commodities. There is no dearth of

Table 2.1: Commodity Arrangements, Inter-Governmental Associations and Consultative Bodies

International Commodity Agreements	FAO Inter-Governmental Commodity Groups	Other International Bodies	Producer Organisations Broad Coverage	Producer Organisations Limited Coverage
1. Sugar	1. Grains	1. UNCTAD Permanent Group of Synthetics and Substitutes	1. OPEC (Oil)	1. Coffee Federation of the Americas
2. Wheat	2. Rice	2. International Rubber Study Group	2. CIPEC (Copper)	2. Inter-African Coffee Organisation
3. Coffee	3. Oilseeds, Oils and Fats	3. International Lead and Zinc Study Group	3. International Bauxite Association	3. OAMCAF (Coffee Organisation of Africa and Malagasy)
4. Tin	4. Bananas	4. International Wool Study Group	4. Association of Natural Rubber Producing Countries	4. Asian Coconut Community
5. Cocoa	5. Wine and Vine products	5. International Cotton Advisory Committee	5. Association of Iron Ore Producing Countries	5. Union of Banana Exporting Countries
6. Olive Oil	6. Meat	6. International Institute for Cotton	6. Asian Pepper Community	6. Primary Tungsten Association
	7. Tea	7. International Wool Secretariat	7. International Sultana Producers Agreement	
Informal Arrangements	8. Hard Fibres	8. UNCTAD Committee on Tungsten	8. International Association of Mercury Producers	
FAO	9. Jute, kenaf	9. GATT Consultative Group on Meat		
1. Tea	10. Citrus Fruit			
2. Hard fibres				
3. Jute, kenaf	*FAO Ad Hoc Consultations*			
GATT	1. Tobacco			
4. Skimmed milk powder and Butter fat	2. Pepper			
OECD				
5. Whole milk powder				

talking shops; only the results are meagre. Out of the 35 commodities, concerted international action has been taken in less than half; only five have had an agreement, and four an arrangement, at some time or other in the past. The possibility of an arrangement has been broached for a couple more. It will be instructive to see how long it took to negotiate even these few agreements and how effective they have been.

The Less Comprehensive Arrangements

The arrangements which have yet to develop into formal agreements are those concerning tea, hard fibres, jute and dairy products. The International Olive Oil Agreement, while executed as a treaty, is also not a fully-fledged commodity agreement. It has no market control provisions, depends on voluntary co-operation rather than on mandatory regulation and, in contrast with the Havana Charter, does not provide for equal representation between producers and consumers. A brief attempt under the agreement to even out temporary shortfalls in some countries by transferring temporary surpluses available elsewhere proved so difficult to implement that the agreements have limited themselves to an information exchange role.

Tea is one of the few commodities that have suffered a continuous decline in the real price throughout the post-war period. Notwithstanding the 20-year history of the International Tea Agreement, the two market leaders — India and Sri Lanka — let it lapse and made no serious attempt to revive it for a long time. The rapid increase in production of tea in the East African countries in the early 1960s prompted a search for means to regulate the market and resulted, in 1969, in a non-binding understanding on limitation of exports. A formal agreement with quota and price provisions has not yet been negotiated, mainly due to an unbridgeable disagreement between the traditional and new producers on respective shares in a static market. The informal arrangement for two of the hard fibres — sisal and henquen — was concluded in September 1967 and abaqa was added in January 1968. The arrangement had an indicative price objective and an informal understanding on quotas. It became inoperative in 1971 and has just been reactivated after a lapse of five years. The vicissitudes of the arrangement are examined in greater detail in Chapter 7, in the context of the problem of competition from synthetics. The regulation of the market for jute is still under discussion between the major producers in Asia and is complicated by the relationship between raw jute exports and exports of jute manufactures as well as by internal conflicts in producing countries on land use. The dairy products' group suffers from having different arrangements, negotiated at different times and implemented in different forums. The Whole Milk Powder arrangement under OECD started in 1963, the Skim Milk Powder one under GATT in 1969 and that for butter fat, also under GATT, in 1973. None of them is comprehensive since they only monitor the operation of minimum export price levels. Since world prices have remained well above the minimum export prices set in these arrangements, they have had little to do.

By their very nature, informal arrangements are unenforceable. They depend entirely on the good faith of the participants for their success. In commodities such as tea and hard fibres the informal arrangements have not operated with sufficient success to give rise to the hope that formal agreements could be concluded in the near future.

The Five Formal Agreements

The classic example of the time it takes to negotiate an agreement is cocoa. If we ignore the abortive attempt made in 1933 at the London Monetary Conference by Trinidad for a buffer stock on cocoa, the first session of the Cocoa Study Group in November 1956 may be said to mark the beginning of consultations. The first UN Cocoa Conference was convened in 1963 and was unsuccessful; so were the second (1966) and the third (1967). In pursuance of a unanimously passed UNCTAD II resolution, the Cocoa Conference was reconvened in June 1968 but again without success. After four failures, the stage was moved back one step and periodic consultations were held among the interested parties to determine when a conference could be recalled with a reasonable prospect of success. The 1969 consultations failed due to a sudden collapse among the exporting countries, Brazil expressing total opposition to almost everything that had earlier been agreed upon. The first session of the Conference in March 1972 was also unproductive; only in the second session in September 1972 was it possible to hold a conference at which an agreed text could be adopted. The first Cocoa Agreement, with a life of three years, came into force on 1 October 1973; but for all three years it remained a paper agreement since market prices remained throughout above the ceiling price inscribed in it. The agreement was renegotiated in September/October 1975 so that it might succeed the first one on 1 October 1976. The future of the second agreement is problematical since a major exporter, Ivory Coast, has reservations on the text as agreed. The United States, the largest importer, accounting for nearly a quarter of the world market, did not join the first agreement and is unlikely to join the second. The reasons why, after 17 years, there are still doubts about an effective Cocoa Agreement will be examined in the context of production cycles and the inverse relationship between market price and the desire to conclude an agreement.

Even in commodities such as sugar and wheat, in which developed countries have a substantial interest as exporters, the process of negotiation is no faster. The earliest international discussions to regulate world trade in wheat, held in London in 1930 following the failure of the World Economic Conference, also failed to agree on a system of export quotas. The International Wheat Agreement, concluded in 1933, in which exporting countries were to accept quotas while importing countries were to limit production and reduce duties when prices rose, soon collapsed owing to the failure of Argentina to observe the quota and to a short crop which made export restrictions unnecessary. Negotiations which began in 1938 were discontinued during the war and a plan drawn up in 1942 by four major exporters – the US, Canada, Argentina and Australia – was discussed in conference in 1945 and 1946 but was abandoned in 1947 because only three of the major exporters – US, Canada and Australia – initialled it; among the importers, the United Kingdom, a major consumer, refused to ratify it. A fresh approach, of the multilateral contract type, was discussed at the Wheat Conference of 1947, but the agreement signed in 1948 never entered into force since this time the United States refused to ratify it. After another conference in Washington in 1949, an agreement actually entered into force.

Thus, discussions which started among the main interested countries, all allies, three years before the end of the war took four more years after it to fructify. Altogether it took seven international conferences to produce this result. Even then two important countries, the USSR and Argentina, stood out, the former dissatisfied with its quota and the latter with the price. Though the 1949 agreement worked well, thanks to the exporters honouring their obligations during the Korean War boom, the renegotiated 1953 agreement lost the United Kingdom as a member on a difference of five cents in the ceiling price between US $2.00 and 2.05. Argentina joined the third (1956) agreement but, in addition to the UK, more importing countries withdrew, leaving it with importers who covered only 25 per cent of the market, as against 60 per cent in the first agreement. The fourth (1959) agreement was modified to meet the importers' criticism and had, except for Russia, a wider membership than its predecessors; Russia too joined the next (1962) agreement as an exporter but, half way through its life, turned into a massive importer. After its initial three-year period the 1962 agreement was extended twice, for a year each time. In 1967 its administrative provisions alone were extended for one more year, but only to await the outcome of the Kennedy Round of negotiations under GATT.

By this time, trade in wheat was no longer a question to be treated on its own but had become embroiled in the whole gamut of economic relationships between the United States and the European Economic Community. The resulting International Grains Arrangement of 1967 was in two parts – a Wheat Trade Convention (WTC) and a Food Aid Convention (FAC). It came into force in June 1968, but without universal membership, since non-members of GATT, such as the USSR, declined to participate in an agreement which they had no part in negotiating and which was presented to them as a *fait accompli*. Shortly after coming into force, the WTC became ineffective since the minimum price provisions were ignored by all major exporters. After this failure, the 1971 WTC which followed wisely refrained from even writing in any price provisions. Since 1971 there has been no effective international agreement on wheat; in this period, world supplies have moved from surplus to shortage and world prices have shot up to unprecedented levels. World trade in wheat is controlled by developed countries, especially the United States and Canada, with considerable resources for regulating national production and holding stocks. If having the resources to control effectively a large part of the export market were the only criterion for the success of an agreement, all Wheat Agreements should have operated equally successfully. In reality, countries have been walking in and out of agreements as if through a revolving door. The failure of the 1967 WTC shows that rich countries can be as indisciplined as the poor. The fact that for the last decade there has been no effective agreement on a vital staple food grain is a sad commentary on the ability of governments to co-operate.

Among the five important formal agreements, continuous existence for reasonably long periods can be claimed for only one other – the International Tin Agreement. Since the end of the war, there have been five such agreements, running for consecutive five-year periods since 1959; the United States, a major importer which adds complications to the market by its policy of surplus disposals, was never a member of the first four agreements. Since the main feature of the Tin Agreements is the use of the buffer stock mechanism, their effectiveness is examined in greater detail in Chapter 9. The general conclusion is that these agreements have been more effective in times of surplus than during periods of prolonged shortage.

The history of sugar agreements has been influenced by a number of factors unique to this commodity. The existence of preferential arrangements accounting for a substantial volume of the trade, a major convulsion which arose out of the shutting off, for political reasons, of Cuban sugar from the US market, the political preference implicit in the Commonwealth Sugar Agreement which has been carried over into the enlarged Community's policy towards some less developed countries, the fact that sugar is both a tropical cane-based product and a temperate zone beet-based one, and the fact that it is one of the most highly protected of agricultural commodities — all these mean that sugar, of all the commodities, exemplifies the full range of complexity of political and economic conflicts of interest. Sugar will therefore be used to illustrate, in subsequent chapters, almost every facet of commodity conflicts. Of the three International Sugar Agreements (1953, 1958 and 1968), only the first had a relatively crisis-free life.

The long history of the negotiations before the International Coffee Agreement could become a reality has been well documented.[7] Because of its political importance to US-Latin American relations, the operation of the agreement has been the subject of more articles in learned journals than any other agreement. It has also been the subject of hearings in the US Senate Committee on Foreign Relations and of Annual Reports by the President of the United States to Congress.[8] Suffice it to note that there was a gap of 14 years between two working agreements. The important milestones in the tortuous negotiations were as follows. A war-time measure called the Inter-American Coffee Agreement existed between 1940 and 1948. Then, for six years, there was not even a proposal for a new agreement. In 1954, a suggestion was made in the Organisation of American States but proved abortive due to total opposition from the US; in 1957, a limited 'Agreement of Mexico' was concluded between seven Latin American countries. A year later, 14 Latin American countries and Portugal (on behalf of its African possessions) signed an agreement at a conference in Rio de Janeiro. But this had no provisions relating to marketing and was soon overtaken by the threatened surpluses. Protracted negotiations then took place between the Coffee Study Group and African producers; these led to a new agreement in September 1959 in which Portugal and the French (African) Community joined. When the United Kingdom on behalf of East African producers also joined it in 1960, the agreement accounted for over 90 per cent of world exportable surpluses. After another two years, a universal agreement with almost all importers and exporters came into force on 30 November 1962. The commitment of the United States to the Coffee Agreement, one of the very few that the US has joined, is a political one and provides a perfect example of a domestic policy conflict between a general dislike of commodity agreements and the imperatives of US-Latin American relations.

The Coffee Agreements also illustrate the thesis that the implementation of commodity agreements is only a continuation of the negotiating process under a formal treaty framework. While every year there are negotiations about the size of the market and quotas, a peak is reached at the time the agreements are renegotiated, when a large number of problems are lumped together. Occasionally renegotiations half-way through are also provided for. Renegotiations are as politico-economic in character as the negotiations that precede the conclusion of an agreement. While it is possible that the operation of an agreement over a period of three or even five years would have shown the participants the advantages that accrue, renegotiation is often seen as a means of correcting 'unfairness' that might have been built into the original set of compromises. Further, some problems which might have been swept under the carpet by an appropriate form of words which permitted a latitude of behaviour might not continue to be susceptible to such treatment. Also, new problems might have cropped up during the operation of the agreement (for example, devaluation of currency or floating exchange rates which mean renegotiating the price clauses); lastly, problems earlier considered insignificant (e.g. the question of exemption from quota provisions for so-called 'new markets' in the Coffee Agreement) might have become more irritating, adding more complications to an already sensitive situation.

The 1962 Coffee Agreement provided for a mid-term renegotiation of basic quotas (that is, the percentage share of the market) no doubt in order to secure the acceptance of these countries which were dissatisfied with the initial allocation. During its life, the agreement also had to deal with two special problems: (i) selective increases in quotas, i.e. differential adjustment of quotas for different types, and (ii) the problem of export of soluble coffee, specifically from Brazil to the United States. The end-of-term renegotiation, apart from some further adjustment in quotas, also made an ambitious attempt to tackle the long term supply problems by creating a Diversification Fund. However, the 1968 agreement, with a life of five years up to 30 September 1973, ran into difficulties in the last year, leading to the abandonment of export quotas. The collapse was partly due to divergencies between exporting members and partly to differences between exporters and importers on the price of coffee at a time of monetary instability. Since the basic economic provisions could not be kept operational, there was no hope of renegotiating a third agreement as promptly as the second. A new text was agreed upon in November 1975 and the Third International Coffee Agreement entered into force on 1 October 1976. However, the disastrous frost in July 1975 in Brazil made it unlikely that the quota provisions of the third agreement would become effective at least for the first two years of its existence. Nature, as much as politics, often interferes with the devout wishes of those who sign agreements.

Before leaving the subject of how long it takes to conclude agreements and how well they operate, it will be of interest to look at the smallest of them all. The International Sultana Producers' Agreement has exactly *three* members, two observers who will not join it and a total annual world export of about a hundred million dollars. By contrast, the coffee trade is worth three to four billion dollars. One would imagine that with only five producer/exporters − the United States, Australia, Greece, Turkey and Iran − with no major political problems between them, an agreement on a fairly minor commodity would be easy. The first two informal meetings between producers in September 1961 and July 1962 failed to produce any agreement, and only the third meeting in June 1963 was successful; even then, the United States decided to be just an observer, and Iran followed suit. In its operation, too, the agreement witnessed a crisis; in 1969, Australia threatened to withdraw if she were not permitted to market her 1969/70 crop before the agreed date of 1 July 1970. Since 1971, this agreement too has lost all its economic provisions and has become another consultative body. Though on the whole the agreement has been beneficial to producers, it appears that it has not kept pace with changing production and marketing conditions. The fact that the market for a commodity is small or the number of exporters very few does not seem to make any difference to success in negotiations.

The history of attempts to negotiate and implement international commodity agreements leads inevitably to the following conclusions.

(i) there are very few commodities for which it has been possible to conclude formal and universal agreements;

(ii) these take a long time to negotiate;

(iii) once negotiated, they frequently break down in their operation, and

(iv) intermediate steps (informal arrangements, producer co-operation) have been tried, but their success has been patchy.

Why Do Commodity Negotiations Fail?

In its Progress Report to UNCTAD III, the Secretariat identified three reasons for the failure of commodity negotiations: 'The reasons for this general lack of progress may be traced to the inherent complexity of many primary commodity markets, the nature of the existing inter-governmental machinery and the lack of political will on the part of interested governments.'[9] Apart from the obvious fact that commodity markets are complex, the other two reasons are vague to the point of incomprehensibility. Since there is no precise criticism of what is wrong with the existing consultative machinery, the second point about its unsatisfactory 'nature' is not at all clear. Does it mean that the machinery does not accurately reflect the bargaining strength of different participants in terms of their importance in a commodity? Or does it imply that the machinery is inadequately democratic and gives too much power to some countries, say, for example the rich?

The Secretary-General of UNCTAD is not alone in blaming 'lack of political will' for lack of progress in negotiating commodity agreements. In a recent report, the Commonwealth Secretariat says three times in a single page:

> Much could undoubtedly be done given the requisite political will on all sides. . . It is often said that to ensure equitable and remunerative terms of trade for primary commodities exported by developing countries is purely and simply a matter of political will. . . Satisfactory arrangements for many commodities would depend on the requisite political will on the side of the exporting countries as well as the importers.[10]

'Political will' is not only a hazy and vague concept but is an example of circular reasoning. All that is said is that an agreement *was not* concluded because it *could not* be concluded; it *did not* work because it *could not* work. The short-hand expression 'lack of political will' hides a multitude of factors which together determine why a solution, even if it is economically viable, cannot be politically implemented. Negotiations rarely fail because appropriate economic solutions are not available. Failures are either because the economic solutions are considered politically unfeasible or because the acceptable solutions are rendered obsolete by changing circumstances.

In attempting to understand why negotiations fail, it is also possible to oversimplify the causes. Fisher, in his study of the 1962 and 1968 Coffee Agreements, comes to the following conclusion: 'In terms of the conflicts between members of the commodity agreement, it would seem safe to generalise that there are two sets of pervasive conflicts that will inevitably arise: conflicts among exporting members over market shares and conflicts between exporting members and consuming members over prices'.[11] This is like claiming that the SALT talks are about numbers of missiles or nuclear warheads; not at all. They are about strategic balance but are written down in terms of numbers of weapons. The pervasiveness of quotas and prices is likewise an optical illusion; commodity agreements deal with trade and so their economic provisions have to be written down in terms of quantities and prices. Preservation or increase of market shares is not a goal in isolation; it is a part of an overall set of goals regarding expectations about total earnings and their predictability. Likewise, low prices are not necessarily the main objective of importers; often, assurance of supply would take precedence over a lower price without the assurance. While it is undeniable that importers generally prefer a lower price and exporters a higher one, the argument is more often about what level of prices would produce the required stability consistent with equity. Further, commodity negotiations are not always resolved strictly in terms of economic self-interest. An example is quoted in Fisher's study, when he describes a conflict among exporters on the principle of selective adjustments of quotas for different types of coffee. 'Privately, however, Brazil moved to flank the Africans by enlisting the support of the United States behind a compromise solution. Thus, Brazil and the United States – in a *separate and secret* bilateral negotiation – agreed . . .' (italics added). This describes not only a case of collusion among participants but an extraordinary one of collusion between the biggest exporter and the biggest importer *against* the interests of a group of exporters. The reason for this alliance was basically political; the United States, having decided for strategic reasons that there should be an effective Coffee Agreement, was willing to throw its weight behind a more important political ally against a group of countries seen to be politically less important. Other examples cited by Fisher describe quite different types of conflicts unrelated to market shares and prices such as the 'crisis over vertical integration' in the case of the soluble coffee problem, conflicts between different regions and between types and a variety of domestic conflicts which influence the attitudes of governments to international negotiations.

A generalised analysis of conflicts of interest in commodity negotiations cannot be based on those that are readily apparent from a study of one tropical beverage. It is obvious that a wholly different set of conflicts arises in the case of temperate zone products that are produced in both developed and developing countries. Recognising this distinction, the Pearson Commission classified primary commodities 'into two groups according to whether they are largely produced in developing countries or in both developed and developing countries'.[12] These are further sub-divided, in the case of non-competing commodities, between those threatened by close substitutes and synthetics and those that are not. For competing commodities, the sub-classification is made on the basis of whether they are protected from international competition in the markets of developed countries. Schematically this can be shown thus:

produced largely in developing countries		produced in both developed and developing countries	
competition from synthetics and substitutes	limited or no competition	protected from international competition	protection not significant

While it might have been adequate for the purposes of the Commission, this fourfold classification is not enough to demonstrate how the inherent characteristics of a commodity and its market generate economic interests and conflicts on which are then superimposed political considerations. A basic distinction which divides the 35 commodities into two groups is whether a commodity is renewable or not. Renewable commodities, i.e. those based on agriculture, forestry or fishing, have problems of production, stockability and marketing that are quite different from the non-renewable minerals and metals. In both groups, substitutability is a problem affecting a large number. Competition from synthetics is only a special example of the general problem of a restraining influence on the market, the degree of restraint varying with the ease and rapidity with which the substitution can be effected. Oil cannot be easily substituted by other fuels except over a fairly long period and with the investment of substantial resources; copper, on the other hand, can be substituted in some of its uses by aluminium, and all edible vegetable oils are interchangeable.

As distinct from the nature of the commodity, the nature of the market often determines the effectiveness of regulatory action. The much larger number of buyers and sellers in a 'free' or 'open' market have influence but less direct control than the large organisations that control the 'closed' market that obtains in some commodities, particularly mineral ores. In another type of closed market, in which the distribution in the importing country is in the hands of a multi-national corporation which is also the producer in the exporting country, the company can not only influence both governments but is also susceptible to political influence by them. The next chapter, therefore, is not only about the position of commodity trade in the international economic system but also about the characteristics of commodities and commodity markets.

Notes

1. It is difficult to be precise about the exact number. Is olive oil to be treated as a separate commodity because there is an International Olive Oil Agreement or as part of the larger group of 'oils and fats'? Are 'dairy products' one group of interrelated products or does one count whole milk powder, skimmed milk powder, butter and cheese as separate commodities? Other such examples are: coarse grains (maize, rye, barley and oats); oilseeds and oilseed cake; wood (conifer and non-conifer or broad-leaved); hard fibres (sisal, abaqa, henequen and coir).

2. IBRD, *Price Forecasts for Major Primary Commodities,* Report No.467, June 1974; see also IBRD Economic Analysis and Projections Department, Commodities and Export Projections Division, *EC/166, Commodity Trade and Price Trends,* Annual, IBRD, Washington DC.

3. William Fox, *Tin: The Working of a Commodity Agreement* (Mining Journal Books Ltd, London, 1974).

4. The *Journal of World Trade Law* has articles and notes relevant to many aspects of commodity negotiation. The progress of on-going negotiations is usually reported in short notes such as those on the International Grains Arrangement 1967 in vol.2, no.2, 1968; the International Coffee Agreements in 2, 1968: no.3, 6, 1972: nos.5 and 7, 1973: nos. 1 and 3; the International Sugar Agreements in 2, 1968: nos. 4 and 3 (1969): no.2; the cocoa negotiations in 3, 1969: nos.6 and 10 (1976): no.3; the International Olive Oil Agreement in 3 (1969): nos. 4 and 7 (1973): no.4; the International Tin Agreements in 5 (1971): nos. 3 and 20 (1976): no.1; the copper consultations in 11 (1977): no.1. Negotiations in the UNCTAD Trade and Development Board and the Committee on Commodities are also reported in notes such as: 2 (1968): no.6, 3 (1969): no.2; 4 (1970): no.1; 6 (1972): no. 5; and 10 (1976): nos. 1 and 6. Longer articles on fats and oils and sugar and the series on competition from synthetics are referred to in subsequent chapters (note 7 to chapter 6 and notes 8 and 10 to chapter 7). For longer articles on other commodities see cocoa 2 (1968): no. 5 and 11 (1977): no.1; tea 4 (1970): no.4; tin 3 (1969): no. 3, and 9 (1975): no.5. The above list is not comprehensive; there are other articles about GATT, the Kennedy Round etc. which also have a bearing on the subjects discussed in this book.

5. J.W.F. Rowe, *Markets and Men* (Cambridge University Press, Cambridge, 1936).

6. J.W.F. Rowe, *Primary Commodities in International Trade* (Cambridge University Press, Cambridge 1965); Food Research Institute Commodity Policy Studies nos.2, 4, 5 and 6: all published by Stanford University Press, nos. 2 and 4, V.D. Wickizer, *The World Coffee Economy with Special Reference to Control Schemes* (Stanford University Press, Stanford, 1943) and *Tea Under International Regulation* (Stanford University Press, Stanford, 1944); nos. 5 and 6, K.E. Knorr, *Tin under Control* (Stanford University Press, Stanford, 1945) and *World Rubber and its Regulation* (Stanford University

Press, Stanford, 1945). See also a set of articles by A.C.B. Maiden, G. Orlando, J. Pederson, C. Burgess and H.G.L. Strange, 'International Wheat Agreements', *International Journal of Agricultural Affairs*, 1, 1949.

7. See particularly International Coffee Council, *The History of Recent International Coffee Agreements*, Document ICC-I-1, Washington DC, June 1963.

8. For a track record of US Congressional interest in the Coffee Agreements see 94th Congress, 1st Session, US Senate Committee on Finance, Sub-Committee on International Trade, *International Commodity Agreements: a Report by the US International Trade Commission*, Washington DC, 1975.

9. See p.3 of the Report by the Secretary-General, 'The Development of International Commodity Policy' in Part I – Commodities, vol. II, *Merchandise Trade, Proceedings of the Third Session of UNCTAD* (UN, New York, 1973).

10. Commonwealth Economic Papers no.4, *Terms of Trade Policy for Primary Commodities* (Commonwealth Secretariat, London 1976).

11. Bart S. Fisher, *The International Coffee Agreement: A Study in Coffee Diplomacy* (Praeger, New York, 1972).

12. The Commission on International Development (The Pearson Commission), *Partners in Development* (Praeger, New York, 1969).

3 ANATOMY OF INTERNATIONAL COMMODITY TRADE

> Thus the Princes recommended that they be let live as hewers of wood and drawers of water for the entire community.
>
> Hosea 9:21

> For no man buyeth their merchandise anymore.
>
> Revelation 18:11

The 35 commodities listed at the beginning of chapter 2 cover a variety of groups — food and beverages, oilseeds, oils and oilcake, industrial raw materials such as fibres and rubber, mineral ores and metals. These 35 differ widely in their economic and technical characteristics. Correspondingly, the attitudes of producers and consumers vary from commodity to commodity. Those who grow or use a renewable commodity are bound to look on their product from a different perspective from that of those who mine or use minerals and metals. Whatever the nature of the commodity, exporters and importers have different, and often antagonistic, interests to safeguard. It is obvious that governments of countries which are net exporters of a commodity will approach commodity negotiations from positions that often conflict with those of governments of net importing countries. The attitudes of governments also depend on the nature of the market for the commodity and how much they wish to regulate it.

It is also obvious that the importance of a commodity to a country's economy as a whole, and to foreign trade in particular, will determine how seriously the government concerned pursues its objectives. A country such as Japan, dependent on imports for a wide range of raw materials, has more interests at stake than continental economies such as the United States, which can produce almost all its requirements within its borders. On the other hand, a commodity may be important to a country because it is a major exporter, even if such exports form only a small part of its total trade. For example, exports of wheat by the United States, even in the recent boom years, accounted for less than 6 per cent of its total exports; but the United States contributes nearly 40 per cent to the total world exports of wheat (26 million tonnes out of 65 million tonnes in 1974). Naturally, the United States has a vital interest in all wheat negotiations; likewise India in tea or Canada in iron ore. Some countries may be small exporters of a commodity but may be heavily dependent for foreign exchange earnings on that one commodity. Burundi exports only US$25 million worth of coffee every year out of a total world market of nearly US$4.5 billion; but that 25 million constitutes nearly 80 per cent of its total exports. To understand commodity trade, one has to know who produces what, who exports how much and how heavy the dependence is. This chapter is therefore devoted to this factual setting. The 35 commodities will be analysed according to the nature of their production and conditions of marketing, their importance in terms of the size of the market as well as the degree of dependence.

What Are Primary Commodities?

There is no universally accepted definition of what exactly are the commodities covered by the term 'primary'. The Standard International Trade Classification (hereafter abbreviated to SITC, Revised) divides all goods which enter international trade into ten sections. Of these, Sections 0 to 4 (0 − food and live animals, 1 − beverages and tobacco, 2 − crude inedible materials, 3 − mineral fuels and 4 − oils and fats) are generally considered to be primary commodities. For example, *International Trade,* the annual survey published by GATT, defines primary products as just these five sections. This leads to the anomalous position in which chocolate and cigarettes are treated as primary products while copper or tin metal is excluded. These anomalies are, in fact, the two main objections to limiting the term 'primary commodities' to these five sections, for they include some obvious manufactures, such as meat and cereal preparations, chocolate, manufactured tobacco and synthetic fibres, and, second, exclude some major commodities, particularly non-ferrous metals such as aluminium, copper, nickel, lead, tin and zinc. The UN Statistical Office tries to achieve a compromise by constructing three different indices.[1] The primary commodities index is still confined to sections 0 to 4, but all manufactures are excluded from the calculations. The non-ferrous metals index is based on the six metals listed above but does not include the ores and concentrates of these metals which are considered to be their primary forms. But the UN also includes non-ferrous metals in constructing the 'manufactures' index. There is apparently no consensus on how to treat these metals; their ores are primary, they themselves are separate yet a part of manufactures. However, another UN organisation, UNCTAD, treats all these metals as commodities; so does the World Bank.[2]

The confusion is not confined only to non-ferrous metals (Division 68 of SITC, Revised). Somewhat illogically, hides and skins (Group 211) are considered a primary commodity, but leather (Group 611) is not. From the point of view of trade, a tanned goat skin is as much a primary product as the untanned variety. Another important question is whether Section 3 (mineral fuels) should really be considered a commodity in the same sense as meat, wheat and oil seeds. Section 3 is mainly composed of sources of energy (petroleum, crude and refined, and natural gas), and these, except to the small extent that crude oil is also a raw material for synthetics and plastics, cannot strictly be considered a commodity. Energy sources have little in common with agricultural products and, unlike metals which can be reused, once the energy is extracted precious little is left. Notwithstanding the fact that the world's attention has been drawn to primary commodities as a result of OPEC's success in regulating oil quantities and prices, oil still remains a unique commodity. Much has been, and will be, written about oil, its economics and politics. While one can learn some lessons from the history of the oil trade and its negotiations, its problems and solutions are of a different order of political and economic magnitude. Hence for the purposes of this study the fascinating complexities of the oil problem have to be set aside and referred to only to the extent of their relevance to the problems of other primary commodities.

By excluding fuels and including metals and leather, a more logical definition of primary commodities would become Sections 0, 1, 2 and 4, Division 68 and Group 611. The first four do include some groups representing either processed forms or even wholly synthetic ones. Some of these products, such as synthetic rubber and synthetic fibres, are direct competitors of similar natural products. Often the problems of a natural commodity arise precisely because such close substitutes compete for the same market. Treating both the natural and the artificial product sharing almost identical markets as primary commodities will not place too great a strain on logic. Nevertheless, some manufactures of food, beverages and tobacco (e.g. 062 – sugar confectionery, 073 – chocolates, 112.4 – distilled spirits, and 122 – tobacco manufactures such as cigarettes and cigars) will be left in the definition. For the most part, the statistics analysed in this study will be the export figures of individual commodities. To the limited extent that aggregate figures are used, the fact that the export value of these few manufactured items are not subtracted will not affect the validity of the conclusions drawn. It is not claimed that the refinements suggested produce a perfect definition of primary commodities. To take a glaring example, if non-ferrous metals are considered 'primary', should not at least pig iron (if not both pig iron and ingot steel) be treated likewise? Such questions can be multiplied. However, this study is about the 35 commodities that the international community has considered to be important. The definition given above is adequate for this purpose.

The question 'what is a primary commodity?' is not just an academic one to be left to be resolved by statisticians. A discussion on commodity problems cannot exclude all reference to manufactures. The concept of increasing the exchange earnings of developing countries by promoting exports of processed and manufactured products is a very relevant one. In discussing vertical integration in developing countries and market access in developed countries, reference will have to be made to synthetic fibres (Group 651), fabrics (652 and 653), wood products (Divisions 63 and 64) and even clothing (841) and footwear (851). There are no clear lines between commodities, processed forms and manufactures. Is soluble coffee a commodity or a manufactured product? If leather is a commodity but shoes are manufactures, what about shoe uppers? In any commodity negotiation such questions do arise and give rise to conflicts. Such demarcation problems also have to be considered as an aspect of resolution of commodity conflicts.

The Characteristics of Commodities

In the light of the arguments advanced in Chapter 2, the nature of production and the conditions of marketing of commodities can be viewed under eight headings. For convenience, these are grouped under three different but interrelated aspects. 'Technical' factors are so called because they are basically inherent in a commodity. Institutional factors are those that are susceptible to change by conscious action by governments, and market factors are those closely related to the economic factors that determine the price of a commodity in the market.

Technical factors

1. Type	(i) Renewable.
	(ii) Non-renewable.
2. Nature of production	(i) Whether subject to periodic surpluses of shortages due to production cycles and/or

natural calamities.

(ii) Elasticity of supply, particularly speed at which production can be increased in reaction to shortage.

3. Storability

(i) Period for which storable without undue deterioration.

(ii) Cost of storage.

Institutional factors

4. Controllability of production

(i) Whether multinational or local investment.

(ii) Whether plantation economies.

5. Location of production

(i) Produced mainly in developed countries.

(ii) Produced in both developed and developing countries.

6. Market access

(i) Protected domestic production in importing countries.

(ii) Barriers to the import of processed forms.

Market factors

7. Market control

(i) Free market.

(ii) Controlled or distorted market.

(iii) Closed market.

8. Nature of competition

(i) Competing types.

(ii) Competition from synthetic substitutes.

(iii) Interchangeable within a group.

(iv) Prospects for market expansion, particularly new uses.

It is possible to draw up a table of the 20 or so possibilities and the 35 commodities and check the appropriate box for each one; the table may look impressive but is of little practical value. While eight different characteristics, each with two or three possibilities, have been identified, it does not follow that all the thousands of possible permutations occur in one commodity or another. Each commodity may have some special characteristic, but, by and large, they do fall into definable groups, because some characteristics are interrelated and in some combinations

no commodity example exists. For example, with the possible exception of tin, virtually all the non-renewable commodities (minerals and metals) are produced in both the developed and developing countries. As regards inter-related qualities, renewable tropical products are particularly susceptible to production cycles and periodic surpluses or shortages arising from natural disasters and generally have storage problems. Conversely, metals are easily storable for long periods at a cost not much higher than the interest charges on investment, and their production in times of surplus can be controlled more easily.
easily.

Price elasticity of demand depends both on the nature of the commodity and the nature of the market. Agricultural consumer products and industrial raw materials whose contribution to the cost of the final product is small have low price elasticities of demand. However low the price, there is a limit to the quantity of coffee or tea that can be drunk or of pepper that can be used. Where there is competition from synthetics or easy substitutes the market sets a limit to the maximum price obtainable without appreciable loss of market. The contribution of the cost of jute carpet backing to the price of the carpet may be small but the existence of synthetic substitutes introduces a higher elasticity. Like the concept of elasticity, the degree of instability in price also often figures in discussions on primary commodities. Undue fluctuations in price are not a characteristic inherent in any commodity. They are a consequence of natural and man-made events. The price may rise sharply because a natural calamity reduces available supply; or it may remain stable because the multi-national companies controlling production and export keep it so. Subsequent analysis, particularly in Chapters 7 and 8, will bring out more clearly how acts of God and men affect the price, its stability and its impact on demand and supply.

A characteristic common to all primary commodities is the denial of access in importing countries to processed and more finished forms. Raw cotton and cotton yarn and fabrics, coffee beans and soluble coffee, cocoa and cocoa butter and chocolate, natural rubber and tyres, leather and shoes, raw and refined sugar, iron ore and pig iron or steel, bauxite and aluminium, copper metal and copper wire bars – in every case protection is the norm. Special attention will be paid to this problem also in the subsequent analysis.

The major groups under which most of the commodities fall are six. In each one, some commodities have special characteristics which are indicated after the list under the main group heading.

1. Renewable food products, mainly produced in developing countries, generally competitive market, least storability, very limited competition from synthetics.

    Bananas
    Coffee
    Cocoa
    Pepper
    Tea

Special characteristics:

Bananas — market control by multinational companies.
Coffee and pepper — more easily storable than the others in the group.
Coffee, tea and cocoa — competition from other beverages including soft drinks.
Coffee — also competition from different types and from different geographical production areas.
Coffee, cocoa and pepper — production cycles and periodic surpluses and shortages.

2. Renewable raw materials for industrial use, mainly produced in developing countries, generally competitive market, better storability than food products, powerful competition from synthetics, high price elasticity.

    Natural rubber
    Jute and similar fibres
    Sisal, abaqa, henequen (hard fibres)

Special characteristics:

Rubber — production control difficult in some areas (e.g. Indonesia).

3. Renewable, produced both in developed and developing countries, generally free market, limited storability, high price elasticity due to interchangeability or substitutability.

Interchangeable within a group
    Fishmeal, oilcake (animal feed)
    Oilseeds
    Edible oils

Competition from synthetics
    Cotton
    Wool
    Hides and skins

4. Renewable, produced in both developed and developing countries, high storage costs, protected domestic production in importing countries and distorted international market, price elasticity not always dependent on the international price.

    Beef
    Maize
    Rice
    Wheat
    Sugar
    Citrus fruit
    Wine
    Olive oil
    Tobacco
    Wood and wood products

Special characteristics

Tobacco — state monopoly trading, the problem of effect on health.
Wood and wood products — degree of protection and distortion of market varies widely.

5. Non-renewable, produced in both developed and developing countries, not easily storable, closed market.
    Bauxite
    Iron ore
    Manganese ore
    Phosphate rock

Special characteristics

Bauxite — production controlled by six vertically integrated multinational companies.
Iron ore — production controlled by multinational companies in some areas, monopsonistic buying practices.

6. Non-renewable, produced in both developed and developing countries, easily storable, market partly closed and partly open.

Tin
Copper
Lead and zinc
Nickel
Tungsten

Special characteristics

Tin – limited production in developed countries.
Nickel – exported almost wholly by developed countries.

Out of the 35 commodities, three do not find a place in the list. The reason for treating oil as a special case has been discussed earlier. Shellac and mica, while interesting from the point of view of competition from synthetics, are not significant commodities in value terms in international trade or the number of countries exporting them.

The identification of the characteristics of different commodities has to serve two purposes. First, it must help to identify the specific attitudes of participants in a commodity negotiation that arise as a direct result. These could be (i) an interest, or lack of it, in regulating the market for the commodity, (ii) an adversary relationship with another participant or group of participants with whom a conflict of interest is perceived; (iii) a co-operative relationship with other participants who share a similar perception; and (iv) a collusive relationship with one set of adversaries against another set. Second, the specific characteristics and relationship they engender must help to identify the possible techniques that could be used to arrive at agreements. As emphasised earlier, conflict, co-operation and collusion in commodity negotiations are not solely the result of economic factors. However, the solving of economic questions is an essential prerequisite; if there are no viable economic solutions to the problems of a commodity, no amount of political 'goodwill' can produce agreement on regulatory measures. It is therefore necessary to look at the economic importance of the trade in primary commodities to world trade as well as to individual countries.

Who Exports Primary Commodities?

Trade in primary commodities is only a part of total world trade which, as is well known, has expanded phenomenally since the end of the Second World War. Total world exports in 1948 were just over US$26 billion; in 1975 they were 33 times that figure – US$878 billion. During this period, the world has also been perceived as being divided into three distinct parts – the rich industrial nations called the developed, the

Table 3.1: Share of Major Groups in Total World Exports

	1950	1960	1965	1970	1971	1972	1973	1974	1975
World	100	100	100	100	100	100	100	100	100
Developed countries	60.9	67.0	68.8	71.9	71.8	71.7	71.0	64.9	66.1
Centrally planned countries	8.1	11.7	11.6	10.5	10.3	10.3	10.0	8.6	9.9
Developing countries	30.9	21.2	19.3	17.6	17.8	18.1	19.0	26.5	24.0
of which									
OPEC	7.0	7.0	6.6	5.6	6.8	7.0	7.4	14.8	13.0
NOEDEC	23.9	14.2	12.7	12.0	11.1	11.0	11.5	11.7	11.0

Sources: UNCTAD, *Review of International Trade and Development*; UN, *Yearbook of International Trade, 1974, and Monthly Bulletin of Statistics*, February and August 1976.

poorer erstwhile colonies known as the developing and the centrally planned countries following a Marxist economic philosophy. How has each group fared in this vast expansion of trade? Table 3.1 gives the figures for the share of the three groups of countries in total world exports for a few selected earlier years and for the six years 1970 to 1975.

Since 1950, the developed market economy countries have increased their share of world exports from 61 to 71 per cent. In 1974 it dropped to 65 per cent as a result of the sudden sharp rise in oil prices, but the disruption it caused was soon overcome and the earlier rising trend was resumed the very next year. Before the oil price rise, the share of the oil-exporting developing countries was about 7 per cent, but it has doubled since then. The share of the centrally planned economies has fluctuated at about 10 per cent. The decline in share of trade has therefore fallen entirely on the non-oil exporting developing countries (hereafter abbreviated to NOEDEC) who have seen their share drop from nearly a quarter to about 11 per cent.

The steadily increasing importance of the developed countries in world trade is seen more clearly when one looks at the changes in the direction of trade. Detailed network tables are usually available in the GATT annual publication *International Trade* and in the UNCTAD annual *Review of International Trade and Development*. A table showing how much of the exports to developed, developing and centrally planned countries comes from each of the three groups is given in Appendix 3. A striking conclusion that is apparent from the table is that in 1955 developed countries accounted for only 15 per cent of all exports to the socialist countries; by 1974, almost two fifths of all exports to these countries came from the developed countries. Correspondingly, intra-socialist trade has dropped, during these twenty years, from four fifths to just over half. The rich countries have always supplied about two thirds of the needs of the poor ones. Thus, the rich countries have gained in what is called the East-West trade and maintained their share of the North-South one. The most important segment is trade with developed countries.

Table 3.2 shows the changes in the pattern of exports of this trade for a few selected years between 1955 and 1974. Exports from the centrally planned countries to the industrial countries have never reached even 4 per cent; exports from the non-oil exporting developing countries stays at about 12 per cent. The phenomenal expansion in world trade is primarily due to a fast growth in trade among the industrial nations themselves, except for the oil price rise in 1974.

Table 3.2: Exports to Developed Countries from Different Economic Groups Percentage Shares

	1955	1960	1965	1970	1971	1972	1973	1974
Total exports	100	100	100	100	100	100	100	100
From other developed countries	69.1	72.7	75.7	78.1	78.1	77.8	76.2	67.8
From developing countries	28.1	23.9	20.6	18.4	18.4	18.9	20.0	28.3
of which								
OPEC	…	…	…	6.5	7.5	7.7	8.2	16.3
NOEDEC	…	…	…	12.0	10.9	11.1	11.8	12.0
From centrally planned countries	2.8	3.4	3.7	3.5	3.5	3.4	3.8	3.8

Sources: UN, *Yearbook of International Trade Statistics*, 1961, 1966 and 1974: *Monthly Bulletin of Statistics*, August 1976.

It is only to be expected that the technological and industrial might of the rich countries would lead to an increase in trade in industrial products among themselves. But to conclude therefrom that all the increase in the share of world exports accruing to the developed countries must be due to an increase in trade in manufactured goods alone would be erroneous. For this conclusion to be true, the share of the different groups in exports of primary commodites would have to remain approximately the same over the years. Table 3.3 shows the share of major groups in world primary commodity exports (excluding fuel and non-ferrous metals, i.e. Sections 0, 1, 2 and 4 only) for 1960, 1965, 1970, 1974 and 1975.

Table 3.3: Share of Major Groups in World Exports of Primary Commodities Excluding Fuel Sections 0, 1, 2 and 4, SITC, Revised

	1960	1965	1970	1974	1975
World	100	100	100	100	100
Developed countries	52.7	56.2	59.0	63.0	66.1
Developing countries	36.2	33.4	31.1	28.0	24.0
Centrally planned	11.1	10.4	9.9	9.0	9.9

Note: For earlier years, the *Yearbook* does not provide export figures for groups of commodities (e.g. 68 and 611); the break-up of figures for 1950 by economic system is also not available.
Source: Derived from UN *Yearbook of International Trade Statistics,* 1974.

It is apparent from Table 3.3 that the share of the developed countries in exports of primary commodities, excluding oil and other fuels, has been rising steadily at the expense of the other groups, particularly the developing countries. The poor countries, which used to export over a third of the world's primary commodities, now export less than a quarter. Since the share of the centrally planned countries hovers around 10 per cent, the shift in shares has been to the benefit of the rich industrialised countries. It should also be noted that one of the years listed in Table 3.3 is 1974 – a 'boom' year for commodity trade; that year is as much a part of the trend as any other. Obviously, the benefits of the boom have not been distributed proportionately; the lion's share has gone to the richer countries. The 'dramatic turnaround' in the terms of trade of the developing countries that some observers predicted when the boom was on did not in practice materialise (see, for example, Angus Hone on 'Gains and Losers in the 1973 Commodity

Table 3.4: Value and Percentage Share of Major Groups in Exports of Primary Commodities Excluding Fuel, 1969 to 1974 Section 0, 1, 2, 4, and Division 68, SITC, Revised

	Value in million US $											
	1969		1970		1971		1972		1973		1974	
	Value	Share	Value	Share	Value	Share	Value	Share	Value	Share	Value	Share
World	77,450	100.0	86,390	100.0	89,090	100.0	105,040	100.0	151,960	100.0	194,640	100.0
Developed countries	44,460	57.4	51,500	59.6	53,930	60.5	64,720	61.6	96,140	63.3	119,900	61.6
Developing countries	25,000	32.3	26,610	30.8	26,120	29.3	30,180	28.7	41,890	27.6	57,210	29.4
Centrally planned	8,010	10.3	8,290	9.6	9,050	10.2	10,110	9.6	13,940	9.2	17,530	9.0

Sources: UN Statistical Yearbook, 1974; UN Yearbook of International Trade Statistics, 1974; UN Monthly Bulletin of Statistics, February and August 1976.

Boom' in the *ODI Review,* no.1, 1974). The distribution of benefits from a commodity boom will be analysed in greater detail in Chapter 8.

Table 3.3 also shows that, by 1974, nearly two thirds of the world trade in primary commodities was in the hands of the rich countries. That this is not an accidental result arising from the choice of the years or the exclusion of non-ferrous metals is shown by Table 3.4, which lists for the latest six years for which statistics are available (1969-74), exports by major groups of primary commodities including metals (i.e. Sections 0, 1, 2, 4 and Division 68).

It is the richer countries that are steadily increasing their share of the total market, the manufactured goods market and also the primary commodities market, excluding that for oil. An obvious conclusion is that the present international economic system operates in a way that leads to a steady improvement in the rich countries' share. If the New International Economic Order in general and commodity agreements in particular are to be designed to benefit developing countries, sheer economic interests dictate that the rich countries will have little interest in it. A 'high official' of the United States, when informed that the poor countries want a New International Economic Order, is said to have remarked, 'So, what is wrong with the old one?' In other words, those who benefit from a system have little cause to change it. The developing countries, however, have long perceived a built-in asymmetry in the present system which seems to them to operate inequitably by enriching the rich and impoverishing the poor. One can understand the rich countries, with their technological and innovative ability, increasing their share of exports of manufactured goods; but they also simultaneously increase the share of primary commodity exports. Figure 3.1, which shows the change in the shares between developed and developing countries, illustrates this graphically – in more ways than one!

Who Exports What and How Much?

Having looked at the broad setting of world trade as a whole and total trade in primary commodities, we can now set out the basic facts of trade in individual commodities – the size of the market and who exports what. Table 3.5 shows the value of total market economy exports and the share of the developed countries in that total for 65 different primary commodities. Though quantities exported are important in determining market shares, value figures are used in this table since a large number of disparate commodities are brought

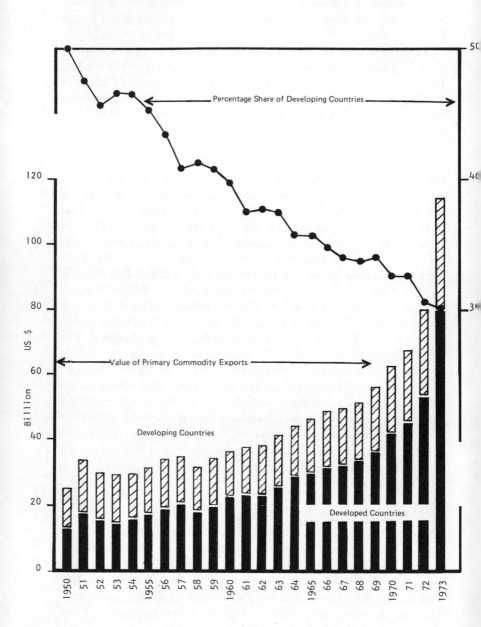

Figure 3.1: Value and Share of Developed and Developing Countries in Primary Commodity Exports (Groups 0,1,2 and 4—1950 to 1973

Data for Figure 3.1: Value of exports Billion US $ — left hand scale.
Share of developing countries — right hand scale.

Year	Developed countries	Developing countries	Total	Share of developing countries — %
1950	12.59	12.55	25.14	49.9
1951	17.66	15.95	33.61	47.5
1952	15.84	13.26	29.10	45.6
1953	15.41	13.49	28.90	46.7
1954	15.73	13.70	29.43	46.6
1955	17.02	14.10	31.12	45.3
1956	18.96	14.49	33.45	43.3
1957	20.29	14.38	34.67	41.5
1958	18.37	13.59	31.96	42.5
1959	19.91	14.05	33.96	41.4
1960	22.12	14.59	36.71	39.7
1961	23.15	13.96	37.11	37.6
1962	23.44	14.26	37.70	37.8
1963	25.67	15.44	41.11	37.6
1964	28.44	16.37	44.81	36.5
1965	29.59	16.42	46.01	35.7
1966	31.62	16.85	48.47	34.8
1967	32.22	16.51	48.73	33.9
1968	33.75	17.18	50.93	34.9
1969	36.83	19.01	55.84	34.0
1970	43.78	22.96	66.74	34.4
1971	47.27	23.24	70.51	33.0
1972	57.09	27.60	84.69	32.6
1973	85.15	38.39	123.54	31.1
1974	107.67	50.34	158.01	31.9

Table 3.5: Value of Market Economy Exports and Share of Developed Countries for Selected Primary Commodities

Annual average of recent years

No.	SITC (Revised) No.	Commodity	Size of market US $ million	Share of developed countries %
Meat, fresh, chilled or frozen				
1.	O11.1	Beef	3,671	81
2.	011.2 to 011.8	Meat and poultry excluding beef	3,016	92
Cereals				
3.	041,046	Wheat and wheat flour	9,765	96
4.	042	Rice	1,956	54
5.	044	Maize	5,726	84
6.	043, 045	Barley, rye, oats etc.	2,760	87
Fruit				
7.	051.1, 051.2	Citrus fruit	1,238	75
8.	051.3	Bananas	673	7
9.	052.03	Raisins	271	61
Sugar				
10.	061.1	Raw sugar	6,318	12
11.	061.2	Refined sugar	1,704	59
12.	Total	Sugar, raw and refined	8.022	22
Tropical beverages				
13.	071.1	Coffee, green or roasted	4,036	0
14.	072.1	Cocoa bean.	1,366	0
15.	072.2, 072.3	Cocoa powder, paste and butter	615	50
16.	074.1	Tea	684	0
Spices				
17.	Ex 075.1	Pepper	174	0
Tobacco				
18.	121	Unmanufactured tobacco	2,112	59
Alcoholic beverages				
19.	112.1	Wine	1,881	90
Oilseeds, nuts and kernels				
20.	221.1	Groundnuts (peanuts)	404	41
21.	221.4	Soyabeans	3,686	84
22.	221.2, 221.3	Tropical tree nuts (copra, palm products)	334	0

Table 3.5 (continued)

No.	SITC (Revised) No.	Commodity	Size of market US $ million	Share of developed countries %
23.	221.5, 221.7	Linseed, castor seed	169	82
24.	221.6, 221.8	Other oil seeds	603	77
25.	Total 221	Oilseeds, nuts, kernels	5,196	74
Fats and oils				
26.	023	Butter	1,261	99
27.	091.3	Lard	164	94
28.	091.4	Margarine	180	84
29.	411.3	Animal oils and fats	672	98
Vegetable oils				
30.	421.2	Soyabean oil	801	89
31.	421.5	Olive oil	420	58
32.	421.4	Groundnut oil	297	27
33.	421.3, 421.6 421.7	Other soft oils	434	93
34.	422.3	Coconut oil	439	19
35.	422.4	Palm oil and palm kernel oil	912	9
36.	Total	Edible vegetable oils	3,303	49
37.	422.1, 422.5 Ex 422.9	Technical oils	297	30
Oilcake and meal				
38.	Ex 081.3	Soyabean cake	1,677	76
39.	Ex 081.3	Groundnut cake	204	8
40.	Ex 081.3	Cottonseed cake	156	13
41.	Ex 081.3	Other oilseed cakes	360	41
42.	081.3	Total oilseed cake, meal	2,397	61
Forestry products				
43.	241, 242	Industrial roundwood @	2,918	44
44.	243	Sawn wood @	4,224	86
45.	Ex 251	Wood pulp @	3,629	98
Rubber				
46.	231.1	Natural rubber	2,570	0
47.	231.2	Synthetic rubber @	970	99
48.	231.1, 231.2	Total rubber @	3,265	31
Fibres				
49.	262.1, 262.2	Wool	2,556	89
50.	263.1	Raw cotton	3,664	33

Table 3.5 (continued)

No.	SITC (Revised) No.	Commodity	Size of market US $ million	Share of developed countries %
51.	264	Jute, similar fibres	182	0
52.	265.4, 265.5	Sisal, abaqa, henequen	232	0
53.	266	Synthetic and regenerated fibres	1,909	99
Hides, skins, leather				
54.	211	Hides and skins @	1,466	81
55.	611	Leather @	1,363	69
56.	Total	Hides, skins, leather @	2,829	75
Minerals				
57.	271.3	Phosphate rock	1,455	21
58.	281	Iron ore	3,761	55
59.	283.7	Manganese ore and	392	45
Non-ferrous metals — ores, concentrates, unwrought metal				
60.	283.1, 682.1	Copper and	7,025	44
61.	283.3, 513.65 684.1	Bauxite, alumina, aluminium	3,526	72
62.	283.4, 685.1	Lead and	854	75
63.	283, 686.1	Zinc	1,675	80
64.	283.6, 687.1	Tin	1,233	17
65.	683.1	Nickel, metal only and	856	97

Note: All figures are averages of the three years 1973 to 1975, except those marked @ and &; @ — average of 1972 to 1974; & — average of 1974 and 1975.

Sources: For agricultural products, FAO *Trade Yearbook,* 1975; for forestry products, FAO *Yearbook of Forestry Products,* 1974; for minerals, metals, synthetic products, hides etc., UN *Yearbook of International Trade Statistics,* 1974 and 1975, supplemented by IBRD and UNCTAD data.

together in one table; the relative importance of different commodities in world trade is more easily seen if specified in uniform dollar terms. Three other comments have to be made about the figures in this table, which will be used as the basis for further analysis. First, the detailed three- and four-figure SITC commodity-wise trade statistics given in the UN *Yearbook of International Trade Statistics* confine themselves to trade in the market economy world; exports of socialist countries are thus excluded though complete figures for agricultural products are available in the FAO *Trade Yearbooks.* The exclusion of the non-market economy world does not affect the validity of the conclusions derived from these figures. In view of their different economic systems, the contribution which these countries can make to the resolving of commodity issues has to be dealt with separately (see Chapter 6). Centrally planned countries, in any case, account for only 10 per cent of world trade and trade in primary commodities. The second clarification relates to the choice of years. Selecting just one year is bound to be anomalous for some commodities; an average is obviously preferable. And the more recent the data the better, though this may also be anomalous since the recent past has had two 'boom' years − 1973 and 1974. It is difficult to avoid them; using the average for a number of years before 1972 will not only mean using five-year-old data but also give a much undervalued picture for the size of the markets. A calculation of the size of the markets for different commodities averaged over 1969 to 1971 showed them to be very much smaller than they are now, in many cases just half the current size. Hence the figures used in Table 3.5 are the average of 1973 to 1975 for most commodities and 1972 to 1974 for some in which the 1975 figures are not available; in a few cases, a two-year average has been used for want of reliable data. Lastly, the export data are all gross figures; re-exports have not been deducted. The figures are therefore to be construed broadly; no accuracy to the last significant digit is claimed.

Based on the size of the market, the commodities can be ranked in importance as follows:

Annual average exports of

Over US $7.5 billion: Wheat

Between US $5 and 7.5 billion: Copper, maize, raw sugar and oilseeds as a group

Between US $4 and 5 billion: Sawn wood, coffee

Between US $3 and 4 billion: Iron ore, raw cotton, soyabeans, |beef, wood pulp, meat and poultry other than beef, bauxite, alumina and aluminium as a group, and edible vegetable oils as a group

Between US $2 and 3 billion: Rough wood, coarse grains other than maize, oilcake, hides, skins and leather, natural rubber, wool, tobacco

Between US $1 and 2 billion: Rice, synthetic fibres, wine, refined sugar, soyabean cake, zinc, phosphate rock, cocoa beans, butter, citrus fruit, tin

Between US $500 million and 1 billion: Nickel, synthetic rubber, palm oil and palm kernel oil, lead, soyabean oil, bananas, animal oils and fats, processed cocoa products, tea

Between US $250 million and 500 million: Coconut oil, groundnuts, manganese ore, tropical tree nuts, groundnut oil, technical oils, raisins

Below US $250 million: Hard fibres, groundnut cake, raw jute, margarine, pepper, lard

In terms of the shares of the markets between the developed and the developing countries, the commodities fall into the following two groups:

Developed countries with more than half the market

Almost wholly exported by them: Wood pulp, nickel, aluminium, butter, synthetic rubber, synthetic fibres, animal oils and fats

Between 90 and 100 per cent: Wheat (including flour), meat and poultry other than beef, lard, wine

Between 80 and 90 per cent: All coarse grains, wool, beef, shaped wood, soyabean and its oil, margarine, zinc

Between 70 and 80 per cent: Lead, citrus fruit, hides, skins and leather, oilseeds as a whole, soyabean cake

Between 60 and 70 per cent: Oilcake as a whole

Between 50 and 60 per cent: Refined sugar, unmanufactured tobacco, iron ore, olive oil, rice, oilseeds, processed cocoa products

Developing countries with more than half the market

Almost wholly exported by them: Green coffee, natural rubber, cocoa beans, bananas, tea, tin, raw jute, pepper, hard fibres, tropical nuts and their oils and cake

Between 80 and 90 per cent: Raw sugar, coconut oil, cotton seed cake

Between 70 and 80 per cent: Phosphate rock, groundnut oil

Between 60 and 70 per cent: Raw cotton

Between 50 and 60 per cent: Rough wood, copper, manganese ore, groundnuts

These facts are more easily visible in the scatter diagram (Figure 3.2) in which the position of each commodity is plotted according to the size of the market in the horizontal axis and the share of developed and developing countries along the vertical. Reading them in bands horizontally produces the second list; read vertically the first.

Dependence on Exports of Developing Countries

The concept of dependence is used in this chapter in the traditional

Figure 3.2: Size of Market and share of Developed and Developing Countries for different Comodities

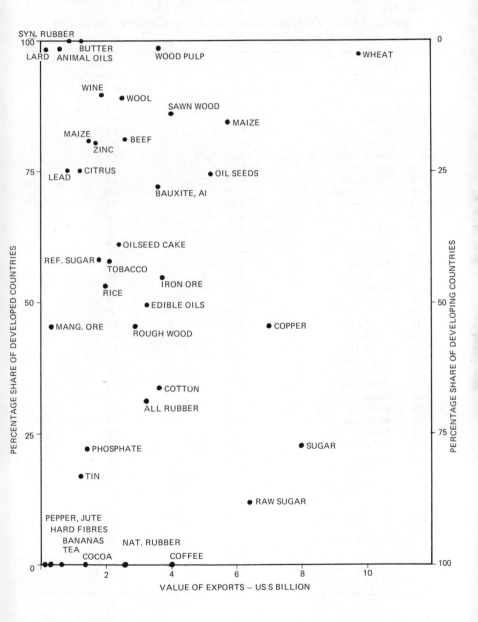

Data for Figure 3.2: Value of exports and share of different groups

Left hand scale: 0 from bottom to 100 at top — share of developed countries
Right hand scale: 100 from bottom to 0 at top — share of developing countries.

No.	Commodity	Value	.Left hand scale share of developed countries
1.	Beef	3.67	81
2.	Wheat	9.77	96
3.	Rice	1.95	54
4.	Maize	5.73	84
5.	Citrus fruit	1.24	75
6.	Bananas	0.67	0
7.	Raw Sugar	6.32	12
8.	Refined sugar	1.70	59
9.	All sugar	8.02	22
10.	Coffee	4.04	0
11.	Cocoa	1.37	0
12.	Tea	0.68	0
13.	Pepper	0.17	0
14.	Tobacco	2.11	59
15.	Wine	1.88	90
16.	Oilseeds	5.20	74
17.	Butter	1.26	99
18.	Lard	0.16	94
19.	Animal oils	0.67	98
20.	Edible oils	3.30	49
21.	Oilseed cake	2.40	61
22.	Rough wood	2.92	44
23.	Sawn wood	4.22	86
24.	Wood pulp	3.63	98
25.	Natural rubber	2.57	0
26.	Synthetic rubber	0.97	99
27.	All rubber	3.27	31
28.	Wool	2.56	89
29.	Cotton	3.66	33
30.	Jute	0.18	0
31.	Hard fibres	0.23	0
32.	Hides and skins	1.47	81
33.	Rock phosphate	1.46	21
34.	Iron ore	3.76	55
35.	Manganese ore	0.39	45
36.	Copper	7.03	44
37.	Bauxite, aluminium	3.53	72
38.	Lead	0.85	75
39.	Zinc	1.68	80
40.	Tin	1.23	17

sense of the importance of a commodity or group of commodities in trade; the higher the share, the greater the dependence. The implication is that heavy reliance on a few commodities makes the country concerned more vulnerable to changes in the international trade in those commodities. The wider concepts of interdependence and sensitivity, which were introduced in chapter 1, are also relevant to the study of commodity conflict. The relationship between commodity dependence and interdependence will be considered in chapter 12.

The well-known facts about dependence on exports of primary commodities are: (i) developed countries, though having a substantial share of the market, are not heavily dependent on them; (ii) developing countries as a whole are more dependent; and (iii) some developing countries are dependent for their export earnings on just one or two commodities. While these conclusions are generally true, there are wide variations in the degree of dependence of various countries. It will also be worthwhile examining the trend of dependence to see whether it is increasing or decreasing for any group of countries.

Table 3.6: Value of Primary Commodities and Manufactures/Exports as Percentage of Total Exports, 1960, 1970, 1972 and 1974

	Exports (Billion US$)				Percentage of total exports			
	1960	1970	1972	1974	1960	1970	1972	1974
All developing countries								
Primary commodities								
(including fuel)	24.7	44.3	57.0	190.9	90.3	83.2	79.2	85.9
Manufactures	2.5	8.4	14.4	30.5	9.1	16.3	20.0	13.7
Developed countries								
primary commodities								
(including fuel)	29.3	59.1	74.6	146.1	34.3	26.4	25.0	26.9
manufactures	54.9	161.3	218.7	388.5	64.3	71.9	73.5	71.6

Notes: Primary commodities —SITC, Revised, 0 to 4 and 68; Manufactures — — SITC, Revised, 5 to 8, excluding 68.
Source: IBRD, *Commodity Trade and Price Trends,* 1976.

Table 3.6 is a brief extract from the World Bank annual publication *Commodity Trade and Price Trends.*[3] It confirms the fact that in a world that is increasingly industrialising and rapidly expanding trade, the share of primary commodities in total exports is steadily diminishing for both developed and developing countries. Of course, primary commodity experts are in the aggregate much less important to developed countries than trade in manufactures; only a quarter of the total exports of rich countries are commodity exports. For the developing countries, both OPEC and NOEDEC, the dependence is still high, amounting to over 80 per cent in 1974. The World Bank's figures include oil exports, which are being excluded in this study for reasons explained earlier. The recalculated figures, excluding oil exports and OPEC countries, for the last six years are shown in Table 3.7.

A comparison of developing countries' dependency when oil is included and when it is excluded leads to the conclusion that oil-exporting countries are very much more dependent on that one commodity for export earnings. For many of them, particularly the large exporters, the dependence is almost total. Table 3.7 also shows that the dependence of non-oil exporting developing countries is steadily declining. Between 1969 and 1974, the ratio of manufactures to primary commodities in non-fuel exports improved from 25:75 to 35:65. This is an indicator of the progress of industrialisation in developing countries in the post-war period and of the fact that their manufactured products are being traded competitively in world markets, albeit with some help from the developed countries. If the reduction in dependence is a good thing, then the trend is welcome and should be encouraged. It is in this context that the question of increased access to processed forms exported by developing countries will be considered in chapter 6. While developing countries as a whole are reducing their dependence on primary commodity exports, progress is not uniform in all poor countries; some are indeed still heavily dependent on the exports of just a few primary commodities. This aspect has been well documented in a variety of ways. One method, adopted by the World Bank, is to list for each commodity the names of countries which are dependent for two-thirds or more of their export earnings on that commodity, then half to two thirds, one third to half and so on downwards. A similar table has been prepared, using World Bank data, for the more normal recent years, 1970-72, and may be seen in Appendix 4. An alternative method is to list the *countries* in order of their dependence, indicating the commodities as appropriate. Since this enables a number of conclusions relevant to this study to be drawn, the data in the Appendix has been used to draw up a list of all non-oil exporting developing countries which have a dependence of more than 50 per cent on primary commodity exports. The exclusion of the

Table 3.7: Exports of Primary Products and Manufactures Non-Oil Exporting Developing Countries 1969 to 1974

(Value in billion US $)

Year	Total Exports	Fuel Exports	Non-fuel Exports	Primary commodities		Manufactures	
				Value	Percentage of non-fuel exports	Value	Percentage of non-fuel exports
1969	33.4	2.6	30.8	23.3	75.6	7.2	23.3
1970	37.4	2.9	34.4	24.5	71.0	9.2	26.7
1971	38.8	3.0	35.8	24.1	67.3	10.7	29.8
1972	45.9	4.0	41.8	27.6	66.0	14.1	33.6
1973	68.1	5.9	62.2	39.6	63.6	22.0	35.4
1974	99.9	17.3	82.5	52.9	64.1	28.9	35.0

Source: UN Yearbook of International Trade Statistics, 1974; Monthly Bulletin of Statistics, August 1976

Notes: Fuel — Section 3, SITC, Revised. Primary Commodities — 0, 1, 2, 4, 68. Manufactures — 5 to 8, excluding 68. NOEDEC inclues a few countries (Bahrain, Brunel, Oman, Trinidad and Tobago) with exports of petroleum over 50 per cent of total exports in 1974.

oil-exporting countries does not imply that their dependence has been ignored. Apart from the fact that all major oil exporters depend almost wholly on exports of that commodity, some oil exporters also depend on other primary commodities. Bananas and coffee are important to Ecuador, cocoa to Nigeria, rubber and timber to Indonesia, cotton to Syria and timber and manganese ore to Gabon. That this dependence is not specifically mentioned is merely an acknowledgement of the fact that, with the oil price rise, their developmental efforts are less constrained by problems arising out of these commodities.

The 59 non-oil exporting developing countries that are dependent for more than half their exports are ranked below in order of dependence. For reasons more fully explained in Appendix 4, the ranking is only generally correct; there could be significant distortions in individual countries, due to the choice of the commodities by the Bank.

Dependence on exports of primary commodities – NOEDEC countries
Over 90 per cent

1. Mauritius *	Sugar 90%
2. Nepal*	Rice 85%
3. Tonga	Copra 78%, bananas 22%
4. Namibia	Copper 63%, lead 26%
5. Sao Tomé/Principe	Cocoa 70%, coffee 28%
6. Equatorial Guinea	Cocoa 70%, coffee 28%
7. Zambia*	Copper 94%
8. Uganda	Coffee 59%, cotton 20%
9. Liberia	Iron ore 73%, rubber 16%
10. Guadaloupe	Sugar 60%, bananas 32%

80 to 90 per cent

1. Togo	Phosphate 33%, cocoa 35%, coffee 18%
2. Peru	Fishmeal 28%, copper 22%
3. Zaire*	Copper 68%
4. Khmer Republic	Rice 60%, rubber 15%
5. Honduras	Bananas 49%, coffee 14%
6. Burundi*	Coffee 73%
7. Sri Lanka	Tea 60%, rubber 18%
8. Cuba*	Sugar 84%
9. Laos*	Timber 80%
10. Gambia*	Groundnuts and groundnut oil 85%
11. Panama*	Bananas 56%
12. Rwanda	Coffee 57%, tin 19%

13. Dominican Rep.*	Sugar 53%
14. Colombia*	Coffee 59%
15. Chile*	Copper 72%
16. Malawi	Tobacco 42%, tea 20%
17. Mauretania*	Iron ore 77%

70 to 80 per cent

1. Ivory Coast	Coffee 33%, cocoa 18%, timber 22%
2. Philippines	Timber 21%, sugar 19%, copper 16%
3. Malaysia	Rubber 28%, tin 18%, timber 16%
4. Bolivia*	Tin 52%
5. Burma	Rice 44%, timber 25%
6. Chad	Cotton 62%, beef 12%
7. Congo People's Republic	Timber 57%
8. Ghana*	Cocoa 62%
9. Costa Rica	Bananas 28%, coffee 28%
10. Yemen Arab Republic	Coffee 35%, cotton 25%, hides 13%
11. Haiti	Coffee 43%, bananas 16%
12. Seychelles Islands*	Copra 70%

60 to 70 per cent

1. Sudan*	Cotton 61%
2. Cameroon	Coffee 25%, cocoa 23%
3. Ethiopia*	Coffee 53%
4. Kenya	Coffee 27%, tea 17%
5. Fiji*	Sugar 56%
6. Uruguay	Beef 34%, wool 21%
7. Nicaragua	Coffee 16%, cotton 14%
8. El Salvador	Coffee 42%, cotton 12%
9. Thailand	Rice 19%, maize 11%, rubber 11%
10. Brazil	Coffee 27%
11. Mozambique	Sugar 15%, cotton 15%
12. Egypt*	Cotton 47%
13. Central African Republic	Cotton 28%, coffee 21%

50 to 60 per cent

1. Guatemala	Coffee 34%, cotton 10%
2. Tanzania	Coffee 16%, cotton 14%
3. Martinique*	Bananas 48%
4. Upper Volta*	Cotton 42%
5. Guyana	Sugar 31%, bauxite 13%

6. Niger	Groundnuts and groundnut oil	46%
7. Benin	Cotton 18%, cocoa 17%	

Of the 59 countries in the list, 23, marked with an asterisk, are dependent on exports of a *single* commodity for the bulk of their export earnings.

Six countries stand out for almost exclusive dependence on one commodity. Copper supplies 94 per cent of all Zambia's exports; 90 per cent of Mauritian and 84 per cent of Cuban exports come from sugar, 85 per cent of Nepal's from rice, 85 per cent of Gambia's from groundnuts and groundnut oil and 80 per cent of Laotian from timber.

When the list is scanned for countries which are dependent on two commodities, some interesting pairs emerge: coffee and cocoa, coffee and cotton, coffee and bananas and sugar and bananas. This pairing has relevance to the problems of land use in developing countries and the effects of actions in one commodity on another. These aspects will be examined in Chapters 5 and 12.

The list is also useful in determining the importance of commodities in terms of the number of countries dependent on them. By far the most important is coffee, since 24 countries are dependent to a significant extent. Next in order of importance are cotton with 17 countries relying on it and sugar, with eleven. Nine countries depend on timber (broadleaved), eight each on bananas and cocoa and seven on copper.

The list contains countries of varying sizes; at one extreme, even a large country such as Brazil is dependent on primary commodity exports. There are 21 countries with populations of over five million. The largest group, however, consists of countries with less than five million population – 33 in all. Of these, eleven have less than a million people.

Though all the countries listed as 'least developed' do not find a place in the list, it goes without saying that they are all heavily dependent on exports of primary products.

Dependence of Developed Countries

When it comes to developed countries, one sees more clearly that dependence is a two-way problem; there is import dependence as well as export dependence. The fact that import dependence has caught the public eye has masked the equally relevant export dependence of the rich countries. Though these are as a whole less dependent than the developing countries on primary commodities exports, the dependence of individual countries varies widely.

There are four categories among the industrialised nations: (i) those that are blessed with abundant natural resources, large territories and are natural low-cost producers — the United States, Canada, Australia and Sweden are obvious examples; (ii) those with fewer natural resources, more dependence on imports and high-cost producers, particularly of agricultural products — many members of the EEC fall in this category; (iii) Japan, with few natural resources and high dependence on imports of energy and raw materials is a category by itself; (iv) countries such as the United Kingdom and the Netherlands have for historical reasons been importers, processors and distributors of raw materials and have an economic dependence different from that of the others.

Even in the first group of countries, the dependence varies enormously, as is shown by Table 3.8, which compares the contribution of primary commodities with total exports of the United States, Canada, Australia and Sweden.

The fact that the United States comes well behind Australia and Canada in Table 3.8 should not lead to the assumption that American economic interests are less. The United States is the single largest exporter of primary commodities in the world, excluding the oil exporters. US exports of such commodities totalled 29 billion dollars in 1974. In a very wide range of commodities, the United States is the largest or second largest exporter, as the representative list below shows. The figures in brackets indicate the US share of the world export market in each commodity listed, based on the average value of exports between 1970 and 1972.

Table 3.8 Exports of Primary Commodities as Percentage of Total Exports — USA, Canada, Australia and Sweden

	1969	1970	1971	1972	1973	1974	Average
Australia	79.9	78.1	77.2	77.5	76.3		77.5*
Canada	40.4	42.7	40.8	39.5	42.2	39.8	41.2
United States	24.5	26.0	24.5	26.1	32.8	29.9	28.0
Sweden	25.8	24.2	23.1	22.6	23.6	23.4	23.6

*of 5 years
Primary commodities — 0,1,2,4,68
Source: UN *Yearbook of International Trade Statistics,* 1974; *Monthly Bulletin of Statistics* February 1976.

US largest exporter of: soyabeans (91 per cent), animals oils and fats (60 per cent), maize (46 per cent), oilcake (37 per cent) of which soyabean cake (62 per cent), tobacco (37 per cent), wheat (32 per cent) rice (26 per cent), cotton (17 per cent).

US second or third largest exporter of: raisins (19 per cent), crude fertilisers (17 per cent), of which phosphates (30 per cent), pulp (17 per cent), poultry (10 per cent), margarine (10 per cent).

Canada is the largest exporter of a variety of forestry products — newsprint (69 per cent of the total market), shaped wood (36 per cent), pulp (32 per cent) and paper and board (26 per cent). Canada is the most important supplier of non-ferrous metals to the market economy world and the largest exporter of lead ore, nickel ore and metal and the second largest of lead metal. One half of the world's export of zinc metal, 40 per cent of zinc ore and one third of exports of copper ore are Canadian. The second largest wheat exporter, with nearly a quarter of the market, is Canada. Sweden also has a major share in the entire range of coniferous wood and products — 16 per cent of the shaped wood market, 32 per cent of the pulp market and 13 per cent of the paper market. Major Swedish non-ferrous metal exports include lead ore and zinc ore. All three — Canada, Sweden and Australia — are major exporters of iron ore, holding between them roughly one half of the world market. Canadian exports of iron ore average 40 to 50 million tons a year, Swedish about 23 million tons. The growth of Australian exports has been phenomenal — 33 million tons in 1971 and 50 million tons in 1972. Australia is also the largest exporter of lead metal and the third largest exporter of wheat. Over half of the wool traded in the world markets is Australian.

Food, oilseeds and oils, iron ore, non-ferrous metals — the developed countries rich in natural endowments have a vital economic stake in a wide range of primary commodities. It is only natural that in negotiations involving any of these commodities they play a role based on their economic interest. The power of the United States is not only a consequence of the overall wealth and industrial might of that country but also of the market power it can exercise on individual commodities. Earlier, an example was cited to show how even in such a minor commodity as sultanas Australia threatened to withdraw from the agreement. The point to note is that it will be futile to expect countries with vital stakes in many commodities to be motivated in international negotiation only by political goodwill, altruism or belief in slogans of interdependence.

Import Dependence

Dependence on imports for economic survival and growth is not a new phenomenon. Immediately after the war, the United Kingdom entered into a number of long-term contracts for supplies of primary commodities in order to ensure their availability for post-war recovery in what were still unsettled world market conditions. Most of these lapsed when conditions became more orderly. Only one, the Commonwealth Sugar Agreement, essentially a seven-year contract, survived; the changes made in the agreement as conditions changed will be referred to in analysing the complexity of sugar negotiations. Dependence on imports suddenly became an object of attention only after OPEC demonstrated it. The share in the industrialised countries of imminent withdrawal of supplies by producers of all commodities, particularly those of minerals and metals, prompted studies such as *Critical Imported Materials,* a Special Report by the US Council on International Economic Policy.[4] The relative import dependence is summarised in this report:

Western Europe, Japan, and the United States share dependence on imports for 90 per cent or more of their supplies of chromium ore, manganese ore, nickel, and tin. In contrast to the US, however, Western Europe and Japan are dependent on imports for virtually 100 per cent of their needs for phosphate rock, 90 per cent or more of their consumption of copper, and 75 per cent or more of their supplies of lead. For none of the minerals and metals listed is Japan's dependence on imported supplies less than 76 per cent and for all but two, it is 90 per cent or more. Western Europe has an advantage over the United States only in bauxite, of which the US imports the bulk of its requirements and Japan 100 per cent. Both the United States and Western Europe produce the major part of their iron ore needs, whereas Japan must import 94 per cent of its growing consumption.[5]

The list of commodities for which Japan is the largest or second largest importer is almost as long as that which shows the United States as the largest or second largest exporter. As in the earlier list, the figures in brackets indicate Japan's importers, averaged over the years 1970 to 1972, as a percentage of total world imports of each commodity.

Japan largest importer of: wood, rough (55 per cent), iron ore (41 per cent), non-ferrous metal ores and concentrates (32 per cent), wool (26 per cent), cotton (25 per cent), oilseeds (24 per cent), maize

(19 per cent), wheat (13 per cent).
Japan second largest importer of: tin (19 per cent), fish (17 per cent), sugar (15 per cent), hides and skins (13 per cent), crude fertilisers (12 per cent).

Japan imports annually over 100 million tons of iron ore, 2 million tons of copper, 1 million tons of zinc ore and 200,000 tons of lead ore. Japan's economic miracle is vitally dependent on imports. But this does not mean, as the Council's Special Report implies, that all the supplies are equally vulnerable politically. The general assumption is that supplies may be threatened by the actions of producing *developing* countries. Less than two fifths (to be exact, 37.5 per cent) of Japan's non-oil imports of primary products come from developing countries; 55 per cent of all its requirements are met by developed country sources. A large part of Japan's investment in raw material resources (mainly in the form of loans for development to be repaid by exports to Japan) has gone to *developed* countries, again with the exception of oil. The United States and Canada supply all the wheat and wood, most of the oilseeds and rock phosphate. A large part of wool and iron ore imports comes from Australia, of non-ferrous metals from Canada, Australia and South Africa. For the sake of proximity, copper ore and timber may be imported from countries in South-East Asia, but these are also available from developed countries. Only in a very few commodities (bananas, sugar) is Japan dependent on imports from developing countries, and, at a pinch, sugar can be imported from the developed and socialist countries, although at a higher cost.

While a great deal has been written about the dependence of developing countries on exports of primary commodities, little mention is made of the import dependence of the poor countries. The dependence on oil imports has, of course, been recognised. The less industrialised countries are naturally importers of manufactures. Yet the import bill of the developing countries is not just made up of petroleum and manufactured goods; one fifth of the total bill is for imports of primary commodities. The obvious reason for this is that not all of them produce all the commodities. There are only six developing countries which export copper and only nine which export tin concentrate or tin metal; most of the developing countries are importers of non-ferrous metals. Many are importers of food, crude fertilisers and fibres, particularly wool. Cereal imports, both commercial and concessional, by the poor countries are an important element of world trade in grains and will be examined in that context. The relevance of the import market in developing countries will become apparent when the question of indexation of commodity prices is discussed. The cost of such indexing will also be borne by many of the poor countries, which have already been burdened with a quadrupled oil import bill which they can ill afford.

Some Conclusions

The purpose of describing in detail the factual setting of commodity trade is to help to determine the economic framework that influences the attitudes of governments to negotiations on regulating international trade. This descriptive process has not only necessitated consideration of statistical data but also classifying the characteristics of commodities and grouping them accordingly. The technical factors of each commodity represent its inherent characteristics and thus determine the practicability of any regulatory action. Market factors further limit the feasibility of such action; these can be ignored only at the risk of becoming theoretical and removed from reality. Institutional factors form the substance of the politics of commodity negotiations. It is the interplay .between these factors, coupled with the dependency factor, that will form the basis of subsequent analysis of commodity conflicts.

The statistical analysis has made it possible to determine the relative importance of various commodities. In terms of the size of the markets the twelve most important commodity groups are: copper, coffee, wheat, wood and wood products, oilseeds, vegetable oils and oilcake, iron ore, bauxite, alumina and aluminium, sugar, phosphate rock and cotton. It is interesting to note that only one of these, coffee, is wholly exported by the developing countries. If looked at purely from the point of view of the poor countries, the list would run differently. Apart from coffee, the important commodities in market size would be: cocoa, rubber, bananas, tea, tin, jute and hard fibres. The alternative criterion —|the *number* of developing countries dependentι—produces this list: coffee, cotton, sugar, bananas, cocoa and copper. The 17 commodities found in one or other of the lists above are the ones most relevant to the study of conflicts; of these, coffee is by far the most important.

Some of the questions that may give rise to conflicts have become apparent in the course of this chapter. These are: access to processed forms, the role of centrally planned economy countries, the land use problem in developing countries, food aid and import dependence, especially that of the non-oil developing countries. A significant conclusion has been drawn that the world is divided into three groups of countries, of which the developed part is becoming increasingly autarkic. The consequence is the pushing back to the periphery of the poor countries, on top of the existing relative isolation of the centrally planned countries. If developing countries are becoming more and more irrelevant to the international economy, is the present international economic system equitable? The difference in perception between the developed and developing of what is equitable is discussed in the next chapter.

Notes

1. See the explanation of the summary tables in the Introduction to the UN *Yearbook of International Trade Statistics.*
2. UNCTAD's definition of what is included in different groups of primary commodities may be seen in Annex 1 of any issue of the *Monthly Commodity Price Bulletin.* For the World Bank definition, see IBRD Economic Analysis and Projections Department, Commodities and Export Projections Division, EC/166, *Commodity Trade and Price Trends,* Annual, IBRD, Washington DC.
3. IBRD, *Commodity Trade and Price Trends.*
4. US Council on International Economic Policy, Special Report, *Critical Imported Materials,* Washington DC, 1975.
5. The list in the report includes, in addition to the minerals and metals considered in this book, chromium, platinum type metals, titanium, cobalt, mercury, columbium, vanadium and fluorspar. While most of these may be important strategically, they are not that significant in terms either of the value of their export trade or the number of countries involved in them. Chromium is also an example of the influence of politics on commodity trade since the major suppliers are Rhodesia (Zimbabwe) and the USSR; dependence on either source creates political problems for the US.

4 EQUITY, EFFICIENCY AND EARNINGS

Herein is that saying true: one soweth and another reapeth.

John 4 : 37

The asymmetry in trade relations between the industrial area and the underdeveloped compared with the volume of intra-trade within each group is significant. What may be a mere ripple for the industrial may seem like a tidal wave for the underdeveloped.

Ragnar Nurkse, *Kyklos* 11,2,1958

All international charters and resolutions about commodity agreements ritually intone the phrase 'stable, equitable and remunerative' prices. Unfortunately the words mean different things to different people. The traditional view, enshrined in the Havana Charter, is a market oriented one. Article 62 of the Charter envisages the use of Commodity Control Agreements only in the exceptional circumstances of a threat of 'burdensome surpluses, unemployment or serious underemployment' which 'would not be corrected by normal market forces'. Likewise, the objective in regulating prices was to prevent or moderate pronounced fluctuations, to achieve 'a reasonable degree of stability on the basis of such prices as are fair to consumers and provide a reasonable return to the producer'. The emphasis throughout is on securing long-term equilibrium between supply and demand and on letting market forces do this to the maximum extent possible. Fairness to consumers and a reasonable return to producers is the attitude a benign government adopts domestically in overseeing the operation of a free market and free enterprise system. The implicit assumption in the Havana Charter was that in an open international trading system similar principles would ensure equity. The principle of an open trading system was, however, jettisoned by its most important and powerful advocate when the United States, in the face of substantial domestic opposition, failed to ratify the Charter. Even within the countries which proclaim an unswerving belief in the open competitive society, regulation of commodity trade is often resorted to. Whenever other objectives (farmers' incomes, allocation of resources, national emergencies) are deemed to have priority, openness has given way to regulation. In the market oriented philosophy, international commodity markets can also be regulated, but only to induce greater stability. This relegates to the background the concept of equity.

Is the post-war economic system equitable to exporters of primary products, particularly the poorer among them? As early as 1949, two distinguished economists — Hans Singer and Raul Prebisch — arrived independently at the conclusion that it was not.[1] The two main conclusions of the Singer/Prebisch thesis were: (i) that there was a structural imbalance and asymmetry in the international economic system and (ii) that this leads progressively and inexorably to a deterioration in the terms of trade of the less developed countries. This thesis was disputed even then by other economists, thus beginning the terms-of-trade controversy which has gone on unabated since then. A consideration of the equitable distribution of the gains from trade necessarily involves the question of terms of trade — of primary commodities in relation to manufactures and of developing countries in relation to the developed. If the terms of trade of developing countries steadily deteriorate, i.e. if the prices of exports from these countries decline relative to the price which they have to pay for their imports, then the developing countries have fewer resources at their disposal to pay for development. A large part of the conflict in commodity negotiations is rooted in this problem. Supposing a commodity agreement designed to stabilise prices results in an inequitable distribution of gains, then two of the three fundamental objectives — stability and equity — cannot be practised at the same time. A controversy is generated about which of the two should predominate. The third concept, of adequate remuneration, also generates conflicts, mainly because it is related to considerations of promoting efficient production. How great a value countries place on increasing efficiency is also a relevant question.

Many arguments between the developed and developing countries revolve around the problems of protection and enhancement of the import purchasing power of the poor countries. Their relevance to commodity trade stems from the debate on whether commodity agreements have any role at all to play in transferring additional resources from the rich to the poor. Often, this is seen as a 'trade versus aid' question. However, export earnings and import purchasing power are not unrelated to the technical characteristics of the individual commodities that make up the export basket of a country. Export earnings are the result of quantities exported multiplied by the price prevailing at the time of export. The economic stake of countries in the production and export of many commodities, analysed in the last chapter, gives them an interest in quantities somewhat independent of that of the overall earnings. Importers too have an interest in quantities since stability of markets depends on adequate supplies becoming available at the right time. Conflicts between importers and exporters on the volume that should enter international trade in an agreed manner are also relevant to the earnings question; the price aspects are examined in chapter 7.

The Free Market Myth

The Singer/Prebisch thesis has been rephrased by B.K. Madan as follows:

> In the distribution of the gains of trade between underdeveloped and more highly developed countries, the latter have reaped the main harvest of benefits flowing from such economic intercourse and the former have on the whole suffered from the excessive degree of specialization of economic activity which restricted the role of the under-developed areas to that of producers of food and raw materials and subjected them to a continued deterioration in their terms of trade with countries having more diversified economies.[2]

In addition to the inexorable deterioration in the terms of trade, the system is seen to have another important effect — the excessive specialisation in production of primary commodities to the detriment of the development of a diversified economy. In disputing the validity of this thesis, other economists have attacked both aspects. The terms of trade controversy is examined in detail in the next section. On the question of the system producing asymmetric effects on economic development, Kindleberger's view is that 'continuous attention to terms of trade is not only a form of hypochrondria but also, in fact, a symptom of incapacity to adapt'.[3] One of his complaints is that interfering in the price system with a view to redistributing income has the normal result of distorting it as an allocative mechanism.[3] Economists like him have a mystic belief in the competitive market as a promoter of efficiency; consequently, they believe that if some people do not benefit under such a system it must be their own fault. G.M. Meier goes further: 'The terms of trade have become a convenient symbol around which a more general argument against free trade for the poor countries has been built.'[4] Here is the crux of the free market economists' objection; anything which casts doubt on the competitive system is heretical and must be wrong. For fear that the debate might have some influence, Meier utters the rallying cry: 'The secular deterioration in terms should not make free traders repentant.'[4] In other words, terms of trade do not matter; they are only a symbol; their deterioration or otherwise is of no concern; even if they do deteriorate, ignore it!

Is the international trade in primary commodities really an open competitive system? If it is, then one can examine whether the asymmetric development is due to deficiencies in the poor countries; if not, the reasons have to be looked for elsewhere. In Table 4.1 the various commodities have been classified according to the type of market control for each one. Five broad groups can be distinguished: generally free market, protected and distorted market, closed market, partly open and partly closed market and oligopolistic buyer market.

A closed market can be defined as one where there is an integral relationship between buyer and seller, either a technical tie-up or of common ownership. The number of traders in a closed market is invariably much smaller than in a more open market. In the case of common ownership, where the buyer (a processing industrial facility) and the seller (the raw material exporter) are both part of the same vertically integrated firm, transfer pricing phenomena, designed to optimise the net earnings of the operation as a whole, prevail; integrated iron and steel and aluminium companies are examples. Bananas are also an example of the closed system because, for a very large fraction of the total trade, the producer/exporter and the importer/buyer/distributor is the same vertically integrated company. Even where such integration does not exist, a closed relationship may obtain due to the unique one-to-one correspondence between the raw material and the processing facility. In such cases, supply of the required raw materials is ensured by means of long-term contracts — for example, the 15-year contracts for purchase of iron ore by Japanese steel mills from mines in Australia, India and Brazil. In this case the Japanese mills function as a monopsonistic buying consortium. Equally on the selling side, wherever long-term contracts for sales at negotiated producer prices exist the market becomes at least partly closed. A fair quantity of metals, such as coppper, nickel and aluminium, are sold under producer price arrangements, and the quantity traded on free markets such as the London Metal Exchange represents only a fraction of the total trade. A different type of closed market exists in commodities where there are very few buyers. Tea is an example; the so-called London 'auction' is not an auction at all; there are just four buyers representing the four major blending and packing companies who meet

Table 4.1 Exports of Major Primary Commodities Classified by Nature of Market

(US $ billion)

Generally free		Controlled/distorted		Closed		Oligopolistic buyers		Partly open and partly closed	
1. Oilcake	2.4	1. Wheat	9.8	1. Phosphate	1.5	1. Coffee	4.3	1. Wood and products	7.1
2. Cotton	3.7	2. Sugar	8.0	2. Iron ore	3.8	2. Oilseeds	5.2	2. Copper	7.0
3. Wool	2.5	3. Beef	3.7	3. Bananas	0.7	3. Vegetable oils	3.6	3. Aluminium	2.0
4. Hides/Leather	2.8	4. Maize	5.7	4. Bauxite	1.5	4. Tobacco	2.1	4. Nickel	0.9
5. Natural rubber	2.6	5. Rice	2.0			5. Cocoa	1.4	5. Lead	0.6
6. Tin	1.2	6. Wine	1.9			6. Tea	0.8	6. Zinc	1.3
7. Jute	0.2	7. Butter	1.3						
8. Hard fibres	0.2	8. Citrus fruit	1.2						
9. Pepper	0.2								
TOTAL	15.9		33.5		7.4		17.4		29.0
Percentage of grand total	17.1		36.0		7.9		18.6		20.4

Source: export figures from Tabl3 3.5; classification by author; total may not equal sum of column due to rounding

in a closed room each day to 'determine' the price of different packets of tea. Since other auction centres such as Calcutta, Colombo and Nairobi are newer and handle much smaller quantities of tea for international trade, their price follows that set by London. The attempts of producer countries to be present at the alleged 'auctions' had been consistently rebuffed. Just a few food-processing companies have worldwide operations and thus control the major part of the markets. Hence, coffee and cocoa also fall under this category. While the domestic trade in oilseeds, edible oils and oilcake may generally be free, the international market is controlled by a small number of vertically integrated companies, members of the International Association of Seed Crushers.

The fourth kind of unfree market is the one distorted by protection. By and large, agricultural commodities which are protected or domestically supported have a distorted market; the quantities imported do not bear a direct relationship to the international price. The costs of production do determine to some extent the international prices for the protected commodities, but the effect of demand on price remains distorted.

Table 4.1 also shows the average annual value of exports of these commodities. Out of a total world market economy exports (i.e. excluding exports by centrally planned countries) of US $ 93.2 billion for the listed commodities, *less than one fifth* can be said to be traded under open free conditions. One twelfth of the world trade is under closed conditions and one fifth in markets with too few buyers. *Over a third* of world trade takes place under distorted conditions, and this proportion keeps growing; less than a quarter was distorted in 1970. Even if the free share of the partly open and partly closed group is added, the value of commodities traded openly is just about a quarter of the total. To proclaim the virtues of a 'free' market when three quarters of the world's exports are traded under unfree conditions either displays ignorance of reality or an unwillingness to perceive it.

One can also examine whether the type of the market depends on the location of production. Table 4.2 shows the number of commodities for each type of market exported predominantly by developing countries, by developed countries and by both. A clear fact that emerges is that the controlled and distorted market is made up of commodities of export interest to the developed countries; sugar and rice are the only exceptions. Even in these two cases, the distortion arises entirely out of protectionism in the rich countries. Those commodities of which more than 75 per cent are exported by the rich

Table 4.2: Number of Commodities Exported by Developed and Developing Countries by Type of Market

Type of market	More than 75% by value exported by developing countries	More than 75% by value exported by developed countries	Exported by both
	(Value in US $ billion in brackets)		
Generally free	5 (4.5)	2 (5.4)	2 (6.1)
Controlled/distorted	1 (8.0)	6 (23.5)	1 (2.0)
Closed	2 (2.1)	–	2 (5.3)
Oligopolistic buyers	3 (6.5)	–	3 (10.9)
Partly open and partly closed	–	4 (4.8)	2 (14.2)

Source: derived from data in Tables 3.5 and 4.1.

countries are either distorted (i.e. protected by governments) or partly closed (i.e. controlled sales by powerful multinational companies); the only exceptions are wool and hides and skins. Though commodities of interest to the rich countries can be found in all types, managed and regulated marketing is the mechanism preferred for products of particular interest to them.

In contrast, developing countries are mainly faced with generally open or wholly closed markets. In the former they are buffeted by instability and in the latter, as in the case of oligopolistic buyer markets, they are under the control of a few trans-national entities. As the quotation from Meier shows, free trade is a doctrine to be preached to the poor, while its frequent breach in the rich countries is taken for granted. The market-oriented economists can have two answers to this criticism: (i) they do not condone such breaches in the rich countries; and (ii) in any case they are mainly concerned with the theoretical losses of efficiency that result from deviations from free competition, whenever they may occur. If these economists are just being theoretical, and consequently Utopian, such views should not be relevant to a practical study of commodity negotiations that take place in this real, unfree world. Unfortunately, this is not the case. Their concepts ignore a vital factor — that international trade is an exchange across borders and that at the borders stand governments. All governments adopt only those professional concepts that suit their purpose. Where regulation is preferred, the free trade concepts are abandoned. Where it is necessary to find something to rebut the poor countries' argument, then the same concepts become useful. In short, those who benefit from the present international economic system use the free trade argument only as an indication of their unwillingness to change the system in a way which they perceive to be detrimental to their interest.

The Terms of Trade Controversy

Developing countries too have a perception. By the late 1950s it was apparent to them that the system was not operating in the non-industrialised countries, many of them newly independent, along the conventionally accepted model of development through rapid industrialisation. The decline in the prices of primary products after the Korean War boom and the recurrent balance of payments crisis of the developing countries confirmed their belief that the Singer/Prebisch analysis was indeed correct. The system was not equitable in its operation. Thus at UNCTAD I, a new and different interpretation of the concept of equity was introduced.

In the view of a large number of delegations the reference in international commodity arrangements to 'stable, equitable and remunerative prices' should be interpreted as referring to prices not merely in absolute terms, but also in terms of import purchasing power, since this was what mattered, in practice, to the primary exporting countries.

In reply, the Havana Charter view was reiterated by the developed countries. 'Some delegations, however, believed that commodity prices could be related only to the characteristics, and market situation of the commodity concerned'.[5] The Conference failed to resolve the conflict but managed to pass the relevant resolution (Annex A.II.1) without dissent, by the well-known expedient of adding a 'chapeau' which left the question of what practical steps should be taken to achieve which objectives exactly as it was before the Conference. According to the Resolution, *a* basic objective of international commodity arrangements was 'to stimulate a dynamic and steady growth', ensure reasonable predictability in the real export earnings of developing countries, while 'taking into account the interests of consumers in importing countries'.[6] This is not one objective; this is not even a set of non-contradictory objectives. This is just a set of words in which every one can read what they want to read in the light of their predilections.

UNCTAD I derived its judgement on the basis of the data that 'from 1950 to 1962 export prices of primary commodities declined by 7 per cent while export prices of manufactures increased by 27 per cent . . . which resulted in a deterioration of 27 per cent in the terms of exchange.' Notwithstanding the passage of another twelve years there is no agreement that the terms of trade of developing countries are in fact declining. A recent 'Expert Group' of twelve economists, convened by UNCTAD to study indexation of commodity prices, came to the conclusion that no detectable long-term deterioration in the terms of trade of developing countries was discernible from the statistics. The UNCTAD Secretariat, however, disagreed with this conclusion and pointed out that its own analysis 'would appear to establish fairly conclusively that the net barter terms of trade of a large number of primary commodities . . . have deteriorated substantially over the last 25 years'.[7] The UNCTAD document which sets out both these contradictory conclusions gives a possible reason – the Expert Group and the Secretariat were talking about different things. While the statistics 'readily available for examination by the group . . . related to world trade in commodities as a whole, and not to the commodity exports of developing countries', the Secretariat analysed statistics of commodities exported only by the developing countries. Further support to the Secretariat's conclusions is adduced by World Bank data. Thus, three different time series, reproduced in Table 4.3, are available for comparison – an all countries one presented to the Expert Group, a World Bank one for 34 commodities exported by developing countries and a Secretariat one for 29. All three series refer to the concept of 'commodity' or 'net barter' terms of trade which expresses the relationship between the evolution of export prices of primary commodities and the import prices of manufactures. All three series agree on the fact that there are substantial short-term fluctuations. A comparison of the first with the other two reveals the range of fluctuation to be much wider for commodities exported by developing countries. This is not surprising as developed countries manage and regulate their own commodities to greater effect. The IBRD and UNCTAD series are quite close for the 1950s and early 1960s but diverge after 1963. Some divergence between the two is inevitable – not only do they use different numbers of commodities, they use different price data and different weights for arriving at the combined index. In the UNCTAD document both series stop at 1972, before the commodity boom. On the whole, the indices show that the terms of trade of developing countries steadily deteriorated in the 1950s, picked up a bit in the

Table 4.3. Comparison of the Indices of the Terms of Trade of Primary Commodities

(1963 = 100)

Year	Expert Group world trade in commodities	IBRD 34 commodities excluding petroleum	UNCTAD 29 commodities excluding petroleum
1950	121	...	...
1951	126	...	...
1952	116	...	...
1953	116	126	122
1954	117	138	137
1955	115	133	130
1956	110	123	128
1957	111	116	118
1958	108	111	111
1959	105	107	110
1960	102	106	106
1961	100	101	98
1962	98	96	97
1963	*100*	*100*	*100*
1964	102	105	109
1965	98	100	109
1966	97	99	109
1967	95	95	100
1968	93	99	102
1969	93	100	104
1970	...	98	102
1971	...	86	89
1972	...	84	87

Source: UNCTAD/CD/Misc.60, *Terms of Trade for Developing Countries*

middle 1960s and started sliding down again until the boom. Yet another survey by the Commonwealth Secretariat confirms 'a deterioration of the terms of trade vis-à-vis manufactured goods, in the 1960s, for many agricultural commodities exported by developing countries, though not for all. If the examination were carried back to the early 1950s, a much greater deterioration of the terms of trade would appear'.[8]

Any number of theoretical arguments have been produced against deriving any conclusions from the statistical data. The UNCTAD paper highlights the following. Are the net barter terms of trade the right ones to use? Should not one use the single factoral terms of trade which would take into account the effect of productivity changes in the export sector or, better still, the double factoral terms of trade which take into account changes in productivity in both export and import sectors? Even assuming that the net barter terms of trade represent a useful index, which period should be used as the base? Should one start from 1950, the height of the Korean War boom, and also include the 1973 boom or ignore both? What weighting system should be adopted? What prices would be used? Should they be actual prices or unit values based on export statistics? How relevant is the UN index of manufactured goods for establishing the prices of manufactured goods imported by developing countries? How does one account for technological changes in the manufactured exports sector? Finally, what is the relevance of the net barter terms of trade or of any other collective indicator to the development problems of individual developing countries and the trade problems of specific commodities?

To continue deeper into this theoretical argument would mean descending into economic theory and straying away from the politics of negotiations, in which the perceptions of participants matter as much as facts. The developing countries pick the terms of trade argument only to describe the facts which they experience in practice — that their import purchasing capacity is both unpredictable and inadequate and that every year they are exporting more raw material to import the same volume of manufactures as the previous year. The Commonwealth Secretariat paper describes the discussion among Commonwealth Heads of Governments at their August 1973 Conference in Ottawa as having been 'conducted in such terms as the number of bales of cotton needed to earn enough foreign exchange to buy a tractor'. However unscientific this may sound, this is the reality that matters to politicians who have to run countries. Do the poor countries have to export more cases of bananas, more bags of coffee, or more tons of vegetable oil to import

Table 4.4. Terms of Trade of Selected Primary Commodities in Relation to Steel Products

Year	From United States		From Germany		From United Kingdom
	Bags of Coffee/ 100 tons	Cases of Bananas/ ton	Tons of Groundnut oil/100 tons	Tons of Iron ore/ per ton	Tons of Tea/ 100 tons
1950	6.1	1.4	13.0	...	...
1955	6.3	1.6	32.4	5.4	6.9
1960	11.9	2.2	32.0	7.5	7.5
1965	9.5	2.0	33.1	10.7	8.9
1969	11.9	2.2	30.3	10.9	10.5
1970	9.5	2.3	33.0	12.6	10.4
1971	...	...	31.1	12.6	13.3
1972	12.1	2.8	37.0	15.0	14.1
1973	12.6	2.8	38.0	19.3	14.3
1974	12.9	3.5	23.5	...	15.0

Sources: UN *Monthly Bulletin of Statistics;* IBRD *Commodity Trade and Price Trends;* EUROSTAT *Iron and Steel Yearbook*

the capital goods they need for their development? Table 4.4 shows the result of such comparison for five different commodities in three rich country markets for 1950, 1955, 1960, 1965 and 1969 to 1974. Complete series from 1948 to 1974, with the actual annual average prices for each commodity in the appropriate market, may be found in Appendix 5. In these tables, the price of coffee and the price of bananas is compared with the price of steel in the United States, that of tea with steel in the United Kingdom and of groundnut oil and iron ore with steel from the Federal Republic of Germany. Standard forms of manufactured steel such as bars and plates have been chosen in order to minimise the quality change problem. Steel products are more standardised than, say, tractors or machine tools or even tyres, in which qualitative improvement may be significant even within a ten-year period.

Table 4.4 shows the deterioration in the terms of trade most clearly for bananas — in 1950 it took 55 lb of bananas to buy a ton of steel; in

1974 140 lb were required. Tea shows a similar decline. At its best, in 1954, 6000 kg of tea bought 100 tons of steel; in 1974, the same quantity bought less than half the amount of steel. Groundnuts and coffee show more fluctuations but even in their case the trend is one of progressive deterioration. What nine bags of coffee bought in 1954 needed 26 bags twenty years later. One would expect some relationship to exist between steel prices and the price of iron ore, its principal raw material. Not so in actual practice. While the average c.i.f. price of iron ore imported from Liberia into the EEC fell from $18 per ton in 1954 to $10 in 1970, German steel prices went up from $92 a ton in 1950 to $125 in 1970 and to $257 in 1974. The fall in iron ore c.i.f. prices may be attributed to progressive decline in transport costs due to the use of larger and larger bulk carriers. Even if this were the sole reason, the figures prove that the benefits of such reduction have gone only to the rich buyer. The system does distribute gains inequitably.

To sum up, the facts do indicate a deterioration in the terms of trade of the developing countries: there have been ups and downs, but, on the whole, the trend is downward. The 1973/4 boom did reverse the trend, but this may be short-lived. World Bank projections of prices likely to prevail in the early 1980s suggest that the boom will be transitory. In saying that the terms of trade of developing countries as a whole have deteriorated and will deteriorate does not imply that this will be true for all developing countries. No figures are needed to prove that (i) the terms of trade of oil-exporting developing countries have dramatically improved fourfold in their favour and (ii) those of the oil-importing developing countries have worsened substantially since 1973 and are likely to stay that way. If the prices of the other commodities that the latter group of countries export do not improve, their perception of the inequity of the system will be confirmed and strengthened.

Commodity Agreements and Resource Transfer

Why do the developed countries refuse to recognise the deterioration of the terms of trade of the poor countries? Partly because it is contrary to their cherished belief in the impersonal and impartially benign free enterprise system that rewards the efficient and punishes the rest. A more practical reason is that acceptance of this fact would imply agreeing to the corresponding corrective mechanism of reversing the decline by increasing the prices of primary products by suitable regulation of the markets. Rich countries do accept the need to transfer additional resources to the poor to accelerate development. They have, after all, accepted, in principle, targets for such transfer (1 per cent of gross national product of each country for total transfer, of which 0.7 per cent is to be official and the rest private), even though the date by which these targets will be achieved recedes further and further, like the horizon. Acceptance of the need for additional transfer does not mean accepting any and every means of doing so. The basic unresolved question is: should an element of protection of the purchasing power of the developing countries be built into commodity agreements? Stabilising the export prices of commodities is only half the answer to the problem of protecting import purchasing power. Even if the export prices were prevented from declining, the prices of manufactured goods imported by the developing from the developed may increase, thereby worsening the terms of trade. This is yet again a question of the definition of equity — is it a two-way proposition covering both imports and exports or just one-way for exports alone?

Pincus, in his *Commodity Agreements — Bonanza or Illusion?*[9] has succinctly summarised the arguments against using international commodity agreements for providing a price higher than the long-term equilibrium price. The main strands of the argument are that the mechanism is unworkable and that it promotes inefficiency. One aspect of the unworkability argument is that commodity agreements cannot be effective in raising prices above market levels, only in stabilising them over a cycle.

> This contention in its extreme form is obviously wrong, as witness the high prices paid to farmers in countries where agriculture is protected ... There is no logical, constitutional, or economic barrier to doubling or tripling the revenues that underdeveloped countries receive for commodity exports ... If the governments of industrial countries want to pay some amount into an economic development fund for each pound of coffee they import that sum can be as large as the generosity of governments allow. It is simply a subsidy to coffee growing countries.

Pincus, however, rejects this method of resource transfer on the grounds that:

> The technique of operating through market prices via supply control is universally preferred because the consequent income transfer ... does not enter as an item in the government budget ... If rich countries want to subsidize poor ones, they can do it by foreign aid

appropriation rather than subsidy to commodity exporter.

The second part of the quotation does not conform with the first; the use of the same word subsidy once again obscures the change that occurs between domestic and international operations. In comparing the preferred mechanism for internal resource transfers with the international system, Pincus forgets that the roles are reversed in the latter. Internationally, it is the foreign aid appropriation that appears as an item in the donor government's budget. A price agreed between importers and exporters, even if it is higher than it would have been without such agreement, would still be collected impersonally through the market. A domestic subsidy to farmers is quite another matter; whether they are price support payments or payments for setting aside acreage, these appear as expenditure in a government's budget. If subsidies are to be excluded because they enter a budget then foreign aid, an even more sensitive item in any donor government's budget, should be even more unacceptable. Pincus's article was, of course, written at a time when foreign aid was more popular. The climate today is one of aid weariness, decline in the real value of foreign aid and an increasing debt burden of developing countries. Even if aid were a better mechanism, in today's conditions it is less practicable. The best, as ever, is the enemy of the good.

The preference for a direct transfer of resources, instead of through commodity agreements, recognises a fact that is not often explicitly stated. Higher prices through commodity agreements do not distinguish between exporters according to their need nor between importers according to their ability to share the burden. Supposing it is agreed that Brazil should receive a higher transfer of resources, using the Coffee Agreement would imply that Colombia, the second largest exporter, would get one third of Brazil's transfer and other Latin American, African and Asian producers a transfer in proportion to their share of coffee exports. Is this the right proportion from the point view of the needs of these countries or their ability to use the resources? Supposing there is also an iron ore agreement providing for higher prices, how does one ensure that the total transfer to, say, Brazil through the two agreements is the right amount? If a higher price is negotiated for bananas so that the developing countries most dependent on banana exports benefit, how does one ensure that an oil and banana exporting country such as Ecuador is not an unintended recipient? Similar problems also arise on the importing side. Should the largest importer of a commodity contribute most to the development needs of the developing exporting countries? If an importing country keeps down imports by protectionist methods, should it be rewarded by a reduced contribution for denying access? Where there are a number of commodities for which higher price arrangements are in force, how does one ensure that there is an equitable sharing of the resource transfer burden among the group of importing countries? The effect of the uniform price rise for all countries, developed and developing, imposed by OPEC is that the poorest of the developing countries who have the misfortune to be energy importers have had thrust on them an unbearable burden. Is this the kind of mechanism that should be emulated?

Another difficult aspect of transferring resources through commodity agreements is that the international price may have little impact on the income of the actual producers in the exporting countries. If a higher international price is related to the total developmental needs of a country, the greater resources need not necessarily be distributed proportionately to the farmers or miners. Income redistribution and relative pricing between various sectors of production are matters strictly within the purview of national economic policies of governments who often impose higher direct taxes or export duties to cream off the difference between a higher export realisation and what is considered a reasonable price for the domestic producer. Governments do make a distinction between a 'reasonable' international price and a 'reasonable' internal price. The temptation to allocate to itself the difference may well be greater in more efficient low-cost producing countries, with the result that a higher international price need not necessarily stimulate more efficient production. On the other hand, a higher price would at least make it easier for high-cost producers to continue in production. The net result on promotion of efficiency will be unpredictable; while governments may well be the best judges of how to utilise their national resources, it does not follow that their collective wisdom is the best for the commodity in question.

Who Wants Efficiency?

The concept of efficiency keeps intruding into these discussions for two reasons. First, it has some inherent validity. More important, free marketeers need it to support their beliefs; efficient allocation of resources is the justification for a competitive system. While this may work well, within defined limits, in a domestic economy, it does not cross frontiers so easily. Does anybody want to promote efficiency internationally?

The argument about promoting efficiency is also important since it gives rise to a number of conflicts and coalition-forming among participants in a commodity negotiation. Since most commodity agreements enforce supply restriction through the quota mechanism they tend to freeze historical patterns of production, thereby discriminating against more efficient producers. The Havana Charter specifically refers to making appropriate opportunities for increasing production from 'sources which can supply in the most effective manner'. The quite different UNCTAD view, in Annex A II.I., refers to increasing market opportunities for efficient *developing* countries but qualifies it by emphasising the need to take account of the trade needs of | traditional producers. The Conference did not define the term 'trade needs' of traditional producers, contenting itself with the vague phrase 'economic development'. It is obvious however, that the qualification moderates and dilutes, if not nullifies, the objective of promoting efficient production. The conflicts thus engendered among exporting countries will be examined in greater detail in the next chapter. For the present, it is interesting to note that the UNCTAD view is that *efficient developing* countries would have the opportunity to increase their share of the market. This implicitly denies it to efficient *developed* producing countries. The thesis that efficiency should be rewarded selectively is not one that is acceptable to the developed countries, particularly the major primary producing ones among them, such as Australia, Canada, Sweden and the United States. While only Australia expressed a reservation on Annex A.II.1, the others let it pass — no doubt because it did not really mean very much with the qualification attached. The result of the selective reward approach was that the developed primary producing countries, who may be expected to have some sympathy for the problems of commodity trade, were firmly placed in the 'developed' camp thus creating simultaneously a conflict between two groups of exporters (developed and developing) and a coalition between developed importers and developed exporters. How a price mechanism could at one and the same time ensure higher than equilibrium prices, promote production in efficient poor countries, protect the share of the traditional producers, inhibit exports from developed exporting countries and prevent burdensome surpluses from arising is not at all clear. Add to this also the criterion, often expressed, that such higher prices should take into account the 'needs of developing importing countries' and the solution becomes all but impossible. Put simply, what this set of contradictory objectives seems to mean is: developing exporting countries should get a higher price because they need it; but developing importing countries should pay a lower price because they cannot afford it; developed exporting countries should get a lower price so that their exports do not increase; but developed importing countries should pay the higher price because they have to transfer the resources. This implies a totally impracticable four-tier system which ignores the fact that for every commodity a market exists where individual buyers and sellers are negotiating specific contracts all the time.

For the consuming countries, developed and developing, the concept of promoting efficiency is not just an abstract one of principle. At the beginning of this century, the United States consumed about 2.5 million tons of sugar with a per capita consumption of 64 lb per annum. By the end of the First World War the annual per capita consumption had risen to nearly 90 lb and total consumption had grown to 6 million tons. In recent years, the United States consumption has been about 10 million tons, or approximately 110 lb per person. Before the First War, the New York wholesale price of raw sugar fluctuated around 4¢ per lb; in 1948 it was 5.5¢ per lb and went up steadily over the next 20 years, reaching a level of 7.5¢ per lb in 1968. The great increase in consumption happened when prices were about the 4 to 5¢ level. This was made possible only by increases in production — and productivity — in beet and cane in the continental US and cane in Hawaii, Puerto Rico, Philippines and Cuba. The United States is not an isolated example. World production of sugar in the early 1900s was less than 20 million tons; currently it is about 80 million tons. It is difficult to believe that had sugar maintained its real value since 1900 such growth in production and consumption would have occurred.

There is, however, a catch in this argument. In global terms, promotion of efficient production is an important consideration. Unfortunately, in the real world, this seems to be the least important consideration for sovereign national governments. During the 1968 negotiations on sugar, the European Economic Community was offered by other exporters an export quota of 300,000 tons. The Community found this unacceptable and stayed out of the agreement, in effect reserving the right to disrupt the market. It cannot be claimed that any country in the Community was so dependent on sugar exports for its export earnings that it was a matter of life and death for the economy. It was merely a case of the EEC saying that they had decided to grow so much high-cost sugar and, since they could not eat it all, they had the right to dump it on the world market. One can only conclude that social priorities are more important to governments than considerations of global efficiency. More such examples of efficiency giving way to social priorities will be noted in chapter 6 in the discussion on the problems of access for processed forms or manufactured goods exported by developing countries.

Conflicts Between Importers and Exporters

The nature of the relationships between participants in commodity negotiations so far discussed relates to export earnings as a criterion by themselves; these have been viewed in the same way as governments do in their balance of payments budget. But the equation that earnings are a product of quantities exported at the prevailing price generates relationships based on the economic fact of whether a country is a net importer or a net exporter. The word 'net' is crucial, for it separates the importers into two classes. Countries which have little or no domestic production of the imported commodity have a different interest from those who produce a substantial part of their domestic demand. Wherever there is sizeable domestic production, the tendency is always to protect it. The conflicts between importers and exporters in protected commodities is discussed in the next chapter. The conflict of interest in the case of commodities which are not produced in the importing countries is simpler. Such conflicts, as has been argued earlier, cannot be limited only to the question of price. Consuming countries also have an interest in securing adequate supplies for their consumption needs of the right mix of types and at the right time. Producing countries too have an interest in quantities since they may have storage and disposal problems.

The annual negotiations in the International Coffee Agreement of 1962 illustrate this point. The Coffee Agreement provides a good example of pure importer/exporter conflict, since all exporters of coffee are developing countries. By assuming that all exporters favour the resource transfer objective while importers back the stability objective, the need to consider cross-relationships is avoided. The 1962 Coffee Agreement was negotiated at a time of high carry-over stocks and declining prices. The total of the Basic Export Tonnages (BET) was set close to world demand at that time. Out of world imports of 47 million bags 45.5 million bags were shared out among the exporters, leaving a small margin for exports to 'new markets' which were not charged to quotas. The first full year for which the International Coffee Council had to decide annual quotas was the coffee year 1 October 1963 to 30 September 1964. However, a substantial change occurred in the supply situation in August 1963; Brazil, the largest exporter, suffered a serious frost and this was followed, in September, by a series of fires which further reduced the crop. These disasters were expected to reduce Brazilian exportable production from 18 million bags in 1962/3 to just 3 million bags in 1963/4. The market price naturally rose sharply in anticipation of the shortage. In the negotiations held in November 1963 in the Council, the importing countries proposed increasing the total of the annual quotas significantly in order to check the price rise. Restoring stability was their main objective. The negotiations failed partly because the importers and exporters could not agree on the quantum and kind of the quota increase and partly because the exporters could not agree among themselves on how to share out the increase between different types of coffee.

The negotiations were resumed in February 1964, and this time the importing countries succeeded in getting the total annual quota raised by 1.4 million bags. At the same time, waivers (exports permitted over and above annual quotas) of nearly a million bags were granted. Total supplies were thus raised by nearly 2.5 million bags. The mix of solutions, part quota increase and part waivers, also helped to resolve the conflict between exporters, since the major share of the waiver quantities went to African Robusta producers and about a fifth to producers of mild coffee other than Colombian. A few months later, in June 1964, shortfalls of 750,000 bags were redistributed, thus increasing the total supplies for the 1963/4 year to 49 million bags or 107.7 per cent of the BETs. To influence market sentiment, the next year's (1964/5) initial quota was also set at a fairly high level of 47.5 million bags (104.4 per cent). The success of these efforts is shown by the fact that the price rise was not only halted but that later in the 1964/5 coffee year quotas had to be reduced to prevent prices from falling too steeply. In these complex negotiations the main interest of the consumers was in restraining the price rise, but they also had a voice in how it was to be effected. The importers could have vetoed any solution proposed by exporters which they considered either unrealistic for achieving the objective or for political reasons unfair to some exporters. They were also able to obtain adequate quantities by waivers and redistribution of shortfalls and ensure a suitable mix of types by promoting a settlement which increased Robusta supplies against the shortfalls in hard Arabicas.

Another element which leads to importer/exporter conflicts is the level of prices to be maintained for ensuring adequate investment for securing future supplies. In other words, there is a conflict over future quantities as well as current quantities. This aspect is more clearly seen in the case of minerals for which the investment requirements are generally higher and more capital-intensive than for agricultural products. An example of the conflict over price in relation to investment needs can be found in the Tin Agreement, a mineral almost wholly exported by developing countries. While the operations of the buffer stock mechanism of this agreement are examined in Chapter 9, it is relevant to note here the relationship between ceiling prices (i.e. the maximum permitted under the agreement) and market prices in times of shortage. There have been many occasions in the life of the four Tin Agreements when market prices were higher than the ceiling, the longest period occurring during the life of the second (1961/6) agreement. The buffer stock had no tin left by the end of June 1961. Prices immediately went above the ceiling of £880 a long ton and stayed above it until early 1962. At that stage, the ceiling itself was raised to £965 a ton. In November 1963, the ceiling was breached again. It was raised to £1,000 a ton to catch up with the market but as this proved inadequate, was raised to £1,200 a year later. The market still stayed above it — in fact, for the whole time between November 1963 and June 1966 the market price was at or above the ceiling. Only when the ceiling was raised to £1,400 in July 1966 at the beginning of the third agreement did it at last catch up with the market. So, for five years the market consistently valued tin higher than the ceiling price in force from time to time. Every failure of the ceiling is an indication that prices in the preceding period were inadequate to promote production and encourage investment. In the Tin Agreement, floor and ceiling prices have to be approved by separate two thirds majorities of importers and exporters. The price range inscribed in the agreement is thus always a compromise between what exporters think they need to promote investment and what importers decide they can afford. Whenever ceilings fail, the conclusion can only be that earlier the importers' judgement on the right price to promote production had been sacrificed for a current lower price.

The question of adequate investment is a somewhat neglected area in commodity regulation. Every surplus situation with its attendant low prices discourages investment in production. Inevitably, in a few years' time, shortages arise, prices boom and frantic investment takes place. This produces surpluses in its turn and the cycle starts all over again. Regulation should have as one of its objectives orderly and adequate investment. But this creates a conflict for participating governments between short-term and long-run objectives. Importer/exporter conflicts are one facet of the problem of current sacrifices for long-term gain.

The Great Divide

In the last chapter, dependency, either on exports or on imports, was identified as one of the economic factors which influenced the policy of any government in commodity negotiations. In analysing the problem of export earnings, two major divisions have been identified. The first is a perceptional, even philosophic, difference which divides the developed from the developing countries in their attitude to the objectives of commodity regulation. The second is the inherent conflict of interest between importers and exporters. The philosophic argument between developed country free traders and developing country advocates of the decline of their terms of trade is less important than the perceptions which give rise to them. The economic language in which the philosophies are expressed only reflects the underlying conflict between the beneficiaries of the present system and the losers in it. Neither accords predominance to concepts of global efficiency. The arguments about principles, between the resource transfer objective and the stability objective, are carried over into the discussions on the appropriate mechanisms to be evolved. The conflict of interest between importers and exporters overlaps the developed/developing division; cross-relationships and coalitions are produced.

When does a country such as Australia or Canada decide that it is a developed country more than a primary commodity exporting one? This is not a theoretical question but one which influences decisions on whether a country will join an Iron Ore Producers Association or what price level it is prepared to accept in the Sugar Agreement. The choice of which of the two conflicting groups its belongs to depends on its self-perception. If it thinks that it has more in common with other members of the developed group than with less developed exporters, it chooses its side accordingly. Why any country chooses to be one or the other is a result of history, sociological make-up, type of political system, strategic considerations and so on. In other words, it is a political choice. Why Saudi Arabia or Kuwait chooses to consider itself part of the developing countries in spite of its riches is also a political choice. Equally, the NOEDEC countries, who have suffered most from the oil price rise, mute their criticism of OPEC purely for reasons of political solidarity. While there is a division between efficient and high-cost producers in both developed and developing camps, in recent history nations have chosen to close ranks under the state of development banner and not under the flag of efficiency. In the following chapters, other conflicts of interest as well as examples of co-operation will be analysed; but all these are enacted across the great divide between the rich and the poor.

Notes

1. H.W. Singer, 'The Distribution of Gains between Investing and Borrowing Countries', *Papers and Proceedings,* Sixty-second Annual Meeting of the American Economic Association. *The American Economic Review,* 40, 1950, pp. 471-85. Raul Prebisch, 'Growth, Disequilibrium and Disparities: an Interpretation of the Process of Economic Development', UN Economic Commission for Latin America, *Economic Survey for Latin America 1949* (UN, New York, 1949).
2. B.K. Madan, Discussion on US foreign investment, American Economic Association *Proceedings,* p.512.
3. C.P. Kindleberger, 'The Terms of Trade and Economic Development', *Review of Economics and Statistics,* 40, 1958, Supplement, p.85.
4. G.M. Meier, Comment on Kindleberger, 'The Terms of Trade and Economic Development', p.88 and 90.
5. UN *Proceedings of the Conference on Trade and Development,* Vol.1, Final Act and Reports, Annex D — Report of the First Committee (UN, New York, 1964).
6. UN *Proceedings,* Annex A.II.1., Resolution on Commodities.
7. UNCTAD, *Terms of Trade for Developing Countries,* CD/Misc/60.
8. Commonwealth Economic Papers No.4, *Terms of Trade Policy for Primary Commodities* Commonwealth Secretariat, London, 1976).
9. J.A. Pincus, *Commodity Agreements — Bonanza or Illusion?* (The Rand Corporation, Washington DC, 1967).

5 CONFLICT AND CO-OPERATION AMONG EXPORTERS

When you dam up a stream of water, as soon as the dam is full, as much water must run over the dam-head as if there was no dam at all.

Adam Smith, *The Wealth of Nations*

It is a well-known fact, proved by many examples quoted earlier, that commodity negotiations as often fail because of conflicts among exporters as because importers and exporters cannot agree. This does not mean that exporters as a class are a more cantankerous lot nor that developing exporting countries are more cussed than the rest. It only reflects the facts that earning money is more vital than spending it and that the tenacity with which developing exporters pursue their objectives is an indicator of their dependence on commodity export. Regulating the market of a commodity implies a degree of restraint on trade (quantities and price) as well as on production. The role of the market place and the factors which determine prices will be considered in Chapter 7.The restraint on the volume can either be controls on quantities imported or on quantities exported; the former is part of the vital question of access to markets, which will be dealt with in the next chapter. The influence of export quantities on the attitudes of exporting governments is the subject of the present one.

For exporting countries, quantity objectives have an independent validity of their own based on current exportable surplus, future production plans and the preservation of market shares. Social and political factors such as farmers' incomes and the limitations and diversification away from a commodity as well as the constraints on ability to store determine the quantity of a particular commodity which a country desires to export. The conflict for market shares among exporters can arise either out of the status of the individual exporter in the market or because different exporters produce different types of the same product. In the conflicts which arise from the status of the different exporters, two different but overlapping strands can be distinguished; there can be conflicts between large and small producers and between established and emerging ones. While all traditionally large exporters are necessarily established producers, the latter group may also include many small exporters. Conversely, emerging exporters necessarily have a small share of the market and may be either large or small producers depending on the amounts they consume domestically. Thus the group of exporters as a whole is one of shifting alliances co-operating and conflicting on different aspects of the negotiations at different times. The shifting alliances between exporters becomes more fluid by reason of the existence of different types of the same commodity, duty to the affinities based on regional association and because of the possibilities of oligopolistic collusion among the very largest exporters.

If co-operation is not confined just to the largest exporters but includes all major exporters, then a producer association such as OPEC is created. While such associations may be viewed as a threat by the importing countries, it is a major achievement for the exporters to be able to resolve their mutual conflicts in the interests of greater gain for all of them. Following the discovery that OPEC had teeth and was prepared to use them, a lot of noise has been generated about possibilities of OPEC-type action on other commodities. It is therefore useful to consider the history of other attempts to create purely producer associations. Generally, conflicts among exporters are considered only within the limited context of a single commodity. This limitation ignores two other types of conflicts, both of which arise in one commodity as a result of actions taken in some other commodity. Where two or more commodities can be grown on the same land, the attitudes of exporting governments to negotiation in either of them is governed by what is likely to happen to the other. The land-use problem and the impact of one commodity negotiation on another are both relevant to an understanding of the motivation of participating governments.

As in the case of the Sultana Producers Agreement, even three exporters can fail to agree among themselves. The increase in the number of exporters in a commodity does not necessarily make conflict resolution proportionately more difficult. However, the larger the number of exporters, the more clear-cut the division between large, medium, small and very small exporters. The number of significant exporters in different commodities varies very widely. For example, in the first three Tin Agreements there were only six producing members – Bolivia, Malaysia, Thailand, Indonesia, Nigeria and Congo (Zaire); when Australia joined the fourth agreement as a producing member there were seven.[1] The major tin producing countries which stayed out of the Agreements are Brazil, Argentina, South Africa, Rwanda, Laos,

Portugal and Burma; between them, these countries cover only 5 to 6 per cent of total world production. Cocoa, like tin, has far fewer significant exporters compared with the number of countries which produce it. The four largest exporters of cocoa hold between them 80 per cent of the world market, and five others are regular exporters. There are 18 other countries each producing less than 10,000 tons; a few of these are potential participants in international trade. The commodities with the largest number of exporters are coffee and sugar. There were 36 exporting countries in the 1962 Coffee Agreement and 42 in the 1968 one; the 1968 Sugar Agreement had 40 exporting members. In these three agreements, every exporting country had some kind of export limitation – either a quota or, for the smallest, exemption from quotas so long as their exports did not reach a significant level. In sugar, the exemption level is 10,000 tons out of a total world market of 20 million tons; in coffee, it is 25,000 bags out of a total world market of approximately 55 million bags. In both cases, one twentieth of 1 per cent of world exports is considered significant.

Market Shares and Attitudes to Negotiation

Whatever the number of exporters, there is a wide range in market shares. The market shares in the 1972 Cocoa Agreement as shown by the quota distribution (though these quotas were never invoked during the three-year life of the agreement) ranged from over one third to less than 2 per cent. The actual distribution was:

Four largest exporters ...		...	83.1%
of which	Ghana	...	36.7%
	Nigeria	...	19.5%
	Ivory Coast	...	14.2%
and	Brazil	...	12.7%
Five smaller exporters		...	16.9%
of which	Cameroon	...	8.0%
	Dominican Republic	...	3.0%
	Equatorial Guinea	...	2.4%
	Togo	...	1.8%
	Mexico	...	1.7%

To take the example of an Agreement with a much larger number of exporters, the 1968 Coffee Agreement market shares were as follows:

Two largest exporters

Brazil	...	38.0%
Colombia	...	12.7%

Medium size exporters

Ivory Coast	...	5.6%
Portugal (Angola)	...	5.0%
Uganda	...	4.3%
El Salvador	...	3.5%
Guatemala	...	3.3%
Mexico	...	3.2%
Ethiopia	...	2.7%
Indonesia	...	2.5%

Small exporters

Between 1 million and 1.3 million bags	...	3 countries
Between 500,000 and 1 million bags	...	7 countries
Between 100,000 and 500,000 bags	...	10 countries

Very small exporters

below 100,000 bags	...	13 countries

The different levels of market shares indicate varying degrees of economic interest which in turn generate different attitudes among the different classes of exporters.

The large established exporters have more at stake; if any one of them does not want an agreement there will not be one. With the power of a large exportable surplus behind them (and thus the threat implicit in their ability to increase their market shares at the expense of all others in unregulated competition) they have a virtual veto over all aspects of a negotiation. This is clearly seen in the negotiations for a Cocoa Agreement where at one point Brazil was responsible for the breakdown and later Ivory Coast decided not to accede to the draft negotiated at Geneva. The early post-war experiences with the Wheat Agreement described in Chapter 2 show that all large exporters have to act together and that any one of them has the power to disrupt. Sometimes large exporters do accept limitations, such as a ceiling of 300 or 400 votes out of a total of 1,000 exporters' votes; these are, for the most part, cosmetic; power can be wielded without being seen to be exercised. When all large exporters collectively share an interest in regulating the market, they are likely to be more forthcoming in seeking compromises with importers. Large exporters have a vested interest in protecting their market shares, and their minimum expectation is likely to be to prevent an erosion in the quantities they had been exporting previously. At best, they may be willing to let all growth in consumption go to other exporters, and, at worst, they may want a proportionate share of the growth also. Having a greater stake in promoting consumption they are more likely to be willing to invest in it. They have a greater interest in developing new markets, in diversification and in development of processing. By and large, this group is likely to be more traditional and 'conservationist' in the sense of wanting to preserve the established order. While they have more to gain, they also have more to lose. For the extra benefits they gain, they also have to carry greater burdens. Stability of the market depends on their prudent stock management policies. If minimum stocks are to be held, they have to carry more physically, even if the proportion of stocks to quotas is the same for all. It is to the large exporters that importing countries turn for assurances on security of supply. At times of shortage, they may have to fulfil supply commitments to importers at less than the prevailing market price. Under the International Sugar Agreement of 1968, importers exercised their options five times during 1972 and 1973, and on each occasion major exporters had to supply at prices below current market levels.

Who are the significant exporters in the different commodities? The list below shows the major exporters for some, along with the 1969-71 average of the quantity share of each exporter as a percentage of total exports of that commodity.

Wheat	...	United States 32, Canada 21
Coarse grains	...	United States 20, Argentina 7
Beef	...	EEC 31, Australia 15
		Argentina 13
Sugar	...	Cuba 32
Coffee	...	Brazil 33, Colombia 12
Cocoa	...	Ghana 30, Nigeria 19, Ivory Coast 12,
		Brazil 11
Tea	...	Sri Lanka 32, India 30
Bananas	...	Ecuador 21, Honduras, Costa Rica
		13
Wine	...	Algeria 29, Italy 17, France
		12.5
Pepper	...	Malaysia 26, India 22,
		Indonesia 18
Cotton	...	United States 19
Jute	...	Bangla Desh 32, Thailand 30

Sisal   ...   Tanzania 37, Brazil 30
Natural rubber   ...   Malaysia 47, Indonesia 29
Phosphate rock   ...   Morocco 33
Bauxite   ...   Jamaica 25, Surinam 12.5
Tin   ...   Malaysia 42, Bolivia 15
     Indonesia 11, Thailand 10

The smaller exporters have less at stake than large exporters and correspondingly less commitment to any agreement. An agreement may survive without some of them, but, if a sufficiently large number stay away, they may disrupt it enough to make it unworkable. Consequently they have a nuisance value which needs placating. To the extent that smaller producers are high-cost producers — not all of them are — they are more interested in higher prices than in long-term growth of the market. Since they have fewer markets, their interest in quota negotiations is more likely to be confined to ensuring that they are able to dispose of the whole of their exportable surplus; they are less concerned about diversification and developing new markets. In particular, they have less interest in control systems, and at least some of them will be less than disciplined. They are more susceptible to political influence. Their bargaining power and voting strength being small and the threat of withdrawal being their only major weapon, they cannot use it often or effectively under normal conditions. All these factors are recognised in any commodity agreement by placing the small exporters in a separate category. In some their quotas and voting strength is protected; in others they are relieved of some obligations such as holding stocks. The agreed text of the 1976 International Coffee Agreement provides some examples: (i) very small exporters (with fewer than 100,000 bags annual exports) are allowed an automatic 10 per cent increase on their quotas each year; (ii) small exporters (between 100,000 and 400,000 bags) are allowed a 5 per cent increase; and (iii) exporters in both groups are allotted a fixed number of votes, unlike larger exporters, whose voting strength varies with the volume of exports in the preceding period.

New exporters, especially those with a potential for low-cost production and rapid expansion of exports, have special problems. Any agreement with quantitative restrictions on exports has to use historical performance as a guide, if not the sole basis, for determining market shares (i.e. basic export quotas). This tends to freeze market shares at current levels, and even where provision is made for growth this is rarely adequate to meet their expectations. Since new exporters can only grow, to their satisfaction, at the expense of established ones, a direct conflict arises between the two. While both groups may be convinced of the virtues of diversification, each may consider the other more suited to diversify away from the commodity. New exporters would point to their low cost of production and favourable natural endowments for their growth, while established exporters emphasise the comparative ease with which growth can be halted in new areas and the social and political problems they themselves have in curtailing production. The bargaining strength of new exporters is small, they may seek to increase support from the consuming countries by a willingness to accept prices lower than those demanded by established exporters. Often, emerging exporters have more to gain by not joining an agreement since they can have the benefits of market stability without the constraints on their growth. Traditional exporters therefore have to decide how small a quota and prospect for growth to allot to new exporters which at the same time is just enough to keep them in the agreement.

G.D. Gwyer, in his study of the East African experience in three international commodity agreements (coffee, tea and sisal), argues that:

> the distribution of gains from restrictive export agreements tends to benefit the larger producing countries because of their considerable voting power in the decision making forums . . . For larger producing countries the choice is between an agreement and no agreement, since their exclusion from an agreement would make it inoperable. For smaller countries the choice is membership in the agreement or non-membership since their membership may not be essential for the continuation of the agreement.[2]

In other words, large and small exporters have different choice options and are in effect playing different games. Gwyer further argues that 'disparities in bargaining power raise the possibility of a large producing country initiating an agreement and disbanding it again to suit its own convenience'. Gwyer does not attribute unequal distribution of gains only to the size of the market share; bargaining skills also matter a great deal.

> East African countries in the coffee agreement were disadvantaged in the determination of basic export quotas by having immature industries with rising production trends relative to established producers like Brazil. For the informal sisal agreement, the roles

were reversed in that Tanzania and Kenya have mature industries relative to Brazil. Thus, it was in East Africa's interests to have export performance measured over a long period to increase their share of the global quota. However, basic export quotas were agreed upon for each producer country calculated on the higher of the figures of their average export performance in two periods . . . The choice of the two periods was clearly to the advantage of Brazil, which, with a rising production trend, chose the [later period] . . . In money terms the failure of East Africa to insist upon [one period] as the base for calculating quota shares meant a 'loss' to East Africa of £210,000 each year and a gain to Brazil of £245,000, assuming a price at f.o.b. of £70 per metric ton.

In order to secure an equitable share of the gains, Gwyer concludes that small countries prepare briefs carefully, send strong delegations and muster all possible support from countries with similar interests.

Quality and Type Conflicts

So far in this study, no reference has been made to the existence of types and quality differentials in different commodities. This is an important aspect of commodity trade, not only because price differentials exist in the market but also because the very differentials are a perennial source of conflict among exporters. Only refined metals, which can be defined as 99.9 per cent pure, escape this problem. All agricultural commodities have varieties, types, grades and quality standards. In some minerals, the specification can vary so widely as to become almost incapable of comparison. For example, the quality of iron ore not only depends on the iron (Fe) content (which itself can vary from 35 per cent for some taconite and magnetite ores to over 68 per cent for the richest haematite ore) but also on the extent of impurities such as calcium and silicon, the moisture content and even the size of the ore (fines or lumps of different sizes). Every commodity has one or two quality types recognised generally as a standard. The quality difference between the standard grade and a particular consignment of the product is indicated by the market as a unit price differential.

The importance of precise understandings about price differentials for the successful operation of a commodity agreement has been clearly brought out in the FAO Commodity Policy Study on *The Stabilization of International Trade in Grains.*[3]

The many wheats sold in world markets and their respective flours differ in protein, gluten and ash content and in other properties which have a bearing on their suitability for specific uses. At the same time, there is a considerable degree of substitutability between these wheats, since a desired quality of wheat flour can be obtained by mixing wheats of different quality and having different properties. Price relationships between the various wheats traded internationally are therefore dependent on their intrinsic qualities and their relative availability in relation to the size and quality of crops in importing countries. Since market preference and supply positions change almost constantly there is no set of 'normal' price differentials which could easily be derived from market price data . . . All International Wheat Agreements in effect from 1949 to 1967 provided for only one basic price range applicable to a specific reference wheat [Canadian Manitoba Northern No.1]. It was left to the exporting and importing members concerned to agree on the appropriate quality differentials to be applicable at the limits of the [price] range. In these circumstances, if and when market prices for wheat dropped below the minimum of the range, it was difficult for the International Wheat Council to ascertain whether any of these prices had actually reached, or broken through, the minimum. In order to give more precision to the minimum price provisions, a schedule of minimum (and maximum) prices was written into the 1967 Wheat Trade Convention for 14 different wheats from 8 exporting countries . . . It was anticipated that when normal trade patterns became distorted, an adjustment in minimum price would provide a 'corrective' competitive advantage to a wheat that was not moving in this market in sufficient volume, by allowing it to sell at a price which was lower relative to other wheats . . . [A comparison of] the highest, lowest and average market differentials for a few representative wheats . . . [shows] that market differentials fluctuate widely and very rarely exactly correspond to the differentials laid down in the Convention. The possibility of establishing fixed price differentials for different wheats had been considered at practically every negotiating conference prior to 1967. In every instance it was thought to be impractical.

In the article referred to earlier, Gwyer gives another example of the importance of price differentials in promoting stability and preventing price declines. Under the informal arrangement on hard fibres, the producing countries agreed in June 1968 to implement a system of minimum prices which would be increased in steps so as to reach target levels by August 1969. A price differential of £5 a ton between Brazilian and East African sisal was also agreed upon. However, both the step-by-step increase and the price differential were abandoned in November 1968, when a minimum price was fixed for East African sisal alone at £75 a ton.

This meant in effect that there was a minimum price for East Africa and none for Brazil. The results of this were soon apparent. With East Africa holding a price umbrella Brazilian sales were reported as surging ahead while the demand for East African supplies remained quiet. This state of affairs continued until . . . April 1969 [when] the differential for Brazil was reinstated.

Attempts were made to revive the market by cutting export quotas but the effect 'on East African sales was only transitory. It seems likely that many buyers had already covered themselves for 1969 from buying cheap Brazilian . . . For the next months, market reports indicate that sales of East African remained at a very low level'.[4]

If the number of exporters in a commodity is large, quality and type differences divide them into conflicting groups, countries producing similar types forming themselves into coalitions. If the range of quality is very wide, as in the case of iron ore, where the product of every mine is unique, the impact on coalition forming is limited. But if the definable number of types is fairly small, large coalitions are more easily formed. The well-known case is coffee, with three clearly distinguishable types – Unwashed Arabicas (major exporters, Brazil and Ethiopia), mild Arabicas (major exporters, Colombia, other Latin American countries and Asia) and Robusta (mainly Africa). Originally just three groups existed, but a fourth was formed when Colombia, as the second largest exporter, decided that its stake in the trade justified it being classified as a group by itself. The 'Mild' group thus became 'Colombian Milds' and 'Other Milds'. With a large exportable quantity of the order of 7 million bags and a reputation for higher quality, Colombia has the power to manage the market in order to maintain a preferred margin between it and other competing types. These four groups conflict with each other constantly, both in the trading arena and on the negotiating stage, on price differentials as well as market shares. A full description of the dispute between exporters of different types of coffee is given in Bart Fisher's book on the coffee agreements.[5] The 1962 Agreement had no clear cut provision for 'selective' adjustment of quotas — i.e. adjusting the export quantities of only one type of coffee, depending on its own price movement, leaving the quantities in other types unchanged. The large exporters, Brazil and Colombia, at first opposed selective adjustments which would only have benefited the other exporters, particularly African Robusta producers. Eventually, the large exporters had to accept a limited application of selectivity in granting waivers to relieve the Robusta exporters of the burden of large surpluses. Towards the end of the first agreement, in 1966, a small part (1 million bags) of the annual quota was set apart to be adjusted selectively on the basis of four price ranges defined separately for the first time. In the renegotiated 1968 agreement, the selectivity principle was specifically written in and the Council was authorised 'to adopt a system for the adjustment of annual and quarterly quotas in relation to the movement of the prices of the principal types of coffee'.[6] An interesting result of the principle was that countries in each group were faced with the problem of the right price for not only their own type but for other types as well. While each group wanted a higher price for its own type, they could not demand too high a price or the next higher type would be made too competitive in relation to their own. Equally the highest priced coffees could not let the cheapest ones be too cheap. It must once again be emphasised that the price differential is not a static concept. As market conditions change and as supplies of one or the other type become plentiful or short, the right differential to preserve market shares varies. Thus, quality- and type-induced conflicts are a permanent feature of negotiations among exporters.

Co-operation among Producers

In the example of coffee discussed above, regional affinities are closely related to the type produced; though conflicts do occur between Latin American exporters, an overall regional affinity can also be detected. The main moves for negotiating an agreement originated in Latin American countries which then had to persuade the African countries to join in. The instrument for the negotiations between the two regions was the Coffee Study Group. Originally conceived in June 1958 as an international forum — with the United States, which had suffered a change of heart from its earlier total opposition, as the chairman — it promptly divided into regional blocs. The failure of the first round of negotiations led to the Latin Americans concluding an agreement among themselves. The Coffee Study Group, however, 'served as the forum in which proposals for coffee agreements, and also studies of the world coffee industry, could be discussed and their terms negotiated by the Latin American, African and European representatives'.[7] Here is a clear example of regional association over-riding other conflicts. The existence of other regional groupings in coffee such as OAMCAF (the Organisation of Coffee Producers of Africa and Malagasy — a francophone group), IACO (the Inter-African Coffee Organisation, which includes all African producers) and FEDECAME (the Central American, Mexican and Caribbean Coffee Federation, an organisation of Latin American smaller producers excluding Brazil and Colombia) all point to some shared interests based partly on economic interest and partly on geography. This is further underscored by the decision of the Pan-American Coffee Bureau not to admit members from other regions but to preserve its regional identity. For both economic and political reasons, the East African tea-producing countries (Kenya, Uganda and Tanzania) tend to act in concert as do the Asian producers, India, Sri Lanka and Indonesia. The ultimate example of course is the European Economic Community, in which regional co-operation has reached the point of regional integration.

In theory, co-operative relationships can be formed between just the largest exporters or between all exporters. The former leads to the possibility of oligopolistic collusion and the latter to the concept of purely producer agreements. Market control by the largest exporters is quite possible in a variety of commodities — the United States and Canada in wheat, India and Sri Lanka in tea, Brazil and Colombia in coffee and Malaysia, Indonesia and Singapore in natural rubber. The surprising fact is that such control has, in fact, not materialised. The success of OPEC in bringing together all exporters is a unique one and is unlikely to be repeated in any other commodity. The sad case of the ease with which multinational corporations were able to break UPEB, the limited banana exporters' group, will be examined in the context of the power of market control. Another case of failure can be found in cocoa. After the failure of the cocoa negotiations in 1963, when the exporters asked for a minimum of 27US ¢ per lb and importers would not go above US¢ 20 per lb, the New York spot price for Ghana cocoa declined to US ¢ 25.4. The major producers then formed the Cocoa Producers Alliance in September 1964 with Ghana, Nigeria, Brazil, Ivory Coast, Cameroon and Togo as members. The Alliance announced the withdrawal of cocoa from the market in October 1964 and the next month announced their intention to destroy stocks of cocoa. None of this had any great effect, and the large production forced the members to resume selling in February 1965. The result was that the New York spot Ghana price declined to US¢ 17.4; even more dramatically, the three-month New York futures which had stood at 22.4 ¢ per lb in January 1963, fell to a record low of 10.5 ¢ in July 1965. The market did not believe that the producers would be able to back their brave words with action, and the market was proved right.

Notwithstanding this failure, major producers of coffee tried it in 1972. When the 1968 agreement collapsed, the largest exporters formed a company called 'Café Mundial' to co-ordinate the sales of all their coffee. This was not a success mainly because the participants, mistrusting each other, did not give the company all their coffee to sell. Creating a company without giving it the necessary power is just a bluff that is easily called by the market. In commodities wholly produced in developing countries, the history of producers' attempts to control the market is one of failure. With their greater dependence on exports, the ever present need for foreign exchange and the very limited government resources for holding on, they just lack the economic muscle. Some commodity observers argue that they lack the necessary economic skills to implement their theories. With developed countries, co-operation among producers is almost instinctive; they are better able to perceive the advantages of market stability which their greater resources make it possible to implement.

Given the limited success of producer co-operation in regulating the market, it is not surprising that commodity agreements consisting only of producers have not made much headway. The Havana Charter does not even contemplate the possibility of arrangements between producers alone. In the climate of opinion prevailing immediately after the Second World War, and given the powerful dominance of the United States in the international economy, any such proposal would have been condemned out of hand as implying 'cartelisation'. In this philosophy, if domestic cartels are illegal, international cartels, especially those formed by governments, amount almost to original sin. Even in the United States, co-operative agreements among firms for export markets was possible under the so-called Webb-Pomerene Act. In actual practice, the greater emphasis on anti-trust legislation and the interpretation of the courts have meant that the Act has been little used for cartel purposes. It should, however, be noted that cartelisation in international trade is anathema only to the United States. European countries have fewer inhibitions about cartels so long as they are carried out beyond their own borders. Arrangements among manufacturers to regulate production and set agreed prices are prohibited only domestically in the United Kingdom, which permits such agreements in foreign trade so long as they are registered with the Department of

Trade. Over 200 such arrangements for sharing the world market are reported to have been registered, but the details have not been divulged even to the British Parliament on the grounds that they are commercial secrets. While the history of the cartel of oil companies is well known, the fact that developing countries have had to pay substantially more for their imports of chemical fertilisers or for electric cables because of cartel action by major manufacturing companies is often conveniently forgotten. In blessing only arrangements in which both producers and consumers take part the Havana Charter went further and specified that there should also be a strict power balance between them: 'Participating countries which are mainly interested in imports of the commodity, *shall*, in decisions on substantive matters, *have* a number of votes *equal* to that of those mainly interested in obtaining export markets for that commodity.'[8] From 1948 until 1963, the type of arrangement permitted by the Charter made so little progress that the disappointment of the developing countries prompted them to include in the Charter of Algiers a call to producing *developing* countries 'to consult and cooperate among themselves in order to defend and improve their terms of trade by effective coordination of their sales policies'. As one would expect, in the discussions during UNCTAD II this was wholly unacceptable to the rich countries.

Opposition to purely producer agreements was not confined to developed importing countries but was also shared by developed exporters who had a substantial interest in the export of primary commodities. The failure of iron-ore-exporting countries to achieve effective co-ordination is a direct result of this conflict of attitudes. The first move to form an association was initiated during the 1968 UNCTAD II Conference; this was followed by a number of meetings between developing countries. None of the major developed exporting countries was willing to participate. The proposal was revived in 1974 and two of the three developed countries (Australia and Sweden but not Canada) have joined the association on the understanding that it would confine itself to exchange of information. In other words, let us talk but not do anything. The fear that out of such humble beginnings an OPEC-type cartel will emerge is not only premature but imaginary. Reference will be made to this history again in the context of price and market behaviour. For the present, the conclusion to note is that exporters' co-operation depends for its success on power, and power is derived from market control and backing resources.

Conflicts between Commodities

All the relationships studied above arise from the characteristics of a single commodity. What has tended to be ignored is the effect of regulatory actions in one commodity on the production and marketing of another. Different commodities can be grown on the same land; for example, rubber and palm (for kernels and oil), coffee and bananas, coffee and tea, sugar and rice, and jute and rice. Production adjustments by relative shifts from one commodity to another are made by the individual grower in response to his anticipated returns. In developed countries the farmers are able to make these adjustments more easily, due to the availability of technical knowledge and financial assistance. For example, the Common Agricultural Policy of the EEC is an attempt to promote the right mix of commodity production by government supported pricing mechanism. The freeing of production controls and the removal of subsidies in the United States is a means of achieving the same end by the market mechanism. As in the case of market control, the resources they command make it possible for rich countries to initiate and promote production changes with greater ease. Mistakes are made, mountains of unwanted commodities do appear but governments are able to pay for these mistakes without too great a dislocation.

The social problems involved in land use adjustments are far greater in developing countries. Bangla Desh illustrates the very real dilemma that poor countries often face. Rice and jute are competing commodities; the bulk of the jute is exported either as raw jute or as jute manufactures, while all the rice is consumed domestically. Low international prices for raw jute coupled with high domestic price for rice in difficult years prompt the farmer to plant more rice than jute. This reduces the export availability of jute the next year, exchange earnings fall and the development effort is stalled. Bangla Desh cannot unilaterally raise the export price of jute because of pressure on prices from competing synthetics. A higher guaranteed price to the jute farmer, irrespective of the international price, would involve heavy subsidies and, at the same time increase costs for the domestic jute manufacturing industry, making Bangla Desh jute fabrics less competitive in the international market. If a higher price is not paid to farmers for rice, production may suffer, making the country more dependent on food imports. The long-term answer is, of course, that productivity in both rice and jute must increase but this does not solve the year to year problem. It is almost impossible to draw up a pricing policy which would simultaneously promote the production of adequate quantities of jute and rice, maintain farmers' incomes, keep down consumer prices for the staple food grain and protect the competitiveness of both raw jute and jute manufacturers. The problem would become more complex if there were an international agreement in one or the other commodity (for example, a Jute Agreement) imposing further obligations on the country.

The inter-relationship between international action in different commodities can be seen in the cases of tea and coffee and bananas. The attitudes which governments adopt in the different commodity negotiations depend on their judgement on how to optimise the country's return in foreign exchange from all commodities as well as optimising the farmers' return in terms of the achievable mix of production. Governments therefore form policies for a number of commodities in an integrated fashion, though internally they have to negotiate them individually. The prospect of the establishment of quotas for export and production ceilings for coffee prompted the East African countries to look for alternatives. They encouraged, with the assistance of the World Bank, a rapid increase in the production of tea, with the laudable objectives of diversifying from coffee and maintaining their farmers' incomes. Unfortunately, tea is one of the few commodities which has shown a steady and secular decline in real price since the end of the Second World War. Attempts to reverse the trend by a suitable market-sharing mechanism face the difficult question of how to accommodate the future planned increase in East Africa at a sacrifice acceptable to the large traditional exporters such as India and Sri Lanka. So far, only some kind of informal arrangement has been worked out. While a great deal has been written about the International Coffee Agreement and its benefits to coffee exporters, very little has been said about how a part of the price has been paid by exporters of tea, all of whom are also developing countries. The chain of interaction does not stop with tea. Faced with quantity limitations in tea and coffee, India has started growing cocoa and the multinational company promoting its production claims that India will be able to export cocoa in a few years' time. In an attempt to diversify the sources of farmers' incomes away from the traditional rubber, rice and palm. Malaysia is also promoting the growing of cocoa. What all this will mean to the already volatile state of the cocoa market and the sad history of international cocoa negotiations can best be left to the imagination. Some Central American countries face an even more acute problem; if they cannot increase their revenues from bananas due to the control exercised by traditional companies and if, simultaneously, they cannot increase the production of coffee due to quota limitations, what can they do to maximise their exchange earnings and raise the standard of living of their farmers?

The problem of promoting appropriate production adjustments is admittedly a difficult one for developed and developing countries. The relationship between beef and dairy products is a constant bugbear in the Common Agricultural Policy of the EEC. The issue relevant to this study is the effect of production changes on commodity negotiations. Production changes happen all the time. While Sri Lanka and India may be large established exporters of tea today, at one time they produced no tea at all until it was introduced by the British. Neither Malaysia nor Indonesia was a rubber producer in 1900. Practically the whole of the world's supply of rubber at that time came from the Amazon valley and Central Africa, where rubber trees grew wild in the forests and expeditions were organised to tap them. Commodity negotiations have to take into account the fact of structural changes. There is a 'punch-bag' effect in which actions in one commodity on a commodity-by-commodity basis lead to situations where success in one may well lead to failure in another.

Conflict and Co-operation among Developing Exporters

Given the technical factors such as quality differences, existence of different types and regional concentration of production, it is possible to visualise where conflict and co-operative situations could occur among exporters. For example, if there were an international agreement on bananas, one would expect some conflicts to develop as a result of market patterns. Central American bananas generally go to the United States, Caribbean and African ones to Europe and Far Eastern ones to Japan. While the Cavendish is the standard variety accounting for the largest part of international trade, other varieties may also become sources of conflicts of types. Coffee exemplifies almost all kinds of conflict, all of them overlaid by the regional distribution of production of different types. In cocoa, there is bound to be the problem of market distribution among major exporters, conflicts between large and small exporters and, looming ahead, the problem of new exporters. In tea, there is a quality conflict, East African teas generally being lower priced than South Asian teas; the beverage also faces large against small and established against emerging exporter conflicts. Pepper, jute and natural rubber are commodities concentrated mainly in South and South-East Asia, and regional co-operation may well become an important factor. In sisal, there is an underlying continental conflict expressing itself as a quality conflict.

This chapter has been devoted to an analysis of the factors which influence the attitudes of exporting countries. The commodities considered are all almost wholly of interest to developing countries, for the reason that exporters' problems are more easily solved by developed primary producing countries domestically with their enormous resources. Without the technical and financial resources to deal with them internally, developing countries have to bring them to the negotiating table. Their attitudes are influenced by their economic interest — whether they are large, small or new exporters and what type they produce. They co-operate when their interests overlap and conflict when they diverge. But political relationships, as when producers belong to the same region, sometimes transcend commodity conflicts. The lack of resources converts problems into conflicts and is also responsible for the failure of producing countries to go it alone. It is the same lack of resources that makes the land use problem in the poor countries well-nigh insoluble. The inability to adjust speedily to changes in the international environment leads to the punch-bag effect. The problems of developed exporting countries are no doubt the same — market control, power to hold on in times of stress and ability to make production adjustments. Apart from devoting greater resources internally, developed countries resolve the conflicts by means of alternative trade-offs outside the commodity sector. In considering in the next chapter the problems of access, the availability of other trade-offs will be seen to be a crucial factor.

Notes

1. Unlike other commodity agreements which divide the membership between exporting and importing countries, the Tin Agreements have producing and consuming members. This classification was helped because of the clear distinction between producing countries which consumed little or no tin and consuming countries which produced little or no tin. The only exceptions are Australia which turned from a consumer into a producer in 1964 and the USSR which is accepted as a consuming member though a large producer of unknown tonnages but importer of known tonnages. For a survey of the membership of the various tin agreements, see Chapter XII of William Fox, *Tin: The Working of a Commodity Agreement* (Mining Journal Books Ltd., London, 1974).
2. G.D. Gwyer, 'Three International Commodity Agreements: The Experience of East Africa, *Economic Development and Cultural Change*, 21, 1973, pp.465-76.
3. FAO Commodity Policy Studies no.20, *The Stabilization of International Trade in Grains: An Assessment of Problems and Possible Solutions* (FAO, Rome, 1970).
4. Gwyer, 'Three International Commodity Agreements'.
5. Bart S. Fisher, *The International Coffee Agreement: A Study in Coffee Diplomacy* (Praeger, New York, 1972).
6. Article 37(2), The International Coffee Agreement, 1969.
7. International Coffee Council, *The History of Recent International Coffee Agreements*, Washington DC, June 1963.
8. Section (b), Article 63, Havana Charter; see Appendix 1.

6 ACCESS, AND MORE ACCESS

> Nearly two thirds of the South's workers were thus employed
> in low value creating jobs in the production of raw materials
> for extractive industries such as agriculture, forestry and
> mining which were characterised by absentee ownership.
> Still, bankrupt Southern communities fell over themselves to
> attract Northern investors...
>
> *Simple Justice,* Richard Kluger's history of
> Brown versus the Board of Education

The conflict of interest between importers and exporters in commodities which are produced in substantial quantities in the importing countries revolves basically around the question of access to these markets. Often this is viewed as one of obtaining access for the *exports of developing* countries in the *markets of the developed* importing countries. Since developed countries are also substantial exporters of primary products, conflicts principally between developed exporting and developed importing countries also have to be considered. Access to markets is also the crucial problem in commodity trade between developing exporting countries and centrally planned countries. Further, unobstructed access to markets for processed forms and manufactures is an integral part of the basic conflict between developed and developing countries.

In Chapter 3, developed countries were classified under four groups, mainly based on their natural endowments. Of these four, one cannot legitimately expect low-cost producers (United States, Canada or Australia) to import the commodities they grow or mine themselves. These countries, as well as import-dependent Japan, do not generally erect barriers against commodities which they do not produce themselves. In general, non-renewable commodities such as metals and minerals are considered by all developed countries to be indispensable for industrial and economic growth and rarely encounter barriers to trade in their raw forms. The problem of access to markets for primary commodities in their unmanufactured state is essentially one of availability of markets in those developed countries with high costs of production. In effect, this is a problem of high degrees of protection for agricultural commodities in the European Economic Community and their effects in drastically curtailing the available markets for developing exporting countries. The economic policies of the centrally planned economy countries have virtually similar effects on the exports of developing countries as the protectionist policies of the EEC.

While only primary agricultural commodities, not mineral ores and virgin metals, encounter barriers to trade in the unmanufactured form, both renewable and non-renewable commodities are subject to discouragement of access in their processed and manufactured forms. The means adopted are cascading tariffs, prohibition of imports, quantitative restrictions on imports, duties or indirect taxes and unusual administrative or health regulations designed to reduce imports. The aim of the importing countries in erecting these barriers is mainly to protect investment and employment in the processing industry. Cascade tariffs also incidentally ensure that the products of the processing industries are export competitive by avoiding undue incidence of taxation on the raw material. The oft-proclaimed interest of the consumer in developed countries is mere rhetoric; in most countries, other indirect taxes such as excise duties, value added tax or sales tax determine the price to the consumer, not the customs duty. The duties on coffee in Germany or the universal fiscal charges on manufactured tobacco are primarily revenue earning measures though they indirectly affect consumption and imports. Thus cascading tariffs are only one element in the variety of measures designed to deny access for the raw material and its processed forms. For the exporting countries there are a number of adverse effects. They are prevented from being able to increase unit values, are unable to industrialise in certain areas and are restricted in their ability to diversify their export pattern and reduce their dependence on one or two export commodities. In theory, the effect on exporters, whether developed and developing, should be the same; however, in practice the rich countries with their greater resources and more diversified economies do not feel the effect with the severity experienced by the poor ones. Where imports from developed countries hurt — steel, automobiles, ball bearings, television sets or whatever — the dispute is usually settled bilaterally by 'voluntary' restraint or, in GATT, the developed countries' forum. The corresponding production adjustments are made without too great a dislocation of the economy. For the developing countries, the effect of restraint on development is more pervasive; not being able to obtain higher unit values reduces their resources for development; non-availability of export markets reduces their scope for industrialisation; inability to diversify the export pattern puts them more at the mercy of the fluctuating fortunes of the commodity market; a lopsided development complicates economic planning and increases social tension: and, lastly, being made to be permanent exporters of raw materials places them in a much weaker bargaining position relative not only to the importing countries but also to the buyers of their commodity. This conflict, therefore, is primarily one between developed importing countries and developing exporting countries.

All the above access-to-markets problems will be analysed in subsequent sections in this chapter. However, note must first be taken of another type of conflict concerning access. Assured *access to supplies* is seen by the importing countries as the answer to the vulnerability posed by import dependence. The analysis of import dependence in Chapter 3 has shown that it varies widely among developed countries. It is almost total for Japan and, with the glaring exception of oil, almost non-existent for the United States. There is an equally wide variation in the import dependence of developing countries, with the added problem, for many of them, of food imports. A large part of the problems of commodity trade pertain to exports from developing countries into developed countries. Food supplies offer an interesting reversal; in this case, developed countries are the exporters and developing countries the importers.

Access to Supplies

In his address to the Seventh Special Session of the United Nations, US Secretary of State Henry Kissinger placed security of supply second in the list of three priorities for ensuring global economic security. The first was controlling inflation in the industrialised nations and the third stabilising the export earnings of developing countries. 'Global economic security depends', he declared, 'on the actions of suppliers of vital products.'[1] Reference was made in Chapter 3 to the Special Report of the US Council on International Economic Policy on *Critical Imported Materials*. In addition, a number of other studies have been made on the so-called threat to supplies of vital materials. The US Department of State produced one on *International Collusive Action in World Markets for Non-Fuel Materials.*[2] The World Bank has done two on opportunities for OPEC-type action on agricultural commodities as well as non-fuel minerals.[3]

Typical of the emotional outbursts that became common after the oil embargo is one called *Eight Mineral Cartels: The New Challenge to Industrialized Nations* by Clarfield and others.[4] It is best to ignore this book's unbridled use of emotive epithets and its venom against developing countries, particularly copper producers. The political perspective of the authors is one that is confined, even in the United States, to an extreme of the political spectrum. Suffice it to say that this is about the only book which considers the International Tin Agreements a cartel! To the authors even the Havana Charter would appear to be dangerously revolutionary! My point in referring to this one-sided study is to emphasise that even these authors did not find any of the seven products (other than oil) studied by them capable of promoting successful cartel action. On tin, they recommended that the United States help the Tin Agreement become more effective; they did not find that cartel action would succeed in bauxite because of the existence of alternative ores in developed countries and of producers of bauxite who may not join in the International Bauxite Association. Even on copper − CIPEC is a particular *bête-noire* − all that they can find is that there may be a potential for cartel action but that the developed world already has many contingency plans up its sleeve to counteract it. The title belies the work; eight mineral cartels turn out to be not a single non-fuel mineral cartel. In talking about vital supplies, Kissinger was referring to oil alone. Apart from OPEC, there is no likelihood whatsoever of developing countries attaining such a degree of control as to enable them to dictate terms.

An essential theme of this book, repeatedly emphasised in earlier chapters, is that non-oil exporting developing countries are becoming increasingly peripheral and increasingly irrelevant to the international economic system as it operates today. Obviously such countries can never obtain the bargaining power to direct the course the system takes. This point needs to be categorically stated in order that further discussion on commodity conflicts is not sidetracked into futile byways of the so-called insecurity of the developed countries in the face of imagined developing country power. Insecurity is a state of mind; the speed and ability with which the developed countries have adjusted to the oil price rise has no doubt helped to allay these fears. Shorn of emotionalism, the problem of security of supply can be put in perspective. Assurance of the availability of imports is a legitimate concern of importing countries. To the extent that importing countries are asked to co-operate in attaining the objective that exporting countries seek, to that extent they too can ask for assurances on supply. In every commercial contract, a delivery date is specified in addition to quantity, quality and price. In commodity negotiations, assurance of supply is the equivalent of the delivery commitment in sales contracts.

If oil is vital to the economic well-being of developed countries, food imports are equally vital to many developing countries. The effect of the technological revolution in this century has been such that today it is the rich countries that have the surplus food and the poor that need to import it. For the most part, the primary commodities imported by the poor from the rich consist of food, particularly cereals. The fact that humanitarian considerations play a large part in these imports should not mean that they are ignored in an analysis dealing with the whole gamut of commodity trade. Until 1968, all International Wheat Agreements covered only commercial sales; the International Grains Arrangement of that year consisted of two parts — the Wheat Trade Convention and the Food Aid Convention. The close relationship between food aid and grain sales which gives rise to a number of conflicts was thus recognised. Conflicts arise among the developed countries because of two separate considerations. The first is the interest of exporting countries in ensuring that concessionary (aid) supplies of food grains do not affect their normal markets. The second is the concern that all countries who can afford to contribute equitably to the food aid programme. As for developing countries, their main interest is in securing adequate supplies of grains at reasonable prices. For some developing countries, particularly large populous ones such as India and Bangla Desh, the adverse economic consequences of the oil price rise in 1974 were made much worse by the very high prices of food grains and fertilisers. These countries did not find the commodity boom an unmixed blessing.

Security of supply and reasonable prices are thus not only a matter of importance to the industrialised countries in terms of industrial raw materials or energy but also to the developing countries for food grains and oil seeds. Conversely, the rich exporting countries also need to have some assurance of markets, as reasonable projections of exports have to be built into their domestic economic policy in relation to production plans, consumer prices, costs of storage and support programmes. Lastly, food as aid has to be reckoned in the context of sharing the burden of transferring additional resources to the poor countries. If the United States stocks millions of tons of wheat and maize as an insurance against famine and starvation elsewhere in the world, this is a contribution to world economic stability. It has been argued that the United States food aid policy is only a direct consequence of the surpluses that have been built up as a result of domestic support policies. Such arguments gain credibility when the US Secretary for Agriculture talks of using food as a weapon. While the volume of food aid does bear a direct relationship to the stocks held, it is also undeniable that most people are motivated by a desire to help others in distress. Particularly when it comes to food aid and starvation, it is difficult to separate humanitarian and self-interest motives. Charity does have a price tag attached to it, and any rational consideration of burden sharing must include it as a contribution to the solving of commodity trade problems. The reason why concessionary sales of food grains (such as under the Public Law 480 of the United States) are not usually included in considerations of the larger primary commodity question are that they have been dealt with only as a conflict between the developed countries as to how much aid and in what form each should provide. Thus the forums for negotiation have been either FAO/UN World Food Program or GATT.

Access Conflicts between Developed Countries

Like food aid, conflicts on access between developed countries have been either a GATT or a bilateral question. In the Kennedy Round a major conflict was one of access for agricultural products, particularly from North America to the European market. The fear of the United States at that time was that the Common Agricultural Policy (CAP) of the European Economic Community (then the Six) with its implicit assumption of high-cost self-sufficiency had given rise to a policy of 'neo-mercantilism'.[5] Being a conflict between rich countries, its resolution was sought in a forum where developing countries had a much smaller voice and the socialist countries none at all. Further, in a GATT context, mutual concessions on the agricultural question were facilitated by the possibility of trade-offs in other fields. Multilateral tariff cutting is a complicated exercise in which the unfulfilled promise to remove the American Selling Price system for customs evaluation on chemicals was as integral a part of the negotiations as access of soya beans into the EEC. Enlarging the area of negotiation made an agreement between the rich countries on access, grain sales and food aid possible, but removing them from an international commodity context also had adverse effects. The consequence of a less than universal participation in the International Wheat Agreement has already been noted. The agreements also had an adverse impact on the developing countries whose products competed in the same market with the developed exporting countries.

Two examples of the resolution of intra-rich country access conflicts can be found in the negotiations between the six members of the EEC and the United Kingdom for the latter's entry into the Community. Of

all the primary commodities, the access problems of only two —
Commonwealth sugar and New Zealand butter — were accorded a place
in the negotiations between the UK and the Six. Both these involved
questions of access for Community production in the British market.
The sugar problem, which concerns exports from developing countries
into the Community, will be considered in the next section. The New
Zealand butter export case is more clearly an intra-developed country
conflict involving the potential for dairy exports from the Six within
the enlarged Community and the market for butter for another entrant
(Denmark) into the UK as well as the share of the UK market to be
made available to New Zealand. The broader context of the negotiations created the possibility of trade-offs in other fields, many of them
not even economic. When the negotiations for UK's entry were
reopened, a fundamental political judgement had already been made by
all the countries concerned — that, within very broad limits, all
problems should be resolved so that the UK could join the Community.
The will to compromise was thus assured. This is, perhaps, one case in
which one can legitimately talk of 'political will' in commodity negotiations in the sense that the totality of the negotiations was a political
act.

Access to supplies also has been a source of conflict between
developed countries. The sudden embargo on shipments of soyabeans
from the US created one between Japan and the US. The reasons for
the embargo were partly domestic considerations in the US and partly
American problems with the international monetary situation. The
conflict was also resolved in the broader context of monetary
questions. It is unnecessary to multiply such examples. The economic
inter-relationships between the countries in the centre are so many that
compensations can be found elsewhere than in the immediate source of
a conflict. Availability of a multiplicity of trade-offs is a source of
economic strength and bargaining power.

EEC's Common Agricultural Policy and Access to Markets

The problem of access for exports of developing countries primarily
results from the protection of high-cost agriculture in the Community.
In terms of importance of market potential, it is worth nothing that the
world's largest agricultural market is Western Europe. The poor
countries are adversely affected by the Community's Common
Agricultural Policy in three ways; the market itself has shrunk, the
competition between developed and developing countries for the
diminishing market has become more acute and the dumping by the

Community of surplus production has reduced the value of other markets. One cannot underestimate the structural impact on world commodity trade of a deliberate policy of protectionism for high-cost agriculture. Maybe the CAP had some reason for coming into being in a continent devastated by two wars within 50 years of each other. Thirty years after the end of the Second World War, that policy looks less and less logical. The frequent piling up of butter mountains and skim milk mountains shows how ridiculous the policy has become. The cost to the Community of the storage and disposal of these huge surpluses may be high, but the rest of the world also has to pay a price. Recently, the European Commission estimated that there was a tendency for the Community to produce 10 per cent more milk than required. As a result, the intervention stocks (i.e. stocks which the Community has had to buy to support the high prices) of butter amount to 200,000 tons and of skim milk to 1.3 million tons. In 1976, the disposal measures for milk products alone were expected to cost the Community 1930 million units of account or over US$2.4 billion Faced with this surplus, does the Commission propose cutting down dairy production? Not at all; it suggests the levying of a 10 per cent tax on all imported vegetable oils as well as an equivalent tax on all imported products containing such oils! This is the essence of the CAP — first produce massive surpluses by high levels of protection and then use the surplus to punish other competing commodities.[6]

Sugar provides the most glaring example of the effects the CAP has on exports of developing countries. In view of the importance of this commodity in world trade and as a source of export earnings to a large number of developing countries, it is worthwhile looking at the Community's sugar policy in greater detail. The brief survey below is heavily indebted to three articles by Ian Smith, two for the Trade Policy Research Centre, London, and one in the *Journal of World Trade Law*.[7] All quotations below are from one or the other of these articles. The European Community's common sugar policy became operative in 1968 and covered production in the then Community (the Six), including the French overseas departments of Guadaloupe, Martinique and Réunion. On paper, the policy had four main objectives: (i) to promote self-sufficiency while avoiding the accumulation of burdensome surpluses; (ii) to stabilise production in regions less suited to beet growing; (iii) to increase production and specialisation in regions best suited to beet growing; and (iv) to keep the cost of the programme within acceptable limits. Leaving aside the question whether the objective of self-sufficiency itself makes economic sense and shows international responsibility, it is important to note that none of the objectives was realised in practice. The reason for reality not even approximating to the principles is that the system devised to achieve the objectives was not designed for self-sufficiency but for over-production. Sugar is the only CAP commodity regulated by quotas. These quotas guarantee a price and a market for a basic quantity equal to the self-sufficiency quantity. However, production up to 135 per cent of the basic quota was *guaranteed* a market at a somewhat lower price. The target for production was therefore 35 per cent over and above self-sufficiency. Naturally, production regularly outpaced the growth in consumption. Between 1968/9 (the first full campaign year under the CAP for sugar) and 1973/4, the Community's beet sugar production increased by 27 per cent – from 6.8 million tons to 8.3 million tons. During the same period consumption increased by only 10 per cent – from 5.9 million tons to about 6.6 million tons. The surplus therefore doubled from 890,000 to 1.7 million tons. If one looks at a longer period stretching back to before the introduction of the CAP, it is seen that the 'common sugar policy has turned the Common Market of the Six from a deficit area of about 350,000 tons to a surplus area of over 1.7 million tons' – a turn-around of 2 million tons. During the recent shortage years, the Community has raised the excess quota to 145 per cent, all of which is to be paid the full price of the basic quota. This could well result in a couple of years in an even more massive surplus.

The growth of this huge surplus is surprising when one considers the market conditions at the time the sugar policy was determined. The average London Daily Price between 1965 and 1968 was only £20 a ton. The negotiations for an international agreement in 1968 contemplated a floor price of only £28 a ton. In contrast, the CAP's intervention price for white sugar, *for areas of greatest surplus,* was £90 a ton in 1968! By October 1974, the intervention price had risen to £135 a ton. Reference was made in Chapter 2 to the Community's refusal to participate in the International Sugar Agreement under negotiation in 1968 even when offered a generous export quota of 300,000 tons. For the equally abortive negotiations in 1973 the European Commission suggested that the Community should be prepared to accept an export quota of 800,000 tons – a nearly threefold jump in just five years. Even this exorbitant demand was considered inadequate by Jacques Chirac, the then French Minister of Agriculture, who called it 'ridiculous'. It is, of course, ridiculous, but not in the way that M. Chirac meant it. A country which is a massive exporter of arms, part producer of the Concorde and sells nuclear processing plants can claim to have the right to dump high-cost sugar on the world markets on only two grounds – that the people of the Community have a right to a higher standard of living at the expense of the poor countries and that national interest should overwhelm international responsibility. A harsh judgement indeed by this author, but one that is easily substantiated. In 1968/9 the Community's degree of self-sufficiency, according to EUROSTAT, was only 102; this rose to 122 in 1971/2 and even in a bad year for beet such as 1973/4 it was 111.[8] This is reflected in the Community's demand for an export quota of more than 300,000 tons in 1968 and more than 800,000 tons in 1973. The actual net exports (exports excluding trade between the countries and overseas Departments covered by the sugar policy) for the five campaign years up to 1973/4 were:

Net exports in white sugar equivalent in 1,000 tons

1969/70	...	497
1970/1	...	944
1971/2	...	1,469
1972/3	...	1,504
1973/4	...	1,516

Even at the comparatively low prices prevailing in the free market in those years, these exports were worth a total of approximately US$900 million. Considering that the dumping itself was responsible for depressing the prices, the loss of export earnings to developing sugar producers would have been well over a billion dollars. By comparison, the total gross food aid of the Six, during the years 1970 to 1974, was only US $850 million. Thus much more than the total food aid by the Community of the Six was taken away by the Community's CAP – on sugar alone. Ian Smith's conclusion that 'the European Community's sugar regulations constitute one of the most flagrant examples of commodity dumping' is incontrovertible.

The fact that the Community's sugar policy came in useful in 1973 and 1974 when there was a world shortage and an extraordinary price rise is not a justification for it, since the sugar policy itself was one of the main causes for the world shortage. The shrinkage of the market, th dumping by the EEC and the consequences of the abrupt shut-off of the US market for Cuban sugar produced a condition when for years even efficient producers were selling in the world market below costs of production. Between 1954 and 1958, the free market price averaged 3.72 US ¢ per lb. But between 1964 and 1968, the price remained at a consistently low level, averaging 2.65 ¢ per lb. Even allowing for the fact that the free market in sugar was a residual market,

> it is difficult to escape the conclusion that the relatively slow growth
> in world production capacity since 1971 has been influenced by the
> depressed free market prices of 1964-68. Moreover, the price
> increase which took place in the next three years 1969-71 (average
> 3.80 cents a lb) was hardly sufficient to justify additional invest-
> ment in sugar cane production.

The EEC sugar policy reached the height of illogicality when it paid
good money for making it unfit for human consumption so that it
could be used as animal feed. Over the five years 1969/70 to 1973/4,
600,000 tons were so consumed. Thus the sugar surplus attacked the
market for other products such as oilcake. Sugar and dairy products are
not the only examples of the Community's support for high-cost
production. Grain prices are maintained above current world prices by
the application of import taxes in the form of variable levies on imports
into the Community. Threshold prices and variable levies also operate
for beef and veal, pigmeat, eggs, poultry meat and olive oil. Export
restitutions (a euphemism for export subsidies) are available for grains
including rice, butter, cheese and skim milk, cattle and meat, white
sugar, fruit and vegetables, vegetable oils and oilseeds, olive oil and
tobacco. Butter mountains and skim milk mountains are only the tips
of the vast iceberg; the magnitude of the adverse impact of the CAP on
the market for agricultural products is incalculable.

The competition between developed and developing countries for
the shrinking European market is an acute one. The number of
products in which there is competitition between the two groups is
surprisingly large. Grains, meat products, wool, citrus fruit, vegetable
oils, oil seeds, tobacco and sugar are the most important ones. In its
1973 *Commodity Review,* the FAO analysed the various markets of the
world from the perspective of competition between the two groups.
The analysis showed clearly that developing countries as a whole
encounter their main competition in the European market. The richest
market is naturally one that attracts the greatest competition. It is easy
to guess who are the losers in this competition. The developing countries
lose partly because of the powerful marketing ability of the rich
commodity exporting countries and partly because market access
decisions are resolved on a plane far removed from them. An example is
the brandy-turkey war; the access for poultry meat in France and the
level of import duty on cheaper qualities of brandy in the United States

have become interlinked. Developing countries cannot offer any such trade-offs. In this lopsided bargaining situation, the rich countries such as the European Economic Community can pursue protectionist policies with impunity. The asymmetry of the system is such that the rich can do what they like and the poor pay.

Will the CAP change? Internal attempts at modifying it, from the days of the short-lived Mansholt Plan, have made little headway. The political conflicts within the EEC are too intense to stand the shock of a major change in the agricultural policy. A chink in the barrier is the incorporation of the Commonwealth Sugar Agreement in the Lomé Convention; but this only protects the access which the Commonwealth sugar-exporting countries have always had in the UK market and does not attack the problem of the dumping of high-cost sugar in world markets. Another encouraging sign is the improvement in access for Mediterranean products, from which the developing littoral countries have benefited. As this is clearly a political gesture, it will be discussed in Chapter 10 in the context of political influence on commodity negotiations.

Access in Centrally Planned Economy Countries

It is not only the industrialised countries of the West that limit access for the products of developing countries. Conceptually, the centrally planned economy countries support the developing countries in the view that commodity agreements should promote development but only to the extent that the responsibility is solely laid on the developed market-economy countries. In the opinion of the socialist countries, the West has an obligation to provide aid as a compensation for their past imperialism and colonialism; not having been guilty of a similar history, they are under no such obligation. The reaction of the developing countries to this thesis varies widely. In general, there is less confrontation between the developing and centrally planned groups. The former, however, do confront the latter with the criticism that they do not provide adequate access to primary products and that they artificially inhibit consumption by high retail prices. Unlike the market economy countries, tariff and non-tariff barriers are not clearly defined in the socialist countries and, in the absence of data on the elasticity of consumer demand, the quantification of denial of access becomes difficult. The characteristics of the import market in the socialist countries are, however, determined by the following objectives of centralised planning: (i) to achieve self-sufficiency to the maximum extent possible within the group as a whole; (ii) to export for hard currency surplus agricultural products and minerals in demand in the world markets; (iii) to import in times of need only the minimum necessary; and (iv) to try to balance trade with each country individually, preferably by means of non-convertible self-balancing trade agreements. Another important aspect of the system is that the price to the consumer of imported products is not related to the cost of import but to a predetermined price differential formula within the domestic system. Together these have the same effect on exports of primary commodities as the policies which protectionist high-cost industrialised countries adopt. A study by the UNCTAD Secretariat indicates that the degrees of self-sufficiency of the USSR in certain primary commodities increased markedly between the periods 1959/61 and 1967/9; rice went from 27 per cent to 67 per cent, sugar from 82 to 94 per cent and tobacco from 70 to 81 per cent.[9]

The relative unimportance of foreign trade to the socialist countries is substantiated by the figures quoted in Chapter 3 (Tables 3.1 and 3.3) of their share of world trade and trade in primary commodities remaining stable about 10 per cent. Unlike the case of Western Europe and Japan, the socialist countries' rapid post-war industrial growth has not led to a corresponding growth in foreign trade. The pattern of trade has, however, changed significantly, as Table 6.1 shows. The share of the developing countries has not changed very much; trade with the industrialised countries has increased two and a half times in the last twenty years mainly at the expense of intra-group trade.

Table 6.1: Exports to Centrally Planned Countries by Developed, Developing and Centrally Planned Groups (Value US$ million)

| Year | Total | Exports to Centrally Planned Countries | | | | | |
| | | By Developed Countries | | By Developing Countries | | By Centrally Planned Countries | |
		Value	Share	Value	Share	Value	Share
1955	8,790	1,320	15.0%	270	6.5%	6,900	78.5%
1960	15,010	2,970	19.8	1,220	8.1	10,820	72.1
1965	21,090	4,990	23.6	2,340	11.1	13,770	65.3
1970	31,420	8,360	26.6	3,150	10.0	19,920	63.4
1973	55,930	18,400	32.9	5,140	9.2	32,390	57.9
1974	70,650	26,590	37.6	7,700	10.9	36,350	51.5

Source: UN *Statistical Yearbook; Monthly Bulletin of Statistics,* August 1976.

As is the case with the market economy world, the socialist world also covers a wide range of countries. The USSR, with its vast area spanning two continents, is endowed with almost every mineral and every variety of climate for growing agricultural products; the others are less fortunately placed and are hence more dependent on imports for selected products. On the whole, consumption in the socialist countries of commodities of interest to developing countries remains substantially lower than in the OECD countries. Table 6.2 compares the per capita consumption of tea, coffee and natural rubber in the USSR and Poland with that in some market economy countries.

Table 6.2: Annual Per Capita Consumption of Tea, Coffee, and Natural Rubber in Selected Centrally Planned and Market Economy Countries (Grammes)

Country	Tea		Coffee		Natural Rubber	
	1962/4	1970/2	1964	1973	1964	1973
Centrally Planned Countries						
USSR	277	399	120	150	1,000*	1,400*
Poland	150	303	n.a.	1,000		
Market Economy Countries						
France	41	71	4,760	5,180	2,600	3,100
German Federal Republic	141	149	4,570	5,480	2,700	3,300
Japan	807	1,018	220	1,200	2,100	3,100
UK	4,296	3,812	1,440	2,190	3,400	3,100
US	308	338	7,150	6,210	2,500	3,300

* USSR and Eastern Europe.
Source: UN *Statistical Yearbook*.

Per capita consumption in the socialist countries has grown, but not by very much. According to the figures for the latest year, per capita consumption of tea in the USSR was only two fifths of that of Japan (mostly green tea) and coffee consumption one eighth. The United Kingdom consumption of tea and coffee is ten and fifteen times that of the USSR. If predominantly coffee-drinking countries are compared, Polish consumption is less than a fifth of that of France or Germany. The retail prices of coffee and tea are so high that any reduction to the levels obtaining in other countries cannot but promote an increase in consumption. The centrally planned countries also derive another benefit at the expense of poor producers; having been classified as a 'new market' under the earlier Coffee Agreements, they were able to import coffee at promotional prices. One estimate indicates that the price of coffee to socialist countries was only $32.90 a bag when the price in the 'quota' markets was US $48.80 a bag. Other commodities of interest to developing countries, such as oilseeds or vegetable oils, do not find a significant market in these countries. The only exception was the access provided by the Soviet Union to Cuban sugar when Cuba lost its entire market in the United States almost overnight. This also clearly belongs to the influence of politics on commodities and will be considered in that context.

The USSR has also experimented with tripartite arrangements of benefit to developing countries, such as spinning and weaving Sudanese cotton in India for import into the Soviet Union. Generally, imports of processed or manufactured forms by the socialist countries also fall under the same four aims mentioned above and so far there has not been a policy of promoting imports from developing countries. Centrally planned countries defend their high consumer price and the policy of limiting imports on the grounds that, as all prices and production quantities are centrally determined in their system, the price level for any commodity is a matter of internal economic policy. But the effect of high consumer prices, whether due to tariff and non-tariff barriers or to the specific nature of the economic system, is the same — denial of access. Imports from developing countries into centrally planned countries are increasing, but only slowly in relation to the demand that is likely to exist. A reason for this slow growth is that, if demand is allowed to be more fully satisfied, it may be difficult to reduce the import quantities in years of foreign exchange tightness. If this reason is related to the increasing share of imports from the industrialised countries, one notes that, when foreign exchange is scarce, imports from the developed countries are given a higher priority than imports from the poor countries. The flexibility of foreign exchange allocation for imports is weighted against the developing countries. This is but another reflection of the asymmetry of the international economic system. A general conclusion that is relevant to the system as a whole is that the centrally planned countries have not been drawn into a global approach to the solution of commodity problems.

Processing in Developing Countries

The importance of a global approach is also the reason why some space has to be devoted to the question of processing raw materials in the producing developing countries. As explained in Chapter 1, the problems of commodity trade are such that solutions cannot be found strictly within the confines of trade in raw materials. In particular, the need to stabilise and increase the export earnings of developing countries can only be met by a variety of measures. Higher unit prices are not the sole means of increasing export earnings at a given volume. Unit values can also be increased by adding more value to the commodity in the producing country. It is unnecessary to repeat here the other advantages of encouraging processing and manufacturing in the poor countries, such as promoting of industrialisation, transfer of technology, raising the level of skills and increasing employment opportunities. Even if the importance of encouraging processing industries in developing countries is conceded, many other questions still arise. How big an increase in earnings is possible? In which products? What are the countries that can take advantage of the opening-up trade in manufactures? What are the constraints on such opening-up? What are the problems of importing countries? And what are the sources of current or potential conflict?

How great an increase in earnings is possible? It is obviously unrealistic to expect that, within any conceivable period, all production of all processed forms will stop in all importing countries and that the whole of the market will become available to the producers of primary products. Developing countries rightly argue that their lack of industrialisation is a direct consequence of colonialism; the industrial and economic development of the metropolitan countries was based on the import of raw material from the colonies to whom the manufactured goods were then exported. The growth of the Lancashire textile industry at the cost of the death of the Indian textile industry is the standard example quoted in this context; Macaulay's minute on the need to develop Indian railways so that the manufactures of Britain could be disseminated to a larger population is a classic statement of this case. While argument about the effects of colonialism provides a justification for encouraging processing and manufacturing in the erstwhile colonies, it still does not answer the question to what extent such production should be encouraged. One relevant fact is that, at least in the recent period, developing countries have expanded their manufacturing industry to a significant extent. The decimated Indian textile industry was in fact revived and in its turn played a part in the decline of the Lancashire textile industry. The decline of the share of primary commodities in the exports of developing countries is shown in Table 3.7; exports of manufactures by the non-oil exporting developing countries have increased from 23.3 per cent of their total exports in 1969 to 35.0 per cent in 1974. This increase occurred in spite of the discouragement of access to the rich country markets.

At this point one question has to be clearly posed and answered. Tariffs on processed forms in importing countries apply equally to all exporters — the few exceptions (preferences between trading zones) are no longer significantly relevant — and they are not specially higher for the developing countries. If the industrialised countries are able to surmount the barriers and export competitively why should the developing countries get a special advantage? One answer is that treating developed and developing countries equally has not led to their development: affirmative action is needed. Secondly, whenever developing countries have surmounted the barriers and increased their exports they have faced additional barriers. Lastly, the principle that a greater transfer of resources from the developed to the developing countries is needed is universally conceded. Considering the decline in foreign aid, the unsuitability of commodity agreements as a sole means of doing so and the fact that no single mechanism can provide all the amounts required, improving access to processed forms is a mechanism by which a part of the transfer can be achieved.

The historical development of processing and manufacturing in the industrialised countries had two facets. Part of the capacity was to meet domestic demand for the manufactured products, part for exports to other destinations, particularly the colonies. The export market can be further sub-divided into the markets in the erstwhile colonies and other markets. To a large extent, the newly independent countries have tended to establish domestic industries at least for simpler manufactures such as textiles, and these infant industries are usually protected from competition from imports. The market for simpler manufactures in a very large number of developing countries is thus rapidly diminishing. To the extent that increasing export earnings is the primary concern of this book, it is the other part of the export market that will provide the first opening for developing countries. In other words, the first target has to be the trade between the industrialised countries in the simpler manufactures. This has the added advantage of not asking for the impossible — that the industrialised countries stop processing even for their domestic consumption. Perhaps the next stage could be for these countries to allocated future domestic growth in the processed products for imports from the poor. Only then can one think of transfer of industries on an accelerated scale.

The development of an export market for a processed form is an indicator of the fact that economic forces have proved that it is cheaper for some countries to import the processed form rather than the raw material; the reasons are a combination of the cost of processing in the importing country, the difference in freight between a bulky raw material and a more compact processed form and the level of tariffs. In any case, these are examples in which an impersonal decision, however unplanned, to shift the processing industry has already been taken. What is the size of this export market? Table 6.3 compares the size of the market for the raw material and processed forms for a few selected commodities. Attention has been focused on the share of this market which developing countries hold because it is this share that has to be increased. The figures in Table 6.3 have to be read with caution. There is no implication that the whole of the export market will automatically be available to the developing countries. All that the sequence of figures in each commodity proves is that, in the aggregate, the share of the non-industrialised countries in processed or manufactured trade declines sharply for every commodity. Though they produce all the cocoa beans, they have only half the market in cocoa products and none at all in chocolate. They produce all the coffee but only export two fifths of soluble coffee; all exports of packaged tea are by the industrialised countries. The poor export 40 per cent of the world's tobacco but have only 10 per cent of the cigarette market. Two thirds of the world's rubber comes from the developing countries but they export few tyres. Take any commodity in the list and one finds the same regression.

In 1970, the developing countries exported 62.5 per cent of the raw materials (US $15 out of 24 billion) in these eleven groups of commodities; the proportion was about the same (61.2 per cent) in 1974. On the other hand, in the processed forms the developing countries' share was 15.7 per cent in 1970 (US $2.5 billion out of 16.3 billion) and 20.8 per cent in 1974. Four fifths of all export trade in processed and manufactured forms was in the hands of the developed countries. It is, however, difficult to estimate precisely from these figures alone the size of the market that the developing countries could have. A part of the export market in processed form is no doubt based on domestic raw materials in the rich countries (e.g. cigarettes from US tobacco or plywood from Canadian wood); even in the case of countries such as the Netherlands or Germany, the processed form could have been produced from imports from either developed or developing countries (e.g. margarine could be made from US soyabean oil, Brazilian soyabeans or other oilseeds from developing countries). All that can

Table 6.3. Export Market for Raw Materials and Processed Forms for Selected Commodities 1970 and 1973 (Value – million US $)

	Export market in 1970			Export market in 1973		
	Total market	Developing countries		Total market	Developing countries	
		Value	Share %		Value	Share %
1. Sugar, raw and refined						
Raw sugar	1913	1726	90.2	3327	2843	85.5
Refined sugar	374	120	32.1	921	196	21.3
2. Green coffee and soluble coffee						
Green coffee	3082	2993	100.0	4332	4111	100.0
Soluble coffee	123	23	18.7	271	109	40.1
3. Cocoa beans, cocoa products and chocolate						
Cocoa beans	862	853	100.0	945	931	100.0
Cocoa powder, paste, butter	279	129	46.2	424	206	48.5
Chocolate	277	0	0.0	478	0	0.0
4. Tobacco, unmanufactured and manufactured						
Unmanufactured tobacco	1147	409	36.0	1667	681	41.0
Tobacco manufactures	654	83	13.0	1976	117	11.0
5. Oilseeds, vegetable oils and processed oils						
Oil seeds	2796	1303	46.5	5428	3397	37.5
Vegetable oils	1389	686	49.4	2452	1239	50.5
Processed oils, margarine	274	35	12.7	498	58	11.6
6. Hides and skins, leather and footwear						
Hides and skins, leather	1408	364	26.0	2836	648	22.8
Footwear	1641	159	9.7	2770	411	14.8

Table 6.3 (Continued)

	Export market in 1970			Export market in 1973		
	Total market	Developing countries		Total market	Developing countries	
		Value	Share %		Value	Share %
7. Natural and synthetic rubber and rubber tyres						
Natural rubber	1127	1127	100.0	1910	1910	100.0
Synthetic rubber	573	0	0.0	885	0	0.0
All rubber	1700	1127	66.3	2795	1910	68.3
Rubber tyres	1981	neg	0.0	2095	neg	0.0
8. Wood, veneers and plywood, wood manufactures						
Wood, rough and shaped	3589	1127	31.4	7716	2363	30.6
Veneers and plyboard (631)	947	248	26.0	2139	646	30.0
Wood manufactures (632)	432	29	7.0	916	115	12.5
631 and 632	1379	277	20.0	3055	761	20.8
9. Raw cotton, cotton yarn, cotton fabrics and clothing						
Raw cotton	2111	1660	79.0	3493	2425	69.5
Cotton yarn	331	182	54.9	822	561	68.2
Cotton fabrics, woven	1436	474	33.0	2766	997	36.0
Clothing	5106	1136	22.0	9821	2989	30.5
10. Copper, and copper wirebars, tubes and pipes						
Copper ores and metal	4111	2887	70.2	5157	3749	72.6
Copper wirebars, tubes, pipes	775	0	0.0	729	0	0.0
11. Bauxite, aluminium and aluminium products						
Bauxite	230	206	89.6	213	168	78.9
Aluminium	2160	116	5.4	3044	159	5.2
Aluminium plate, sheet, strips	412	0	0.0	660	0	0.0

Note: Re-exports ignored.

Source: UN *Yearbook of International Trade Statistics*; GATT

be guessed from these figures is that the market for processed forms based on raw materials from developing countries is likely to be of the order of several billion dollars, at least US $7 or 8 billion. In the eleven commodity groups alone, encouragement of processing and manufacture in the poor countries will within a reasonable period of time increase unit values by one third.

Can the poor export competitively? A few success stories can be recounted. The earliest, and consequently the one to suffer most from discrimination at the hands of the developed countries, is cotton textiles. It is unnecessary to repeat the history of the Long-Term Textile Agreement or its successor, the Multi-Fibre Agreement (both concluded under GATT), the main aims of which were to limit the industrial and export development of the poor countries by putting a break on growth. With a few exceptions, the United Kingdom being the major one, most of the developed countries used the LTA not to promote development but to stop it. In spite of this, the developing countries have proved their ability to export competitively not only fabrics but also clothing; in 1973 Hong Kong alone had 14.3 per cent of the world's clothing market. This kind of rapid growth is also seen in other products. In 1970 Brazil and Korea exported a negligible US $6 million worth of footwear; in 1973 their exports were US $90 and 110 million respectively. Korea also dramatically increased its exports of rubber tyres from US $2.8 million in 1970 to US $60 million in 1974 and emerged as the largest exporter (US $281 million) of veneer and plywood in 1973 with 13.2 per cent of the market. Given the right internal and external conditions there is no reason why one or the other of the developing countries cannot produce any of the processed and manufactured forms.

The General Scheme of Preferences

The solution to the external problem at first sight appears straightforward; remove the tariff barriers for developing countries and everything will be all right. That is the principle of the General Scheme of Preferences (GSP), one of the few concrete schemes to be negotiated under UNCTAD. Unfortunately, there is a great gulf between principles and practice. The limited utility of the GSP is a result of the structure of industry and pattern of manufactured exports in developing countries in relation to the nature of the scheme itself. Table 6.4 compares the manufacturing output pattern and export pattern of manufactured goods in developed and developing countries in 1972. The food processing, leather, clothing and footwear industries account

Table 6.4. Manufacturing Output Patterns and Trade Structure in
Developed and Developing Countries in 1972

	Manufacturing output pattern % of total		Exports % of total manufactures exports	
	Developed	Developing	Developed	Developing
Food processing	10.8	21.8	7.7	22.4
Textiles	4.6	11.8	6.2	10.8
Clothing, leather, footwear	4.0	6.3	2.4	6.1
Wood products, furniture	4.2	3.3	2.0	3.5
Printing	4.4	3.1	0.8	0.7
Rubber, plastic products	3.1	3.2	0.9	0.5
Miscellaneous light industry	2.1	1.6	5.5	5.8
Total light industry	33.2	51.1	25.5	49.8
Paper	3.4	1.8	3.9	0.7
Chemicals	9.8	9.4	11.2	4.1
Petroleum products	1.7	7.2	1.9	14.5
Non-metallic minerals	4.1	5.2	1.8	1.0
Basic metals	8.0	6.2	11.4	19.1
Machinery	21.0	8.9	19.4	4.4
Electric equipment	8.7	4.2	8.0	3.2
Transport equipment	10.1	6.0	16.9	3.2
Total heavy industry	66.8	48.9	74.5	50.2

Source: Tables 2 and 4, UNCTAD IV, TD/185/Suppl.1, *The Dimensions of the
Required Restructuring of World Manufacturing Output and Trade in order to
Reach the Lima Target,* Nairobi, May 1976

for two fifths of all manufacturing in developing countries but only one fifth in the developed countries. The proportions are reversed for heavy industry – machinery, electrical and transport equipment make up two fifths of all manufacturing industry in the industrialised countries but only one fifth in the non-industrialised ones. By virtue of their state of development, the latter countries can only export what they make. Bhagwati summarises this in the statement that a less-developed country will produce whatever it imports and will export whatever it produces.[10] The export pattern in Table 6.4 provides some proof of the truth of this statement. Forty per cent of manufactured exports from the developing countries is processed food, textiles, clothing, leather and footwear. This group accounts for only one sixth of the exports of developed countries, two thirds of all their manufactured exports consisting of chemicals, machinery, electrical and transport equipment. The hypothesis that the share of manufacturing exports by the less-developed countries in their total exports will tend to reflect their share of manufacturing value added in GNP has been tested by Bhagwati and Cheh and found to be plausible.[11] It is unrealistic to expect that the LDCs will quickly be able to enter the export market for capital goods and chemicals however much these imports are encouraged by the rich countries. If the objective is to increase their export earnings in a short period of time, schemes to encourage exports of manufactures from developing countries must be specifically directed to those sectors where manufacturing exists or can be easily established. It is here that the GSP fails.

Generalised tariff preferences apply in principle only to manufactures and semi-manufactures with certain exceptions. These exceptions are indicated by the countries granting the preference in the form of negative lists. These countries have generally assumed that the GSP was not in principle intended to cover primary commodities, particularly agricultural and fishery products and their processed forms. Preferential treatment could be given to selected processed and semi-processed agricultural products, these being indicated in the form of positive lists. The effectiveness of the scheme therefore depends entirely on what specific items donor countries put in the (negative) exceptions lists and in the (positive) processed agricultural goods list. A detailed country-by-country description of the lists is given in the Report of the UNCTAD Secretariat to UNCTAD III.[12] All donors except the EEC exclude textiles and footwear from the coverage. The EEC, however, limits the application of GSP on textiles to only seven signatories of the LTA; since these seven have 'voluntarily' agreed to restrict their exports of textiles, the EEC scheme does in practice exclude textiles. The positive lists of most preference-giving countries cover only a few items, mostly vegetable oils and some preparations of tropical beverages. It should also be mentioned that the depth of the tariff cuts varies widely and that all countries have some kind of a 'safeguard' or 'escape' clause. The EEC and Japan apply limitations in the form of tariff quotas, i.e. a ceiling beyond which the GSP is not applicable. A typical escape clause is in the UK scheme, in which the United Kingdom reserves the right to withdraw preferential treatment unilaterally if a product is imported 'in such increased quantities and under such conditions, as a result of preference, as to cause or threaten to cause, in the opinion of the British Government, serious injury to domestic producers of like or directly competitive products'.

Comparing the GSP schemes as operated by the preference-giving countries with the structure of production in developing countries, one sees that most of the products that the poor countries can export are excluded one way or another. In his study, 'How Helpful is the Generalised Scheme of Preferences to Developing countries?', Murray has analysed the degree of correspondence between products qualifying for preference and products exported by the LDCs.[13] Out of total developing country exports of US $23 billion in 1967, US $14 billion worth of goods were already entering the markets duty free, being primary commodities or unprocessed raw materials. Of the balance, only US $5.4 billion were manufactured items; the rest were agricultural products not covered by GSP (the positive list items account for only a tiny amount, about US $60 million). When all the excepted items in the negative lists are excluded, the size of the market eligible for preference is reduced to US $1.8 billion or just 7.7 per cent of the LDCs' total trade. After analysing the schemes of the EEC, Japan, the UK and the Nordic countries, Murray concludes that these may generate increased export earnings of approximately US $100 million. Rachel McCulloch has estimated that the cost to the United States of the GSP would only be about US $100 million a year.[14] The net additional transfer of resources from all preference giving countries to *all* the developing countries is thus likely to be about US $200 million. Considering the magnitude of the problem in increasing export earnings and the size of the potential market available, it is obvious that the GSP can only play an extremely limited role.

The exceptions are the trouble with the GSP. In general, there is a direct correlation between the ability of the developing countries to export and the degree of restraint imposed. For example, the United

States scheme excludes some products of significant export interest to developing countries, particularly shoes. The peculiar thing about imports of shoes into the US is that the largest exporters of footwear to that market are not developing countries but Spain and Italy. Thus, if the American shoe industry is threatened by imports from developed European countries, the solution is found by excluding it from the GSP for Brazil! Import controls on shoes from Spain or Italy are more difficult to impose because of GATT regulations. Since GATT, being a rich country instrument, is sacrosanct but UNCTAD/GSP is not, an action is taken which reaps internal political advantages without, of course, solving the problem of the industry. Making Brazil or Korea less competitive will do nothing to hinder European imports. Yet again, the greater vulnerability of the developing countries to restraint and damaging action by the developed countries is seen to be a basic element of the international economic system.

Problems of Adjustment

There cannot be a uniform solution to a complex problem in which the nature of the solution must depend on the degree of processing of a particular commodity, its importance to the local economy of the importing country, the capability of the exporting country to undertake the processing and lastly on the extent of encouragement the exporting countries are permitted to give. To take the degree of processing, at one extreme there are cases in which little additional processing is required except packaging. There is no reason why blended ready-to-sell packaged tea should face a higher tariff than bulk tea which is then repacked in the consuming country. Encouraging packaging in the producing country will immediately give a slightly higher unit value, encourage the packaging industry and, in due course, the packaging materials industry. At the other extreme, it is futile to expect that Japan, whose economy is built on the import of raw materials and export of finished goods, will forthwith stop importing iron ore and import steel instead; apart from anything else, the exporting developing countries do not have the resources or skilled manpower to invest in steelmaking of the order of tens of millions of tons. Between the two extremes lies a variety of possibilities. Where natural endowment in energy is favourable, bauxite or alumina can be converted into aluminium and its fabricated versions. Most metals could be fabricated and exported as sheets, strip, tubes or pipes rather than as ingot metal. Vegetable oils could be made into margarine and soap and cocoa and sugar into chocolate. The range of possibilities for any one exporting country will be fairly narrow. Equally, the ability of the importing countries to relax barriers will also be limited.

The limitations in the developed importing countries arise from economic and social factors. Encouraging imports of a processed or manufactured form of a commodity involves two economic losses to the government — loss of revenue from the tariff reduced and an adverse impact on the balance of payments. On top of the losses, there is an additional cost to the economy from the adjustment assistance that may have to be given to the area of the declining processing industry, either through programmes for training workers or through incentives to alternative industry to move into the depressed areas. An instructive example of how such change can be brought about in an orderly manner is the decline of the jute industry in the United Kingdom. Historically, the jute industry was concentrated in Dundee in Scotland. While the total additional cost of importing jute manufactures rather than raw jute was not considerable for the United Kingdom as a whole, the social cost for this one area would have been totally disproportionate. The United Kingdom government therefore followed a deliberate policy of negotiating with the exporters of jute manufactures (mainly India and the then Pakistan) for a restrained but orderly increase in their exports while simultaneously promoting alternative employment in the Dundee area. Over a period of years, there was a steady and gradual decline in Dundee's dependence on this one industry. A similar example is the decline of the Lancashire cotton textile industry, which started before the LTA came into force as a result of the encouragement provided by Commonwealth preferences to the textile industries in Hong Kong, India and Pakistan. In the beginning the decline was not a co-ordinated effort. The respite afforded by the LTA, changes in the pattern of consumption from cotton textiles to synthetics and mixtures and vertical integration of the industry all subsequently helped to mitigate the social consequences of the decline. In addition to social and economic factors, there are also political complications which arise on grounds of national security. An argument for protecting high-cost production, both agricultural and industrial, is that in times of hostilities a country cannot be dependent on imports. No importing country would be willing to wind down the rubber tyre industry just because tyres could be produced more cheaply in the rubber-exporting country. So long as the industrialised nations continue to believe that a major war is possible, a limit is automatically placed on the degree of liberalisation that one can reasonably expect.

While security considerations establish the political limit on the *extent* of adjustment, the *pace* of adjustment is determined by internal politics, mainly by the influence which the processing industry and the labour employed in it possess. The greatest resistance in the United States to liberalising imports of textiles or shoes comes from the labour unions. Protectionist moves are suggested to Congress with the argument that the wage levels in the exporting countries are low. How unions, which rhetorically uphold the virtues of free trade, can deny the law of comparative advantage passes all economic understanding. The assumption of unions in the industrialised countries generally is that, if any exporting country is competitive, it must be because labour is exploited or the government subsidises exports — anything except the fact that, sometimes at least, there can be genuine comparative advantage. The hypothesis of Bhagwati and Cheh

> suggests that countries tend to export what they produce — a conclusion which is compatible with either the theory of comparative advantage or the observed fact that several LDCs, having import substituted in manufacturing, tend to move quickly thereafter, under balance of payments difficulties, into subsidization to export the very manufactures whose production they have been encouraging in a sheltered market.[15]

Either there is a genuine comparative advantage or there is a genuine need for increased export earnings. Emmanuel has rightly pointed out that the greatest opposition to the poor countries comes, not from the governments or businesses of the rich countries, but from their working people.[16] The most vocal and persistent demand for import controls during the recent economic crisis in the United Kingdom came from the Trades Union Congress; this the government has had to resist. Emmanuel's argument may lead some to rejoice that the *embourgeoisement* of the proletariat had proved false the Marxist concept of the international solidarity of the proletariat; but the proving or disproving of European politico-economic theories is of less interest to developing countries than the fact that it is their earnings that are affected. This point is emphasised because Pincus, in listing the arguments against using commodity agreements as a means of transferring resources, adds the following: 'The income redistributing effects of higher commodity prices may mean in effect that low-income consumers in industrial countries are forced to pay for improvements in the living standards of high-income producers in the underdeveloped countries.'[17] In other words, the poor of the rich countries pay for the enrichment of the rich in the poor countries. This view was expressed, in just these words, by one of the contenders in the 1976 election campaign for the US Presidency. This is just demagoguery. Of course, in any transfer of resources, somebody from the transferring country pays, be it the taxpayer or the consumer. The emotional playing to the gallery comes in the contrasting of the 'rich of the poor' as the only recipients of payments from 'the poor of the rich'. In fact, as the world turns now, it is the comparatively poor in the rich countries who are against the very poor of the poor countries.

This said, however, the fact that processing industries are economically important to a few of the industrialised nations must also be recognised. In the classification of developed countries made earlier, special mention was made of the United Kingdom and the Netherlands as two countries where, historically, processing industries had developed. For example, the Netherlands is the largest exporter of margarine, cocoa powder, cocoa butter and chocolate and the second largest exporter of processed oils and tobacco manufactures. In suggesting that the export market for processed forms is the best area for starting to promote development in the developing countries, the impact this may have on the economy of the Netherlands is an important factor. On the other hand, though Germany is the largest exporter of processed oils, soaps, copper products and aluminium, one would presume that the strength of the German economy and the diversity of its exports would enable Germany to withstand a greater degree of disruption. All these preceding arguments only underline the fact that the adjustment problem is very complex. The attempts made hitherto, both on the importers' and exporters' sides, have been unco-ordinated, unplanned and lacking in discrimination about the feasibility and extent of adjustment.

Along with the elimination of the degree of protection in importing countries, an associated problem is the extent and manner of encouragement that exporting countries can give. The well-known case of the soluble coffee dispute between the United States and Brazil illustrates this. The US, having removed the small tariff of 3 ¢ per lb on soluble coffee soon after joining the International Coffee Agreement, found that increasing exports of soluble coffee from Brazil were assisted by the fact that soluble coffee paid no export tax while green coffee paid a contribution to the exchequer. The US considered this unfair subsidisation, but Brazil contended that the 'contribution' was not a tax but literally a contribution to a fund to help the coffee industry. The conflict led to protracted negotiations, bilateral and multilateral, as well as to arbitration proceedings in the International Coffee Council. Eventually, Brazil imposed an export tax of 13 ¢ per lb on soluble coffee, though the US thought it ought to have been 30 ¢ per lb. The conflict was not strictly one of principle between governments but only reflected a conflict within the US coffee industry. It could not make up its mind whether to take advantage of Brazil's investment policies by investing in soluble coffee production there or to fight for protection through the US Government. In actual fact, it hedged its bets and did both. The final solution of the soluble coffee dispute was that Brazil agreed to export 560,000 bags of green coffee duty-free to the US; these were distributed pro-rata among American coffee manufacturers. The market leader — General Foods — got the biggest share of the imports of cheaper coffee and was thus placated.[18] While this illustrates the influence a processing industry has on its own government it also raises the important question of whether there should be comparability of export taxes between the raw material and the processed product. If greater liberalisation of access to processed forms does occur, the question of when encouragement becomes a subsidy will also increasingly recur. Given the social, economic and political constraints, the industrialised countries cannot all adopt uniform policies on the encouragement of processing industries in the developing countries. Equally, only some of the developing countries — in fact only the more developed among them — will benefit from such encouragement. The problem therefore has to be attacked in a far more discriminating fashion than has hitherto been the case.

Patterns of Conflict

It is difficult to summarise the arguments in this chapter. Under the broad umbrella of access, a variety of relationships has been analysed. Dividing the world into developed and developing on the one hand and importer and exporter on the other gives rise to a maximum of six relationships. (i) Exporting countries, whether developed or developing, share some common interests; (ii) so do importing countries. (iii) Developed exporting countries have conflicts with other developed but importing countries on access to markets and on burden-sharing. (iv) At the same time, developed exporting countries have a different kind of relationship, based on food aid, with developing importing countries. (v) Developing exporting countries have a variety of conflicts with developed importing countries; from the developed side, most of these are viewed as demands for concessions or demands for resources. The poor countries see them as matters of equity and right. (vi) The last of the six relationships is that between developing exporting and importing countries. This is at the moment significant only in one important aspect. Some of the developing countries are exporters of oil, of whom some are very rich. The oil price rise has imposed a great burden on those developing countries which have to import oil. There is a clear possibility that resources are being transferred from some of the poor developing countries to some of the very rich developing, oil-exporting ones. This conflict has not surfaced and has, in effect, been submerged in the greater divide between the developed and developing groups.

In this chapter, the special case of trade in primary commodities with the centrally planned countries has also been analysed. A large part of it has also been devoted to the problem of promoting exports of processed and manufactured goods from the poor countries. Whenever a relationship was studied, consideration of some aspect has had to be deferred on the grounds that the actions and decisions were more political than economic. The distinction between economics and politics has worn quite thin. Before the political aspects are analysed, it is essential to devote some attention to a neglected sector of commodity negotiations – the market place.

Notes

1. 'Global Consensus and Economic Development', address by Dr Henry A. Kissinger, Secretary of State, before the Seventh Special Session of the United Nations General Assembly, New York, 1 September 1975, reproduced in 94th Congress House Committee on International Relations and Senate Committee on Foreign Relations, *Report by Congressional Advisers to the Seventh Special Session of the United Nations,* Washington DC, 1975.
2. US Department of State, *International Collusive Action in World Markets for Non-Fuel Materials,* Washington DC, 1974.
3. IBRD, Commodities and Export Projections Division: Analysis and Projections Department, Commodity Paper no.1, *Opportunity for OPEC-type Action in Agricultural Commodities,* Washington DC, March 1973; *What are the Opportunities for Raising LDCs' Earnings from Exports of Non-Fuel Minerals through OPEC-type Cooperation?* Washington DC, February 1972.
4. Kenneth W. Clarfield, Start Jackson, Jeff Keefe, Michele Ann Noble and A. Patrick Ryan, *Eight Mineral Cartels: The New Challenge to Industrialized Nations* Metals Week, (McGraw-Hill, New York, 1975).
5. Harold B. Malmgren and D.L. Schlechty, 'Rationalising World Agriculture Trade', *Journal of World Trade Law,* 4, 1970, pp. 515-37.
6. The facts on the Commission's proposal are from a statement in the UK Parliament by the Minister of Agriculture, Fisheries and Food. See the Parliamentary report in *The Times,* London, 22 October 1976.
7. Ian Smith (with Simon Harris), *World Sugar Markets in a State of Flux,* Agricultural Trade Paper no.4 (Trade Policy Research Centre, London, 1973) and

The European Community and the World Sugar Crisis, Staff Paper no.7 (Trade Policy Research Centre, London, 1974); also 'Sugar Markets in Disarray', *Journal of World Trade Law,* 9, 1975, pp.41-62.

8. Self-sufficiency and net export figures from EUROSTAT, *Yearbook of Agricultural Statistics,* various years.

9. UNCTAD TD/B/C.1/108 and Corr.1, 'Trends in Markets of Selected Temperate Zone Products in Five Importing Areas'; see also 'Access to Markets' in *Proceedings of the Third Session of UNCTAD* (UN, New York, 1973).

10. J. Bhagwati and V.K. Ramaswami, 'Domestic Distortions, Tariffs and the Theory of Optimum Subsidy', *Journal of Political Economy,* 71, 1963, pp.44-50.

11. J. Bhagwati and John Cheh, 'LDC Exports: A Cross-sectional Analysis' in Luis Eugenio Di Marco (ed.), *International Economics and Development: Essays in Honour of Raul Prebisch* (New York, Academic Press, 1972).

12. 'Generalized Scheme of Preferences: Report by UNCTAD Secretariat' and 'Addendum to the Report', vol.II, *Proceedings of the Third Session,* pp. 104-40.

13. T. Murray, 'How Helpful is the Generalized System of Preferences to Developing Countries?' *The Economic Journal,* 83, 1973, pp.449-55.

14. Rachel McCulloch, 'United States Preferences: The Proposed System', *Journal of World Trade Law,* 8, 1974, pp.216-25.

15. Bhagwati and Cheh, 'LDC Exports'.

16. Arghiri Emmanuel, *Unequal Exchange: A Study of the Imperialism of Trade* (The Monthly Review Press, New York. 1972).

17. J.A. Pincus, *Commodity Agreements – Bonanza or Illusion?* (The Rand Corporation, Washington DC, 1967).

18. Stephen D. Krasner, 'Business Government Relations: The Case of the International Coffee Agreement', *International Organization,* 27, 1973, pp.495-516.

7 THE PRICE AND THE MARKET PLACE

> The uninitiated often fail to understand that, within pure theory, the economics of firms is not about actual firms and the economics of households is not about households. The theory, therefore, is not meant to be tested by looking at actual firms or households.
>
> from a review in *The Economist*

> Exact no more than that which is appointed you.
>
> Luke 3:13

There is often a strange dichotomy between commodity trade and international commodity negotiations. Trade takes place in the 'market' — a collective definition for any means, an exchange of letters or telexes an auction on personal negotiation — by which a transaction for exchanging quantities at an agreed price happens. A commodity negotiation occurs mainly between government delegates in a setting which sometimes bears little resemblance to the market place. For example, when the international price of sugar was 2 ¢ per lb, the argument between negotiators for the International Sugar Agreement was whether the floor price would be 3.25 ¢ per lb or 3.50; in other words, they were negotiating what ought to be. In 1975 a very large number of governments solemnly negotiated a new International Coffee Agreement which has a price objective of about 75 ¢ per lb; the price in October 1976 was over 150 ¢ a pound and was still rising. There is no possibility of any of the regulatory provisions of the agreement coming into effect for another two years. It has been ratified by the required number of countries in the full knowledge that most of what is written in it will remain just words for years.

Why do governments go through the complex process of negotiating, approving and ratifying an unreal and unimplementable agreement? The charitable explanation is that they are legislating for a visionary world — again, for what ought to be rather that for what will be. The cynical explanation is that it is a political act for the political benefit of the two main participants. The United States, the largest importer, promotes the agreement because it is in its interest to show, after the Seventh Special Session of the UN at which the US Secretary of State made 41 proposals, that something is being done in line with what

161

developing countries say they want. Since the market price of coffee is in any case going to remain high, the United States gets a political pay-off at no additional economic cost. Brazil, the largest exporter, needs time, after the disastrous frost, to build up the coffee industry and stocks so that when the inevitable collapse of the market occurs there will be some agreement that will preserve a large part of Brazil's traditional share of the market. Brazil's pay-off is partly economic and partly political in terms of her relations with the US.

The dichotomy does not mean that governments are being foolishly unrealistic. While one part of the government is negotiating for the ideal, another part is devising policies to cope with the real world. The International Coffee Agreement 1968 broke down in December 1972 because importers and exporters could not agree on the right price level taking into account the devaluation of the US dollar. But trade did not stop, awaiting an agreement on the price; all exporting countries continued to export, and the major ones did so by 'managing' the market. The two games – the negotiating game and the market management game – were being played simultaneously. For all the Algerian insistence on indexing commodity prices with those of manufactured goods, SONATRACH, the Algerian government corporation for petroleum and natural gas, continues to enter into contracts with French, Italian and American buyers at prices negotiated to mutual satisfaction. There is no indication that Algeria is refusing to sell gas unless indexation is built into the contracts. If they do win the indexing game, then the pay-off in future market games will be greater; in the meantime, they are optimising the pay-offs in the current market game.

Are commodity negotiations concerned about drawing up a blueprint for the ideal world, or should they stick to reality? There is no clear-cut answer to this question; most negotiations attempt the former while trying to stick, as closely as possible, to the latter. To the extent that the solution diverges from reality, the negotiations fail or an agreement collapses at a later date. Failures have so far been more numerous than successes; in order to minimise the chances of failure in future negotiations, this crucial gap between reality and negotiated solutions has to be analysed. The reality is the 'market' – a hypothetical place where buyers and sellers can agree to buy or sell stated quantities, to be delivered at stated times, at an agreed price. It is not an impersonal entity, with a volition of its own, 'setting' prices. The 'market price' of a commodity, at a particular moment, is the result of a large number of transactions – each one of which is a double subjective judgement between one buyer and one seller. The collective result of a moment ago, or a month ago, may influence the individual judgement, but the next collective result is still a sum of the subjective judgements just preceding. The above is, again, the ideal state, which, as usual, is not always found in reality, particularly in commodity trade.

Before discussing the conditions, such as the nature of the market and the nature of the competition, which determine the price of a product, it is essential to see how far reality differs from the ideal market. Five phenomena which affect prices will therefore be analysed. These are: (i) closed markets and multinational corporations; (ii) the effect of protection in importing countries on prices; (iii) preferential trading arrangements; (iv) interchangeability between products; and (v) competition from synthetics. Divergences from the ideal market, as well as these five phenomena, affect the prices of commodities in three ways: (i) instability; (ii) secular decline; and (iii) asymmetric distribution of gains between exporter and importer. Analysis of these three effects, together with the differential pricing arising out of quality variations and type differences (considered in Chapter 5), will provide an understanding of how prices are arrived at in the unideal real world.

The Real and the Ideal Market

The ideal or totally free market is one in which nothing extraneous (a government for example) intervenes to influence the rational economic judgements of the buyer and seller. So far as international commodity trade is concerned, such a free market exists only in the minds of some economists and politicians who find the concept useful to support what they do not want to do for other reasons. The classification of the nature of the real market for different commodities in Chapter 4 (in particular Table 4.1) has shown that any analysis based on the assumption that commodity trade is free would be so unreal and theoretical as to be of little practical utility. This chapter will therefore be confined to a study of the commodity markets as they exist — closed, protected, discriminated against, subjected to technological disruption and made unpredictable by natural disasters. Significant unpredictability is perhaps the one quality that distinguishes the market for commodities from that for manufactured goods. This leads to another beloved concept of economists, particularly of the free-market variety — that of the long-term equilibrium price. Is there such a thing?

Because the collective judgements of traders determine the market price at a given time, it does not necessarily follow that there is an ideal equilibrium price. The concept of 'long-term' equilibrium is a static one;

it assumes that everything would remain the same until the ideal situation is reached. After that everybody will live happily ever after in a blissful state of equilibrium. In the commodity world nothing remains the same. In commodities such as coffee, cocoa and pepper natural ups and downs occur. What is the long-term equilibrium in these cases — one that assumes that every so many years there will be a frost or a cyclone which will have the identical effect on supply? That the instability in prices which accompanies these fluctuations will not change consumption patterns? The proponents of the long-term equilibrium view neglect or ignore a whole number of factors — productivity changes may occur leading to a drifting down of real prices, new producers may emerge able to satisfy the market at a different price, the sudden discovery of a synthetic substitute may endanger the market for a commodity, consumer preferences may change. There is no predictability about any of these changes, all of which have occurred in one or other commodity. As will be seen in the next chapter, influences such as international monetary instability may even make it impossible to determine what exactly the so-called equilibrium price is at a given time; a calculation in pounds sterling may give quite a different answer from one in US dollars. Wars and hostilities and international tension may change the supply situation drastically, and all the beautiful curves showing the long-term equilibrium will have to be thrown out and redrawn, only to be thrown out again when the next unpredictable change occurs. In any case, what does long-term equilibrium mean? That the price will remain stable for three years, five years, ten years? In real terms or current terms? If the argument is that this price is one which under ideal free market conditions will align supply and demand, the answer is: (i) ideal free market conditions rarely exist in international commodity trade; and (ii) supply and demand change constantly, often in unexpected ways. An equilibrium price which shifts every time there is a change in the assumptions on which it is based cannot, by definition, be a 'long-term' equilibrium.

The confusion arises because of the usual mistaken transference; the successful operation of a free market system in a domestic economy with a stable and reasonably predictable socio-economic system does not mean that it can be transferred to the international system. It is strange that the developed nations which have had to abandon the concept of fixed exchange rates as impracticable in an ever-changing world and which laugh at the idea of a long-term equilibrium price for steel or automobiles still cling tenaciously to it for primary commodities. This is not to deny the validity of market and equilibrium concepts to economists, who need to idealise the real world for purposes of theoretical understanding; the protest is against its misuse by political negotiators in order to add a spurious intellectual content to a political attitude. The Federal Republic of Germany, for example, vehemently opposed during UNCTAD IV the proposal to set up a Common Fund for commodity stabilisation on the grounds that it would disturb the free market system. But Germany has, however reluctantly, subscribed to the greatest of all deviations from the market — the CAP of the Community. Obviously the political and economic dividends for Germany from the CAP outweigh any adherence to the free market principle. There are no such political dividends from abandoning it in favour of the developing countries. Apart from condoning protectionism, the developed countries have until recently not even noticed the existence of closed markets in commodity trade.

Closed Markets

How does a closed market affect prices? The simple answer is that nobody knows what the price would have been had the market been a free one. The 'closed' 'market' is a contradiction in terms; the resultant price is equally unreal. For example, how does one know what the proper price for bauxite is, in an industry characterised thus by the US Council on International Economic Policy.

> The aluminium industry is highly integrated, with six firms controlling the majority of the non-communist world's production capacity for bauxite, alumina and aluminium. The six firms own about 60 per cent of the non-communist world's bauxite mining capacity, 70 per cent of its alumina capacity and 63 per cent of its aluminium smelting capacity... Bauxite, alumina and aluminium are not traded on commodity exchanges and only aluminium has a published price.[1]

The report points out, however, that even the published prices for aluminium are not effective selling prices, 'wide discounts from published prices' being offered. The whole price structure of the bauxite, alumina and aluminium industry of the six sisters is mythical.

How total is the degree of control by multinational corporations of the aluminium industry is shown by this graphic description from *Eight Mineral Cartels*.

Look at the steps involved in turning Jamaican bauxite into Reynolds

Wrap. . . Today Reynolds Jamaica Mines, Ltd., owns 67,000 acres of bauxite land in Jamaica — 2.5% of the entire island — which it mines with Reynolds-owned equipment. The bauxite is shipped on a Reynolds-owned six-mile-long overhead tramway to the Reynolds dock at Ocho Rios. There the bauxite is loaded aboard a bulk carrier of the Caribbean Steamship Company, owned 100% by Reynolds, and shipped to Reynolds' alumina refinery at Corpus Christi, Texas. The refined alumina is then transferred to Reynolds' San Patricio, Texas, reduction plant, where it is smelted into aluminium and cast into sheet ingot. This sheet ingot may be shipped to the Reynolds sheet and plate plant at McCook, Ill., to be processed into reroll stock and then shipped to the Reynolds foil mill at Louisville, Ky., where it is rolled down to household foil, packaged, and delivered to super-markets all over the United States to be sold as Reynolds Wrap.

The report goes on to add: 'Some companies even provide their own power for smelting. Alcoa owns and operates a coal mine in southern Indiana which supplies fuel to the Alcoa-owned power plant which runs Alcoa's Evansville, Ind., reduction plant.'[2] Where such a total degree of control exists, transactions between the different parts of the same firm are governed by considerations totally removed from the concept of a 'market'.

The operations of multinational corporations have been examined at length in a UN study which has the following to say on intra-corporation trade:

Trade between parent firms and their affiliates, as well as among the latter, represents a major component of the total operations of multinational corporations. Since the goods and services entering intracorporation trade do not involve 'arm's length' transactions (that is, transactions with non-affiliated firms at market prices), their prices are not determined by the market mechanism but by the corporations themselves. A firm's transfer prices are designed to satisfy a variety of requirements; and a number of factors are taken into account in determining their level, including the tariffs of the importing country, absolute and differential tax rates, actual or expected exchange rate differentials, government policies on royalty payments and profit transfers, the need to satisfy equity holders both in the home and the host countries and numerous others. Transfer prices can also include payment for part of the corporations' global overhead cost much of which is incurred by the parent firm.[3]

In such a context, concepts such as 'free market' and 'equilibrium' can be seen to be chimerical.

The impenetrability of intra-corporation transactions is brought out by George Beckford in his remarkable study of plantation economies.[4] In the course of the study, he asked several firms about the extent and nature of their plantation activities and the contribution of these activities to the relevant plantation economies.

> Several firms cooperated somewhat but several were extremely reticent. The United Fruit Company indicated that they do not break down their operating figures in a way that would readily indicate the degree of vertical integration of the enterprise nor their profits by country of operation; and added that some of those figures are regarded as 'classified' information. Unilever indicated that whereas they do not 'reveal all', their subsidiaries in 'major (metropolitan) countries' provide more public information on operations than their plantation subsidiaries located in Third World countries.

Beckford offers two explanations for this double standard of revealing more information in the home metropolitan countries and less in the Third World. The first is that it is in the company's interest to appear not to be withholding information in their own countries; the second is that governments in the plantation countries seem to demand less information than their counterparts in the industrialised world. If the Third World countries do not know about transfer pricing and other injurious phenomena it is because they do not compel disclosure of relevant information; in some cases, they have even signed away their right to do so in their eagerness to attract foreign capital. Vertical integration is not confined to minerals alone. Describing the growth of Unilever, Beckford has shown that it was an organic process in an agricultural commodity − from growing groundnuts, to acquiring the shipping to carry it, to extracting the oil, making soap then margarine, to making other cleansing products such as detergents, marketing all of them, right down to owning its own advertising agency. The control over the entire range of activities is therefore pervasive and complete.

Even where vertical integration is not total, the close technical tie-up between an importing processing industry and the raw material supplier imposes constraints which place the seller in a weak bargaining position. When monopsonistic buying cartels are superimposed on this situation, the concept of free market determination of prices virtually disappears. The best example of such practices is the Japanese iron ore consortium, though the total control over Canadian mining by US steel interests might prove equally instructive. All the Japanese steel mills buy their iron ore under a single negotiating umbrella; they spread their risk against insecurity of supply and improve their bargaining position by buying from Australia, India, Brazil, Chile and South Africa. Each seller is allotted a share of the total market, and an unwritten rule that no country can export more than 40 per cent of the total is said to exist. On the other hand, the sellers cannot spread the risk for geographical reasons of proximity; the United States gets its iron ore from Canada or Venezuela and Europe its from Sweden or West Africa. The sellers nearest to Japan — India and Australia — are effectively tied to that market, though the increasing use of very large capacity ore carriers may change the situation somewhat. One result of the superior bargaining position of the Japanese buyers is their determined attempt to prevent the sellers from getting a higher share of the realisation from carrying more of the ore in their own bottoms. Protracted negotiations have only led to a share for the exporting countries of 15 per cent of the ore exports. There is no logical reason why a seller should sell on f.o.b. basis and not on c.i.f. — that is, carry all the ore and deliver it at the port of destination. Since the ore can be sold either on f.o.b. or c.i.f. basis, an equitable distribution of the gains would imply sharing the shipping on a 50:50 basis. The fact that, in actual practice, it is 15:85 in favour of the rich buyer is yet another example of the asymmetry of the system. At least in iron ore one can say that the bargaining strength of the rich is seven times that of the poor sellers.

Faced with impenetrable vertical integration, control over production and marketing of both raw material and the finished product, monopsonistic buying practices and often oligopolistic collusion as well, opening up closed markets is not an easy task. Developed countries do not welcome attacks on multinationals, though they may have the purpose of making the closed market freer, a goal which they profess to cherish. Attempts to control multinational corporations are thwarted by the developed countries because these companies are an integral part of the asymmetric international economic system and have, in fact, helped to accumulate greater power in the hands of the countries in the centre. The methods tried so far by the developing countries include: (i) breaking up vertical integration by bringing raw material production under local control; (ii) unilateral action to increase revenues from exports; and (iii) co-ordinating action among producing countries to increase relative bargaining strength against the power of the firms. The effectiveness of these methods will be examined in Chapter 9, on the mechanisms for dealing with commodity problems. The conclusion can be anticipated: the effectiveness is directly related to the degree of market control that the co-operating producers can effectively exert.

Protectionism, Preferential Markets and Prices

If closed markets camouflage true prices, protectionist policies distort them. For all the commodities protected in developed countries, particularly in important markets such as the EEC, the essential detriment is the reduction in the market and the consequent denial of access. However, one should not ignore the distorting effect of such protection on the world market price for the protected commodities. 'The most important of the distortions is the downward pressure of world market prices. For some products the downward pressure is so strong that these prices have no meaning at all for guiding the allocation of production in the world or for estimating the efficiency of national agriculture.'[5]

Once again two familiar conclusions emerge — that the concept of from market determination of prices is mythical and that efficient use of the world's resources bothers governments the least. A study by FAO and UNCTAD of the estimated price effects in 1980 as a result of a hypothetical removal of the 1970 levels of protection shows that the world market price of various commodities would rise as follows:

Wheat	+ 28 per cent
Sugar	+ 54 per cent
Rice	+ 64 per cent
Coarse Grains	I 24 per cent
Vegetable Oils	+ 11 per cent
Beef and Veal	+ 20 per cent

While these figures cannot be expected to be precise estimates of possible price changes, at least they indicate the order of magnitude of the price-depressing effect of protectionism. The study also estimated that the export gains in 1980 of the removal of protection would be of the order of US $17 billion. In world market economy exports of US $80 billion in 1970, this would represent an increase of 20 per cent in the earnings of exporting countries. Of course, not all the benefit would flow to the developing countries; in fact Asian developing countries would *lose* about US $6 billion while African and Latin American developing countries would gain about US$10 billion. Low-cost developed producing countries (the United States, Canada and Australia) would also gain US $10 billion.

A more recent study of the World Bank indicates that the dismantling of protection for nine major primary commodities would lead to an annual growth rate in export earnings of 15.5 per cent; without the liberalisation it would only be 12.5 per cent. This 3 per cent extra growth is significant. The study shows that 'in f.o.b. value terms there would be an increase of $7.1 billion in LDC export earnings from $19.7 to $26.8 billion in 1980 in constant (1974) terms which is equivalent to an increase of about $12 billion in current (1980) terms'.[6]

To some extent preferential trading arrangements help to minimise the price distorting effect of protection. The only commodity for which such arrangements have been tried consistently is sugar – under the erstwhile US Sugar Act, the Commonwealth Sugar Agreement and the arrangement included under the Lomé Convention. The following brief summary of the benefits of the US Sugar Act to the exporting countries is from the detailed *History of Sugar Marketing* by Roy A. Ballinger of the US Department of Agriculture.[7] Until its recent abolition, imports of sugar into the United States were paid for at the same price as domestic sugar. For a brief period between 1962 and 1964 there was an import fee calculated as a percentage of the difference between the world and domestic US prices; however, for much of the period world prices were higher, and consequently the import fee was zero. Foreign holders of US sugar quotas generally obtained a price higher by 1 or 2 ¢ per lb over the free market price, and in some years, such as 1966 and 1968, the difference was as high as 4.5 ¢ per lb. For example, in 1959 and the first half of 1960, Cuban sugar received a quota premium which averaged about 2.29 ¢ per lb, amounting to over US $250 million for 5.6 million tons of sugar sold over the 18-month period.

In the case of the Commonwealth Sugar Agreement, imports into the United Kingdom of specified quantities (Caribbean Commonwealth countries 659,000 tons, Mauritius 335,000 tons, Australia 300,000 tons, Fiji 120,000 tons, Swaziland 85,000 tons and India and East Africa token quantities) were paid a 'negotiated price' defined as one which was 'reasonably remunerative to efficient producers'. In practice, it was calculated by taking into account increases in costs of production over the base price of £30 10s a ton in 1950. The price was, in fact, 'indexed' to proved increases in costs; another innovation of the CSA was that less developed exporting countries were paid a special premium of £4 a ton when the world price was low, progressively scaled down if the world price increased, falling to a minimum of £1 10s a ton when the world price reached a level of £39 a ton. Thus the CSA not only provided a higher than world price for Commonwealth exporters but paid a still higher price to the developing exporters and protected them from the vagaries of the free market. It is also important to note that there was a built-in sharing of growth in consumption between domestic and Commonwealth suppliers. As an enlightened example of reducing the distorting effects of protectionism by providing guaranteed access, share of growth, minimising price depressing effects and indexing to costs of production, the CSA was unrivalled. The CSA has now been subsumed in the Lomé Convention between the enlarged EEC and the 46 African, Caribbean and Pacific countries with a guaranteed access for 1.4 million tons at a price related to the Community's own target price for domestic sugar.

Interchangeability and Substitutability

Just as the nature of the market — closed, preferential or protected — affects prices, so does the nature of the competition faced by a commodity. If a commodity is substitutable, its price is obviously governed by that of other products. In theory, everything is substitutable in the long run; for example, changes in consumption between tropical beverages and soft drinks are a long-term trend. In the market place it is the immediate substitutability that has an impact on the price. In this two categories can be distinguished — 'interchangeability' and 'competition from synthetics'.

The best example of a product group with a large number of mutually interchangeable products is 'oils and fats'. Some oils such as linseed oil, castor oil and tung oil are mainly used for industrial purposes and their interchangeability with edible oils and fats is limited. Even if these are excluded, the variety of edible products is staggering. These are either of animal or of vegetable origin. Edible animal fats include products, such as butter and lard, from domesticated livestock and marine products such as fish oil, whale oil and sperm oil. Edible vegetable oils also cover a very wide product range. Some are tree crops with productive lives ranging from 25 years in the case of the oil palm to 100 years for the olive tree and 200 for the babassu palm. Other vegetable oils are plant crops; some, like cottonseed oil, are by-products of a crop grown mainly for some other purpose (e.g. fibre). Oil can be extracted from over 100 varieties of plants, including tomato pips and grape seeds. Oil-bearing commodities are grown in every variety of climate, tropical, semi-tropical and temperate. Their oil content varies widely, some produce more meal than oil and are thus 'meal seeds' rather than 'oil seeds'. The quality of the different oils, in terms of the

Table 7.1: Edible Vegetable Oils

Oilseed	Type	Oil content %	1974 production Crop (million mt)	1974 production As oil (million mt)	Main producing areas
Soft oils, poly-unsaturated					
1. Soyabean	Temperate, plant	18-20	57.3	9.2	USA, Brazil
2. Cottonseed	Plant, by-product	18-20	25.6	2.9	USSR, China, USA, India, Pakistan, Brazil, Turkey, Egypt, Sudan
3. Sunflower	Adaptable, plant	35-45	11.1	3.8	USSR
Soft oils, mono-unsaturated					
4. Groundnut (peanut)	Tropical and temperate, plant	65-68	17.9	3.0	West Africa, India, China, USA
5. Olive	Subtropical, tree	25-30	7.7	1.5	Mediterranean
6. Rapeseed	Adaptable, plant	40-45	7.3	2.3	Canada, West Europe
Lauric oils, highly saturated					
7. Copra	Tropical, tree	65-68	3.6	2.4	Asia and the Pacific
8. Palmkernel	Tropical, tree	45-50	1.4	0.5	West and Central Africa, Asia
Other highly saturated oils					
9. Palm	Tropical, tree	45-50	—	2.7	West and Central Africa, Asia

Source: Compiled from A. Langstraat, 'Characteristics and composition of Vegetable Oil Bearing Materials', *Quarterly Supplement*, Asian and Pacific Coconut Community, Jakarta, 30 September 1976

proportion of fatty acids, also varies widely. The characteristics of some of the important oil-bearing crops are summarised in Table 7.1. Edible oils, with such widely different characteristics, have become interchangeable parts of a single edible oils and fats market because the same end products can be made from a suitable mixture of different oils. The invention of margarine was mainly responsible for the growth of world trade in oils, though they are also important in soap manufacture.

One purpose of classifying commodities according to their characteristics (Chapter 3) was to relate the 'technical factors' to the market for each commodity and so, in turn, to determine their effect on commodity conflicts. The relationship between the characteristics of different oils and the market for oils and the consequent effects on international negotiations have been clearly brought out in two articles by M.P. Cracknell in the *Journal of World Trade Law*.[8] The analysis which follows is substantially the same as in these articles (which also provide the quotations, unless otherwise specified); the data has, however, been updated.

The competition for the available market between the different oils, the effect on prices for different oils and the impact on the conflict between developed and developing countries − all derive from the change in the nature of the market since the Second World War. Total world production of edible vegetable oils has grown exponentially over the last 20 years and has now reached 30 million tons a year.

The main production areas, in descending order, are North America (soyabeans, cottonseed, animal fats), Asia (soyabeans, palm and palmkernels, copra), Eastern Europe (soyabeans, sunflowerseed, animal fats), Western Europe (animal fats, olive oil), Africa (groundnuts, palm and palm kernels, cottonseed) and Latin America (animal fats, fish oil).

The one significant change since the above passage was written is the emergence of Latin America (i.e. Brazil) as a large producer of soyabeans. A large part of the increase in production since the Second World War has occurred in the developed and centrally planned countries for autarkic reasons.

The increase in American production during the Second World War was partly to insure autarky of supplies of vegetable oils. A similar preoccupation inspires the policy of other main importers today, chiefly European countries, except Great Britain. Both in the EEC and in Eastern Europe, oilseed production is encouraged. In Western Europe this is above all to insure supplies of seeds to the local crushing industries: in eastern Europe it is part of the general policy of attaining a fairly high degree of independence from outside supplies. It is evident that in spite of interchangeability, imports of oilseeds face more competition from national seed production than they do from national production of animal fats. Thus, encouragement of production of oilseeds in importer countries goes directly against the interests of tropical exporting countries.

Most of the oil produced in the various countries is consumed domestically. World trade in edible vegetable oils is a little over a third of total production — about 11 million tons in 1974. Of this quantity, about 6.5 million tons are exported as oils, the balance being the oil equivalent of the seeds exported. The only oil exported in substantial quantities by the centrally planned countries is sunflower seed oil. Developing countries export mainly groundnut, coconut, palm and palm kernel oils. Developed countries export either the seed or oils extracted from soyabeans, cottonseed, rapeseed, and, increasingly, sunflowerseed. Out of total exports of 11 million tons, soyabean accounts for over 40 per cent — 4.7 million tons, made up of 1.5 million tons as oil and about 3.2 million tons as oil in the beans exported as such. The ever-increasing importance of the soyabean in the oils and meal market is a result of three causes: first, the extremely rapid rise in US production of oilseed during and after the Second World War; second, the emergence of the US as a large net exporter of oilseeds and oils gave the products an important place in the administration's support programmes, thus boosting production further; and, third, the fact that while the oilcake market has expanded that for oils has slowed down considerably. Since the markets for oilseeds, oils and oilcake are closely related, a table, combining the value of exports of the different varieties, from developed, developing and centrally planned countries, for the years 1970 and 1974, is given in Appendix 6. Table 7.2 is an extract showing the share of developed and developing countries (i.e. excluding centrally planned countries) for five oilseed varieties for the two selected years. The predominant position of soyabean products in the world markets is clearly seen from the figures. The rapid increase in exports of developing countries of soyabeans, from almost nothing in 1970 to US $600 million in 1974, is entirely due to the 'Brazilian miracle'; but for this, the share of the developing countries

Table 7.2: Exports of soyabean and competing products 1970 and 1974

(Value US$ million)

Oilseed	Exports in 1970			Exports in 1974		
	Total	Developed	Developing	Total	Developed	Developing
Soyabean products						
Soyabean	1,251	1,221	30	4,150	3,546	604
Soyabean oil	311	306	5	1,069	1,042	27
Soyabean cake	51	46	5	176	145	31
Total	1,613	1,573	40	5,395	4,733	662
Copra and products						
Copra	170	—	170	263	—	263
Coconut oil	189	20	168	614	94	519
Copra cake	28	3	25	65	4	61
Total	387	23	363	942	98	843
Palm products						
Palm kernel	67	—	67	135	—	135
Palm oil	201	9	191	894	51	843
Palm kernel oil	51	14	37	226	50	176
Palm kernel cake	17	7	10	41	7	34
Total	336	30	305	1,296	108	1,188
Groundnut products						
Groundnuts	210	41	169	431	190	241
Groundnut oil	143	24	119	305	86	219
Groundnut cake	131	5	126	205	8	197
Total	484	70	414	941	284	657
Competing products Total	1,207	123	1,082	3,179	490	2,688
All four products Total	2,820	1,696	1,122	8,574	5,223	3,350
Share of the market	100	60	40	100	61	39

Note: Trade of centrally planned countries excluded; differences in totals due to rounding
Source: FAO Trade Yearbook, 1974

would have shown a marked drop in 1974.

Why is soyabean so important? It contains much less oil than tropical oilseeds; if oil were the main product required, then coconut oil and groundnut oil would be the most important ones. The reason is the expanding demand for oilcake and the stagnant demand for oil. 'In Western Europe, the main importing area, demand for oilcake has increased rapidly because by buying temperate, low-oil content seed, European crushers can face demand both of oil and of cake with no problem of surplus oil.' Worldwide, the balance cannot always be maintained. If total demand for oilcake is much stronger than for oil, then soyabean is crushed to produce the required quantity of cake; a surplus of oil results. In effect, the oil has become a by-product.

The rapid rise in production in the US and the even more miraculous increase in Brazil in just a few years share an important characteristic of annual plant crops — an ability to adjust to changes in demand. Similar examples can be found in the successful development of types of rapeseed in Canada and of sunflowerseed in Eastern Europe. Tropical tree crops are quite different.

> It is necessary to distinguish between tropical and temperate oils because it happens that this distinction also largely covers the economic division into rich and poor countries... In the main temperate oilseeds come from annual plants whereas tropical oilseeds are more generally tree crops, with the big exception of groundnuts. This means that temperate oil producers can more easily adapt their production to market conditions, for their production cycle is shorter; tropical producers, on the other hand, must tie up big capital investments for a long period before receiving any returns.

The competition between temperate plant oils and tropical tree oils has been graphically described by Siegfried Mielke, editor of *Oil World,* thus: 'Nowadays the fight for the market is taking place between soyabean oil on the one hand and lauric oils and palm oil on the other hand.'[9]

The structure of the oils and fats market is thus a complex one comprising by-product oils, marine oils, livestock animal fats, plant oils and price inelastic tree oils. Of the major oils and fats, soyabean oil has joined cottonseed oil, lard, fish oil, tallow and greases as by-product oils. Fish oil, whale oil and sperm oil production are dependent on the catch of fish and whales. The production of a competing fat such as butter is dependent on milk production on the one hand and on the manufacture of fat-containing milk products on the other. In an important market such as the EEC, the quantity of dairy products produced also depends on the Community's policies on beef and veal production. A very large part of the market requirement is thus filled by oils whose supply depends on extraneous factors. 'There remain only four vegetable oils which are produced as the main product and the raw material product of which therefore can be adjusted to demand from year to year — namely, groundnut oil, rape oil, and sesame oil (the latter also only partly).'

What happens to prices of individual oils in this complex market? As a group, fats and oils showed remarkable price stability until 1972. There was a sharp increase in 1973 and 1974, the years of the commodity boom; prices have since declined. The stability of prices of the group as a whole is not a matter of great interest; since most countries export only one or two types, it is the behaviour of the individual oils that is relevant.

> Taken individually, oilseeds prices tend to fluctuate considerably. . .
> Price sensibility of individual oilseeds varies according to the degree of possible substitution with other oilseeds and the extent of particular uses in which a given oil is indispensable. In case of limited supply, where a particular oil is indispensable, users tend to bid high prices when supply falls; this has been the case with laurics; when substitution is possible, after a varying period of price rise, during which technical changes in 'recipes' of the finished product intervene, the price of a rare but interchangeable oil tends to drop into line with the mean level of the substitute oils; this is usually the case of fluids such as groundnut, soyabean and cotton seed oils. . .
> Another element of price formation is speculation. Forward sales tend to dominate the market, spot transactions being somewhat limited. . . As far as price elasticities go, on the demand side and for fats and oils as a whole, this is low. But for any particular oil, demand elasticity is usually high when substitution is possible and decreases as substitution becomes more difficult.

Yet another factor in price determination is the existence of multinational corporations.

> Though no controllable figures are available on this point, it has been estimated that 75 to 80 per cent of consumer goods based on

fats and oils in North America and Western Europe are more or less directly controlled by three firms. In order of size based on turnover these firms are Unilever (Anglo-Dutch), Procter and Gamble (American) and Colgate-Palmolive (American). Naturally, these firms do not 'control' 80 per cent of the world market, but their size and importance are such that their decisions cannot help influencing short-term market trends and developments.

It is interesting to note that the International Association of Seed Crushers, formed in 1910, is serviced largely by personnel of Unilever, London, which also provides office facilities. 'The membership consists of associations, firms and even private individuals; membership is mainly European but American associations are well represented and even a few firms based in developing countries are members. There is a virtual absence of exporters' representatives from developing countries.' On the producers' side, the only associations are the Asian and Pacific Coconut Community and the African Groundnut Council. Neither has market power remotely approaching that of the crushers' Association.

In this complex situation, one fact stands out: for technical reasons, autarkic protectionist reasons and for reasons of powerful competition from the developed countries, the developing producers of edible vegetable oils have suffered decreasing markets, declining prices and price instability. What has been the international reaction to this situation? A FAO Study Group on Oilseeds, Oils and Fats has been in existence since 1966. Like other study groups it has met many times, analysed the market situation and even agreed on the objectives, in vague general terms. But the Study Group has not been able to agree on a set of recommendations on the actions that need to be taken. After UNCTAD II in 1968, the Study Group made a determined effort to find solutions in two special meetings but with no positive result.

One of the main difficulties is that it is not possible to tackle the problems of oils and oilseeds without considering the market for oilcake. But the oilcake market itself is a complex one, partly because of the varieties of oilcake but more so because it is part of a wider animal feed market. Farm fodder, grains and grain wastes such as bran are other important constituents of the animal feed market. As seen earlier, even sugar made inedible for human consumption can compete for the animal feed market. Apart from the general economic conditions which affect personal disposable income in the rich countries and, consequently, the demand for meat, demand for oilmeals is determined mainly by (i) the farm fodder supply situation and (ii) the price level of oilmeals in relation to that of feed grains and in relation to that of livestock and livestock products. The high prices of grains in 1973 and 1974 increased the demand for oilmeals; so did the drought in 1976 in Europe which reduced the availability of farm fodder. The reverse could easily happen; plentiful farm fodder and cheaper grains would decrease the market for oilcake. Total world trade in oilcake, as such, was about 15 billion tons in 1974, with a value of US $2.8 billion. In addition, the element of cake in seed crushed in importing countries was worth approximately US $3.5 billion. The value of trade in both forms at US $6.3 billion should be compared with total world exports, in 1974, of coarse grains (maize, barley, oats, sorghum and rye) of about US $9.5 billion. In the total oilcake market, almost all the increase in the last ten years has been, as one would expect, on account of soyabean meal. The share of this meal has increased from 49 per cent in 1966 to 61 per cent in 1976. During this period, the share of all other oilmeals, except rapeseedmeal, has declined quite significantly. Since the complexity of the oils and fats market has been analysed in detail, it is unnecessary to go through the same exercise for the equally complex meal market.

The close relationship between the various products provides another example of the punch-bag effect. To take a triangular example, an important dairy fat, butter, is a direct competitor with edible vegetable oils; at the same time, the cost of production of butter depends to some extent on the price of oilmeals; the price of oilmeals and the price of oil are, of course, inter-related. If the market situation is so complex and if solutions are going to be almost impossible to find, why bother about having international negotiations at all? There are two reasons why one should persevere with attempts to regulate the markets. First, the size of the markets for oilseeds, oils and oilcake is a considerable one. Table 7.3 shows that the value of the total market was over US $5 billion in 1970 and over US $12 billion in 1974. In terms of size, this product group is more important than copper or coffee. A global attempt to resolve commodity conflicts cannot afford to ignore this group. The second reason is the high dependence of a number of developing countries on exports of one or two oils. The dependency list in chapter 3 gives some examples of the importance of groundnuts and groundnut oil to a number of West African countries. Copra is an extremely important product in the economy of many of the smaller countries in the Pacific, and of the Seychelles Islands, though their share in world trade may be tiny. The problems of the smallest, and often least developed countries, deserve special attention.

Table 7.3   Market Economy Trade in Oilseeds, Oils and Oilcake (US $ million)

	1970	1973	1974
Edible oilseeds	1,962	4,425	5,681
Edible vegetable oils	1,219	2,025	4,074
Oilcake and meal	914	2,683	2,474
Total oilseed, oils, oilseedcake and meal	4,095	9,133	12,229
of which			
Developed countries	2,582 (63.0%)	5,942 (65.1%)	7,956 (65.1%)
Developing countries	1,510 (36.9%)	3,189 (34.9%)	4,296 (34.9%)

Note: Oilseed cake and meal includes all cake, i.e. including castor and linseed
 cake. Oilseeds and oils edible varieties only
Source: FAO *Trade Yearbook,* 1974

Do any feasible solutions exist at all for such a complex problem? The FAO Study Group studied a number of techniques such as buffer stocks, using surpluses as food aid, means of liberalising trade and levying an import or consumption tax to be used to compensate developing countries. It is clear that there cannot be a single set of solutions to all the problems of the markets which will ensure that the right countries benefit and also protect the economic interest of developed exporting countries. The problems are of different kinds — access problems, tariff problems, protection levels, competition from synthetics, price fluctuation and declining prices. No single commodity agreement on the traditional pattern can conceivably attack all these. Only a variety of specific measures, each designed to deal with a single aspect, can achieve some success. All these measures may be under an overall umbrella of a general agreement on oilseeds, oils and oilcake, but individually they must be commodity-specific and country-specific.

Competition from Synthetics

It will be recalled that one of the four major groups into which the Pearson Commission divided all commodities consisted of those produced mainly in developing countries and facing competition from synthetics. The spectre of synthetics depriving the natural product of its traditional market haunts many a primary commodity. Among edible oils, lauric oils face competition from synthetics in that part of the market where the end-use is soap making, because of the development of synthetic detergents and similar cleaning preparations. Oilcake also faces increasing competition from synthetic protein. When both oils and oilcake are threatened, the effect on each is cumulative. Among the threatened products, by far the best-known are natural rubber and jute, both of significant importance to countries in South and South-East Asia. Plastics threaten the market for hides and skins; plastics, as well as paper-based products, threaten the market for a variety of wood products. Even sugar suffered for long under the threat of the cyclamate group of artificial sweeteners until reprieved by the discovery of the adverse effects on the health of consumers by its excessive use in prepared and processed foodstuffs; iso-glucose is the latest threat. The nature of the competition from synthetics for a variety of commodities (textiles, hides and skins, rubber, hard fibres and jute and lauric oils) has been examined by Ursula Wassermann in five articles in the *Journal of World Trade Law*.[10] The technical conditions of the competition may vary from commodity to commodity, but some general conclusions apply to all of them.

The question why synthetics develop has been answered succinctly by Enzo Grilli in his World Bank study on *The Future of Hard Fibres and Competition from Synthetics*.[11]

Synthetic substitutes are developed whenever research has created the technological basis and the marketing factors justify their use. The critical impulse to their development usually results from supply shortages, from large fluctuations in prices of the natural product, or from both. Whatever the reasons behind these temporary disruptions of the normal market situation, the result is the same: investments for the production of synthetics are made and low variable costs of operation allow synthetics producers to stay in the market even if prices of natural products decline. Further investments for synthetics production are not made generally until the next scarcity. Past experience clearly shows that the investment cycle in the synthetic-fibres industry is correlated quite closely with the price cycle of the various natural fibres. Once synthetic production on a sufficiently large scale is started, the strategy of natural-fibres producers shifts to one of containment, of maintaining a certain share of the market for the natural product. The fact remains, however, that the technical, financial, economic, and managerial advantages of the synthetics industry make it hard for producers of primary commodities to compete effectively.

For commodities encountering competition from synthetics, an extra dimension is added to existing conflicts. For example, the conflict between low-cost and high-cost producers is complicated by the realisation that both have an interest in preventing prices rising to levels that would encourage further production of synthetics. The sacrifices required from high-cost producers are then greater, and the point at which burden sharing becomes equitable differs from that when there is no competition from synthetics. The conflict on price differential due to quality variations is also sharpened since different qualities have to compete for a diminishing market on which a price ceiling is set by the competing synthetic substitute. The interest of the importing countries is complicated by the existence of different pressure groups within the country — producers of synthetics and processors of the natural product. An alliance may thus develop between the processors in the importing countries and the exporters of the natural product. Faced with conflicting pressures, importing countries often find it politically inadvisable to take a stand; consequently there is much less interest in negotiating international arrangements. There is no clear divergence of views between developed and developing countries on this question. While some developing countries, as exporters, may criticise the development of synthetics, they do not generally inhibit the growth of synthetics to compete with products in which they have little or no export interest. Such growth is justified usually on grounds of import substitution and promotion of new technology in the less industrialised countries.

The most important area of competition is, of course, textile fibres. The rapid development of first artificial (e.g. rayon) and then wholly synthetic (e.g. nylon, polyester) fibres and yarn in the last 30 years has affected the market for all natural fibres, particularly cotton, jute and wool. A study of this problem would be too extensive since (i) synthetic fibres themselves compete with each other and (ii) a whole new technology of mixtures of artificial and natural fibres has been developed. One important conclusion, of relevance to other commodities also, can however be drawn. Some of the synthetic fibres have technical qualities superior to those of the natural product. However, once the synthetic is developed its use is not confined only to those applications in which the special qualities are really required; the competition extends to areas in which the natural product is still adequate. A fibre group less complex than textile fibres is 'Hard Fibres' — sisal, abaqa and henequen. The group is also interesting since an informal arrangement regulating the market has been tried with limited success. A product which exemplifies the problems of adjusting the relative production of synthetics and the natural product is rubber; the International Rubber Study Group, one of the earliest such groups to be formed, has been discussing this question for the last two decades. Rubber also has a long history of attempts to regulate international trade, dating back to the inter-war period. Attempts have also been made to co-ordinate producer action by forming an Association of Rubber Producers. Hard fibres and rubber will be used as examples to study commodity conflicts arising from competition from synthetics.

Sisal, abaqa and henequen, all perennial crops, are produced commercially in only a few developing countries.[12] Sisal, the most important of the three, accounts for 66 per cent of total production and 83 per cent of total exports of all hard fibres; Tanzania and Brazil are the two largest producers. Henequen, similar to sisal and the second most important variety, accounts for 17 per cent of total world output of hard fibres and 5 per cent of world exports; about 90 per cent of all production is in Mexico's Yucatan Peninsula. Abaqa, accounting for about 8 per cent of world production and 10 per cent of world exports, is produced almost exclusively in the Philippines. The main use (three quarters of world consumption) of hard fibres is in the manufacture of cordage. The bulk of the fibres is exported in the raw form, though Mexico, Tanzania and Brazil also export significant quantities of manufactures. The two largest producers of sisal are also the two largest exporters, holding between them two thirds of the raw fibre market. Developed countries are the main importers of the fibres, absorbing 85 per cent of all exports. In terms of export earnings, hard fibres are important to the economies of only a few of the producing countries. Tanzania and Haiti are the only countries which draw a substantial share of their total foreign exchange earnings from exports of these fibres. Nonetheless, hard fibres are of crucial importance to some producing countries because they often represent the main source of employment and income in particularly poor regions in which alternative production possibilities are limited.

Abaqa began to be displaced by nylon in the 1950s and by polyester fibres in the 1960s. Sisal was unaffected for a time; the 1963/4 price boom — largely caused by political uncertainties in East Africa — coincided with the development of polypropylene and high-density polyethylene. These new products had a combination of special characteristics — light weight, high tensile strength, versatility in applications and, above all, low production costs. The parallel development of new packaging and cargo-handling techniques also reduced demand for hard fibres and hard fibre goods. World fibre import demand fell rapidly, at an average rate of 3 per cent a year between 1964/6 and 1968/70. The consumption of polypropylene resin throughout the world rose more than fourfold between 1965 and 1970. Translated into its hard-fibre equivalent, the product weight increase in consumption of synthetic cordage in developed countries alone represented about 115,000 metric tons of hard fibres displaced by synthetics. Hard fibres are among the few agricultural products the demand for which actually is falling in total volume. The price behaviour hard fibres follows the usual routine of shortage and high prices followed by excess supply and sharp drop in prices. The price rise during the Korean War boom set in motion a strong increase in acreage which led to the production boom and price fall in the mid-1950s. The high prices of the early 1960s triggered another planting cycle; prices fell in the mid-1960s, accelerating the development of synthetic substitutes. Low prices prevailed up to 1972, when prices rose rapidly as a result of two consecutive years of drought in East Africa. Since 1974, prices have declined sharply. The excessive fluctuation in the last six years is seen in the price of sisal:

Sisal — East African E.G., c.i.f. European ports, US$ per metric ton

1970 —	152
1971 —	170
1972 —	240
1973 —	527
1974 —	1,039
1975 —	729
1976 —	500

The Informal Agreement on Hard Fibres was referred to in Chapter 5 in connection with the conflict on price differentials. The collapse of the sisal market in 1967 led to the conclusion of the agreement under the auspices of the FAO Study Group. It was informal in the sense that it did not take the form of a binding treaty; instead the participants pledged themselves voluntarily to respect and implement the recommendations unanimously agreed on by the Group. The unanimity required is an essential distinction between formal agreements where decisions are possible by majority voting and informal ones. The agreement, which was mainly among producers (consumers participating in a kind of observer/adviser role), consisted of a non-binding understanding on export quotas and an indicative target price for sisal to be reached 'as soon as practicable' by stages. The agreement was in effect from January 1968 to end of 1969; it broke down temporarily in 1970 but was reactivated in May 1971. The high prices prevailing from 1972 to 1975 made the informal quota and price arrangements inoperative. It was reactivated again in February 1976. The limited success of the agreement is due to the fact that, being informal, it depended entirely on the voluntary exercise of discipline on the part of all exporters. In practice, neither quota nor price provisions were respected by all; both overshipments and underselling were resorted to by some exporters, including a major one, Brazil.

In the Hard Fibre Agreement, the developed importing countries, who are the main producers of the competing synthetics, have not undertaken any responsibilities, except that of giving advice. In the case of rubber, a similar stand-off attitude would mean that the problems of natural rubber could not be tackled at all. Not only are the markets for synthetic and natural rubber too closely integrated but the production of the substitute has reached a point where the natural product is pushed into an almost residual status. The facts about rubber production and marketing can be briefly summarised as follows: 85 per cent of all natural rubber is produced in South-East Asian countries, the three largest producers being Malaysia (44 per cent), Indonesia (25 per cent) and Thailand (11 per cent). (All percentages are 1972/4 averages.) These three countries also have similar shares in total world exports — Malaysia (49 per cent), Indonesia (26 per cent) and Thailand (12 per cent). An important technical factor in the production of natural rubber is that, while large plantations do exist, a considerable part of the production comes from smallholder units. The problems that this pattern of production create in supply regulation have been referred to earlier. As for synthetic rubber, the world's largest producer is the United States (34 per cent), followed by the EEC (22 per cent) and Japan (12 per cent). The major exporters of synthetic rubber are the United States (15 per cent of the market for such rubber), France and Japan (about 14 per cent each) and the Netherlands (11 per cent). The developed countries account for 80 per cent of world imports of both natural and synthetic rubber — the former from developing countries, the latter from other developed countries. About half the world consumption of rubber is for the manufacture of tyres, while a large proportion of the other half is for other components for automobile and commercial vehicle industries. The role of the tyre manufacturing companies in rubber production and trade is therefore crucial. Prices of natural rubber show the same violent fluctuations as other natural commodities. Just after the Second World War, the price was about US $480 a metric ton; it jumped to a peak of US $1,300 during the

Korean War boom but declined to US $520 by 1954. Political uncertainties in the next few years kept prices between US $600 to 800. Since 1960, there has been a steady decline reaching a low point of US $399 in 1971. During the recent boom, it jumped to US $868, declined to US $634 in June 1975 but rose again to about US $900 in 1976.

The extent of the competition faced by natural rubber can be seen from the trends in production of the two kinds – natural and synthetic. Table 7.4 shows that in the 25 years between 1948 and 1973 world production of natural rubber increased by 125 per cent, but that of synthetic rubber by 1,250 per cent! Just after the war, there were only

Table 7.4 Production of Natural and Synthetic Rubber (million metric tons)

	1948	1951	1961	1966	1971	1973	1974
Natural rubber wholly in developing countries	1.55	1.92	2.13	2.40	3.08	3.51	3.44
Synthetic rubber Total world production	0.57	0.97	2.13	4.21	6.16	7.71	7.55
of which							
Developed countries	0.54	0.92	2.00	3.31	4.59	5.69	5.29
of which							
United States	0.47	0.86	1.43	2.00	2.28	2.61	2.42
Centrally planned Europe	0.03	0.05	0.12	0.82	1.28	1.73	1.90
Developing countries	–	–	–	0.08	0.20	0.27	0.31

Sources: UN *Statistical Yearbook;* International Rubber Study Group, *Rubber Statistical Bulletin.*

three producers of synthetic rubber – the United States, Canada and East Germany, all of whom had started because of war-time demands. The production of synthetic rubber rapidly caught on in all developed countries. This is shown by the fact that the share of the United States in production in this group fell from 87 per cent in 1948 to only 46 per cent currently, even though US production itself quintupled from less than 500,000 tons to about 2.5 million tons. The centrally planned countries were the next to start production, increasing sixtyfold in 25 years. Though it started much later, production in developing countries is also increasing rapidly. The displacement of natural rubber by the synthetic substitute is shown by the percentage of synthetic rubber consumed in 1974 as a proportion of all new rubber; Eastern Europe has the highest percentage consumption of synthetics at 82 per cent. In the United States, Canada and Brazil, it is about 75 per cent and in Japan and the EEC about 66 per cent. By contrast, India, a natural rubber producing country, uses only 14 per cent synthetics. In countries which do not produce natural rubber synthetic production rises rapidly until it captures 75 to 80 per cent of the market; exceptionally, Brazil's behaviour is like that of a non-natural rubber producer in spite of the fact that this was one of rubber's original homes. While the developed countries have been chiefly responsible for denying markets to natural rubber, other groups are following along the same path some way behind.

Two points are generally made about the inevitability of the growth of the synthetic rubber industry, and a third is left unstated. The first is that the rapid growth in the car-owning population of the developed countries and the corresponding increase in demand for automobile tyres could not have been met by any conceivable increase in natural rubber production. Even if this is assumed to be true, it is obvious that the increase in synthetic production was far more than was justified to meet any gaps; had it been so, natural rubber would not have suffered from violent fluctuations or periodic surpluses. A second argument advanced is that natural rubber does not have the technical characteristics that some special uses require. It is true that synthetic rubbers do have some special characteristics; but natural rubber is also superior in some respects. It is estimated that 45 per cent of total demand for rubber currently goes to synthetic rubber on technical considerations and only 20 per cent to natural rubber for similar reasons. But for 35 per cent of the demand, both kinds are equally suitable. The development of synthetics is not purely a response to technical demands; monopolistic and political considerations also play a significant part. For example, the development of polyisoprene rubber, an almost direct chemical duplicate of natural rubber, was not prompted by a search for a superior product. The tyre manufacturers exercise a considerable degree of control over the supply of raw material, owning natural rubber plantations whenever possible (e.g. Firestone in Liberia) and also, more importantly, by building captive synthetic rubber factories. In the United States, about half the synthetic rubber capacity is owned by tyre manufacturers; in European countries the proportion is even higher. With captive synthetic production, the inclination of the manufacturers is to use this capacity to the maximum at the cost of the natural product. In this way natural rubber is becoming a residual market. As in the case of edible oils, the existence of very few large companies controlling the raw material supply introduces monopolistic tendencies in what is mistakenly often referred to as the 'free market' in rubber. The tyre manufacturers have been encouraged to develop synthetic production by the governments of the developed importing countries for the third reason, which is often left unstated. Since the automobile industry is a key one in both peace and war, these countries do not want to be dependent for a vital raw material on imports from distant tropical countries.

The effect of the rapid growth in synthetic rubber production has been to deny to natural rubber a legitimate share of the growing mass market. It is also undeniable that, if only a fraction of the resources expended on research and development of synthetics had been devoted to improving the qualities of the natural product, it could have been adapted to many of the new uses. Malaysia has made commendable efforts in promoting a programme of research support to natural rubber users. By improving plantation techniques and by developing new processes for converting raw rubber into the commercial product, a superior natural rubber SMR (Standard Malaysian Rubber) has been successfully developed. The total investment a developing country can make still remains meagre compared with the resources of the giant companies. On the whole it is difficult to avoid the conclusion that the growth of synthetics has been unbridled and unplanned, both in terms of technical need and the quantity required to meet world demand in the most efficient manner. The International Rubber Study Group has from time to time considered the possibility of co-operation between producers of the two types with a view to evolving an accceptable 'code' of fair practice. There has been no desire on the part of developed, advanced developing or centrally planned countries to regulate the production of competing synthetics even to the extent of at least ensuring that natural rubber is provided with a stable market and a reasonable share in the growth of the market for all types of rubber. The developed countries argue that, with their free market economies, it is impossible to control industrial production; this is not very convincing. It must not be forgotten that there are tax incentives to spending vast amounts on research to develop synthetic substitutes; there are few incentives for importing a natural product. If developed countries can use fiscal measures either to control or to step up production of agricultural commodities there is no reason to assume that appropriate levels of indirect taxation would not succeed in regulating the production of any industrial commodity. Housing starts are controlled by raising or lowering mortgage rates; durable appliance production is regulated by altering the level of the tax or by changing hire purchase requirements; surely it is not impossible to devise an appropriate mechanism to regulate synthetic rubber production, ensuring, at the same time, a proper balance between natural and synthetic so that the cost to the consumer does not rise appreciably. The present time is favourable for re-thinking this question; with the sharp increase in the price of the raw material for synthetics, crude oil, there may now be a financial incentive to consider the possibility of a more balanced and efficient use of the world's resources.

Price Instability and Price Decline

Closed markets mean artificial prices; protected markets depress them; preferential arrangements raise them and protect earnings to some extent; and substitutability puts a ceiling on them. All these not only determine the price of a commodity at a particular moment but also influence the movement of the price over time. Two aspects of the variation over time of the market price figure in international commodity negotiations. The price can either exhibit violent fluctuations or can show a long-term secular declining trend in real terms. Violent fluctuations are generally considered to be detrimental to orderly marketing and disadvantageous to both exporting and importing countries. Even the UNCTAD Expert Group on Indexation, which did not detect any decline in the terms of trade of developing countries, agreed that violent fluctuations should be avoided, thus implicitly blessing regulation of the markets.

The number of commodities which exhibit a substantial degree of instability is quite large. Violent fluctuations, not only from year to year but often within a year, sometimes day to day, occur in many. In its report UNCTAD III, the Secretariat has listed them as follows:[13]

Substantial Instability	*Moderate Instability*
Sugar	Coffee
Copper	Groundnut oil
Pepper	Palm Kernels
Rice	Coconut oil
Palm oil	Groundnuts
Cocoa	Sisal
Tungsten	Tea

Lead metal   Tin
Bananas
Rubber
Copra

The range of fluctuation can be seen from the fact that since 1950 the annual average price of raw sugar has ranged from less than 2 ¢ per lb to over 30 ¢ per lb; cocoa prices have varied from under 13 ¢ per lb to 44 ¢ per lb; and coffee from 27 ¢ per lb to well over $1 per lb. If the daily variations in price are taken into account, the range between highest and lowest will be even greater. Particularly violent fluctuations and excessive instability occurred after 1974.

Table 7.5, compiled by the World Bank, summarises the fluctuations in prices, volume and earnings for some primary commodities. The fluctuation in iron ore, a closed market commodity, is seen to be very small; as one would expect, artificial prices are not subject to market pressures. On the other hand, where only a part of the commodity is traded under free conditions, the fluctuation in price of that limited quantity is more intense; copper prices on the free market varied over 13.4 per cent while producer prices remained relatively more stable. The variation in the US preferential price for sugar was only 3.5 per cent but in the free market it was 23.1 per cent. Tin, with an international buffer stocking arrangement and the US strategic stockpile behind it, had more limited price movements. The table also shows the clear correlation between fluctuation in prices and fluctuation in earnings. The importance attached in this book to earnings stabilisation for developing countries is thus justified. A comparison of the list of commodities which, according to the World Bank and UNCTAD, show substantial instability with the nature of the markets for these commodities (as in Table 4.1) does show that the nature of the market has a direct bearing on instability. Generally, oligopolistic buyer market commodities show greater instability than closed markets of the vertically integrated variety. The unstable commodities are those in which the developing countries have a significant export interest. Correspondingly the commodities in which developed countries have a preponderant *export* interest (not just protected production interest) are relatively more stable.

The relationship between price instability on the one hand and stock policy and national stabilisation policies on the other has been discussed by D. Gale Johnson in his 'World Agriculture, Commodity Policy and Price Variability'.[14]

Table 7.5 Fluctuation Indices in Selected Commodity Prices, Volume
and Earnings

(% Deviations from 5 year moving average)

Commodity	Prices[a]	Volume[b]	Earnings[c]
Copper	13.4	8.2	11.4
Tin	6.2	4.7	8.7
Lead	12.9	2.7	10.6
Zinc	13.2	3.4	15.9
Iron Ore	4.2	6.5	8.0
Manganese Ore	7.7	9.7	12.9
Coffee			
Santos 4	9.5		
Angolan 2AA	8.7		
Cocoa	16.2	5.9	9.9
Sugar			
World ISA Daily	23.1		
U.S. Preferential	3.5		
Beef	6.7	12.2	9.8
Rice	8.2	6.7	5.2
Vegetable Oils			
Groundnut Oil	8.2	11.0	6.9
Soybean Oil	10.4		
Coconut Oil	8.0	8.4	9.0
Palm Oil	7.1	4.0	8.2
Cotton	4.0	5.7	3.9
Jute	10.5	8.6	10.0
Sisal	13.4	3.7	11.4
Rubber	12.9	3.5	12.4
Timber	6.9	4.4	9.1

a. The period covered is 1950 to 1973 except for cotton (1952 to 1973), rice
(1951 to 1973) and jute (1955 to 1973).

b. The period covered is 1950 to 1972 except copper (1952 to 1972), tin, lead,
zinc, iron ore, manganese ore (1953 to 1972) and timber (1953 to 1971).

c. The period covered is 1950 to 1972.

Source: International Bank for Reconstruction and Development, 'Price
Forecasts for Major Primary Commodities', 19 June 1974, Commodities and
Export Projection Division, Report no. 467

Past behaviour of most governments and even a cursory examination of policies and programs designed to stabilize prices indicate that there is far less concern with the stability of prices outside and inside national boundaries ... In fact, the concern of most governments with internal price stability, with little or no regard for external effects, is comparable to the primary concern of governments with internal resource adjustments in agriculture ... There has been little recognition of the extent to which one nation or region achieves price stability at the expense of instability to others. This has not been an important issue in international negotiations or in trade negotiations ... The world need not have a period of price instability for major storable farm products such as it has witnessed since 1972 and is likely to have over the next year or more. If there were substantial liberalization of trade in farm products, price instability would be significantly reduced for internationally traded products.

Liberal access to markets is thus one way of reducing instability.
The more controlled a market the more stable it is. Why are fluctuations so violent in the commodities that are unregulated? This question cannot be answered without looking at the role of speculative forces in international trade. The standard defence of speculation is that it helps both buyer and seller by moderating violent changes and thus introduces stability in the market. If this were true in international trade — as opposed to domestic trade — then free market commodities should not present double-digit variations. There are a number of reasons why speculation in international trade does not encourage stability. First, price determination in the exchange is not always the result of open and free competition. In the London Metal Exchange there are only 28 'ring' dealers who 'fix' prices daily. In the words of the Chairman of the Exchange's Committee: 'It seems incredible at first sight that the fate of the world, in the form of prices of raw materials, is determined by such a procedure, but the practicability of this method has had many years to prove itself.' It is, no doubt, practical: commodity dealers, he said, earn more than £100 million in invisible earnings for the United Kingdom each year.[15] The question is whether the 'fixing' is equitable to raw material producers. Second, in some commodities, the quantities traded are not very large; in copper they are only part of the market and in sugar a residual market. Supply variations which may be small in terms of total exports become a much greater proportion of the residual market. The prospects of a

disproportionate price increase for much diminished supplies provoke feverish speculative activity and magnify rather rather than dampen an already unstable situation. Third, the expectation of stability in an international market is much less; it is more volatile because there is no ultimate power, as in the case of a government in a domestic market, that can be expected to intervene if things get out of hand. When the Paris refined sugar market collapses or the Maine potato futures fail, there is a fear that some government department or an authority such as the Commodities Exchange Commission may intervene and regulate the entire futures markets. The threat of unwelcome action usually guarantees good behaviour. Fourth, the exchanges themselves are under-regulated and subject to much less control compared with domestic operations. In his UNCTAD study on *Speculation and Price Stability in International Commodity Future Markets*, W.C. Labys comments: 'There also appear to be wide discrepancies among countries regarding the public availability of useful published data describing international hedging and speculative operations.'[16] In other words, even knowledge about international speculative activity is scanty and unreliable; naturally control, if any, is minimal. Lastly, monetary instability and inflation add an extra dimension to speculation.

An example of the magnitude of profits and losses in speculation in commodities is provided by the London cocoa market in which one of the largest chocolate companies in the world lost 80 million dollars in the course of a few months! How this came about is described by *The Economist* thus:

As the price rose in 1973 (from £330 a tonne in December 1972, which was already high) he [the Rowntree cocoa buyer] expected a turnround to come — and gambled on it by selling forward cocoa that he hadn't bought. But the price took off with the world boom, and hit nearly £600 a tonne in mid 1973 . . . Rowntree panicked and closed out its future contracts as quickly as it could, driving the price up against itself. Its next annual accounts revealed losses of £32 million simply on transactions in the cocoa terminal markets.[17]

Nobody can claim that speculation helped to 'moderate' the market in this case. Two conclusions that Labys arrives at are: '(i) there would seem to be a case for the wider application of government regulation of futures markets and (ii) regulation of future markets can also make a contribution to any overall approach to international commodity stabilisation.'[18] The stability which speculation is said to induce in domestic trading does not so easily transfer itself when trade crosses frontiers. The Chicago commodity exchanges, where there are a large number of buyers, sellers and middlemen, trading in substantial quantities in an environment which is basically acceptable to all participants and with the ever present threat of sanctions if things go wrong, is no guide as to how the international market in cocoa, pepper or copper would operate.

A few commodities have suffered a steady decline in prices in the post-war period. A long-term secular fall, particularly when not compensated by corresponding increases in volume that would keep total earnings at least constant, has a significant adverse impact on exchange earnings and on the resources needed for development. The problem is obviously acute in the case of developing countries which are dependent on the export earnings of one or two commodities. The following commodities have been listed as suffering from 'greatly unfavourable long-term price trends': bananas, bauxite, jute, phosphate, tea, citrus fruit, iron ore and manganese ore.[19] Of these, phosphate rock has escaped from the trend. As one example of the unfortunate commodities, Table 7.6 shows the money price and real price (money price deflated by the UN all commodities index) of tea from 1951 to 1975. Since the mid-1950s, the real price of tea has been steadily falling relative to the prices of other internationally traded goods; it was halved between 1956 and 1974. The price declined for a variety of reasons, mainly, in the case of tea, because of the inability of exporters to resolve the market share conflict between traditional and new exporters. Where there is consistent excess production, supply regulation is the appropriate solution. Declining consumption has to be met by promotion or by finding new uses. There does appear to be connection between closed markets and declining prices for the commodity. Vertical integration, monopsony and cartel buying generally involve decreasing prices in real terms for the producers. These can only be countered by breaking up the closed market or by equalling it through exporter cartelisation. The escape of phosphate rock from the declining trend was in fact the result of efforts of the market leaders to raise price levels.

The Share of the Exporter

The third and last question regarding the price is the share of the exporter in the price paid by the importer. This had recently become a contentious point between the Group of '77' and the developed countries and within the Group of '77' itself. As originally phrased, the

Table 7.6 Current and Real Prices of Tea, 1951 to 1975 (new pence/kg)

Year	Money Price	Real Price	Year	Money Price	Real Price
1951	40.24	37.26	1962	49.00	49.49
1952	33.54	31.94	1963	46.5	46.50
1953	40.14	40.14	1964	47.2	46.27
1954	58.02	58.61	1965	46.0	44.66
1955	55.82	56.38	1966	44.8	42.67
1956	53.17	52.64	1967	45.7	43.52
1957	48.78	47.36	1968	43.5	41.83
1958	50.47	50.47	1969	40.5	37.85
1959	50.03	50.54	1970	45.7	40.44
1960	50.68	50.68	1971	43.3	36.39
1961	48.51	49.00	1972	42.2	32.97
			1973	43.4	28.18
			1974	59.8	26.66
			1975	62.4	24.86

Note: Current prices — London average tea prices; real prices — current prices
deflated by UN all commodities index, 1963 = 100.

Source: G.P. Tyler, 'Recent Developments and Future Prospects for the World
Tea Economy', *Oxford Agrarian Studies,* 5, 1976, pp.99-123.

Group's view appeared to be that the exporter should receive a 'real and proportionate' share of the 'final consumer price'. This is too broad a demand since the 'final consumer price' may well include, in most countries, an element of consumer taxation. For example, it might imply that every time a government, developed or developing, puts up the excise duty or VAT on cigarettes for revenue purposes, a part must be passed on to the exporting country. This is unlikely to be acceptable to any government, rich or poor, since this amounts to taxing one's own citizens for a foreign country. In any case, governments are most reluctant to reduce collection from indirect taxes, as witness the unwillingness of the Federal Republic of Germany to reduce its duties on coffee. On the other hand, in some commodities the increases in the price paid by the consumer, without government intervention, have wholly accrued to the importers. In effect this concerns earnings on shipping, distribution and marketing. In the case of bananas, the grower receives only 11 ¢ out of every dollar spent by the consumer; the balance is shared as follows: ripeners 19 ¢; shippers 40 ¢; and retailers 30 ¢. If the retailers' margin is excluded, the multinational company which ripens and ships the bananas gets 84 per cent of the price paid by the importing country and the grower only 16 per cent. How much of this is a result of the transfer pricing phenomenon is, as seen earlier, an impenetrable mystery. The case of exports of iron ore to Japan, where only 15 per cent of the ore is carried in the exporter's (India, Australia or Brazil) ships, shows that earnings from exports of commodities need not necessarily come just from selling it. If increasing earnings, and unit values, of the exporting countries (particularly developing ones) is a valid objective then a coherent approach must take note of the decreasing share of the c.i.f. price received by the exporting country.

A reason for the declining share must be that developing countries as a whole have not been active participants in the actual marketing of products in the consuming countries. Most have been passive sellers on the international market; very few have even contemplated a market management policy. But all of them stop at the shores of the importing country, leaving the processing, packaging and promotion of the product to national firms in the importing countries. There is no reason why this should be so. The investment made by developing countries in promoting consumption of their products is negligible compared with what is spent by competitors. Even if they devoted say only 2 per cent of their realisation from exports of primary commodities, they would have a billion dollars a year to invest. Most governments, however, do not consider such expenditure as an investment but take the short-term view that the money spent is earnings foregone. In tropical beverages, if the coffee and tea producing countries devoted a fraction of the amount that soft drink manufacturers spend on advertising and promotion, they might well avert the long-term decline in per capita consumption and incidentally improve their prices. Very often attempts to promote such products (e.g. the Coffee Promotion Fund of the International Coffee Agreements) get bogged down on controversies about whether the promotion should be generic (promote coffee as such), uninational (promote, say, Colombian coffee) or by brand name. The controversy seems pointless, nobody buys tea because they have heard of the Taj Mahal. In most market economy countries brand consciousness and brand loyalty are facts of life. A reason for the reluctance to promote branded products is the very heavy investment required to launch a new brand against established ones. But promotion need not always take the form of a new brand; co-operation with a distributor with a small share of the market against the market leaders is one possibility. In many primary commodities which are not consumer products but raw material for some industry, promotion by providing market support, research and development is not an expensive proposition. In short, developing countries, with a few exceptions, have not been aggressive sellers. Many of them cannot play the market game according to its rules because they lack the necessary skills. The asymmetry in the development of world trade inhibits the acquisition of such skills by developing countries. The success achieved by some countries (e.g. Brazil, Korea) is proof that marketing skills can be learnt.

The reality of the market place has been the theme of this chapter. It may be closed; it may be open; it may be distorted; it may be uncomfortably competitive; it may be violent; but it exists. The people who act in it, whether government corporations, private companies or individual speculators, base their judgements on two things – facts and expectations. Facts are overhanging stocks, natural phenomena which affect supplies or acts of government which disturb the market. Expectations include judgements about how all these will change in the near future. This is where the market often diverges from the hopes of commodity negotiators. The buyers and sellers ignore what governments say they *intend* to do but act on what they think the governments *will* actually *do*. The dichotomy with which this chapter started boils down to this – how much confidence do the traders actually have in the proclaimed intentions of governments acting collectively? If commodity negotiations fail and agreements collapse it is often because the credibility gap is too wide.

Notes

1. US Council on International Economic Policy, Special Report, *Critical Imported Materials,* Washington DC, 1975.
2. Kenneth W. Clarfield, Stuart Jackson, Jeff Keefe, Michele Ann Noble and A. Patrick Ryan, *Eight Mineral Cartels: The New Challenge to Industrialized Nations* Metals Week (McGraw-Hill, New York).
3. UN, Department of Economic and Social Affairs, *Multinational Corporations in World Development* (Praeger, New York, 1974).
4. George L. Beckford, *Persistent Poverty: Under-development in Plantation Economies in the Third World* (Oxford University Press, London 1972).
5. UNCTAD *Review of International Trade and Development 1973.*
6. Wouter Tims, *Possible Effects of Trade Liberalization on Trade in Primary Commodities,* IBRD Staff Working Paper no.193.
7. Roy A. Ballinger, *A History of Sugar Marketing,* Agricultural Economic Report no.97 (US Department of Agriculture, Washington DC, 1971).
8. 'M.P. Cracknell, 'Fats and Oils: The Legal Framework of the World Market' and 'The Slippery Path to an Oilseeds Agreement', *Journal of World Trade Law,* 2, 1968, pp.401-44, and 4, 1970, pp.743-69.
9. Siegfried Mielke, 'World Supply and Demand Situation for Oilseed, Oils and Fats', *Quarterly Supplement,* Asian and Pacific Coconut Community, Jakarta, 30 September 1976 (mimeographed).
10. Ursula Wassermann, 'The Challenge of Synthetics: I — Textiles; II — Hides and Skins; III — Rubber; IV — Hard Fibres and Jute; and V — Lauric Oils', *Journal of World Trade Law* 5, 1971, pp.397-426, 672-93; 6, 1972, pp,300-26, 405-26; 7, 1973, pp.63-85.
11. Enzo R. Grilli, *The Future of Hard Fibres and Competition from Synthetics,* IBRD Staff Occasional Papers no.19 (Johns Hopkins University Press, Baltimore, 1975).
12. The debt to Grilli's book for almost verbatim extracts on the facts about production, marketing and competition from synthetics is acknowledged with gratitude.
13. See Table 2 in 'Pricing Policy, including Price Stabilization Measures and Mechanisms', Part I, Vol.II *Proceedings of the Third Session of UNCTAD* (UN, New York, 1973) pp.43-60.
14. Gale D. Johnson, 'World Agriculture, Commodity Policy and Price Variability', *American Journal of Agricultural Economics,* 1975, pp.823-8.
15. See the report on the speech by the chairman of LME in the Business Diary of *The Times,* 10 November 1976.
16. UNCTAD TD/B/C.1/171, W.C. Labys, *Speculation and Price Instability in International Commodity Futures Markets,* (Geneva, February 1975.
17. *The Economist,* 23-29 October 1976, 261 (6947), p.26.
18. Labys, *Speculation and Price Instability.*
19. Ursula Wassermann, 'Multi-commodity Approach to International Agreements', *Journal of World Trade Law,* 9, 1975, pp.463-7.

8 ACTS OF GOD AND MEN

I saw seven ears of grain full and fine growing on a single stalk. After them sprouted seven withered thin ears, blasted by the east wind. The thin ears swallowed up the seven fine ears.

Genesis 41 : 22, 23, 24

The international market watches politics as closely as it studies meteorology. Whether rain falls at the right time in India or a frost occurs in Brazil is important to any trader for judging expectations. Equally, a *coup d'état* in a producing country that might affect supply, or a war that might influence both demand and supply, are valid inputs for guessing what the future will bring. Acts of God and acts of man do affect commodity trading intimately. One need not go to extreme lengths to prove this point — such as considering the effect of a change in the US President or the case of a multinational company changing the government of a small country for a more amenable one. Production cycles, natural disasters, commodity booms, monetary instability and some kinds of international tension affect commodity trading more directly. In short, this chapter is concerned with the influence of the immediate extraneous environment on commodity negotiations.

Production Cycles

Production cycles appear to be as old as human agriculture; the Old Testament understanding of seven fat and seven lean years was based on the observed fact of a cyclical pattern of yields attributable to factors outside human control. Olive oil has a two-year production cycle. Cyclones and typhoons are annual events; monsoons in South Asia appear to fail in roughly two out of every five years; dust bowl conditions may occur once in 50 years. In 1975, the USSR had a bad grain crop due to an adverse 20-year drought cycle; in 1976, there was a potato famine in Western Europe. There are a few fortunate places in this world where climate does not affect production; for the most part, the occurrence of too much rain or too little, frost cyclones and even earthquakes is widespread. To these natural phenomena the distinction between perennial crops and annual crops adds its own cycle. Perennial crops, as seen in the case of oil-bearing trees, have long gestation periods; so does coffee, for it takes five years for a tree to become productive. Rubber and tea are other examples.

Production cycles affect supply and consequently prices, the effect depending on both the duration of the cycle and the magnitude of the change between the peak and the trough. If the cycle is as short as two years and the magnitude of the change is also manageable (as in olive oil), a simple solution — transferring surpluses to temporary shortage points — may suffice. If, on the other hand, the cycle is longer and the variation in production large, violent fluctuations in prices result. The phenomenon of a time lag between a price boom which encourages new planting and the crash which follows when the new crop is produced is one that recurs again and again in many agricultural commodities. Though they do not experience strictly a production cycle in the same sense as agricultural commodities, minerals also exhibit a similar time lag between the start of investment and the commencement of production. With the rapidly increasing costs of developing large mineral deposits, the delay in obtaining returns governs investment decisions more and more. A fluctuating price cycle, whether in renewable or non-renewable commodities, induces its own production cycle.

Commodity negotiations are influenced by production cycles in a number of ways. An important one is the way in which the attitudes of the exporting and importing countries change at different points of the cycle. To take an example, Table 8.1 shows the total world production of cocoa and the New York spot price for a standard quality for different years. While total world production has been gradually expanding, the ups and downs are clearly visible. World production averaged only about 800,000 tons in the early 1950s; it rose to an average level of 1.2 million tons by the early 1960s. This rapid growth was matched by a rising demand for cocoa until 1964-5, when exceptionally favourable weather resulted in a record crop. In that year, world new supplies of over 1.5 million tons far exceeded demand leading to a severe fall in prices. In the previous year, at the UN Cocoa Conference in September 1963, the exporters had sought a price target of 27 ¢ per lb, higher than the then prevailing prices but below the prices of 1955-7; the importers were offering 20 ¢ per lb, below even current prices, a price that anticipated a fall fairly soon, since a good year was imminent. The price did fall; in the futures market, which is a better guide of market expectations, the New York 3-month futures fell from 22 ¢ per lb in January 1963 to an all-time low of 10.5 ¢ per lb in July 1965. Such low prices, though they stimulated demand, curtailed

Table 8.1 Cocoa Production and Prices

Year	Total World Production (in thousand tons)	New York spot price (Ghana — US¢ a lb.)
1955-7 average	853	31.8
1962	1212	21.0
1963	1215	25.3
1964	1520	23.4
1965	1225	17.5
1966	1345	24.4
1967	1364	29.1
1968	1214	34.4
1969	1416	45.7
1970	1464	34.2
1971	1520	26.8
1972	1589	32.3
1973	1412	64.4
1974	1441	98.1
1975	1549[a]	74.8
1976	1465[b]	96.4[c]

a — Preliminary   c — January to September
b — Estimate
Source: FAO *Commodity Review,* various issues

plans for expanding production. The 1964 bumper crop was followed by four consecutive years of shortage, when production was less than the requirement for current consumption and normal stocks. There was a slight surplus in 1969/70 and the 1970/1 crop turned out to be even bigger. By this time world grindings had reached a level of 1.5 million tons. There was a balance in 1972/3, but the subsequent decline in output during the boom pushed up prices to over $1 per lb. Even a long cycle can be managed if other factors do not intervene. Provided consumption continues to grow at trend levels, new exporters do not emerge and civil wars and disturbances do not happen in producing countries, a stocking policy might work. Unfortunately, all these misfortunes do happen to cocoa.

The above example shows that production cycles sharpen the importer/exporter conflict on prices. The exporters have the greatest interest in concluding a regulatory agreement when there is a large surplus accompanied by low prices. They attempt to obtain a floor price which will approximate to the high prices they had enjoyed a few years before. On the other hand, the importers are guided in their counter-offer by current prices and the expected direction of movement in the near future. Neither exporters nor importers are infallible in predicting the future supply and price movements. One example of importer fallibility cited earlier (chapter 4) was the consistent over-estimating of future supplies by consuming countries in the Tin Agreements.

Another effect of production cycles is that conditions may change drastically between the time an agreement is negotiated and the time it comes into force, or during its life. Two examples of how the supply situation changed suddenly while an International Coffee Agreement was being negotiated have been cited earlier; both the 1962 and 1976 Agreements started in the first year after a substantial fall in Brazilian export surplus. This raises an interesting question – at what point in the production cycle should an agreement start so that it has the best chance of survival? If the agreement starts at a wrong point – wrong in the sense of the price level not being valid for the life of the agreement – then it is bound to feel the strains when the market price diverges too far from that written in it and a collapse follows. The life of the agreement itself has something to do with it; normally agreements are concluded for a period of five years (coffee, sugar, tin), sometimes for three (wheat). Indeed, the Havana Charter lays down the law thus: 'Commodity Control Agreements *shall* be concluded for a period of *not more than five years.*' Why? Those who framed the Charter must have intended that the period should not be so long that changes in production and consumption would make the agreement unrealistic nor too short for it to achieve the objectives of restoring stability; five was as good a number as four, six or seven. The mistake was in assuming that this dictum was applicable to all commodities at all times. This is one more example of the rigidity that characterises the Charter's conception of commodity agreements.

Commodity Booms

If the price of a commodity rises sharply, it is just an upward fluctuation; if this happens to a number of commodities simultaneously it is generally called a 'commodity boom'. Since the end of the Second World War, there have been two short periods when there was a general upswing in commodity prices – the Korean War boom and the recent one, as yet unnamed, of 1973/4. The Korean War boom came about for a number of reasons. The return of peace released a certain amount of pent-up demand for consumer goods and the infusion of the Marshall Plan money promoted rapid industrial recovery in Western Europe; demand for food, fibres and industrial raw materials rose sharply. Production increases requiring a longer gestation period could not keep pace with increase in demand. On top of this, the politics of confrontation of the Cold War added a further demand for purposes of stockpiling. The Korean War pushed prices up still further. In contrast, the 1973/4 boom occurred at a time of reduced international tension. As in the Korean War boom there was a sharp increase in demand; in 1973 and 1974, this was brought about by the simultaneous upward swing of the business cycle in leading industrialised countries. The gap between increased demand and available supply was exacerbated by the fortuitous coincidence of shortages in a number of commodities. Other contributory causes were worldwide inflation and international monetary instability. The second boom was also less universal than the first and left some commodities (e.g. tea, jute and iron ore) virtually unaffected.

The fact that not all commodities benefit from the boom prompts the questions − who gains and by how much? Most observers implicitly assume that a commodity boom, being of a generalised nature, must benefit all exporters equally. The corollary is the assumption that the gains of the boom are distributed equally between the developed and developing countries. Are these assumptions borne out by the experience of 1973 and 1974? The answer to this question is one more test of the fairness of the operation of the international economic system. In the analysis which follows, oil, for reasons reiterated earlier, is again excluded. An additional reason is that, while the oil price rise and the commodity boom may have happened at the same time, they arose out of different causes. Co-ordinated action by producers to raise prices and control supplies is quite different from a fortuitous coincidence of high demand and supply shortage in a number of commodities.

There are a number of ways of looking at the distribution of gains during a boom. Table 3.4 show that primary commodity exports earned developed countries US $51.5 billion in 1970; earnings increased by 86.7 per cent to US $96.1 billion in 1973. The increase in 1974 over 1970 was even higher − by 133 per cent to nearly US $120 billion. The increase in earnings over 1970 for developing countries was significantly smaller − 57.4 per cent in 1973 (from US $ 26.6 billion to US $41.9 billion) and 115 per cent (to US $57.2 billion) in 1974. The centrally planned economy countries had average gains in 1973 but were worse off than even the developing countries in 1974.

The fact that, as between market economy countries, the richer ones had greater gains could be because (i) the commodities exported by them experienced higher than average price rise, (ii) their market shares increased at the expense of the developing countries, or (iii) because of both causes. Table 8.2 shows the value of market economy exports and the share of developed and developing countries for the years 1970, 1973 and 1974 classified according to type of product. Since both the latter years were boom years, the average of the two years is used to deduce the following conclusions. Overall, the share of the developed countries increased from 66 per cent to 69.5 per cent. The increase was most marked in agricultural commodities, 63.5 per cent to 68 per cent. In non-ferrous minerals and metals too the rich countries' share increased from 52 per cent to 56 per cent. There was a fall in the share of the market for forest products, though by 1974 it was almost made up. The increase in raw material costs in the case of synthetic rubber and synthetic fibres did not reduce the competitiveness of the rich countries.

These broad aggregates are broken down into individual commodities in Table 8.3; for the sake of simplicity in presentation, only the total value of exports and the share of the developed countries is shown in the table for the selected years. These figures too tell the same story. Overall, in the 59 commodities listed (accounting for about 70 per cent of all primary commodity exports), the share of the developed countries increased by over 5 per cent; while they registered a gain of 220 per cent in the two boom years, on average the developing countries managed only 178 per cent over 1970.

The table shows clearly that there was no boom in tea and jute and only a limited one in iron ore. For most of the other commodities, both 1972 and 1974 were boom years; 1974 was almost always the better of the two. Only meat, wine, hides and skins and oil cake showed a reduction in 1974 compared with 1973. The most dramatic increases happened in natural phosphates (sevenfold in 1974 compared with 1970), sugar, maize and zinc (three and a half times) and wheat (over three times). Increases of three to four times were common in many oilseeds, oils and oilcakes. Many other commodities doubled their earnings. In contrast, coffee and cocoa experienced an increase of only one and a half times. With the exception of phosphates and sugar, most of the commodities with higher than average increases are of predominant export interest only to developed countries.

This conclusion is also substantiated by contrasting the commodities

Table 8.2. Market Economy Exports of Primary Commodities during a Boom (Value US $ millions)

Source		1970 Total Exports	1970 Developed Value	%	Developing Value	%	1973 Total Exports	1973 Developed Value	%	Developing Value	%	1974 Total Exports	1974 Developed Value	%	Developing Value	%
FAO	Total Agricultural products	49210	31299	63.6	17911	36.4	89280	61518	68.9	27762	31.1	107486	72130	67.1	35356	32.9
FAO	Total Forestry products	11213	9724	86.7	1489	13.3	19999	16525	82.6	3473	17.4	25818	22248	86.2	3571	13.8
UN	Hides, Leather, Synthetic rubber and fibres	2987	2542	85.1	445	14.9	5953	5126	86.1	827	13.9	6691	5981	89.4	710	10.6
UN	Non-ferrous base metals, ores, concentrates	10660	5528	51.9	5132	48.1	13225	7431	56.2	5794	43.8	19974	11150	55.8	8824	44.2
UN	Iron ore and natural fertilisers	2676	1386	51.8	1290	48.2	3379	1820	53.9	1559	46.1	5658	2392	42.3	3266	57.7
	Total	76746	50479	65.8	26267	34.2	131836	92420	70.1	39415	29.9	165627	113901	68.8	51727	31.2

Table 8.3. Changes in Size of Market and Share of Developed Countries during a Boom

No.	SITC (Rev.) No.	Commodity	Size of Market (US $ million)			Share of Developed Countries %		
			1970	1973	1974	1970	1973	1974
		Meat, fresh, chilled or frozen						
1.	011.1	Beef	1797	3937	3709	70	71	82
2.	011.2-.8	Other meat and poultry	1440	2946	2865	92	91	92
		Cereals						
3.	041,046	Wheat and wheat flour	3055	7796	9893	95	95	97
4.	042	Rice	999	1385	2287	55	58	53
5.	044	Maize	1691	4247	6038	72	86	82
6.	043,045	Barley, oats, rye, etc.	953	2193	2999	84	87	85
		Fruit, fresh or dried						
7.	051.1, .2	Citrus fruit	653	966	1022	75	69	75
8.	051.3	Bananas	476	622	638	8	6	7
9.	052.03	Raisins	130	276	323	66	58	59
		Sugar						
10.	061.1	Raw sugar	1913	3327	6916	10	15	9
11.	061.2	Refined sugar	382	921	1464	68	79	68
		Tropical beverages						
12.	071.1	Coffee, green or roasted	3081	4322	4469	–	–	–
13.	072.1	Cocoa beans	862	945	1585	–	–	–
14.	072.2, .3	Cocoa powder, paste, butter	279	424	660	54	51	49
15.	074.1	Tea	640	693	793	–	–	–
		Spices						
16.	Ex.075.1	Pepper	93	144	194	–	–	–
		Tobacco						
17.	121	Unmanufactured tobacco	1146	1667	2189	64	59	59
		Alcoholic beverages						
18.	112.1	Wine	829	1929	1755	79	88	90

Table 8.3 Continued

No.	SITC (Rev.) No.	Commodity	Size of Market (US $ million)			Share of Developed Countries %		
			1970	1973	1974	1970	1973	1974
		Oilseeds, nuts and kernels						
19.	221.4	Soyabeans	1252	3297	4150	98	85	85
20.	221.1	Groundnuts	210	319	431	20	35	44
21.	221.2, .3	Copra, palm nuts and kernels	237	278	400	—	—	—
22.	221.6, .8	Cotton seed, sesame, sunflower seed	105	181	277	25	40	42
23.	Ex.221.8	Rape and mustard seed	158	350	425	85	100	100
24.	221.5, .7	Linseed, castor seed	79	169	204	85	78	82
		Vegetable oils						
25.	421.2	Soyabean oil	311	374	1069	99	87	98
26.	421.5	Olive oil	173	406	454	85	63	53
27.	421.4	Groundnut oil	143	217	305	17	27	28
28.	422.2, .4	Palm oil, Palm kernel oil	251	457	1120	9	10	9
29.	422.3	Coconut oil	188	264	614	11	19	15
30.	421.3, .6, .7	Other edible oils	152	307	511	73	87	94
31.	422.1, .5	Technical oils (linseed, castor, tung)	116	275	368	20	25	32
		Butter, lard, animal oils						
32.	023	Butter	586	1038	1232	100	100	100
33.	091.3	Lard	101	113	194	100	100	100
34.	411.3	Animal oils and fats	337	498	847	85	95	100
35.	091.4	Margarine	55	106	184	79	88	86
		Oil cake						
36.		Soyabean cake	505	1843	1756	91	77	82
37.		Groundnut cake	131	264	205	4	5	4
38.		Other oil cake	289	576	513	23	34	35
		Rubber						
39.	231.1	Natural rubber	1509	2580	3140	—	—	—
40.	231.2	Synthetic rubber	573	892	1347	100	100	100

Table 8.3 Continued

No.	SITC (Rev.) No.	Commodity	Size of Market (US $ million)			Share of Developed Countries %		
			1970	1973	1974	1970	1973	1974
		Forestry products						
41.	241,242	Industrial roundwood	1540	3334	3610	47	43	43
42.	243	Sawn wood	2126	4699	4894	84	86	86
43.	Ex.251	Wood pulp	2418	3182	5294	98	98	97
		Fibres						
44.	262.1, .2	Wool	1435	2808	2863	88	89	90
45.	263.1	Raw cotton	2112	3493	4271	21	31	35
46.	264	Jute and similar fibres	215	227	229	—	—	—
47.	265.4, .5	Sisal, abaqa, henequen	90	170	362	—	—	—
48.	266	Synthetic and regenerated fibres	936	1910	2508	99	99	99
		Hides, skins and leather						
49.	211	Hides and skins	777	1695	1417	71	82	82
50.	611	Leather	701	1456	1419	70	66	72
		Minerals						
51.	271.3	Phosphate rock	271	470	1940	35	28	16
52.	281	Iron ore	2109	2943	3786	60	57	55
53.	283	Non-ferrous base metal ores	3386	4570	6367	48	50	48
		Metals — unwrought						
54.	682.1	Copper	3941	4309	7238	33	39	45
55.	683.1	Nickel	760	850	991	97	97	97
56.	684.1	Aluminium	1259	1538	2247	94	92	91
57.	685.1	Lead	393	455	714	80	87	80
58.	686.1	Zinc	327	773	1196	79	90	89
59.	687.1	Tin	594	730	1221	21	20	19
		Total listed commodities	52,270	93,156	122,112	57.4	63.2	61.8
		of which						
		Developed countries	30,555	58,906	75,414			
		Developing countries	22,715	34,250	46,698			

Sources: for agricultural products, FAO *Trade Yearbook,* 1975; for forestry products
FAO *Yearbook of Forestry Products,* 1974; for minerals, metals, synthetic products
hides etc, UN *Yearbook of International Trade Statistics,* 1974 and 1975, supplemented by IBRD and UNCTAD data.

which are almost wholly (over 95 per cent) exported by the rich countries with those almost wholly exported by the poor. Wheat, woodpulp, synthetic fibres, synthetic rubber, butter and lard registered an average increase in 1973 and 1974 of 133 per cent over 1970. (Even if the synthetic products are excluded on the grounds of the impact of the oil price rise on costs of production, the figure for the rest is still 131 per cent.) On the other hand, the increases in tropical beverages, pepper, natural rubber and jute, which the developed countries do not export at all, was only 51 per cent.

Did the boom lead to shifts in market shares? Taking only those commodities in which there was a change of more than 5 per cent, one sees that the rich countries increased their share of the market in beef, maize, wine, oils, cotton, hides and skins and zinc. The poor countries increased their share of the market in tobacco, phosphates, copper and oilcake; the change in the share of the soyabean and products was not due to the boom but to the emergence of one new exporter, Brazil. On the whole, the developed countries increased their share in more products and more valuable products.

Whichever way one looks at it — overall increase in earnings, the quantum of increase in different commodities, the change in market shares — the developed countries did significantly better out of the boom than the poor ones. It may be argued that developed countries show a greater short-term efficiency in booms, i.e. they are better able to take quick advantage of improved market conditions. Even if this were true, the inequitable distribution of gains, even during a boom, cannot but strengthen the perception of the developing countries that the international economic system is unfair and tends to push them to the periphery faster. This basic inequity does not imply that the distribution within the developing world was any more equitable. It is undeniable that exporters of sugar and phosphates fared much better than exporters of tea, jute or iron ore. The difficulty arises in assuming that the increase in prosperity of a few large exporters of sugar and a couple of exporters of rock phosphate is shared by the bulk of the developing countries. Angus Hone's judgement, in the paper quoted in Chapter 4, is that 'the losers are a small group' is not substantiated by his own conclusion. 'The commodity boom has increased the resources of 800-900 million people in the Middle East, South East Asia, Latin America and parts of Africa . . . The Prospects for the 900-1,000 million in South Asia and the least developed world will be very bleak indeed.'[1] If one excluded the OPEC countries, the gaining group is not as numerous as is made out. There are many more losers, both in terms of the number of countries and the number of people involved. It must also be emphasised that, among the developing countries, the richer have gained and the poorer have lost. This is another proof that the international economic system operates in such a way that, in any segment of the spectrum of nations, the richer gain more than those further down the line.

If in a single commodity an upswing in prices reduces the keenness of exporters to conclude agreements, the effect of a boom should be similar and more widespread. The price range that could be inscribed in any agreement, with the consent of the importers, would be much less than the prevailing boom prices; exporters are unlikely to agree to this since they do not want to forego a short-term gain and since an agreement might have the effect of moderating the boom itself. One would expect that commodity negotiations in general would receive a setback at such times – existing agreements would fail to function and no new ones would be concluded. This is clearly seen in the Korean War boom. The Inter-American Coffee Agreement was liquidated in 1948 and negotiations were not revived for six years, i.e. until after the boom had abated. The first post-war UN Conference on Sugar was only held in 1953. A proof of the reluctance of exporters to delay concluding an agreement until the boom was about to spend itself was the failure of the 1950 UN Tin Conference. The negotiators at this Conference agreed on the mechanisms of control including the creation of a buffer stock and the role of the buffer stock manager. The Conference was unable to reach full agreement partly because of the attitude of the United States and partly because of exporters' hesitations. By 1953, when the International Tin Study Group met again, the boom was over and the First Tin Agreement became possible.

The vicissitudes of the International Sugar Agreement 1968 provide another example. The agreement contained supply commitment provisions to take care of situations in which market prices rose above the ceiling price written in it. Quotas were then suspended, exporting members' minimum stocks released and they were obliged to supply member-importers' requirement at agreed commitment prices. This set of provisions introduced a degree of flexibility to protect the interests of consuming members even when conditions were abnormal. During 1972 and 1973, importers exercised their options during five 30-day periods. As against a price range of 3.25 ¢ to 5.25 ¢ per lb the original commitment price was 6.50 ¢ per lb. This was raised to 6.95 ¢ per lb in 1971 and again in 1972 to 7.60 ¢ to take account of dollar devaluation. But by October 1973 the London Daily Price had shot up to the equivalent of 9 ¢ per lb, by early 1974 to 24 ¢ per lb and, in the panic that gripped the market, some shipments were exchanged at even higher prices. When the divergence between the market price and the commitment price became too great, the commitment provisions also collapsed. This careening of prices had its effect on the 1973 UN Conference on Sugar. The exporters started negotiations with a price ceiling objective of 11 ¢ per lb, clearly influenced by boom prices. They later brought it down in negotiations to first 9.5 ¢ and then to 9 ¢. The importers started with a ceiling offer of 7.0 ¢ per lb and were thought to be willing to raise it to 7.60 ¢. A compromise 'split-the-difference' proposal for a range of 5.40 ¢ to 7.90 ¢ failed to gain acceptance.

Inflation and Recession

The 1973/4 boom occurred at a time of great instability in the international economic system, with worldwide inflation and international monetary instability. The boom continued in 1974, with the energy crisis superimposed on an already chaotic world economy. The high rates of inflation in the industrialised countries may also have contributed to the rise in commodity prices. They were clearly a factor, in the eyes of the developing countries, in the deterioration in their terms of trade. In the decade 1950-9, the UN unit value index for manufactured goods (1953 = 100) moved from 96 to 107, an increase of about 11 per cent; in the 1960s the rate of increase was again 11 per cent. In fact, in the 20 years 1950 to 1969 the prices of manufactured goods (1950 = 88 and 1969 = 110, both on 1963 = 100 basis) went up by just 20 per cent. The index then shot up as follows:

$$(1963 = 100)$$
$$1970 = 117$$
$$1971 = 124$$
$$1972 = 134$$
$$1973 = 156$$
$$1974 = 186$$
$$1975 = 213$$

In the first six years of the 1970s, the increase was nearly 80 per cent. To the extent that the commodity boom was not just one which raised commodity prices but was part of a worldwide inflation, the developing countries did not gain any additional import purchasing power.

If inflation in developed countries affects the poor countries, what about recession? The survey of international trade 1975-6 by GATT provides the answer.

In 1975, almost all commodity prices continued the decline begun in 1974 from their peaks of the 1972-74 commodity boom; this was the result of the recession in industrial areas and, for some raw materials, of the strong tendency to run down stocks. Although demand in the main industrial countries had been recovering since mid-1975, commodity prices began to rise only at the beginning of 1976 . . . The value of exports of primary products by industrial countries rose by 3 per cent in 1975, due to an increase of 8 per cent in exports of food . . . In 1975, the recession in industrial countries brought about the steepest contraction of the post-War period, roughly 8 per cent, in the volume of exports from developing countries taken as a group . . . The value of exports of oil-importing developing countries remained in 1975 at about the same level as in 1974. Their share in world exports, which had slightly increased (to almost 12 per cent) in 1973 and 1974, fell back to its level (11 per cent) in 1971 and 1972 . . . The combined trade deficit (f.o.b. − c.i.f.) of the oil-importing developing countries, which had almost trebled between 1973 and 1974, reaching $34 billion, rose further to $45 billion in 1975. This record deficit occurring in spite of the decline in the volume of imports, resulted from the stagnation of export earnings and the continued rise in prices of imports, which in 1975 was concentrated on manufactures.[2]

Inflation reduces the import purchasing power of developing countries; recession cuts down their export earnings but manufactured goods' prices continue to increase. It is a permanent state of 'heads you win, tails I lose.' The rich countries argue that controlling inflation, combating recession and pursuing policies of growth will do more for the problems of the developing countries than commodity agreements or indexation. Maybe so; growth without inflation may solve some problems. The only nagging doubt is whether this alone will suffice; so far the history has shown that it has only led to an increasingly autarkic economic system, mainly benefiting the rich.

The International Monetary System

The international monetary system is also an essential part of the immediate economic environment and is intimately related to commodity negotiations. For the purposes of this book, it is not necessary to go into the whys and wherefores of the chaos that has characterised the system for the last five or six years. It is sufficient to note that it is highly unstable; fixed exchange rates have been abandoned; the dollar has lost its primacy as a stable trading currency; much trumpeted 'agreements of the century' — the Smithsonian of December 1971 — collapse within a few months. Everybody floats; they cannot decide whether to sink or swim; in any case, *terra firma* does not enter into anyone's calculations. It is argued that traders make their own adjustments in a floating world and cover themselves suitably by forward purchases. This does not help commodity negotiations in which one has to deal with price objectives in some acceptable currency. Price ranges have to be written down in pounds and pence or dollars and cents. So long as there was a reasonable certainty of exchange rates, negotiators could attempt to project three or five years ahead and seek a solution to their already complex conflicts. Isolated changes in parity were troublesome but were not insoluble problems. Every time the pound was devalued the prices in the International Tin Agreement had to be renegotiated. It was never a simple case of just multiplying old prices by the new ratio. It is a fact of life that whenever a subject is reopened negotiations have to start almost from scratch; every part-icipant seeks to obtain the maximum advantage from the revision process. The change in the supply commitment price of sugar, quoted earlier, provides another example. If the price were changed by the extent of the US dollar devaluation, it would not necessarily have been fair to Canada or Japan, who are major buyers of free market sugar. Monetary instability affects other commodities also; one of the reasons for the collapse of the 1968 International Coffee Agreement in December 1972 was the difference of opinion on the price range after the devaluation and floating of the dollar.

So far no attempts seem to have been made to relate prices in commodity negotiations to special drawing rights (SDRs). To link prices to a theoretical currency standard may not be of much help, since very often agreements contain triggering mechanisms. For example, quotas are automatically enhanced or reduced and buffer stocks released or bought if prices remain for a number of days above or below a level. If monetary floating uncertainty is also to be superimposed on the commodity fluctuation, decisions may not be clear-cut and no action may be taken even if warranted. While the EEC has successfully used a mythical 'unit of account' for its transaction, its use of a set of 'green currencies' for the CAP has not been a happy one. When the value of one national currency drops in relation to others but its 'green' rate stays the same, the country in effect gets a subsidy on its imports. For example, the United Kingdom with a steadily depreciating currency has been gaining more than £500 million a year in subsidies, or

Monetary Compensation Amounts (MCAs) in EEC jargon. Between the country with the strongest currency (the German mark) and one with the weakest (the pound) the distortion is a massive 43 per cent.[3] With this experience, the use of a standard rate for a variety of commodities on a worldwide scale does not look like a feasible proposition.

From the developing countries' point of view, the impact of monetary instability is more serious. The concept of assuring earnings is based upon protecting the import purchasing power from fluctuations in price. If prices are expressed in a depreciating currency, the very concept loses its reason for existence. Hence the suggestion fron oil-producing countries for an 'OPEC dollar' or from the International Bauxite Association for a 'bauxite dollar'. These ideas have met with predictable resistance from the importing countries; given a choice, every buyer would rather pay in a depreciating currency than in a stable one. But the illogicality of the position has to be recognised. One cannot claim to protect the earnings of poor countries while simultaneously paying them in an uncertain coin. The developing countries have little economic muscle to do anything about the chaotic monetary situation. It is only the rich countries which can restore some semblance of order so that even a floating market can be anchored to some fixed point.

The Political Environment

The immediate environment of commodity negotiations also includes the political environment, especially in the exporting countries. A war in Angola affects supplies of coffee as much as frost in Brazil. The conflict between Bangla Desh and Pakistan affected the jute market as much as cyclone damage. It is true, however, that all international disturbances do not affect commodity negotiations in the same manner or to the same extent. The Korean War is forever associated with the boom and the West Asian crisis with oil. Other international crisis, such as in the Congo or Vietnam, had much less impact on commodity negotiations because they did not involve a very large exporter. On the other hand, the fact that Cuba was the world's largest exporter of sugar and the United States the largest importer meant that the tension between the two would bedevil sugar negotiations for a very long time. The rights and wrongs of the dispute are not relevant to this book — only its effect on the sugar market, in which, apart from Cuba and the United States, a host of other countries were, and are, vitally interested.

The point stressed in relation to sugar is that trade was mostly under preferential arrangements and that only a small residue was traded freely. The effect of the US – Cuban tension was to change structurally the shares of the free markets. Table 8.4 shows the changes in the major preferential markets during the three crisis years – 1959, 1960 and 1961. In 1969, Cuba exported over 3 million tons of sugar to the US. The US Sugar Act was amended in July 1960 and the President, on the same day that he signed the law, reduced the Cuban quota to zero. Almost overnight an additional quantity of 2.5 tons was thrown on the open market. The US

Table 8.4 Imports of sugar by preferential markets 1959, 1960 and 1961 (Thousand tons)

| Year | Total | United States | | UK net imports | USSR net imports |
		Cuba	Others		
1959	4474	3215	1259	2194	148
1960	4900	2390	2600	1973	1602
1961	4420	0	4420	2191	2917

Source: Roy A. Ballinger, *A History of Sugar Marketing,* Agricultural Economic Report no.97 (US Department of Agriculture, Washington DC, 1971).

preferential market continued to exist after the Cuban cut-off and the Cuban quota was redistributed. At that time possession of a US quota was money in the bank; it not only meant assured sales but also higher prices than in the free market. The redistribution was therefore done in accordance with the political priorities of the United States. In the words of the US Sugar Act, special consideration was to be given to 'countries of the Western Hemisphere and to those countries purchasing United States agricultural commodities'. Most of the redistributed quantities went to the Dominican Republic, Mexico, the Philippines, Peru, Brazil, the British West Indies and British Guyana. The re-distribution had the effect of stimulating production in those countries. But the Cuban sugar which could not be sold to the United States did not disappear. The net result was over-production and very low prices for the next decade, except for two years (1963 and 1964) when there was a shortage because of natural causes. The Cuban cut-off was the economic consequence of a political decision; as a result of the same political environment, the Soviet Union provided greatly enlarged access to Cuban sugar. To the extent that a large part of the sugar found another preferential haven, both Cuba and other exporters derived some benefit. The USSR did re-export some of the Cuban sugar to world markets. Between 1961 and 1963, USSR exports were about a million tons each year, whereas between 1954 and 1959, before the onset of the crisis, exports had averaged only about a quarter of a million tons. Thus about 750,000 tons of Cuban sugar were re-exported to world markets. The USSR's imports of Cuban sugar were substantially more — in 1961 4 million tons and in the first three years of the crisis an average of nearly 3 million tons. The USSR thus absorbed between 2.5 to 3 million tons in the first three years and over 2 million tons thereafter. 'Nearly all imports by the USSR and Mainland China came from Cuba and appear to have been intended as a means of assisting that country economically.'[4] The offtake by the USSR reduced the pressure on the free market, thus preventing prices from collapsing to even lower levels.

The Cuban sugar crisis contains examples of the whole gamut of conflicts of interest in commodity negotiations. When there is an insoluble political conflict between the biggest importer and the biggest exporter, the whole market for the commodity is shaken to its foundations and it takes a very long time to recover. Conflicts among exporters were sharpened; there was a scramble for the redistribution of the Cuban quota and another one for sales in the free market overburdened with supplies. More countries acquired a stake in preferential markets; international agreements had to exclude these and concentrate only on the free market. A global approach to sugar marketing became impossible. Not until 1969 could a new International Sugar Agreement be negotiated. Even then it was full of holes: the United States did not become a member; the EEC decided to stay out and dump sugar on the market; exports to centrally planned countries were outside the agreement and the USSR was allowed to re-export 1.1 million tons of Cuban sugar imported by that country.

Sugar is thus super-power politics. Where the super powers do not intervene, the effects of international tension may not be so long-lived. In the Bangla Desh crisis of 1971, the largest exporter of raw jute was involved in a conflict. Had it persisted for a long time, the continued disruption of supplies and high prices would have prompted a permanent shift to synthetic substitutes. However, no importers were directly involved. The relatively smaller disruption in the export of jute manufactures from India, the short duration of the conflict and its confinement to a limited geographical area all helped to prevent a major structural change in the jute market. Thus one can conclude that duration, extent of involvement and the importance to a commodity of the countries involved in a conflict determine how much it will be affected.

The political environment also has a relevance to production prospects, particularly in the case of minerals. As more developing countries became independent, they ceased to be automatic recipients of investment from the metropolitan countries; at the same time, their own limited resources were needed for increasing food production, commencing industrialisation and urgent social welfare programmes. The investment needs were sought from foreign capital, primarily through multinational companies. In deciding to invest in a developing country, such companies are not only influenced by the long-run price trend which determines profitability but also by the so-called investment climate. The evolving disenchantment with the operation of the companies, described in the last chapter, has had an impact on investment, made more serious by the ever-increasing size of the financing required. One way of coping with this problem, through an International Resources Bank, is referred to in Chapter 13.

To say that wars, hostilities and international tension affect international economic relations is commonplace. The purpose of drawing attention to these factors is not to arrive at the equally trite conclusion that these should be avoided. No one can predict when political tensions will erupt; nor can one predict with any degree of certainty when a frost or a drought will occur. One can only examine the effect of unpredictability of the immediate environment on commodity negotiations. The effects often last a long time; the delay in return to normalcy and a degree of stability is detrimental to the health of the international economy. A constructive approach to the resolution of international commodity problems must include adequate flexibility to cope with abnormal conditions and speed up a return to a more orderly state.

Notes

1. Angus Hone, 'Gainers and Losers in the 1973 Commodity Boom: Developing Countries Prospects to 1980', *ODI Review* 1, 1974, pp.24-37.
2. GATT, *International Trade 1975-76.*
3. For details of the gap between 'green' and actual exchange rates and details of MCAs see *The Economist,* 19-25 February 1977, 262 (6964), pp.56-8.
4. Roy A. Ballinger, *A History of Sugar Marketing,* Agricultural Economic Report no.97 (US Department of Agriculture, Washington DC, 1971).

9 TECHNIQUES OF REGULATION

Labham prajanam aupaghatakam varayet.
(Exploitation of markets or consumers is prohibited.)

Kautilya's Arthasastra (3rd century BC)

He is a merchant and balances of deceit are in his hand.

Hosea 12:7

The 35 commodities chosen for this study were classified in Chapter 3 under nine different characteristics on the grounds that these, and the relationships they engender, must help to identify the possible techniques that could be used to arrive at agreements on regulation. It is therefore appropriate to consider the mechanics of regulation before discussing the feasibility of their implementation. The whole range of available techniques will be analysed with the obvious proviso that not all techniques are applicable to all the commodities. Indeed, the same ones may not be applicable to the same commodities at different times.

The need for a flexible mix of techniques to deal with different problems at different times was emphasised in the last chapter as a result of the analysis of the unpredictability of the immediate environment. The aim in this chapter is not to produce a theoretical study of the mechanisms, treating them as operating under ideal conditions. For example, in discussing quota mechanisms, one can draw theoretical supply/demand curves for different prices over a period and draw conclusions on the quantities that should ideally be exported at any given time. But such projections, however valid theoretically, often fail either because the participants do not behave as the curves demand or because the unexpected happens. Here the techniques are examined for their effectiveness as they have operated and can be expected to operate in the real world of traders and governments.

Commodity Characteristics and Regulatory Techniques

The first classification made in Chapter 3 was a basic one between renewable and non-renewable products, mainly justified by the argument that the problems of the two types are significantly different; consequently the mechanisms best suited to either group are also different. The second characteristic identified was the occurrence in a commodity of periodic surpluses or shortages. The shortages problem is

218

more easily resolved in non-renewable commodities by adequate investment in increasing production; the price of the commodity at all times has to be such as to provide the appropriate incentive to invest, assuming that there are no political disincentives and that it is not so high as to encourage over-production. This is more easily said than done, and the problem is made more difficult in agricultural commodities by the additional factor of shortages occurring from natural causes. For these commodities something more becomes necessary. Production surpluses can only be regulated by controlling the quantities entering the market. Three kinds of inter-related control techniques can be distinguished. In the short term, quantities exported can be controlled by quota mechanisms, in the medium term by quotas and control of stocks and in the longer term by production control and encouragement of diversification. It goes without saying that there is also an integral relationship between the quota and stock mechanisms and the regulation of prices in the free market. Whether production control succeeds or not depends on the degree to which the producer is susceptible to control; this was identified as the third group of characteristics. Likewise, the success of stock arrangements depends on the fourth characteristic — the cost of storage as well as the period for which a commodity can be stored without deterioration.

Just as the first four characteristics have an inter-related bearing on the techniques that can be used, those identified under location of production, market access and future growth are also inter-related. The demand aspect of quantities traded was examined in chapter 6 primarily as a case of access. In chapter 7 mention was made of increasing the demand for commodities produced mainly in developing countries by market development, promotion of consumption and research and development of new uses. For commodities produced in both developed and developing countries, it was seen that access and prices were closely associated with protectionism, sometimes mitigated by the effects of preferential arrangements. In discussing prices, competition from synthetics, fluctuation and decline were identified as three main problems, in addition to the need to tackle the artificiality of prices in closed markets.

Throughout this study, it has been emphasised that earnings are a target by themselves and not merely a result of the regulation of quantities and prices. Reference has been made to increasing unit values by promoting processing and earnings by a greater share in shipping and distribution. Measures specifically directed to assuring stability of earnings have yet to be considered. At various points reference has also been made to the form in which the appropriate set of techniques are to be put together — in a formal treaty framework, informal arrangements or through producer co-operation. The main distinction between formal and informal arrangements is that the commitments are more binding in a treaty; consequently, it is more usual to include penalty provisions and mechanics of discipline in such agreements. The nature of the supervisory mechanisms and the effectiveness of disciplinary provisions must also be examined. The circumstances in which many of the techniques above work — or fail to work — have been described in examples in earlier chapters. Only the conclusions about their effectiveness will be stated in this chapter. Techniques not illustrated earlier (such as production control and diversification, buffer stocks and other stock control mechanisms, earnings stabilisation schemes and problems of supervision and control) will be analysed in greater detail.

The various techniques can be listed and grouped as follows:

1. Regulation of export quantities by controlling supply

   (i) Quota mechanisms
   (ii) Production controls
   (iii) Diversification

2. Regulation of export quantities by controlling stocks

   (i) Buffer stocks
   (ii) National stocks under international financing and control
   (iii) National stocks under national financing and control
   (iv) Orderly disposal of surpluses

3. Demand aspects of quantities

   (i) Quantitative assurance of access
   (ii) Removal or reduction of non-tariff barriers
   (iii) Assuring security of supply and supply commitments
   (iv) Market improvement by promotion of consumption and research and development

4. Improving the market condition

   (i) Opening up of closed markets by transferring control of production
   (ii) Controlling production of competing synthetics

5. Regulating prices

   (i) The multilateral contract

(ii) Indicative price ranges
(iii) General indexation (i.e. relating the prices of commodities to that of manufactured goods in general)
(iv) Particular indexation (i.e. relating the price of a single commodity to that of its finished product)

6. *Assuring and improving levels of earnings*

(i) Compensatory financing schemes
(ii) Stabilisation schemes
(iii) Increasing unit values by promoting processing
(iv) Preferential arrangements

7. *Supervision and discipline*

(i) Invigilatory mechanisms
(ii) Penalties for non-compliance

It is necessary to indulge in this degree of elaboration in order to afford the maximum flexibility in terms of both the techniques suitable to each commodity at different times and the techniques acceptable to different countries developed, developing or centrally planned. In approaching commodity problems from a systemic perspective, what governments can or cannot do often becomes the crucial factor.

The Export Quota Mechanism

The export quota is the most widely used of all control mechanisms. It is found in formal international agreements on coffee, sugar, tin and cocoa as well as in the informal arrangement on tea. The Wheat Agreement is the only one which uses the multilateral contract approach, though even in wheat the export quota was the first technique to be considered. It was abandoned in favour of regulating prices rather than quantities for reasons peculiar to that grain. The export quota mechanism succeeds quite often: an example in chapter 4 described a situation in which a considerable shortage of exportable surplus in Brazil was successfully overcome by selective adjustment of quotas and waivers in favour of other types of coffee. The success of the Coffee Agreement in dealing with a specific type-shortage situation does not mean that all agreements have been successful in dealing with overall shortage conditions. In the 20 years of its existence, the International Tin Agreement, which is essentially a buffer stock arrangement supported by export quotas, repeatedly failed to defend the ceiling price. On the other hand, when the Tin Agreement came under sustained pressure against the floor price — i.e. a situation of excess supply — it was successful in defending the floor by an application of export quotas. The distinction to make is whether there is an overall shortage in the commodity as a whole or a selective short supply. If demand as a whole exceeds available supply, an export quota has no meaning.

Both in shortage and surplus situations, an essential criterion for the success of the export quota mechanism is the *quantum* of surplus or shortage. In 1974, when the world shortage in sugar was not within controllable limits, no amount of regulation could have prevented prices from going through the roof; equally, all the brave intentions of the Cocoa Producers Alliance in 1964 could not prevent prices from crashing, because the surplus was overwhelming. This points to the crux of the problem — the discipline of the exporting countries bears an inverse relationship to the quantum of surplus or shortage. In a time of deficit, some exporter is bound to find the higher price irresistible and break ranks; others follow suit. In a time of surplus, some exporter is going to find the cost of holding on too high and will again break away. The reason why the Wheat Agreement survived the Korean War boom was that neither of the major exporters — the USA or Canada — found the cost of holding stocks beyond its capacity. Thus export quota mechanisms can work only when the variation between current demand and total supply is fairly narrow. The mechanism obviously cannot deal with a structural shift in the market. Again the case in point is sugar; tinkering with a quota mechanism meant for a residual free market was no solution when the avalanche of hitherto preferential quota-free Cuban sugar hit the quota-bound free market.

A point to note about the quota mechanism is that its effectiveness is also dependent on the details of its operation in relation to the price. Most quota-type agreements provide for a trigger mechanism by which changes in the market price cause changes in the quotas.[1] An elaborate example, which triggers action on both quotas and the buffer stock, is found in the Second (1976) International Cocoa Agreement. The price range of 33 to 55 ¢ per lb in this agreement is divided into five sectors, and, along with the provisions for situations when the market price is below the minimum or above the maximum, seven different combinations of quota and buffer stock action are written in it.[2] In general, the principles of quota adjustment are: (i) when the market price is above the maximum of the price range, quotas are suspended — i.e. all available export surplus can enter the market without restrictions; (ii) there is a middle range when 100 per cent of quotas are effective; between the top of the middle range and the ceiling specified percentage increases in quotas may be provided for; likewise, between the bottom of the middle range and the floor, specified percentage cuts in quotas can be effected; and (iii) below the minimum of the price range substantial cuts in quotas are made. It is obvious that the effectiveness of the mechanism depends on how realistic the price level in the agreement is in relation to actual market conditions.

Production Control

If export quotas can be effective only within a limited range, the obvious corollary is to control production so that the variation is kept within the domain of effectiveness. Unfortunately, production control by international agreement is one of the most difficult aspects of commodity negotiations. It involves acceptance of international supervision over a country's own internal economic policies, a supervision which entails difficult political and social decisions. The first prerequisite for an international production control agreement is a successful working market regulation agreement. One cannot have production control if the countries concerned cannot even agree on the regulation of the export market. It is no wonder that of the five commodities covered by formal international agreements, only the International Coffee Agreements have made an attempt to control production. Even this was tentative; while the 1962 Agreement propounded it and the 1968 Agreement made elaborate provisions for it, the latest one (1976) has simply abandoned it.

The 1962 Agreement devoted a whole chapter (XI) of three articles in eight sections under which the producing members undertook to adjust production and the Council had the authority to prescribe production goals for each member, along with a timetable for their implementation. The members had to report progress, and failure to implement the right production policies invited a penalty of withholding of quota increases. The chapter (XII) on 'Production Policy and Control' in the 1968 Agreement was more elaborate and contained eleven sections. The Council assumed powers to impose production goals if it did not agree with the one proposed by the member; it also assumed the power to impose goals even on members who did not export any coffee. The penalties were increased to include the loss of voting rights and the threat of expulsion from the agreement. All this serious endeavour came to naught when the economic provisions of the agreement collapsed early in its fifth year. The 1976 Agreement has *no* chapter on production policy, and the single article dealing with it has been lumped together with 'Other Economic Provisions' relating to processed coffee, promotion, stocks, co-operation with trade, studies and information gathering and such miscellany. The article itself is very short – unlike the 1962 and 1968 agreements, in which the members undertook 'to adjust production', in 1976 they undertook only 'to use their best endeavours to adopt and implement a production policy'. 'Best endeavour' is only agreement jargon for a pious wish. Gone were the powers of the Council to impose production goals; it could only co-ordinate the best endeavours – whatever that may mean. The abandonment of the production policy was not based on economic grounds; just because the agreement comes into force at a time of shortage it does not mean that a production policy should not be adopted. The high prices during the shortage may encourage a glut and lead to the inevitable collapse of the market a few years hence. One reason for abandoning all production control policies was the position of the largest exporter. When there was a threat of excess supply and Brazil's main interest was in preserving her market share, controlling production in all areas was a desirable objective. But when Brazil had suffered tremendous damage and had to rebuild her coffee production, any attempt at production control could have given other exporters an opportunity to say that Brazil might go slow on replanting.

Production controls do not work. Most small and medium exporters, as noted earlier, have little interest in the long-range goals for the commodity as a whole. Large exporters have an interest in it only when they themselves are not in the process of increasing production. As inscribed in the Coffee Agreements, there were *no incentives* to stop increasing production – only *penalties* for failure to do so. In a similar domestic situation, the usual method adopted is not to threaten the farmer with punishment but to pay him for taking acreage out of production. Such a method is unlikely to work internationally – it will be difficult to negotiate, impossible to finance and incapable of being policed.

The attitude of the Coffee Agreements to production *encouragement* is quite interesting. In the 1962 Agreement, the Council had to 'maintain close contact with international, national and private organisations' which could finance production. This was considerably tightened up in the 1968 Agreement.

Members *shall refrain from offering directly financial or technical assistance or from supporting proposals* for such assistance by an international body to which they belong . . . whether the recipient country is a member of the International Coffee Agreement or not . . . The Council shall maintain close contact with international bodies with a view to seeking maximum cooperation.[3]

In other words, the United States should not assist the production of coffee; nor should the World Bank or the Inter-American Development Bank; if any proposal for supporting coffee production comes before these bodies, the United States, U.K., Canada, Germany, etc. should all vote against it! Obviously the large exporters took fright at the financial assistance provided by the World Bank to East African countries for tea production. They had seen that, while it did help the recipient countries to increase and diversify their export earnings, the result was low prices for all. The cost of East African development was borne by traditional exporters of tea, and the major coffee exporters had no desire to be placed in the same position. All these provisions have literally been swept away in the 1976 Agreement; for now Brazil itself may well need financial and technical assistance to rebuild her coffee industry.

Diversification

Closely related to production control is diversification; if a country is to forego planned expansion in the production of one commodity it must be helped to grow alternative crops. Here again, the Coffee Agreements made a brave start and again ended by abandoning it. The 1962 Agreement set up an international Coffee Fund, made up of voluntary contributions, to 'further the objective of limiting production of coffee in order to bring it into reasonable balances with demand for coffee'. The Fund idea, a brainchild of the big exporters, was resisted by the smaller ones and by the developed countries which did not want to contribute to yet another resource transfer mechanism. During the life of the 1962 Agreement, the Council also decreed, against the opposition of the smaller exporters, to compel countries which had been granted a waiver (i.e. permission to export stated quantities over and above the quota) to segregate 20 per cent of the foreign exchange earnings and contribute them in free currency for promoting diversification. Some US $6.5 million was thus collected. The 1968 Agreement went further; a Diversification Fund was created with *compulsory contributions from only exporting members* at the rate of US ¢ 60 for every bag exported, a sum which could later be raised to one dollar a bag. Four fifths of the contribution was to be spent in the member's country and one fifth, in free currency, could be used anywhere. By the end of the 1968 Agreement, the Fund had about US $130 million. But very little of it had actually been used for financing schemes of diversification. As one would expect from the attitudes of the major exporters, in the 1976 Agreement there is no diversification programme. The old Fund has been liquidated. Thus ended another brave attempt — the victim of a natural calamity and national self-interest.

National Stocks

In discussing the role of stocks in regulating commodity trade, it must be made clear that control stocks are not only different from 'normal' stocks but, in fact, are an addition to commercial stocks, which are held as a part of the process of production or consumption. The object of holding a regulatory stock is to control the flow of the commodity into the market. The distinction between the two is not always clear-cut. Traders may 'hoard' in anticipation of a shortage; large multinational corporations, particularly metal companies, often hold back supplies in a weak market. While such private sector regulation may have international implications, they are by and large directed towards the domestic market. The analysis of stocks as an international regulatory mechanism is therefore limited to stocks held by governments and those held internationally. Though government stocks, particularly those held by a major exporter of a commodity, influence international trade, the motivation for building up the stock need not always be the regulation of trade. For example, there are two views about the build-up of wheat stocks in the United States. One is that it was the unplanned result of domestic farm support policies and that grain sales, particularly concessionary sales under Public Law 480, were a consequence of the high level of stocks. Another view is that the United States, the world's most important exporter of grain, holds stocks because in addition to a steady demand from Western Europe and Japan there are also sudden calls on her supplies from Russia, China and India. At least in the case of the EEC, it is clear that the emergence of butter or skim milk powder mountains was not motivated by any consideration of their implications for international trade in these commodities.

Nationally financed and controlled stocks play an important role in commodity negotiations and commodity markets. Such stocks form the basis of the multilateral contract type of commodity agreement; they are also an essential element in assuring security of supply to importers and in supporting supply commitments. The size of the nationally held stocks is a factor which determines market sentiment. If the total exportable stock is such as to assure exports to meet current demand it induces stability; if it is too low to compensate for any anticipated shortfall it encourages bullishness, particularly in the futures markets; if there is too much stock of any commodity — that is, if it 'overhangs' — the market is induced to be bearish. If a large exporter with enough resources holds a large amount, this has less impact than if a number of smaller importers have excess stocks. In the latter case, the chances are that some of them will be willing to dispose of them at a lower price. The ability of different categories of exporters to hold on becomes a crucial factor. All commodity agreements have some provisions relating to stocks and disposal of excesses. The Coffee Agreements provide for verification of national stocks and the granting of waivers in specific cases to relieve the burden of holding excess stock. The Sugar Agreements provide for a compulsory holding of a minimum level of stock related to the export quotas of the exporting members. The minimum stock is really an assurance to importers that supplies will be available if unforeseen circumstances reduce the availability from current production. The assurance of supply is embodied in 'supply commitment' provisions whereby exporters obligate themselves to give priority to the requirements of importing members in times of shortage; in return for the burden of holding such stocks, the supply commitment price is higher than the ceiling price applicable to trade under normal conditions. It was seen earlier that the Sugar Agreement supply commitments worked reasonably well for some time, until they were overtaken by the pressure of events.

Though in theory nationally held stocks need not necessarily be financed only by the holding government, international financing of nationally held stocks is a concept which has not yet gained general acceptance. This has been proposed and implemented partially in the context of the Food Security Scheme. The Federal Republic of Germany has provided US $5.4 million through the FAO for financing grain stocks in four Sahelian countries in addition to contributing to food security support in Bangla Desh. The Netherlands has contributed US $3.2 million and a number of other European countries have promised to support similar schemes.[4] While international financing for holding food stocks may be more readily available on humanitarian grounds, its extension to other primary commodities is likely to be much less acceptable to the rich countries.

Buffer Stocks and Surplus Disposals

By far the most discussed type of regulatory stock holding is the 'international buffer stock'. Its name defines it – it is a buffer financed by more than one country that holds back supplies from the actual user market in times of excess supply, stores it and releases it when there is a shortage. Thus it moderates fluctuations, and since the purchases are always when the price is low and the sales when it is higher it can in theory do so without making a loss. In practice, carrying costs and deterioration in storage can affect profitability.

The best-known example – and the only commodity for which it has been tried over a long period – is the buffer stock in the International Tin Agreements. It was noted earlier that the quota provisions in this Agreement had to be invoked to protect the floor prices. The reason for doing so was that the resources of the buffer stock were inadequate to hold more than a limited quantity of supplies. Since 1961, the buffer stock manager's resources have consisted of 20,000 tons of tin (or equivalent cash at the floor price).[5] The manager could also borrow from the banks against the tin held, thus adding to his cash resources. The floor and ceiling prices, the average London price, the quantity held in the buffer stock and quotas in force, if any, from 1956 to 1976 will be found in Appendix 7. In these 20 years, there have been three periods when quotas had to be imposed (October 1957 to September 1960, December 1968 to December 1969 and March to September 1973). In the first of these, the buffer stock started buying in June 1957 and bought 23,000 tons over a year. This was not enough to arrest the price decline and quotas were imposed, first at 27,000 tons a quarter, gradually reducing to 20,000 tons a quarter during the last months of 1958. If he had had to buy all the tin that the producers were holding back at their cost by the quota mechanism, the manager would have needed much larger resources. In other words, when the buffer stock's resources are exhausted the burden of holding stocks is transferred to the producing countries. At the other extreme, the manager has no similar backstop provision; if he has no metal to sell, he can do nothing to arrest a price rise, even if it shoots above the ceiling. The many occasions in the life of the Tin Agreements when this has happened have been described in Chapter 4. In these circumstances it is the consumer who bears the burden of the higher prices. The fact that the price of tin was so often and for so long above the ceiling indicates that the buffer stock mechanism in the Tin Agreements was not particularly successful in moderating price fluctuations. Other commodities might have had more violent movements, but the instability in tin was also quite marked. The movement in tin prices above the ceiling and below the floor was in addition to the 'permitted' fluctuations; as the table in Appendix 7 shows, the gap between floor and ceiling prices have been quite wide, as high as 37.5 per cent and as low as 13.6 per cent; in general, however, the ceiling has been 20 per cent higher than the floor. Thus a fluctuation of 10 to 15 per cent is considered normal before the buffer stock manager starts taking serious action. The actual fluctuations in the market are shown by the low and high points in tin prices between July 1956 and July 1976 in Table 9.1; a range of £1,400 to £4,750 a ton in five years does not indicate any great stability.

Table 9.1 Market Prices of Tin (Monthly averages — £ per long ton)

	Low Points			High Points	
Month		Price	Month		Price
July	1956 ...	749.9	November	1956 ...	852.3
November	1957 ...	730.5	March	1962 ...	962.0
September	1962 ...	851.3	October	1964 ...	1584.1
February	1965 ...	1230.6	March	1965 ...	1529.7
September	1967 ...	1185.4	December	1969 ...	1616.3
October	1971 ...	1402.0	September	1974 ...	4014.2
May	1975 ...	2971.0	July	1976 ...	4760.0

Source: International Tin Council

One of the reasons for the comparative ineffectiveness of the buffer stock was the existence of a much bigger overhanding stock — the United States stockpile. Disposal of surplus or strategic stock by some countries is a direct intervention in the market; it is, in effect, 'exports' by a non-producing country, since, even if released for domestic consumption only, it reduces the available export opportunity to genuine producing countries. On the other hand, the exporting countries export more than the normal demand in the period when the holding country buys for stockbuilding. Thus, building up and releasing surplus or strategic stocks affects demand substantially. Purchases and disposals complicate commodity negotiations during both periods, create a set of conflicts between the producers and the holding country and influence the conflicts between exporter and importers.

Of all the holdings of surplus stocks, the largest, most varied and most important are those of the United States, which holds a variety of metals (aluminium, chromium, cobalt, copper, manganese, nickel, platinum, tin, tungsten, vanadium and zinc), minerals (bauxite, fluorspar and mica) and natural rubber. Some of these stocks are very large; there is enough tungsten for eight years' normal peace-time consumption and sufficient tin and chromium for three years. Any commodity negotiation on bauxite, copper, manganese, tungsten or mica has to take the existence of these stocks into account. The experience of the only commodity which has been the subject of an international commodity agreement and has been stockpiled by the United States is worth examining. The United States acquired huge quantities of tin during the post-war period up to 1952. The possibility that the US might discontinue purchases for the stockpile acted as a spur to the conclusion of the First Tin Agreement. At that time, there was a significant excess of production over consumption, with no prospect of the excess being removed by US purchase. The United States did not join the first four Tin Agreements (1956-76), arguing that it could not subject national sovereignty regarding the disposal of stocks to international control. Only in 1976 did the President propose and the Senate concur in US ratification of the Fifth Tin Agreement.

Just as buying for stockpiling had an impact on the negotiations for an agreement, so too did disposals from it affect the functioning. In 1961, the United States made the first announcement about the release of tin from stock, and the market immediately fell from £991 a ton to £935 a ton. By early 1962, the US announced that out of the 349,000 tons of tin in stock 164,000 were considered surplus to its requirements. The magnitude of the quantity which threatened the market can be seen from the fact that world production in 1961 (excluding USSR, China and other socialist countries) was only 136,000 tons. Even though the United States did not dispose of 15 months' production immediately, the availability of such a large quantity acted as a strong depressant on the market. The anguished reaction from the producing countries made it necessary for the US to negotiate with them. Such negotiations for orderly marketing of the surplus were held throughout the period of disposals. It is interesting to note that the negotiations with the US were held with the Tin Council as a whole, that is with representatives from both exporting and importing countries. This implies that the groups inside the Agreement were able to arrive at compromises before negotiating with an important non-member. Here at least is one example of a successful co-operation between two usually conflicting groups.

The actual quantities disposed of over the years since the programme began in September 1962 are shown in Table 9.2. Of the total quantity of nearly 145,000 tons, approximately 125,000 tons were sold commercially; most of the balance was sold to AID. By July 1976, almost all the tin authorised by Congress had been disposed of. At this time, the United States held three years' consumption equivalent, though the target is only one quarter of that − i.e. nine months' equivalent; a proposal for further disposals was therefore submitted to Congress. From Table 9.2, it is seen that the disposals were highest between 1963 and 1966 and in 1973/4. A comparison of the rate of US disposals with the market condition would show that on balance the US has followed a cautious policy and has released tin without too great a dampening of prices. Indeed, the disposals were an important stabilising

Table 9.2. Disposals of Tin Metal from|US Stockpile (Long tons)

Year	Total disposals	Year	Total disposals
1962	1400	1970	3038
1963	10626	1971	1736
1964	31347	1972	361
1965	21733	1973	19949
1966	16276	1974	23137
1967	6146	1975	575
1968	3495	1976	2809
1969	2048	(January to July)	
Total disposals, September 1962 to July 1976			144,476

Source: International Tin Council

factor in times of tin shortages. Without this extra availability tin prices in these periods would not only have been much higher but the Tin Agreements would have been even less effective.

Two further aspects of the operation of buffer stocks are of interest − the question of financing them and the actual mechanics of operating them. In the case of tin, the burden of financing has been borne solely by the producers, all of whom are developing countries. Since stability of the market is conceded to be of benefit to importing countries too, the failure to support stockholding with resources must be viewed as a refusal by the importing countries to undertake their share of the burden. For a long time, there was no international financing support either. Since June 1969, the International Monetary Fund (IMF) has permitted member countries to borrow from it for financing an international buffer stock operated by an International Commodity Agreement. The conditions under which money can be drawn and the repayment terms are stringent; only if a member is in dire need, after borrowing its gold tranche, can it avail itself of the facility. The whole scheme is a short-term one. Since its inception, the facility has been used only once — there being only one international agreement with a buffer stock — and the exporting members of the Tin Agreement drew only a small amount, US $37 million, all of which has been repaid. The effect of throwing the burden of financing on exporting developing countries has been to require them to tie up resources that could be used for development. While on the one hand mechanisms for assuring earnings and transferring resources are being promoted, immobilising a part of the existing resources is a contradiction.

The mechanics of operating a buffer stock are an important but neglected question. When does it buy? When should it sell? Should it make a profit or break even? If it makes a loss, who bears it? How is control to be exercised on the operator of the buffer stock without denying him the flexibility of dealing in the market? In the first three Tin Agreements, the price range between the floor and the ceiling was divided into three ranges — in the lower the manager could buy but not sell, in the middle he could do neither, and in the top range he could sell but not buy. The middle range corresponds to the theoretical conception of a 'free market' — in actual practice it was not so, since any dealer in the market knew how the price would move as it approached either of the outer ranges. Speculation often became betting on a certainty. In the Fourth Agreement therefore the manager was given greater flexibility to operate — buy or sell, cash or forward — in the outer ranges also. This raises the question of how much the manager should actually buy or sell at a given time. His primary objective is, of course, to stabilise the market; but he needs to balance it with profit and loss considerations. Even if it is assumed that he need not make a profit on every deal, how often and what quantum of losses can he be permitted to make? He can no doubt be given guidelines, but a supervisory body cannot control every transaction; it can only conduct a post-mortem examination. This was dramatised in the last Tin Agreement when the buffer stock manager and his deputy were suddenly suspended and the Chairman of the Tin Council took over all their functions. Presumably, they had been behaving in a manner considered inconsistent with the standards expected of an international civil servant. To control an international official who operates in a volatile commodity market while giving him adequate flexibility is very difficult.

How effective has the buffer stock mechanism been in the Tin Agreements? It is essential to have a clear answer to this question since this technique has acquired a reputation for effectiveness, particularly among the developing countries. The Dakar Conference recommended the creation of a fund for the financing of buffer stocks of commodities exported by the poor countries. The evolution of the Common Fund concept and the importance given to it to the detriment of other mechanisms will be examined in detail in Chapter 13. Any conclusion drawn on the basis of tin experience cannot automatically be deemed to be applicable to other commodities, since few of them will have a supporting US stockpile. In his book on the working of the Tin Agreements, William Fox has a chapter assessing the effectiveness of tin control.[6] After examining the tin market in the 50 years between 1924 and 1974 (except for the extraordinary period of the Second World War and its immediate aftermath), Fox asks and answers four questions. Has international control produced a greater tendency for production and consumption to keep in better natural balance? In the pre-war period the surplus averaged about 13,000 tons a year and the shortages about 11,500 tons; post-war, the average surpluses were slightly smaller at 10,500 tons, but the shortages were substantially larger at 19,000 tons. The relative balance during the Third Agreement was merely a coincidence of high production and high consumption. Have the agreements promoted efficiency? Fox's answer is: 'To expect the Tin Council to be able (or even willing) to change the world pattern of production is expecting too much'. Have the agreements given the tin industry longer-term price stability which the other non-ferrous metal industries have not had? 'Tin does not seem to have attracted the general flow of new capital that might have been expected, and there are no signs that the other non-ferrous metals, without the advantages of a floor price, have found any difficulty in raising capital to maintain or expand production.' What have the Agreements achieved? 'So far as the use of the buffer stock has eased some of the problems (of wide short-term and long-term fluctuations in prices, great depression in production and consumption, excessive dependence on the upswings and downswings of industrial activity in the developed countries) or the use of export control ... has preserved part of the world tin mining industry from extinction, the weapons of the tin agreement have been justified.' Fox further points out the 'slow and, indeed, reluctant approach by so many members of the agreement to considering the need for providing in adequate quantities the money and metal without which the buffer stock cannot function effectively'. In short, the buffer stock, like the quota mechanism, can operate successfully only within a limited range of variation between supply and demand; it can do little to promote consumption, improve efficiency or attract investment. It needs adequate resources to be effective.

Improving Market Conditions

Improving access to markets either by quantitative assurances or by reduction of barriers, market improvement by promotion of consumption and research and development and by regulating the production of synthetics have all been dealt with extensively in the earlier chapters. All these require action by individual countries according to the degree of their responsibility by specific measures best suited to their economic structures and political philosophy. The particular case of the EEC's policies on access towards countries associated with it will be considered in the next chapter.

In dealing with the artificiality of prices in closed markets (Chapter 7) three approaches to the problem of opening them up were identified. Of these, the first — increasing openness by separating the producing unit from the other vertically integrated sections — involves the consideration of the complicated question of the relationship of multinational corporations with their host governments and, in particular, the issue of compensation. To venture into the pros and cons of this question, which is not susceptible to a standard solution, will mean straying too far from an analysis of commodity conflicts. Only the other two approaches will be examined here, by considering two specific examples, bauxite and bananas, since oil, the best known example, needs no elaboration. The success of OPEC is a result of effective co-operative action by the governments of exporting countries accounting for most of the market economy trade. The bauxite case illustrates both the unilateral approach by one exporting country and an attempt to enhance producer co-operation. As a market leader in bauxite, Jamaica, which accounts for one fifth of the world's production and over half of world exports, has succeeded in increasing tax and royalty payments by the producing companies by appropriate domestic legislation. A levy of 7.5 per cent of the price of aluminium ingots has also been imposed on each ton of bauxite mined, thus ensuring that a part of the increase in the price of the end product accrues to the country suffering resource depletion. Other actions by Jamaica include production control by imposing minimum production levels and gradually acquiring a stake in the mining companies. Jamaica's success in increasing revenues as well as its control over production is due to its superior bargaining power in bauxite. Jamaica is the world's second largest (after Australia) supplier of bauxite; half of the total requirements of the United States comes from this source; and to the aluminium companies Jamaican bauxite is important in terms of quality, proximity and price. It must be noted that notwithstanding a substantial increase in the revenues of the producing country, the impact on the companies or importing countries is very little; the net effect of doubling the price of bauxite is an increase of less than 10 per cent in the price of aluminium. An International Bauxite Association was established in March 1974 by seven producing countries – Jamaica, Surinam, Guinea, Guyana, Sierra Leone, Australia and Yugoslavia. A proposal under discussion in the IBA is the possibility of a minimum price for bauxite designated in a 'bauxite dollar' to protect it from the fluctuations in the major trading currencies.

In contrast with the moderate success of some members of the IBA, the attempt made in 1974 by some Central American banana producers, members of UPEB, proved abortive. In order to increase the returns to the producing countries, the UPEB members sought to impose an export tax of US $1 per box, a fraction of a cent on the price of one banana. The major American companies – United Brands (formerly the United Fruit Company), Standard Fruit and Del Monte – threatened and carried out boycott action against the governments which tried to put the tax into effect. Subsequent revelations, following the suicide of the President of United Brands, indicate that other unsavoury methods of influencing governments were also used. The coercive threat of ruining the economies of small countries by total stoppage of production and exports naturally threw the members of UPEB into disarray; some abolished the tax and some others reduced it to varying levels. United Fruit actually stopped cutting and shipping bananas in Panama, the only country to make a serious attempt to collect the tax. One reason for the failure of UPEB was that its membership was limited to a few Central American countries and other major producers such as Ecuador, Surinam, the Philippines and Ivory Coast did not join. The group as a whole lacked adequate market control and, in addition, was composed of countries more vulnerable to coercive action by powerful transnational companies. The lesson to be learnt from the oil, bauxite and banana examples is that in order to succeed against multinational corporations operating a closed market the producing countries must control a significant share of the market and must have sufficient holding power.

The Multilateral Contract

The main objective of regulation of quantities — exports, imports, or stocks — is the stabilisation of the price of a commodity; the four mechanisms listed under 'regulation of prices' attack the problems of the price level directly. Of these the multilateral contract type of commodity agreement also has to deal with quantities, at least to the extent of allocating approximate shares of the total guaranteed quantity among exporters. The quantitative control over production, stocks and total exports is, however, left to be determined entirely by the individual exporting countries. The International Wheat Agreements are the only examples of regulation through this mechanism.

The Wheat Agreements embody two sets of balanced obligations — importers agree to buy certain guaranteed quantities at not less than the agreed minimum price and exporters agree to sell guaranteed quantities at not more than the agreed maximum price. Thus the quantity set consist of guaranteed access by importers and assured supply by exporters; the price set is a mutual obligation to observe the price range. The earlier (1949, 1953 and 1956) Wheat Agreements expressed the reciprocal quantity obligations in absolute terms. The later (1959 and 1962) agreements had more flexible provisions; so long as the price was within the range the exporters agreed to supply all the commercial requirements of the importing member countries, who in turn undertook to purchase a specified percentage (usually 80 per cent) of their commercial purchases. When the price went above the ceiling, exporter obligations were reduced to selling at the maximum price certain minimum quantities based on past average importers, and the importers were relieved of their percentage purchase obligations. The success of a multilateral contract type agreement rests entirely on the ability of the major exporters to hold stocks in times of surplus and to obey the supply obligations in times of deficit. The earlier Wheat Agreements worked because the major exporters, particularly the United States and Canada, had the resources to hold considerable stocks and also the discipline to forego higher than maximum prices for some quantities in times of shortage. The success of the wheat agreements was not repeated by the International Grains Arrangement 1967. Since then the wheat situation has swung from one extreme — surplus and low prices up to 1971 — to the other — global shortages, depletion of stocks and rocketing prices since 1972.

Indicative Price Ranges

Like the multilateral contract mechanism, the indicative price range also has a price objective, but in this case supplies are even less controlled. Such agreements do not attempt to allocate, even approximately, market shares, though there may well be an informal understanding on this question. The achievement of the objective is left entirely to the exporting governments who regulate exports and stocks as they wish. The GATT-sponsored intra-developed country 'Arrangement Concerning Dairy Produce' (skimmed milk powder and butter fat) has an indicative price/earnings target and the importing countries co-operate by ensuring observance of minimum prices. The informal international arrangements for jute-type fibres and sisal-type fibres also have indicative price ranges, but the degree of co-operation offered by importing countries is much less. The Gentlemen's Agreement on whole milk powder also has an indicative price, but 'gentlemanly' behaviour cannot be defined; for all one knows, it is just an informal cartel. A contrast is provided by the informal International Arrangement on Tea — there are informal quota understandings but no agreement on an indicative price range. The unavoidable conclusion is that informal arrangements work only among the rich countries; their cartelisation does not have to be spelt out in so many words — it is just 'understood'. It is interesting to note that co-operation by developed importing countries is more readily forthcoming for commodities exported by other developed countries.

Indexation

There are two techniques of price regulation which have nothing to do, *on the face of it,* with quantity regulation. Relating the price of a single commodity to that of its finished product and relating the price of all primary commodities to those of manufactured goods can both be called 'indexing' techniques. But common usage has reserved the term 'indexation' to the latter alone. There has so far been one successful attempt at single commodity indexation — that of Jamaica in bauxite. This concept can readily be applied to a few more commodities. Since India exports iron ore to Japan and imports steel from Japan and since, as time goes by, India has to export more and more tons of iron ore to import one ton of steel, it is obvious that there is a deterioration in the terms of trade for India, at least in this integrated product group. This example is not as far-fetched as the usual bales of cotton to tractors one, so easily attacked by the rich countries. At least in the field of minerals, an asymmetry is easier to prove and a correspondence between mineral and metal easier to establish.

The concept of 'indexing' the prices of all primary commodities to that of manufactured goods is not new; the UNCTAD study on indexation has an Annex which traces it back to 1949, to an expert group appointed by the Secretary-General of the United Nations which recommended a proposal for preserving the import purchasing capacity of a country experiencing a shortfall in export proceeds by transferring resources from countries which had experienced a balance of payments improvement.[7] Needless to say, the proposal was not given any serious consideration. The technique of indexing as a means of protecting the import purchasing power has of late become a focus of confrontation and contention between the developed and developing countries. In December 1973, the General Assembly adopted − 95 countries voting for, 5 against and 26 abstaining − a resolution calling for 'a study . . . of ways and means whereby unit prices of manufactured imports from developed countries and unit prices of exports from developing countries could be *automatically* linked' (emphasis added).[8] Much has been written about the pros and cons of this proposal; the Secretary-General of UNCTAD also appointed an expert group of economists to advise him; the group did not even acknowledge the existence of a deterioration in the terms of trade of developing countries, let alone find indexation feasible. An illuminating examination of the question can be found in *Terms of Trade Policy for Primary Commodities.*[9] The paper defines the concept as 'guarantees by countries importing primary commodities to pay prices related to the price index of manufactured goods imported by developing countries' and analyses possible methods of indexation, their feasibility, the costs and the adverse effects. The main conclusions are:

(i) Deliberate action to turn the terms of trade in favour of exporters of primary products will meet political resistance in the importing countries on the grounds that (a) the cost of living will increase and (b) the importers will get nothing in return.

(ii) Payment of guaranteed prices depends on some intervention in the operation of the market by the governments of the importing countries. (The paper does not add that this is unacceptable, as a general principle, to some important developed countries, e.g. the United States.)

(iii) There is a problem of selecting (a) the basket of manufactured goods, (b) the price quotations to which the prices of primary commodities would be linked and (c) the appropriate parity for each commodity, keeping in mind quality differentials and the relativities between different commodities.

(iv) In primary commodities facing competition from synthetics, it will be necessary for the importing countries to impose controls over expansion of synthetic production or taxes to reduce their competitiveness.

(v) In primary commodities produced in both developed and developing countries, the problem of unintended benefit to the rich countries would arise.

(vi) A guaranteed price cannot be open-ended on quantities; otherwise it will lead to over-production.

(vii) If markets diminish because of higher prices, some exporting countries will be tempted to sell below the guarantee and the whole system will be undermined.

(viii) Higher guaranteed prices will depress demand and have adverse employment and social consequences in the developing countries.

(ix) If the scheme is limited to stated quantities of imports, quantitative restrictions on exports will have to follow in order to allocate market shares equitably, and inevitably production control must follow quotas.

(x) It will be difficult to ensure that the benefits of the higher prices for a large number of commodities will be equitably distributed among the many developing countries.

(xi) A general rise in commodity prices will have inflationary effects.

There are two fundamental objections to the concept of overall indexation. The assumption that indexation will benefit *all* developing countries and *only* developing countries is false. Table 3.3 shows that developed countries account for nearly two thirds by value of exports of primary commodities and developing countries for just over a quarter. Any indexation of all primary commodities will benefit mainly the rich. Further, a large number of developing countries are also importers of raw materials. A country such as India exports tea and iron ore but imports oil, food grains, copper, tin, lead and zinc and so on. To increase the price of tea or iron ore is, on the basis of evidence adduced earlier, more difficult than to do so for oil or metals. If the prices of all primary commodities are indexed, some developing countries are bound to be losers. In short, indexation as proposed will benefit the developed countries and some developing countries, while some others will suffer a large net loss. This is very similar to the finding of the FAO study on the costs and benefits of removal of protectionism. The second objection is that indexation is unworkable. If the world cannot achieve concerted action for a few commodities with few types or quality differentials, if it cannot tackle the problem of one major commodity facing competition from synthetics, if it is unable to regulate the market for a group with a large number of interchangeable products, it is difficult to believe that it will be able to fix the right parities for the whole range of primary commodities, taking into account the effect of coffee on tea and copper on aluminium. Indexation is a blunderbuss which hopes to kill one bird by scattering shot in all directions; it is not a magic spell that will make all the complications and conflicts of commodity regulations disappear. The puzzling question is why the developing countries attach so much importance to this concept, which is politically non-negotiable and practically non-enforceable? As usual, there is a charitable and a cynical answer, both of which are partly true. The charitable one is that the proposal is only a reaction to the deep-seated frustration at the lack of action, or even acceptance, by the developed countries of the problem of deterioration in terms of trade. To the developing countries the decline is real and tangible, whatever economists may read from their figures. The cynical answer is that it is a brilliant political manoeuvre by some OPEC countries to divert attention away from the economic adversity they have visited on oil-importing developing countries by seeming to champion the cause of all primary commodity exporters. There is no better way of doing it than by choosing the most impracticable method, one that has the added advantage of being politically unacceptable to the developed countries.

Earnings Stabilisation Schemes

It is possible to argue, theoretically, that most of the techniques of regulating quantities or prices are concerned with the returns to the producer of the commodity rather than with the foreign exchange earnings of the exporting country. This is true only in theory since there does not exist a single country which does not intervene in one way or another (regulating production, marketing, taxes or exchange rates) between the producer and the final consumer. Of the techniques considered so far, indexation comes closest to recognising the importance of export earnings to the exporting country, since its main aim is to protect the import purchasing power of countries. It is generally conceded that fluctuations in export earnings affect development since 'the benefits of price rises do not seem to offset the disadvantages of price falls even if both variations appear to be of the same magnitude'.[10] Fluctuations disrupt investment planning, upset the internal balance of public finances and exacerbate balance of payments difficulties. Schemes for direct stabilisation of countries' earnings have been discussed internationally for a long time. The 1949 expert group proposal, cited earlier, was a direct stabilisation scheme. Subsequently, another expert group recommended the creation of a Development Insurance Fund providing for partial, but automatic, compensation of export shortfalls below the average of the immediately preceding years.[11] A proposal recommended by UNCTAD I in 1964 for 'Supplementary Financing Measures' and studied by the staff of the World Bank in 1965 was not acceptable to the developed countries. The two schemes of practical importance are the Compensatory Financing Scheme of the IMF and the recent Stabex scheme of the Lomé Convention.

The Compensatory Financing Facility of the IMF, started in 1963, is geared to the balance of payments problems of countries dependent on raw material exports, especially those arising from sudden shortfalls due to natural causes. The conditions of drawal from the facility were quite stringent until recently. The period of repayment was quite short at five to seven years and the interest rate high. Further, the country had to be in dire need on its overall balance of payments; that is, if the shortfall in earnings from one commodity were offset by increased earnings from another the country was not eligible. The amount that could be drawn was limited by fixing the maximum drawal at 25 per cent of the member's quota; in effect, the richer the country, the more it could draw. The shortfall was calculated not with reference to past earnings but also taking into account forecasts for earnings in the following two years. Because the scheme was so restrictive, the Fund had allowed drawings of only US $1.25 billion in the twelve years since the inception of the facility; by the end of 1975, about half the drawals had been repaid. A hundred million dollars a year for all the members of the Fund, poor and rich (so long as they fulfilled the requirements, developed countries could also borrow, as New Zealand once did), is not much of a transfer of resources. Indeed, the shortness of the repayment period shows that the principle of the scheme is not a 'transfer' but only a temporary tiding-over loan, that too at near market rates of interest.

That the terms were onerous at last came to be recognised; the most important member of the Fund suggested, as part of Secretary of State Kissinger's proposals to the Seventh Special Session of the UN General Assembly, that the terms ought to be liberalised. This suggestion was implemented in December 1975.[12] The limit on drawings was increased from 25 to 50 per cent of the member's quota and the maximum amount outstanding correspondingly increased from 50 to 75 per cent. Though the principle of projecting the earnings for the two following years was maintained, the projections were henceforth to be based on the assumption that growth in earnings would be at the same rates as in the recent past. Other improvements include making the assistance more timely and also making it available to countries whose trade data are not up to date. The proof that the terms had, in fact, been liberalised is seen by the sharp increase in drawings; in the first six months of 1976, approximately US $1.1 billion were drawn by 25 countries.

An innovative feature of the Lomé Convention not found in its predecessor, the Yaoundé Convention, is the Stabex scheme. In essence, the scheme seeks to guarantee a level of earnings for the ACP countries on their exports to EEC — not global exports — of a selected group of primary products. The scheme also has the novel feature of providing more generous treatment to the least developed (24) countries among the ACP, the landlocked and island developing countries (10 more), as compared with the less disadvantaged (the remaining 12). The products covered by the scheme are: fresh bananas, cocoa (beans, paste and butter), coffee (raw, roasted, extracts etc.), raw cotton, groundnut products (nuts, oil and cake), raw hides, skins and leather, palm products (oil, nut, kernel oil), sisal, tea, wood and iron ore. The inclusion of the last commodity was agreed to by the EEC 'only for the sake of not jeopardising the achievement of overall agreement, for it remains firmly opposed to the extension of the system to mineral products'.[13] The basic principle of the scheme is to compensate, by a transfer from a special fund, shortfalls in earnings in any year of exports of these products to the Community.

The first condition that any ACP country must meet before it is eligible to request a transfer is to prove that it is dependent on the product in which a shortfall had been experienced. A country is defined as being dependent when its earnings from the export of the particular product to all destinations are at least 7.5 per cent of its total earnings from exports of goods. The exceptions are: the dependence threshold is reduced for all products to 2.5 per cent for the 34 least developed, landlocked and island developing countries; and for sisal the threshold is reduced to 5 per cent for all countries. For an eligible country to claim a transfer, it must prove that the earnings from a particular product on its exports to the Community have declined in relation to a reference level which is defined as the average of earnings (of exports to the Community) over the preceding four years. If the earnings have declined by more than 7.5 per cent it can request a transfer; the exceptions are: the 34 specified countries can claim if the decline is 2.5 per cent or more; for five countries (Burundi, Ethiopia, Guinea-Bissau, Rwanda and Swaziland) global exports and not merely exports to the Community are compensatable.

The percentages indicated above are again threshold levels; that is, no transfer can be claimed if the shortfall is lower. But the amount of the transfer itself is based on the actual shortfall, i.e. the difference between actual earnings in the shortfall year and the reference level. However, a transfer will not be sanctioned, or its amount can be altered by the EEC, if (i) the fall in earnings is due to trade policies that discriminate against the EEC; (ii) if the product does not meet the strict conditions of rules of origin; (iii) if the product was not consumed or processed in the EEC; and (iv) if the trend of the country's trade reveals 'important changes'. The total amount available for transfer for all the countries over the five-year life of the Convention is 375 million units of account; each year, therefore, 75 million units of account are available on an average.

Balances unutilised in any year can be carried forward to the following years, except, of course, from the last year. The transfers are interest free. The scheme also provides for repayments to the fund, though the 24 least developed countries do not have to repay; in their case they receive a grant. Repayments are to be made, up to a maximum of the transfers actually received, over a period of five years after the transfer, if the prices in any year exceed the prices of the product in question at the reference level *and* if the volume of exports to the Community is at least equal to that of the reference level.

The main differences between the IMF and Stabex schemes are: (i) the Fund scheme deals with overall balance of payments shortfalls while Stabex covers each commodity group individually; (ii) the Fund scheme applies to all exports while Stabex guarantee earnings only on exports to the Community, with a few exceptions; (iii) Stabex calculates shortfalls with reference to past earnings while the Fund projects possible earnings into the future for two years; (iv) the terms of the Stabex loan are much more liberal and in many cases a grant is given; (v) even when a loan, not a grant, is made, it is interest free.

The criticisms of the Stabex scheme are: (i) the amount available each year, about US $90 million, is very small (less than 4 per cent) compared with the value of exports of the covered products by the ACP countries to the Community of approximately US $2.5 billion; compensation to the full extent of shortfalls is unlikely to be available to all the applicants; (ii) the product coverage is restrictive and excludes in many cases all but the most rudimentary processing; examples of the products excluded are: carded or combed cotton, linters, sisal products, wood which is processed beyond being squared or sawn lengthwise; (iii) some of the conditions, such as those dealing with trade policy measures and important changes in trade patterns, are vague and likely to lead to conflicts in interpretation; and (iv) in combination with the free access provision the scheme places one group of developing countries at an advantageous position to the detriment of earnings and market shares of other developing countries exporting the same commodities. One judgement of the scheme is that 'it is a technically cumbersome, bureaucracy ridden and politically sensitive scheme for making transfers, the concessionary element of which is variable, to a selected group of countries without regard to any sensible criteria covering overall need for aid'.[14] This does seem a somewhat over-harsh judgement.

In its first year of operation, the Community signed 24 transfer agreements with 17 different countries for a total value of 71.8 million u.a. The largest amount (15 m.u.a.) went to Ivory Coast, followed closely by Ethiopia (14.4 m.u.a.). Congo (7.4 m.u.a.), Benin (7.1 m.u.a.), Niger (5.95 m.u.a.) and Ghana (5.18 m.u.a.) were other large recipients. Twelve of the 17 countries were 'least developed'; the grants to them account for over half of the total transfer. Nine different commodities figure in the list as suffering export shortfalls; wood was by far the most important with 43.35 per cent of the total. Coffee, cotton, hides and skins and groundnuts were the other important commodities. At least its first year of operation indicates that transfer agreements were not too difficult to negotiate, that substantial transfers could be made and that the least developed countries benefited as much as the more advanced developing countries.

Invigilation, Deterrence and Punishment

This analysis of the various techniques began with the assumption that not all the techniques would be applicable to all the commodities. During the course of analysis, the inter-relationship of the different techniques was also noted. Indicative price ranges go with informal arrangements, national stock policy with multilateral contracts and a quota system with production control, diversification and stock policy. The choice of techniques to be put into a given set depends on the characteristics of the commodity as well as the political acceptability of the set as a whole. The choice of *form* depends on the degree of enforceability considered necessary and acceptable by the participants. Enforceability is a crucial element in commodity regulation. It can vary from a 'gentlemen's agreement' to a treaty with elaborate provisions for invigilation, deterrence and punishment.

Why is there a need for policing provisions at all? To answer this question, one has to look at the nature of the membership of the international understandings (agreements, arrangements, understandings of whatever degree of rigidity). The examples studied show clearly that in order to be successful any understanding will have to cover a very substantial part of the total trade in that commodity – the more the better. But it is neither essential nor practicable to achieve total coverage. No understanding is universal, in the sense of including 100 per cent of the total trade, all the exporters and all the importers. There will always be members and non-members. The main difference between the two groups is that members accept obligations which non-members do not. The latter, however, do get the benefit of the results of the understanding; if the price of a commodity is stabilised, if marketing becomes orderly and if prices are held above a floor by controlling supplies, non-members also reap the benefits. Indeed, they benefit more because they do not have to bear any part of the cost of regulation. This is analogous to non-members of a trade union getting the higher wages negotiated by it without having to pay the union dues. There does come a point, however, when it is not equitable for non-members to get away without paying a price, particularly if they jeopardise the members' efforts by disruptive marketing. A second reason for policing is that, even among members, there are two groups – those who obey the provisions of the understanding and those who evade them. The distinction becomes particularly relevant in cases in which costs are associated with membership – supply restriction, stock-holding and production control. The analysis of the motivation of the different categories of exporters in Chapter 5 shows that the point at which compliance gives way to evasion is different for each one. No country can be classified as belonging permanently to one category or another. The temptations against complying vary as times change, and the success of any understanding depends on encouraging the former and discouraging the latter. Supervisory and control provisions therefore have to deal with the three categories of countries: (i) compliant members; (ii) recalcitrant members; and (iii) non-members.

All understandings, however loose, have adequate provisions for reporting so that information is available to contemplate action, if necessary, to guard against the inroads of non-members, to reward the compliant and punish the recalcitrant members. There is no need to elaborate on reporting procedures except to note that they have to include forecasts (anticipated production) as well as information on past events (exports already made, stock held) and that such information must be prompt and timely.

As far as non-members are concerned, two things must be watched: they must not increase their market share at the expense of members and they must not undermine the understanding by exporting below the minimum price objective. The quantity problem is usually sought to be safeguarded by providing for a limit on imports from non-members by member-importing countries. The limit is based on past performance, generally the average of the preceding three years. Ensuring that non-members do not undercut members is more difficult. The only point at which control can be exercised is at the importing end. Importing members alone can take action to prohibit imports from non-member, or even member countries, below the accepted price level. Controlling imports quantitatively and prohibiting imports if made at low prices both involve import control mechanisms. The degree to which importing countries accept such obligations varies: countries such as the United States dislike import controls and usually plead absence of bureaucratic machinery. The argument is not a credible one for, when it suits them the United States has not hesitated to use import controls (e.g. oil) or even export controls (e.g. soyabeans). The degree of co-operation received from importing members is shown by the example from the 1962 International Coffee Agreement shown in Table 9.3.

While the quantity of excess imports may seem small in relation to

Table 9.3 Excess Imports above Non-Member Limitation International Coffee Agreement, 1962 (60 kilo bags)

Importing Country	1966-7	1967-8
United States	337,832	103,869
Germany (Federal Republic)	144,511	27,786
France	50,710	8,590
United Kingdom	29,723	1,420
Switzerland	28,667	5,261
Sweden	13,261	34,189
Italy	11,730	16,718
Others	33,323	4,694
	649,757	202,527

Source: International Coffee Organisation.

total exports of over 50 million bags, these excesses were in addition to the clandestine and diverted quantities which are described in the next paragraph. As in the case of exporting countries, it only needs one major importer to break ranks; others then feel obliged to follow suit. From the point of view of the exporting countries, full co-operation by the main importing countries is essential if their efforts to gain benefits that are commensurate in relation to the obligations they undertake are not to be frustrated. To be fair, one must add that in the subsequent agreement there was more and better co-operation from the importing member countries. In most other agreements, importer support has been minimal.

Dealing with recalcitrant members, on the face of it, should be an easier problem — after all they have accepted the obligations and the penalties for not fulfilling them. In actual practice, however, disobedience turns out to be an even more difficult question to tackle. Once again the Coffee Agreements provide an example, because only they have made the most consistent attempts to improve control methods. In the 1962 Agreement, control over exports was minimal for the first couple of years and, with the introduction of the certificate of origin system, developed into one of checking performance after the exports had taken place. Both exporting and importing governments had to report quantities exported or imported by them so that the two could be matched. Overshipments by exporters carried a penalty of deduction of equal amounts from future quotas for the first offence, double deduction for a repetition; after the third such offence, the member became liable to expulsion. But the agreement also provided two loopholes for overshipping indirectly. Since exports to 'new markets' were outside the quota, coffee could be exported, on paper, to non-quota markets and diverted on the way. The second loophole was clandestine shipping to a non-member country which appeared as exports from these non-members — the so-called 'tourist' coffee. All three types (one blatant and two indirect) of overshipments occurred during the life of the agreement, the peak coinciding with the year of the highest total exportable surplus — showing the inverse correlation between high stocks and resistance to temptation. For example, Liberia, which had never had an exportable production of more than 60,000 bags, exported 798,000 bags of coffee in 1966 — all of it from Ivory Coast. Nearly half a million bags were imported by one US company — General Foods — on false certificates of origin. About 40 per cent of all Ugandan coffee exported in 1966 is estimated to have come under the Kenyan imprint — at that time Kenya was a non-member. Colombian coffee took a tourist ride to Aruba, which exported 300,000 bags to the United States in the two years 1965 and 1966. In most years an additional two million bags were diverted from new markets. The active connivance, and even encouragement, of American companies in frustrating the agreement must be noted. It was therefore surprising that the United States should take the initiative in proposing a system for controlling shipments *before* exports took place. Under the 'stamp plan', which came into effect on 1 April 1967, each exporting country was distributed 'stamps' equal to the quantity of permitted quota exports in any quarter; the stamps had to be fixed to every shipment at the time of export. Importing countries agreed to prohibit entry to exports from member countries not having the requisite stamps. In practice, therefore, when an exporting country had exhausted its stamps it could over-ship only if it was prepared for the shipment to be denied entry; the deterrent, in fact, was imposed on the importing companies, since they could not risk paying for coffee that they might not actually receive. The ingenious plan did work since it attacked both the over-shipping exporting country and the conniving importer. While this solved one problem, the question of non-member exports remained. The 1976 Agreement tried to avoid this by having just two categories of markets — member-quota and non-member-non-quota; how well this will work remains to be seen. Human ingenuity being what it is, if a country wants to ship more and if a company wants to connive at it, no doubt ways will be found.

Two important points arise from the above — the inadequacy of penalties and the importance of importer co-operation. Commodity arrangements are international treaties; short of war there is no way by which the international community can impose its will on a government that has decided to evade its obligations under the treaty. The ultimate punishment in any agreement is the threat of expulsion; but in reality this is no punishment at all. After all, a country can withdraw from any agreement by giving appropriate notice. Expulsion or withdrawal will be a credible penalty only if this is followed by a tangible loss of market. So far experience has shown that importing countries are unwilling to co-operate to a full extent. Tourist coffee and non-member coffee cannot find markets unless coffee-importing companies in the developed countries, with the tacit blessing of their governments, disregard the provisions which the governments have undertaken in an international treaty. Importing companies treat the agreements signed by their governments with cynical disdain. Such action would not be tolerated by any government with respect to domestic legislation. But all market economy rich countries happily condone this when it comes to international obligations. So, when one talks about the lack of discipline among developing exporting countries, one must also remember that importing countries give equal encouragement to their citizens. If exporter indiscipline has a snowballing effect, so does importer illegality. Domestic enforcement of accepted international obligations must however be a willing exercise. No amount of penalties or threats of punishment can force governments to honour commitments which they feel, rightly or wrongly, to be against their national interests.

The analysis of the effectiveness of the various techniques has shown that some do not work and cannot be expected to work in the foreseeable future. These are: production controls, diversification, an integrated buffer stock for many commodities and indexation of all commodity prices. Other techniques sometimes work and sometimes fail. Export quota mechanisms, buffer stocks for individual commodities that are easily storable and multilateral contract agreements backed by adequate national policies of exporting countries – all work within certain limits of supply and demand. Producer co-operation can be successful at reasonably high levels of market control. Informal arrangements succeed mainly among countries with similar systems and similar philosophies. Single commodity indexation is practicable. Some techniques, such as the Stabex, benefit a large number of developing countries, though not all, and help to solve problems of regulation for some commodities; in a less liberal manner, the IMF Compensatory Financing Scheme does the same. One area in which improvement is needed is the equal sharing of burdens between importers and exporters. This applies both to costs of operation and to mechanics of control. Ability to hold on is essential in making many of the techniques work. Examples have been cited of both exporting and importing countries being moved by short-term considerations to the detriment of long-term goals. In both groups, failure of one important country to hold the line has a snowballing effect. Countries sometimes comply with international understandings; at other times, pressures induce them to evade or disobey. Evasion cannot be enforced by just threats of punishment. There are no credible punishments that are purely economic and have no political consequences. It is in this context that the political compulsions that influence the attitudes and decisions of governments in commodity negotiations are analysed in the next chapter.

Notes

1. The usual trigger mechanism is the average price over 15 consecutive market days of the specified standard quality of the commodity; the use of the average over a fortnight avoids too frequent adjustments when the price teeters around the trigger level.
2. The middle range when there is no regulatory action either on the buffer stock or on quotas is 47 to 53 US cents. The four possible actions when the price is below the non-intervention level are as follows: (i) between 45 and 47 ¢ is a warning period when the full extent of annual quotas will be in effect but a quota cut becomes possible if prices decline further; (ii) between 43 and 45 ¢ annual quotas are cut by 3 per cent and the buffer stock will absorb the cut; (iii) between 39 and 42 ¢ the buffer stock will buy up to 4 per cent of annual quotas; and (iv) below 39 ¢ the buffer stock will keep on buying till it is exhausted. The possibilities when the price is in the upper part of the range are: (i) between 53 and 55 ¢ the buffer stock will sell up to 7 per cent of annual quotas; and (ii) when the price goes above 55 ¢ the buffer has to continue selling until it is exhausted.
3. Section 10 of Article 48 of Chapter 11 'Production Policy and Controls' in the International Coffee Agreement 1968.
4. FAO *Report of the Conference – Eighteenth Session* November 1975, C 75/REP; see the Report of the First Session of the Committee on Food Security.
5. In the first (1956-61) Tin Agreement, the buffer stock manager's resources were higher – 25,000 tons of tin or cash equivalent at the floor price then in force. In all Agreements, producing countries could contribute either metal or the cash equivalent to the quantity multiplied by the prevailing floor price.
6. See Chapter XIX 'An Assessment of Tin Control' and 'Post-script' in William Fox, *Tin: The Working of a Commodity Agreement* (Mining Journal Books Ltd., London, 1974).
7. UNCTAD TD/B/503/Suppl. *The Indexation of Prices.* The history of proposals recommended by various expert groups is in Supp.1/Add.1. Annex I, *Previous Studies related to Indexation.*
8. UN General Assembly 3083 (XXVIII).
9. Commonwealth Economic Papers, no.4, *Terms of Trade Policy for Primary Commodities* (Commonwealth Secretariat, London, 1976).
10. Commission of the European Communities, Information Directorate-Generale, Information – Development and Cooperation 94/75, *The Lomé Convention – Stabilization of Export Earnings,* Brussels.
11. See the summary of the recommendations of the Expert Group (Sir J. Crawford, I.H. Abdul-Rahman, A.C. Flores, A.G. Hart, S. Posthama, M.L. Querishi) in the document UNCTAD TD/B/503/ Suppl.1, *The Indexation of Prices.*
12. *IMF Annual Report* 1976, Chapter 3, 'Activities of the Fund', pp.52-3.
13. Commission of the European Communities, *The Lomé Convention.*
14. David Wall, *The European Community's Lomé Convention: Stabex and the Third World's Aspirations,* Guest Paper no.4, Trade Policy Research Centre, London, 1976.

10 THE POLITICS OF COMMODITY NEGOTIATION

> Allies of equal resources also may differ in their readiness to help, the magnitudes and attitudes of assistance and their acceptability to appeals.
>
> The Arthasastra

A recurring theme in this study has been that, while economic interests may determine the basic attitudes of governments to commodity negotiations, these are then modified by political considerations. Even when we sought to identify only economic interests politics kept intruding. For example, in Chapter 4 it was seen that the choice a country makes in belonging either to the developed or developing camps was a political one. Even when the specific economic interests of a country as an exporter (or importer) coincided with those of a group of exporting (or importing) countries, attitudes were motivated by feelings of solidarity based on identification with one camp or another. The solidarity of the centrally planned economy countries is essentially a political solidarity underpinned by a similar economic system; in any case, the inter-relationship between politics and economics is more clearly recognised in Marxist philosophy. The fundamental political difference, which affects commodity regulation as much as any other aspect of international relations, is between the developed, the developing and the centrally planned. For reasons of greater economic interdependence, the analysis in this book has been concentrated mainly on the relations between the first two groups, though without totally ignoring the third. By the time, in Chapter 6, the question of access came to be considered, the distinction between politics and economics was beginning to wear thin. In analysing other aspects, attention has been drawn whenever political considerations outweighed economic ones. One example of this was the conclusion that the sugar trade was not just politics but super-power politics at that. The use of the word 'politics' is perhaps inappropriate, because there is a presumption that the influence of politics is always to the detriment of good economic solutions; words such as 'politics' and 'politicking' have come to acquire pejorative overtones. No such presumption is made herein; 'politics' is used here only as a catch-all phrase to cover all other national interests, extraneous to commodity interests, that influence commodity negotiations.

Apart from the politico-ideological division between developed and developing countries, there are at least three identifiable political relations that cut across economic interests. These are the strategic power relationship, historical association and regional solidarity. In this chapter, specific examples of the three types will be analysed. The influence of politics on the forums in which commodity negotiations take place and their influence on choice of techniques will also be considered.

The most fascinating example of regional solidarity and the influence of politics on commodity negotiations is provided by the European Economic Community, particularly by its Common Agricultural Policy. A report in *The Economist* on an EEC farm ministers' meeting sub-titled 'Farming is Politics', says:

> France's Mr Christian Bonnet sought — and obtained — a higher milk price despite existing surpluses. Why? Because the other ministers recognized his position would have been intolerable if he had to go back with empty hands to French milk producers. Mr Peart's career seemed to hang on retention of the beef premium — so his colleagues gave him that, albeit in diluted form. Germany's Mr Josef Ertl agreed to a reduction of border taxes; but only a partial one, so that he could argue to German farmers (who benefit from retention) that the system had not been abolished.[2]

The extent to which politics diverges from economics is shown by the following further quotations from the same report:

> The Council fixed a higher milk price than the Commission proposed. So the prospect is more surpluses. The Community already has more than 1 million tons of surplus milk powder in its stores. So the Council agreed to mix 400,000 tons of it into animal feed and to stockpile some of the soya which would otherwise have been used for the feed. This is to try, probably unsuccessfully to appease the Americans, who are key soya exporters . . . The wine war between France and Italy seems to be over despite the riots and several deaths in the Midi while the meeting was going on. France imposed a special tax last September on imports of cheap Italian wine to placate the wine growers of the Midi, to the fury of the Italians. Now 4 million hectolitres (about 90 million gallons) of wine are to be distilled into industrial alcohol to mop up the wine lake.

The complications of the CAP and its financing are infinite; since it is impossible to summarise them all within this study, one has to take refuge under the excuse that the EEC is a case of regional integration and not a pure case of international trade. Thus the focus in this chapter is limited to those aspects of the Community's policy which have a direct bearing on commodity negotiations with the external world.

Historical Association

The EEC's relationship with the less developed countries is the best example of the effects of a historical association. In contrast with the high drama of every commodity negotiation among the members of the Community, that between the importing European countries and the exporting former colonies is much less dramatic; none the less it is important. For one thing, the Community's approach, whether of the Six or the Nine, is generally less dogmatic and doctrinal and more pragmatically oriented towards finding specific solutions. The reason is historical association. Colonialism established economic inter-dependencies which have an imperative of their own. Achievement of politicial independence could not change these overnight. The erstwhile metropolitan countries still remain the major trading partners of the former colonies. Shipping lines, airline routes, telephone and telegraph communications — all radiate like the spokes of a wheel from the centre to different points on the periphery. The close political relationship that subsisted after the achievement of independence was strongly underpinned by economic interdependence. *Mutuality* of dependence does not imply that there was *equality* of dependence. In the nature of things, the metropolitan countries were less dependent, collectively with all the former colonies and individually with any one of them; consequently they had a superior political position. So the negotiations necessarily had to take the form of more 'giving' by the rich countries and more 'taking' by the former colonies.

Within this general framework, some special issues must also be noted. All negotiations of commodity problems with the less developed world are subservient to (i) all negotiations between the Community's members on the same commodities and also (ii) to commodity negotiations between the Community and other developed countries. The first priority is obvious; the second is due to the inherently greater importance of trade with developed countries compared with trade with the developing world. The less developed countries around the Mediterranean have a special place. While only some of them were fully fledged colonies (others were mandated or condominium states), all have a special political, strategic and economic importance to the Community. But, these, in turn, are less important than other countries around the Mediterranean — Spain, Portugal, Greece and Turkey are all aspirants to full membership of the Community. The EEC therefore has to balance its political interests with the various groups in some order of priority. To take a specific instance, increased access to olive oil from Tunisia and Morocco affects oil imports from Spain or Turkey and also the Community's own production. Imports of wine from Algeria add a further dimension to the hot dispute between France and Italy. The citrus fruit question affects every country in the mediterranean — including Israel. So the Community's ordered set of priorities in dealing with commodity problems seems to be:

(i) Intra-Community problems on the whole range of the CAP (with varying degrees of enthusiasm among the members for the CAP as it exists and on the need for change);

(ii) Intra-rich country problems (grains, oilseeds etc.);

(iii) The candidate Mediterranean states;

(iv) Other Mediterranean states;

(v) Former colonies in Africa (to which have been added former British colonies in the Caribbean and the Pacific);

(vi) The rest of the world, in the following order: (a) the proximate countries in Central Europe; (b) Asia (the former British colonies); (c) Latin American countries.

The Community has Special Trade agreements with each one of the non-candidate Mediterranean states. With the fifth priority group it has made collective agreements.

The evolution of the collective agreements between the Community and an increasing number of developing countries, mostly in Africa, is a good example of the adaptation of historical colonial association to changing circumstances.[3] When the Treaty of Rome which created the Community was negotiated, special arrangements were written in, at the insistence of France, to protect the benefits which the colonies had as members of the Franc zone. Two principles of the first association convention — compensation for benefits lost and a European Fund for Development — have also remained the cornerstones of subsequent conventions. By the time the first convention ended in 1963, most of the colonies had become independent. The Community offered to continue the association and 18 developing countries (the Association of African States and Madagascar, or AASM) signed, with the EEC of the Six, The Yaoundé Convention which came into force on 1 January

1964. This Convention continued the benefits of the earlier scheme with the addition of a new principle: the AASM countries were also to grant 'reverse preferences' for EEC products imported by them. The second European Development Fund under this Convention had additional resources of 150 million u.a., thus making 730 m.u.a. available for the five years of its life. The two principles recognised in this agreement were: (i) a country's prior colonial status was a justification for the establishment by the EEC of discriminatory trading preferences in its favour; and (ii) these preferences together with financial aid were appropriate tools for compensating countries for the consequences of the Community's policies, particularly the CAP.

During the life of the First Yaoundé Convention, attempts were made to enlarge the number of countries benefiting from it, prompted by the criticism that it was merely a continuation of colonialism. A three-year negotiation with Nigeria led to the signing of an association agreement in 1966, but this was never ratified. In 1969, the Arusha Convention was signed between the EEC and the countries of the East African Community (Kenya, Uganda and Tanzania); this was less comprehensive than the Yaoundé Convention as it had no financial transfer provisions. The first Yaounde convention was itself renegotiated between the EEC and the AASM with no significant changes and lasted till 31 January 1975. During the ten-year life of the two Conventions so many changes had taken place that any instrument that followed had to be significantly different. The main changes were: the negotiation by the Community of a number of preferential trading schemes with various countries around the Mediterranean, the GSP which gave preferential treatment to imports of manufactures from all developing countries; the gradual erosion in the value of the preferences to AASM countries due to repeated tariff cuts in different rounds of GATT, and, most important, the enlargement of the Community itself through the accession of the United Kingdom, Denmark and Ireland. Since the principle that a former colony was entitled to compensation for loss of preferences had been recognised, the UK demanded similar treatment for the Commonwealth countries. The dilution of the benefits by the addition of a large group of countries was unacceptable to both the EEC of the Six and the AASM. As a compromise, it was agreed that only 20 Commonwealth countries in Africa, the Caribbean and the Pacific were entitled to the same treatment as the AASM. The seven Commonwealth countries in Asia were thus excluded. Eventually, 46 countries (19 AASM including Mauritius, 21 Commonwealth including Bahamas and six other African countries) negotiated with the

Community of the Nine an agreement that has come to be known as the Lomé Convention.[4]

While the Lomé Convention contains seven Titles and as many protocols, the main ones are those dealing with access, earnings stabilisation and financial aid. Of these, Stabex has been analysed in the last chapter. In theory, the Convention provides totally free access into the EEC for all products originating in the ACP countries. For example Chapter 1 of Title I states:

> Products originating in the ACP states shall be imported into the Community free of customs duties and charges having equivalent effect . . . The Community shall not apply to imports of products originating in the ACP states any quantitative restrictions or measures having equivalent effect other than those which the Member States apply among themselves.

In practice, the free access provisions are circumscribed by a number of important qualifications. The rules of origin which determine whether an ACP product is eligible for free access contain an enormous list of prohibited processing activities, including a large number in which the ACP may be expected to have a competitive advantage. Processed meat products, flour made from cereals, cigarettes containing more than 30 per cent imported material, even aluminium utensils if the import content is more than 50 per cent − all these exported products are ineligible. Again, all commodities protected by the CAP are excluded. The value of the free access provisions is also whittled down by the access provided to other countries under zero duty, the Mediterranean treaties, the GSP and the free trade agreements with many European countries. Lastly, the Community has reserved the right to impose protective measures in what is, perhaps, the widest safeguard clause ever drafted;

> if, as a result of applying the provisions . . . *serious disturbances* occur in a sector of the economy of the Community or of *one or more* of its Member States, or *jeopardise* their external financial stability, or if *difficulties* arise which may result in a *deterioration* in a sector of the *economy of a region* of the Community, the latter may take, or may authorise the Member of State concerned to take, the necessary safeguard measures.

The effectiveness of the free access provisions will only be proved by experience; in its immediate operation, the Community has shown understanding of the problems of the exporting countries. For example, in applying the safeguard clause for beef, the special position of four countries to whom the commodity is important was recognised by giving them a quota equal to their best performance.

An important change in the Lomé Convention is the abolition of the reverse preferences. The reason for this is not so much generosity but US opposition to the idea that developing countries should grant preferences in a discriminatory manner to only some industrialised countries. Since any developing country granting such preferences could have been debarred from the benefits of the US scheme, ACP countries could not afford to grant them to the EEC. The Fourth European Development Fund, under the Convention, is substantially bigger, with resources of 3,000 m.u.a. (including the Stabex amount of 375 m.u.a.) for the 46 countries, compared with 905 m.u.a. in the Third Fund for the eighteen AASM countries. The bulk of the amount, 2,100 m.u.a., is non-repayable grant aid. The incorporation of the main provisions of the Commonwealth Sugar Agreement within the CAP pattern is also a significant part of the Convention.

The Lomé Convention is important in many ways. First, it covers a large number of developing countries in different parts of the world. An agreement between 46 poor nations and nine industrialised ones is a hopeful sign that constructive action is possible. Second, the fact that the 46 negotiated as one group, in spite of the wide differences in economic conditions among them, shows that unity of approach can be maintained; the group system need not always be confrontationist. Third, the Convention clearly recognises the inter-dependence of trade, earnings stabilisation and aid. There are two main criticisms. It is overly restrictive on access for processed and manufactured goods, thus making the Title on Industrial Co-operation more a pious wish than one of operational significance. The second criticism is that, by choosing a set of developing countries for special treatment, it discriminates against the rest, particularly the populous, poor nations of Asia. A conflict is thus generated between two sets of developing countries. While it is true that the excluded countries are placed in a position of comparative disadvantage, it is equally true that the Convention represents, on the whole, a valuable package for the 46.

The historical relationship between metropolitan countries and former colonies does not endure at the same level; as time passes and the countries develop new economic and political relations, the old economic ties diminish. This is best seen in the British Commonwealth, for the obvious reason that the process of decolonisation started there earlier. The imperial preferences of the pre-war period, transformed into Commonwealth preferences, have gradually lost their value. For a long time, the Commonwealth Sugar Agreement and the Colombo Plan were the main symbols of the Commonwealth association. The former has now been subsumed in the Lomé Convention and the latter overshadowed by other newer programmes of technical assistance. The United Kingdom membership of the Community is the clearest indication of the weakening of the old economic ties, though a political connection still persists. The importance of the CSA as an example of guaranteed access, guaranteed higher prices and a built-in advantage to the less developed countries has been discussed earlier. The CSA also performed a useful bridging function in international negotiations on sugar. Since the group contained developed importing countries, developed exporting countries and developing exporting countries, it acted as an effective producer-consumer coalition and was able to perform mediatory roles. It is for this reason that one should take particular note of historical associations. They are the few bridges across the great divide between the developed and developing.

Strategic Power Relationship

Even when ties of economic inter-dependence weaken there is still a residue of political co-operation which can make a positive contribution to reducing the level of confrontation. Political co-operation can also exist without the history of colonialism and its economic after-effects. This can be classified as the 'strategic power relationship' and is exemplified by the interaction between the United States and Latin American countries. The United States has a philosophic dislike of commodity agreements, a dislike overcome only in two special circumstances: (i) when it has a substantial economic stake in a commodity; or (ii) when there is overwhelming political compulsion. The United States has not only been a loyal member of the International Wheat Agreements but an active promoter, but only because it is the most important exporter of that commodity. It did not join the first four International Tin Agreements; it has been a member of the Sugar Agreements only on the condition that its own sugar policy was not regulated by them. Though it is a very important producer of copper, the US has no intention of joining the Council of Copper Producing Countries (CIPEC). But one should not assume from this that US hatred of producer associations is even greater than its dislike of commodity agreements. The US is an 'observer' in the International

Sultana *Producers'* Agreement, because California is the largest producer of raisins. The US participates in the Management Committee of the Arrangement on Dairy Products. If the US has not chosen to become a full member of such agreements it is because effective participation can be achieved without going through the arduous exercise of submitting treaties to the Senate for ratification. There are two examples of political compulsions prompting the US to join a commodity agreement. One is the decision to join the Fifth Tin Agreement. The reluctance to join the earlier agreements was seen in the last chapter to be due to the desire to retain freedom of action regarding releases from the strategic stockpile and not be called upon to justify them in the Tin Council even when they were perfectly justifiable. The political imperative which overcame that reluctance was the need to be seen to be doing something for more than one commodity, as a part of the 41-point package presented to the Seventh Special Session of the UN.

The second example – the change in the US attitude to an international coffee agreement – clearly shows the strategic power nature of the political compulsion. Since the termination of the war-time Inter-American Coffee Agreement in 1948, United States policy on any kind of a coffee agreement was that enunciated in the Randall letter. In April 1956, IA-ECOSOC voted to draft an international coffee agreement. The position of the United States was stated in the letter dated 27 April 1956 sent under the signature of the US Ambassador to IA-ECOSOC: 'The United States could not take the lead in negotiating an international agreement on coffee or become a participant in such an agreement.'[5] The refusal to associate the US with a coffee agreement was categorical; even if others succeeded in negotiating one, the US would not join it. By the end of the 1950s, the situation in Latin America was changing rapidly; on 1 January 1959, Batista fled Cuba and the revolution succeeded. It was then that opinion in the State Department and in the coffee trade became alive to the fact that coffee was vital to many economies in that part of the world. A collapse of the market might well affect the US strategic interests with the prospect of 'Latin America going Communist'. On Kennedy's election as President, a further positive thrust was given as a result of the report of the Latin American Task Force appointed by him. The Alliance for Progress that followed had to have a proposal relating to coffee that could be seen to benefit many countries in Latin America, particularly the largest among them. So the President said: 'The United States is ready to cooperate with the Latin American and other producing country governments in a serious case-by-case examination of the major commodities and to lend its support to practical efforts to reduce extreme price fluctuations.'[6]

Latin American countries had always relied for their developmental effort on the stability of the coffee market, both at the time of the Randall letter and after. The only change was that, after 1960, not doing anything about it affected the United States politically and strategically. The complete reversal from the position of the Randall letter came in Treasury Secretary Dillon's statement to the OAS-IA-ECOSOC meeting in August 1961: '[The United States] is prepared to join in a workable coffee agreement, to use its good offices to urge the participation of other consuming countries and to help in the enforcement of export quotas through the use of import controls.'[6] The extent of this change is shown by the willingness shown to use import controls as a means of helping to police the agreement, a significant departure from the attitude to all other agreements on commodities which the US imports. The United States has continued this policy of full co-operation in the functioning of the Coffee Agreements. Two examples of the help given to the Latin American producers have been cited earlier — US collusion with them to impose a settlement on African producers and the 'stamp plan' for exercising control over exports prior to shipment.

Regional Affinities

Apart from the coffee case, the relationship between the US and Latin America is weaker than that between the European metropolitan countries and their former colonies. In fact, regional ties either tend to be very strong (as in the case of the EEC) or very weak. Even where regional co-operation is tenuous, the fact that major producing countries all belong to the same region is helpful in tackling commodity problems. The largest producers of oil are in the Middle East; the very largest, with the power to withstand cutbacks in supplies (equivalent to the ability to hold stocks in other commodities) and the power to control the market, are all Arab countries. The lead taken by the Latin American countries was crucial to the successful negotiation of the Coffee Agreement. The ESCAP region provides four such examples — the Association of Natural Rubber Producing Countries, the Asian Coconut Community, the Pepper Community and the informal jute producers' meetings. Barring a few exceptions, regional co-operation in the developing world is still at a tentative stage. Promoting such co-operation may well be a necessary first stage for a successful negotiation in a wider forum.

Choice of Negotiating Forum

This leads to the problem of the multiplicity of forums which were described in Chapter 2. The industrialised countries prefer to settle their commodity problems under GATT. Developing countries prefer to handle them under UNCTAD. The choice of a forum is a political decision made by the countries mainly interested in the trade in a particular commodity. In theory, UNCTAD, as the successor to ICICA, has the sole responsibility for recommending the convening of a UN Commodity Conference and for servicing it. This is a decision of the United Nations, accepted by all member countries. However, when a conflict arose between the United States and the EEC (of the Six) on access to agricultural commodities, the forum chosen to settle it was GATT. The ostensible reason was that trade in agricultural commodities was primarily a case of quantitative restrictions and other non-tariff barriers to trade. An additional reason, as explained earlier, was that under GATT the developing countries were much less important and the centrally planned countries were excluded, thus creating possibilities of trade-offs between the industrial and agricultural sectors of the two main contenders. The 'Gentlemen's Agreement on Whole Milk Powder' was negotiated under the auspices of the OECD and is serviced by it.

Why do the rich countries prefer the OECD or GATT? Because the OECD, and for the most part GATT, are perceived by the rich as well as the poor to be rich men's clubs. The history of the OECD shows how these perceptions developed; it is the successor to the OEEC (the Organisation for European Economic Co-operation) set up in 1948 to co-ordinate the recovery policies of Europe with the aid of the Marshall Plan. The OEEC had 17 members, the US and Canada being associated with it; the OECD has 24, membership consisting solely of developed countries. Two of the objectives of the OECD are 'to achieve the highest sustainable economic growth' and 'to contribute to the expansion of world trade on a multilateral non-discriminatory basis'. This echoes the preamble to GATT which includes, as objectives, the following: 'expanding the production and exchange of goods' and 'the elimination of discriminatory treatment in international commerce'. Since it came into force on 1 January 1948 and until the adoption of Part IV (on Trade and Development) in November 1964, GATT and OECD were not dissimilar in spirit and attitudes. Even the adoption of Part IV, rightly hailed as a significant departure, was only a reaction to events. As Kenneth Dam remarks:

There can be little doubt that this step was a reaction to the preparations, already in progress, for the 1964 United Nations Conference on Trade and Development and that the increasing grandeur of the format [of Part IV] during the year and one half of drafting was a reaction to the growth of UNCTAD from an isolated United Nations Conference to a permanent body commanding the allegiance of the entire less developed world.[7]

GATT changed but OECD did not. What the OECD thought of UNCTAD was: 'Many individuals regarded the United Nations Conference on Trade and Development as a confrontation between two opposing groups. In fact, one government representative reported at the Annual Aid Review that the impression had been given in his country that the industrial countries were being made *defendants.*[8] (emphasis added) When the rich countries wanted to form a pressure group against OPEC, they narutrally turned to the OECD; the International Energy Agency was created under its auspices. There is no indication that the OECD or IEA ever thought of asking developing oil importing countries whether they wanted to join the IEA, an organisation supposedly representing the interests of *all* importers of oil, not only the rich countries. Much as Dr Kissinger would like every one to believe that confrontation between the rich and poor nations was entirely the result of the oil crisis and the intransigent rhetoric of the developing countries, it was always implicit in the creation of the OECD. Every change of policy in the rich countries — the change in GATT, Kissinger's own 41 proposals — came about only after the developing countries had brought the matter to the surface. No wonder developing countries get the idea that unless one *confronts the rich with their own policies* nothing gets done. Confrontation became a settled policy and was first identified as such in the OECD, not in any forum of the developing countries. The OECD has thus, for all practical purposes, become the Secretariat of 'Group B' (rich industrialised countries' group) in UNCTAD; the developing countries' Group of '77' lacks a similar institution. The group system did not originate in UNCTAD. The 15-year existence of the OECD and its threatened total hegemony in international trade and economic matters inevitably provoked those who were left out to get together. Thus, if the rich countries prefer the GATT, there is a reason for it; it is *their* organisation. If the poor prefer UNCTAD, the reason is the same; it is *their* organisation.

Reference to international organisations in commodity negotiation would not be complete without mentioning the role of the Secretariats of Commodity Councils in the functioning of International Commodity Agreements. One vital function that they perform is the collection of all relevant information and its presentation in an acceptable objective form. The importance of this information-conveying role should not be under-estimated; they not only gather facts but also information on the attitudes of the negotiators and their limits. Especially during the conduct of negotiations on vital questions such as quotas and prices, the Secretariat can influence the negotiations towards what they perceive to be an acceptable compromise. The successful chief executives of the Secretariats are those who, having built up a position of trust among the various parties, are able to perceive the possibilities of a compromise. An example quoted in Fisher's book on the Coffee Agreements is the successful attempt made by the executive director to resolve the deadlock on the selectivity issue. 'His active secretariat brokerage resulted in a plan for a quota review – known as the "Santos document" – which served as a useful lightning rod in the ensuing discussions.'[9] The role of the international civil servant in commodity negotiations is generally not understood and often misunderstood. He cannot create a solution where none exists, nor propound one which is politically unfeasible. He can only promote those that have a reasonable chance of success; in fact, Fisher is right in characterising him as a 'broker'.

Positive Politics

In considering the influence of politics on commodity negotiations, emphasis has deliberately been put on its positive aspects. There are at least two successful examples whose complexity is as great as any so far described. Both concern the European Economic Community, whose machinery – the Commission, the Councils of Ministers, the Summits – has often been described as a nightmare. But the thing somehow works. Conflicts there have of course been and will continue to be; the surprising thing is that the CAP has survived in spite of exchange rate adjustments, border taxes, conflict with other developed countries, admission of new members to the Community, wine wars and butter mountains. There are two reasons for this success. First, the participants have always considered that the benefits of regional integration outweigh the sacrifices they are called upon to make under the CAP. They fight to minimise the sacrifices to the last drop of ink in their pens, but ultimately they agree, even if it means resorting to stratagems such as stopping the clock. There is, in short, a political will to succeed, because the will in this case comprehends pay-offs in other areas –

strategic, political and industrial. The second reason for success is that negotiations are always on-going; they can even be said to be permanent. In this context, a wine war is nothing but a continuation of negotiation by other means; it is only a signal that the sacrifice demanded of one party is too great. This unequal sharing of the burden is consequently corrected in the next round. Within an accepted framework, adjustments are constantly being made. This is the lesson that one can learn from the CAP; commodity negotiations cannot be once-for-all or infrequent affairs. The essence of the flexibility that has been consistently advocated in this book means continuous adjustment.

The second example of the successful negotiation of a complex agreement is, of course, the Lomé Convention. There were many conflicts among the 46 and among the Nine. A great many negotiations had to be gone through before the ACP and the EEC could harmonise their separate positions; only then could they attempt to reconcile the two. But it was done. One reason for the successful result was the disaggregated approach to different parts of the package. Small groups of interested countries negotiated the different bits on the understanding that agreement on any part was subject to agreement on the whole. In other words, a satisfactory re-aggregation was implicit. If 55 countries could agree on a complex package, it should not be totally impossible for 125 to do the same. Another example of historical association, described in Chapter 7, is the Commonwealth Sugar Agreement, which guaranteed access to all Commonwealth sugar exporters, usually paid a higher than world price for such exports, paid an even higher price to developing countries, granted them a share of the growth in the market and even indexed the price to increases in costs of production. A favourite preoccupation of 'free marketeers' is the chastising of preferential arrangements, whether they be the US Sugar Act, the Lomé Convention or the CSA. It is not necessary to equate them all with original sin. It all depends on how one looks at them. If the Lomé Convention is seen as a conflict between the 46 and the rest of the '77', a conflict is all that one will find. If, on the other hand, one recognises that the 46 have gained something, supports the gains and then asks what is to be done for the rest, perhaps one can build a structure on a constructive foundation.

The importance of perspective also applies to other kinds of political associations. The strategic interest of the United States in Latin America can either be looked upon as an unfortunate effect of power politics or as a positive factor in promoting commodity arrangements which benefit them. In commodity negotiations, no relationship is totally adversary. Importers and exporters were able to get together in the Tin Agreement before negotiating with an important non-member; a mixed exporter-importer group such as the CSA performs a useful bridging function; if all the major producing countries belong to the same region this is helpful in promoting international co-operation.

This analysis of political influence points to a neglected aspect of the relationship between developed and developing countries – the 'constituency problem'. In a sense, the Mediterranean and the ACP countries can be construed as a constituency of the Community, which is prepared to undertake some obligations towards their development. To a lesser extent, the United Kingdom has a constituency in the former colonies, and, more tenuously, the United States has an interest in the development of Latin American countries. In theory, South-East Asian countries could provide a constituency for Japan and Australia, if these countries are prepared to accept a special role in the development of ASEAN and Indo-China countries. This leaves the populous South Asian countries without an identifiable sponsor; a recent article, however, considers them as a constituency of the World Bank.[10] Perhaps, lacking a single strong sponsor and having relations with all, multilateral financial institutions automatically become their main source.

This emphasis on the positive aspect of politics shows that there are many factors which help commodity negotiations. Food aid is essentially humanitarian in motivation, but its contribution to global economic stability is a positive one. Historical association, regional co-operation, altruistic motivation – all these can be harnessed. The question posed is simply: if countries want to do good for political reasons why not accept it instead of fighting it?

Notes

1. Even the phrase 'commodity interest' is a vague one; it does not mean strictly economic interests. For example, social problems affecting land use, run-down of processing industries or diversification have also been considered a part of legitimate commodity interest.
2. *The Economist,* 13 March 1976, 258(6916).
3. For a description of the earlier Conventions see David Wall, *The European Community's Lomé Convention: Stabex and the Third World Aspirations,* Guest Paper no.4, Trade Policy Research Centre, London, 1976.
4. For a background to the negotiation and the details of the Lomé Convention see: (i) Commission of the European Communities Information Directorate-Generale, Information – Development and Cooperation 99/75 *The Lomé Convention – ACP/EEC;* (ii) Overseas Development Institute ODI Briefing Paper, *The Lomé Convention;* (iii) David Wall, *The European Community's*

Lomé Convention; and (IV) Commission of the European Communities, Information Directorate-Generale, Information – Development and Cooperation 94/75, *The Lomé Convention – Stabilisation of Export Earnings,* Brussels.
5. See International Coffee Council, *The History of Recent International Coffee Agreements,* Document ICC-I-1, Washington DC, June 1963.
6. For the full text of President Kennedy's Alliance for Progress speech and Secretary of State Douglas Dillon's statement see the appropriate US State Department Bulletin.
7. Kenneth W. Dam, *The GATT: Law and International Economic Organization* (The University of Chicago Press, Chicago 1970).
8. OECD, Development Assistance – Efforts and Policies 1965, Review by the Chairman of the Development Assistance Committee, September 1965.
9. Bart S. Fisher, *The International Coffee Agreement: A study in Coffee Diplomacy* (Praeger, New York, 1972).
10. Ronald T. Libby, 'International Development Association: A Legal Fiction Designed to Secure an LDC Constituency', *International Organization* 29, 1975, pp.1065-72.

11 POLITICAL WILL AND BARGAINING POWER

> The poor, whether they are countries or individuals, have little place in the world.
>
> Jawaharlal Nehru

The most common reason given for failure of commodity negotiations is that 'political will' was lacking. This vague explanation was shown, in Chapter 2, to be unsatisfactory because it is not a single tangible entity but covers a multitude of factors which together determine why viable economic solutions are often not deemed to be politically feasible. In blaming political will, it is rarely made clear whether the lack is that of individual governments or the aggregate will of all participants. It is unrealistic to expect that in a multilateral negotiation all participants will have an equal level of commitment to achieve success. In practical terms, the level of commitment is also not static. Governments have interests; out of these interests, some of them conflicting, is born an attitude or a policy. The policy may vary from total opposition to a commodity agreement at one extreme, to lukewarm acceptance or 'let us go along if most others do' in the middle, to the very rare total commitment to an agreement at the other. Attitudes may swing between 'let us wait and see' to going all out to succeed in ngotiations. These may well represent the individual political will; it is when one looks at negotiations in the aggregate that difficulties appear. The political will of the respective participants is not all equally important. Some countries are more important than some others and sometimes groups of countries may acquire a special, if temporary, importance. In other words, the political wills have 'weights'. The totality of political wills is thus a weighted result of individual wills, which may themselves fluctuate over time. Without analysing the causes and interests that influence the attitudes and policies of the various participants, it will not be possible to give content to this concept.

The reasons why commodity conflicts have to be analysed as a problem of *political economy* have been explained in the first two chapters. Summarised briefly, the theme is: the attitudes of governments to negotiations are determined by their economic interest in a commodity, which influences and is itself influenced by political considerations, all under an overall umbrella of systemic perceptions

267

and ideological beliefs. That the economic importance of a commodity to a country is the main factor in influencing its attitudes to regulation is so obvious as not to need much elaboration. An example is the attitude of the United States in promoting agreements in commodities in which she has a vital interest — wheat, sultanas; the US does not join the Tin Agreements because of an economic interest in preserving freedom of action on the disposal of surplus stocks. Having pursued policies which produce large quantities of surplus high-cost sugar, economic interests dictate that the EEC cannot join a sugar agreement that can restrain the freedom to export sugar at whatever cost. Any country, developed or developing, that produces synthetic rubber is bound to be reluctant to consider control on synthetic production. Japan is naturally apprehensive about iron ore producers getting together, given the fact that a large part of her economy is so dependent on imports of cheap ore; this dependence is also the reason why a tight control is maintained on the shipping of the ore.

It is equally obvious that the higher the dependence of a country on a commodity, the greater the tenacity with which it will pursue the economic objectives of preservation of market shares and optimistion earnings. The relationship between the character of the exporter — large or small, established or emerging — and the different attitudes adopted to different aspects of regulation have been described in Chapter 5. The change in the attitude of Brazil from pursuing production control and diversification in the 1962 and 1968 Coffee Agreements to their total abandonment in the 1976 Agreement is a direct result of the change in production in that country. The reasons for this change, discussed in Chapter 9, illustrate one other interesting aspect of the impact of economic interest on political wills. Do countries follow a short-term interest or a long-term goal? The Brazilian example would indicate that in a reasonably stable environment large exporters may follow long-term objectives but that in an unstable situation short-term advantages take priority. The example of the attitudes of importing governments in the Tin Agreements shows that the short-term advantage of lower prices is often preferred by consumers to the long-term one of promoting production by agreeing to higher prices. By and large, countries generally opt for policies that have short-term advantages, perhaps because they realise that in the ever changing commodity markets a long-term objective is intrinsically unobtainable. To paraphrase Harold Wilson ('A week in politics is a long time'), five years is a long time in commodity trade. Political will, in relation to economic interests, is what a country thinks is likely to happen in the course of the next two, or at most three, years.

How are these economic interests modified by politics? Without repeating the many examples quoted in the earlier chapters, the conclusions can be briefly stated as follows. Sometimes political considerations override ideological commitments and induce an interest in regulation when there are no vital economic interests precluding it. In some cases, commodity negotiations even have political pay-offs unrelated to economic advantage. In rare cases (e.g. sugar), political interests may even override significant economic interests. Chapter 10 was devoted to a consideration of the special aspects of political associations that act to the advantage of primary commodity exporting countries, particularly some developing ones. Where a set of developing countries are clear beneficiaries, politics determine the choice of recipients. In all cases, the influence of politics on the attitudes of governments depends on who the participants are. Once stated, this is self-evident, but the obvious is rarely said in so obvious a fashion. It is usually cloaked under a vague concept of political will.

The Individual Will

Political will, even that of a single country, is not a constant, invariant to time. The mere fact that most governments take a short-term view of the commodity market and its regulation is an indication that attitudes change as circumstances change. At times of high prices, the keenness of exporters for regulatory mechanisms declines sharply; at times of low prices it is the importers who lack enthusiasm for regulation. If in a single commodity an upswing in price reduces the 'will' of the exporters, in a boom period the effect is more widespread. In booms, all commodity negotiations receive a setback and running agreements face severe strains and usually collapse. Political will is also directly related to the ability to hold on. The discipline of the exporting countries as a whole bears an inverse relationship to the total quantity of surplus or shortage. The higher the stocks the greater the temptation to break ranks. The temptation to evade international obligations is not confined only to developing exporting countries.[1] Examples have been given of the rich importing countries encouraging, or at least condoning, the evasion of obligations by companies in their countries. If one major importing country obtains large quantities of cheap 'tourist' coffee, all others are encouraged to do so. Exporter indiscipline has a snowball effect; so does importer indiscipline. Thus, the political will of the participants changes if that of others change. From this it was also concluded that no country could be classified permanently as being either a compliant member of an agreement or a recalcitrant member. The temptations against complying vary with time, and the success of any commodity understanding depends on encouraging observance and discouraging evasion. This cannot be achieved by threat of penalties or punishment. Nothing can force governments to honour commitments which they feel, rightly or wrongly, to be against their national interest. Perceived national interest often overwhelms international responsibility.

Thus the number of factors which go to make up so-called 'political will' are many. Before one can even attempt to determine what the will of any country is, at any given time, a series of questions has to be answered first:

Overall attitudes

(i) Is it a developed or a developing country?

(ii) What is its attitude to commodity agreements in general and to the resource transfer objective in particular?

(iii) Is the country an exporter or an importer?

State of the market

(iv) What is the level of prices – high or low?

(v) Which way are prices expected to move in the near future?

(vi) What are the total stocks of the commodity? Are they adequate, overhanging or insufficient?

(vii) Is there a prospect of a downturn in production due to natural calamities or production cycles?

(viii) Is there a likelihood of political turmoil in a major producing or consuming area?

(ix) Is the market threatened by synthetics or substitutes?

The country's situation

(x) What is the degree of dependence on exports or imports?

(xi) What is the economic interest in the commodity?

(xii) If an importer, does it protect home production?

(xiii) If an exporter how large? established or new?

(xiv) What is the level of stocks in the country in relation to its holding power?

(xv) What are the relative strengths of different domestic pressure groups – producers, processors, importers, consumers?

(xvi) What is the degree of control over production and marketing?

(xvii) Who are its political allies? adversaries?

In functioning agreements

(xviii) What importance do importers attach to the agreement?
(xix) Who is most likely to break away?
(xx) Who is most likely to follow suit?

This list of 'twenty questions' is not meant as a joke; every one of them has a relevance to the shaping of the political will. In Chapter 3, the 35 commodities were classified under nine major characteristics in order to assist in determining how they affected the attitudes of governments to commodity regulation and towards the other participants in a negotiation leading to such regulation. The 20 questions listed above are not only related directly to these characteristics but have also been modified to suit the influence of political considerations. If these can be answered with reasonable accuracy, one can predict the attitude of any country to a specific negotiation in view at that time. Unfortunately, this judgement is not wholly quantifiable. In theory, one could grade the country, say from one to five, for each of these questions and then assign arbitrary weights to each one. For example, the level of stocks could be postulated to be more important than expectations of political turmoil; or, for a small exporter, dependence can be accorded a very low weight and so on. A composite number that would be roughly indicative of the 'political will' of a country towards a negotiation could then be produced.

No doubt drawing up a matrix and playing around with weights would be a fascinating exercise, but the utility of this forced mathematics is doubtful. In order to tackle the problem of variation in time, the 'will' has to be monitored continuously throughout the period of protracted negotiations. Attempting to measure changes implies the belief that something can be done about them. If the temperature of the patient rises sharply, i.e. if the political will drops alarmingly, one must know which of the 20 causes – and in what degree of importance – were responsible for the deterioration. While answers to questions relating to the status of the country (developed or developing, exporter or importer) will not change, the group of questions under the heading 'state of the market' will have a major impact on attitude changes. What causes the change is often unclear; it may be something as simple as a change in the minister dealing with the subject. Sometimes, even the fact that the will has changed comes as a surprise to other participants in the negotiations.

The Collective Will

The quantification of the 'political will' of any one country by itself is inadequate to determine the prospects of success for any negotiation. As noted earlier, it is the 'collective will', or the totality of individual 'wills', that matters. While it is obvious that there can be no meaningful coffee agreement without Brazil and Colombia or a sugar agreement without Cuba, how does one assign weights to medium and small exporters? What importance is to be attached to coalition forming among them? What weight is to be given to preferences between different mechanisms of regulation, to the controversy between stability and resource transfer, to the importance of obtaining the co-operation of the major importing countries? An attempt can, of course, be made to devise another list of questions. But the problem is not a quantifiable mathematical exercise in which 'lack of political will' is denoted by

$$\sum_{i=1}^{i=n} w_i P_i < A$$

Where w_i is the weight assigned to a given country, P_i is its political will and A is an arbitrary number below which there is a lack and above which there is a sufficiency.

Cannot the weights be determined empirically by analysing past negotiations — successful ones as well as failures — in all the commodities? The range of variation is so wide and the number of negotiations so few that any result based on historical evidence is bound to be subject to a very large margin of error. The ability of such a formula to predict, with any reasonable degree of accuracy, the outcome of a future negotiation is highly questionable.

Bargaining Power

Though the attempt to create a theoretical framework is not being pursued, it is necessary to devote some attention to the bargaining strength of participants in a commodity negotiation, if only because this has achieved a certain vogue after the success of OPEC in raising oil prices. Further, examples of adversary, co-operative and collusive relationships have been identified as playing an important part in commodity negotiations. It is also illuminating to discuss bargaining power in the overall systemic context of the division between developed and developing countries. The system elaborated in the Havana Charter imposed an absolute equality between importers and exporters of a commodity to the extent of prescribing equality of total votes between the two groups and requiring that decisions on substantive matters should be taken by separate two thirds majorities in each group. Equality of power between the two groups does not always induce equality of responsibility. For example, the degree of co-operation shown by importers varies; developed importing countries show greater readiness to co-operate in negotiations which involve commodities of interest to other developed countries. Importer co-operation is minimal in commodities mainly produced in developing countries. The cases discussed in detail in earlier chapters prove that rich importing countries are generally reluctant to accept any significant obligations to ensure the observance of the terms of an agreement. They do not contribute to promotion funds, diversification funds or buffer stock finances; they do not normally (with one exception) undertake any responsibility in the quota policing functions. They do not agree to co-ordinate the production of synthetics. All that they seem to do is to agree to continue to provide a market; in other words, their contribution is keeping the doors at least partly open for products of developing countries. The implicit threat is that, if an agreement is not to their liking, access can be shut off. Obviously, this threat cannot be applied in the case of products of developed countries for fear of retaliation in other fields; hence the greater co-operation provided for these commodities. Once again, the asymmetric effects of the system are evident; power derives from being near the centre, having possibilities of trade-offs and making the rules of the game.

It is in this context that the prospects of commodity regulation by co-operative action by producing countries alone become relevant. The conclusion arrived at in Chapters 4 and 9 was that the success of producer action depended entirely on the ability to control a substantial share of the market and the ability to hold on. This aspect of controlling the market, as distinct from just having a share of the market, is an important one. For example, in the case of commodities where production and marketing is controlled by multinational companies, the share of the market that a country has is no indication of its ability to control the trade in it. The case studies on bananas, bauxite and iron ore prove that, in order to succeed against multinational corporations operating a closed market, the producing countries must first obtain *control* over a significant share of the market and also build up their holding power. Control of the market is not synonymous with share of the market in cases in which a ready synthetic substitute is available. Equally, in a broad group such as oils and fats, share of the market for any one oil does not provide a corresponding ability to influence the decisions of the market.

In commodities wholly produced in developing countries, the history of attempts by producing countries to control the market has been one of failure (e.g. the Cocoa Producers Alliance, Café Mundial). With their greater dependence on exports, the ever present need for foreign exchange and the very limited governmental resources for holding back supplies, the developing countries just lack economic muscle. In developed countries co-operation among producers is almost instinctive; the United States and Canada pursue parallel policies for regulating the wheat market without actually forming an Association of Wheat Exporting Countries. As Rowe remarks: 'For all exporters the US "free" price was the bulls eye and thus the world "free" price was really set by one seller and not by four large exporters in competition with one another.'[2] (The word 'free' was put in quotes by Rowe — not by this author, who has been inveighing against the mythical concept of the free market!) Thus, exporter co-operation depends for its success on power, and power is derived from backing resources.

It is necessary to reiterate that the main effect of the international economic system on developing countries is to increase their sense of vulnerability; and vulnerability implies decreasing bargaining power. The success of OPEC has tended to obscure this basic fact. The fear that followed the discovery of dependence on imports for energy prompted a rash of studies that elevated all developing countries to a power status similar to OPEC's. The US Council on International Economic Policy devoted its entire study on 'Critical Imported Materials' to an analysis of the possible bargaining and control power of producer groups in the various commodities. It is now accepted wisdom that what worked in oil will not work for the other commodities. On the other hand, it is not generally realised that the oil-exporting countries are no less vulnerable than other developing countries. Even after their wealth has increased, they still depend on the developed world for the financial institutions to manage the money, for the greatly increased imports which they can now afford and for arms. Their attempts to invest in the developed world produced predictable xenophobic reactions. In fact, their wealth itself has become a hostage. They may have gained some power and moved a little nearer to the centre in monetary matters, but in all others — trade, industrial power, technology, management — their dependence and vulnerability continues to be as great as ever.

The bogey of producer power is only a reflection of the confrontation that was created and developed by the OECD. Every time the frustrations of the excluded show themselves in some action — creation of UNCTAD, oil price increase — they are accused of creating confrontation. A system whose basic momentum is centrifugal cannot but divide. Those who benefit from the system do not want its asymmetric effects brought to the surface; those who suffer have no option but to confront the centre with the results of a system they had no hand in shaping. To talk about bargaining power in this context is another meaningless red herring. There is no equality or even commensurability of economic power between the developed and developing, and this is increasingly so in commodity trade.

The inequality of bargaining power between the developed and the developing in commodity negotiations is only a reflection of the inequality that exists in the international economic system. The point that the richer, more industrialised and more technologically advanced countries have a superior bargaining position is also obvious. It is all the more surprising that the bogey of developing country power has such a hold on the imagination of the public and the media in the better-off world.

The patent incommensurability of bargaining power between the rich and the poor does not imply that, within the two groups, all countries have a superior bargaining position is obvious. It is all the the same in all commodities. Enough examples have been cited earlier to prove the point that major exporters or importers of a given commodity have a predominant, often decisive, voice in the conduct of negotiations. The whole range of economic, political and ideological factors comes into play in determining the actual power that a country can wield in negotiations. Often this is instinctively felt by the other participants rather than explicitly quantified. As in the case of political will, it is not possible to propound a theoretical formula for quantifying bargaining power that could be of practical utility.

Is the effort to understand the factors behind 'political will' or bargaining power a futile endeavour? The temptation is to declare that commodity negotiations are so complex that attempts at understanding them should be given up. But agreements, however few, have been concluded in the past; even though many have failed to run the course, some have worked successfully at least for reasonable periods of time. In all cases in which negotiations have been successful, the collective political will was, in fact, adequate. Therefore, in abandoning the search for a theoretical framework which will supposedly explain everything one need not also abandon the search for a constructive approach which might increase the chances of success. This can only be done by looking for the positive elements in the past history of commodity negotiations and by building a structure that will include those while eliminating as many of the negative ones as possible. The next chapter therefore is in the nature of a summary of the analysis thus far undertaken. It places commodity conflicts in the systemic context outlined in Chapter 1 and attempts to identify the constructive strands which will promote success in commodity negotiations as well as the limitations that might inhibit it.

Notes

1. The classic example of evasion by the rich industrialised nations is one not directly related to commodity trade. The so-called 'voluntary restriction' on trade between developed countries in manufactured goods (e.g. exports of automobiles, steel) would be a direct violation of Article XIII of GATT on 'Non-discriminatory Administration of Quantitative Restrictions', had they been imposed as an import quota against a single exporting country.
2. J.W.F. Rowe, *Markets and Men* (Cambridge University Press, Cambridge, 1936).

12 ASPECTS OF CONFLICT RESOLUTION

> The United States is ready to cooperate in serious case-by-case
> examination of the commodity market problems.
>
> President Kennedy, Alliance for Progress speech,
> 13 March 1961

> The United States proposes to discuss new arrangements
> in individual commodities on a case-by-case basis.
>
> Dr Kissinger, US Secretary of State,
> Address to the Seventh Special Session of the
> UN General Assembly, 1 September 1975

The more things change, the more they remain the same. In 1961, the
United States declared its readiness to examine *seriously* commodity
problems on a 'case-by-case' basis. Fourteen years later, the United
States, as part of a much heralded new initiative, proposed to discuss
new arrangements in individual commodities 'on a case-by-case basis'.
On both occasions, the not-so-stirring words were accompanied by
fanfares of trumpets proclaiming great breakthroughs and changes of
position. What breakthrough? In 1961, the United States proposed the
conclusion of a new International Coffee Agreement; in 1975, Dr
Kissinger declared that 'we are actively participating in negotiations on
coffee'. In the 1960s, the United States was participating in cocoa and
sugar negotiations and in 1975 it continued to do so. The only addition
in 1975 was the declared intention to sign the International Tin
Agreement, 'subject to Congressional consultations and ratification' and
with the proviso that 'we will retain our right to sell from our strategic
stockpile.' President Kennedy said in 1961: 'Frequent violent changes
in commodity prices seriously injure the economies of many Latin
American countries, draining their resources and stultifying their
growth.' Dr Kissinger said in 1975: 'The development programs —
indeed the basic survival — of many countries rest heavily on earnings
from exports of primary products, which are highly vulnerable to
fluctuations in worldwide demand... The unpredictability of export
earnings can make a mockery of development planning.' So, after 14
years, what is new?

What is new is that the developing countries see themselves as
gradually becoming less and less important in international trade in the

277

entire period since the war. Reference to the statistics given in Chapter 3 will recall the facts that the share of the non-oil exporting developing countries in total world exports shrank from a quarter in 1950 to just over 10 per cent in the mid-1970s; their share in primary commodity exports, excluding fuel, declined from two fifths to just over a quarter in the same period. Is trade important? Cannot developing countries achieve progress even if their share of exports and imports decreases? There may well be divergent views on whether there has been adequate total development in developing countries – both growth in economic terms and improvement in social welfare, in nutrition, health, education, employment opportunity and income distribution. But progress there has been; defined narrowly as economic growth, significant advances have been made in national income, agricultural production, particularly food production, industrial development and in dissemination of technology. Even though growth has occurred in the face of declining importance in trade, it still matters for a number of reasons. Given the facts that aid is becoming more unpopular and the debt burden is increasing, the role of the international trading and monetary system in promoting growth is obvious. Secondly, decreasing trade shares and declining terms of trade are two main reasons for the developing world's perception of its vulnerability. Few countries can, or even want to, adopt the total self-reliance model; if countries see themselves as part of an interdependent market economy world, their decreasing participation in it cannot but be a source of frustration. Lastly, there is reason to be concerned at the political consequences of a system that is becoming increasingly closed as the rich countries trading among themselves in manufactures as well as primary commodities push back the peripheral countries to the outermost edges of the system.

Apart from peripherality, some other concepts were identified as being relevant to the conflict between developed and developing countries over the international system as a whole. These were: asymmetry, vulnerability, insensitivity, economic inefficiency and inseparability of politics and economics. Some conclusions applicable to the system in general were also indicated. Do these conclusions apply to the commodity trade sector also, or is it free from any or all the blemishes? While it would be unduly repetitive to summarise here all the conclusions reached in the earlier chapters, it is nevertheless necessary to relate them specifically to commodity trade. The inter-relationship between politics and economics in commodity negotiations has been amply demonstrated. In fact, it can even be argued that they are even more inextricably intertwined than, say, in the field of trade in manufactures. Commodity production and trade occupy a special place in the domestic policies of most governments. In agricultural commodities, the social problems of the farming communities have always been given, in developed and developing countries, at least as high a priority as the economic aspects of agriculture. Minerals have a special place, just because they are non-renewable resources. It is no wonder that the post-war economic system, devised by the rich industrial countries, concentrated on liberalisation of the industrial part of international trade and tacitly recognised the right of governments to be as protectionist as they pleased in agriculture. Since autarky is more the norm than the exception, commodity trade is likely to be more blemished than other parts of the system; consequently, asymmetry is more likely.

The distribution of gains from commodity trade has been analysed to see whether the system was as asymmetric in its operation in this sector as it is elsewhere. The perception of asymmetry by the developing countries is strengthened by their awareness of a number of effects — decrease in terms of trade, erosion in import purchasing power, instability in commodity prices, unequal distribution of productivity gains and declining share of the exporter in the returns. An extraordinary effect of the system is that both booms and recessions affect the peripheral countries adversely; contrary to popular belief, boom periods also benefit mainly the rich commodity exporting countries in terms of increases in earnings as well as in shares of the market. However, the asymmetric distribution of gains is not solely a result of the inequities of the system; attention has been drawn earlier to the developing countries' failure to take action to obtain the advantages which the system can provide. Lack of aggression in selling, inadequate investment in product and market development and inability even to extract information from multinational companies were some of the shortcomings identified.

The vulnerability of developing countries in commodity trade has been repeatedly stressed in the earlier chapters. A characteristic common to most developing exporters of primary products, except oil, is their lack of ability to hold on in times of stress; this decreases their ability to regulate the market for any length of time. Every external force — international monetary instability, inflation in developed countries, violent price fluctuations — increases this vulnerability. On top of this, the widespread denial of access for processed and manufactured forms exported by the poor countries has a pervasive effect on development restraint. Not being able to obtain higher unit values reduces resources; non-availability of export markets limits scope for industrialisation; inability to diversify the export pattern puts poor countries even more at the mercy of the fluctuations in the commodity markets; lop-sided development complicates economic planning and increases social tension and, being made to be permanently exporters of raw materials places them in a weak bargaining position in relation not only to the importing countries but also to the buyers of the commodities.

If there is more politics than economics in commodity trade, if protection of farming communities is promoted regardless of cost and if protection of employment is more important than the burden on the consumer, the goal of efficiency must rank very low indeed in the eyes of governments. While there is no dearth of domestic pressure groups, there is no international public interest in efficiency; there never has been. The two casualties of the system as it operates in commodity trade are 'the law of comparative advantage' and the 'rewarding of efficiency in production'. Whether cotton textiles and footwear can be manufactured more efficiently and at less cost in developing countries is irrelevant to most governments of rich countries, whose sole objective is the protection of employment. In the contest between the comparatively poor in the rich countries and the poor in the poor countries, the latter always lose; as Emmanuel rightly remarks, there is no longer any international solidarity of the proletariat. Except in isolated instances, governments always take the easy road of protectionism rather than the more complicated route of shifting labour from agriculture to industry or from low technology to high technology industries. Where is the promotion of efficient production, if the Community pays its farmers £100 a ton to produce beet sugar which it then proceeds to dump on the world market at £20 a ton? The saga of the dairy products' mountains is even more horrific; in spite of a stock of 46,000 tons of butter and nearly half a million tons of milk powder, the EEC *raised* prices by 7.5 per cent in 1976; by February 1977, the mountains had grown to 190,000 tons of butter and over a million tons of milk powder, all acquired at a cost of 1.5 billion US dollars. Since the EEC intervention price for butter is four times the world price, every export sale is another flagrant example of dumping. One can only conclude that the Community reaches for its gun whenever somebody mentions efficiency! Not that abandonment of the concept of efficient production is confined only to the developed countries. The fact is that in all countries there are no votes to be gained by promoting global efficiency.

That the developing countries see the rich ones as insensitive to their problems does not also require much elaboration. The long list of failures in negotiations and the repeated attribution of lack of political will are proof enough. Two other points add strength to this belief about insensitivity. The developed countries have rarely, if ever, taken any initiative to propose solutions to commodity problems; they have only reacted to the proposals of the poor countries, often tardily. The developed countries also have a habit of postponing consideration of any proposals either by demanding more studies or by using any forthcoming event — some conference or other, some election somewhere or other, a summit meeting of some rich group or other — as a pretext for arguing that everyone should await the results of that event; usually there is no positive result. Insensitivity is also apparent in the refusal of the rich countries to apply various techniques to the developing countries which they have no hesitation in using either domestically or among small groups of developed countries. Informal arrangements, minimum price support schemes and use of fiscal measures are examples. After all, the only 'Gentlemen's Agreement' is under the OECD; presumably wealth is a prerequisite of being a 'gentleman'! The same insensitivity is at the root of the unco-ordinated development of synthetic substitutes.

In its characteristics, operation and effects, commodity trade is no different from the other parts of the international economic system; in fact, in many instances it. is worse. The point that resolution of commodity problems cannot be tackled in isolation from the system is thus reinforced. In attempting such conflict resolution, account has to be taken of some general conclusions that have emerged from the analysis in previous chapters.

The Real and the Ideal World

The commodity trade system described in this book is not an idealised vision of the Havana Charter but the one which exists in reality, with protectionism, closed markets and omnipresent distortions of the free market. Of the total trade in primary commodities, only about a sixth can be said to be traded under free conditions. A quarter of the total trade consists of 'closed' markets or is controlled by oligopolistic buyers; over a third is distorted by protectionism. The interesting fact is that the commodities mainly produced in the developing countries are either subjected to the full buffeting of market forces, made more violent by speculation, or are under the firm grip of a few multinational corporations. In contrast, the controlled and distorted market is predominantly made up of commodities of export interest to developed countries. Protectionism exerts a significant downward pressure on international prices in addition to reducing the available market. One is therefore forced to the conclusion that in the real world the virtues of a free market determination of prices are more mythical than real. Regulation of a commodity market is the preferred method if the country or group of countries interested in a commodity have the market power to enforce it.

The dichotomy between the real world and the idealised vision of commodity agreements was seen clearly in the examination of the success of techniques of regulation in Chapter 9. A crucial point stressed in the examination of the market place was that the success of any technique of regulation depended on the view of the market. It is not enough if a technique is said to be acceptable by many governments; the market makes a judgement not only on the desire of the different governments to implement the mechanism but also on the possible changes in time of the desire. There is a difference between what governments say they intend to do and what the market believes they actually will do. If the negotiated solutions are so rigid that they cannot but diverge from reality as circumstances change, failure is built in. In spite of the proved limitations of the various techniques, the hold which some patently impractical ones have on the minds of governments is astonishing. For example, the Dakar Declaration of developing countries calls for the establishment of international stocks and market intervention arrangements and suggests: 'Stocking operations could be organised on a multi-commodity basis whereby a central agency would buy and sell stock for a number of commodities in accordance with agreed criteria on operations.'[1] A multi-commodity international trading agency is a financial monstrosity and an administrative nightmare.

This divergence from reality is also seen in the faith which many governments have in the transferability of tested domestic solutions to similar international problems. Many examples have been cited to illustrate the wrong assumption that what works well in a stable domestic politico-economic environment will work equally well when transferred to the international system. For example, in a predictable environment, commodity exchanges and speculative trading may help to stabilise the market; in an international exchange, with its greater volatility and limited quantities, speculation usually magnifies price changes. Equilibrium, even long-term equilibrium, is a reasonably valid concept when the environment is stable; long-term equilibrium has no meaning in an international commodity market in which nothing can be assumed to be constant for any length of time. In most developed countries, the market mechanism of higher prices at the expense of the consumer rather than a direct subsidy from the exchequer to the farmer is preferred for transferring resources to the agricultural sector. This cannot be assumed to be equally practicable in the international system; otherwise the whole argument about the use of commodity agreements as a mechanism to transfer resources need never have taken place. The absence of overall authority, the inability to arrive at and implement decisions quickly and the fact that governments distort activities at the border — all these make it impossible for domestic solutions to cross frontiers and still retain their efficacy.

The preference of governments for solutions based on their own experience is understandable. It is not only generals who are always fighting the last war; bureaucrats and politicians are also forever solving the last crisis. The result, however, is an unproductive rigidity in thinking. Even though the Havana Charter and its International Trade Organisation were summarily jettisoned by its principal promoter, the United States still holds the principles of the Charter sacrosanct. The Charter's insistence on a five-year maximum duration for commodity agreements is not necessarily good for all commodities at all times; nor is the absolute equality between importers as a group and exporters as a group a condition that should hold true irrespective of the obligations of the two groups. The rigidity which the Charter has imposed on thinking about the form and mechanics of commodity arrangements is itself responsible for many of the failures. The reason why the United States abandoned the ITO was that it discovered that the real world bore little resemblance to the ideal world of the Charter. The implicit assumption in the Charter was that in an open international trading system the principle of 'fairness to consumers and a reasonable return to producers' would operate as successfully as it does in a domestic free market economy. In this assumption at all valid? One will never know the answer to this hypothetical question. In this world of nation states, the international economic system has never approached that degree of freedom which could test the relationship between openness and equity. Those who believe in it can do so only as an article of faith; those who lack such lodestars of certainty can only point out that the real world is so far removed from the ideal vision as to make the concept meaningless in actual practice.

The real world is also a world politically divided into three parts — one isolated, another vulnerable and the third insensitive. The world has so far failed to approach commodity conflicts with a global perspective. Global, in this context, not only refers to political divisions but also means an approach that covers all aspects of commodity negotiations.

The Punch-Bag Effect

The two quotations at the head of this chapter illustrate the hold which the commodity-by-commodity approach has on thinking about commodity regulation. At first sight, it has a strong appeal, mainly because commodity negotiations are extremely complex. The characteristics of the commodities are so different, the markets so varied and the techniques applicable so diverse that it does seem better to tackle them one by one. Two things are wrong with this reasoning. First, the success of the commodity-by-commodity approach has been very meagre. The assumption that picking on commodities one by one and solving the problem of each on its own merits simply has not worked. Second, this very approach ignores the effect of regulation in one commodity on others. This is what in this book has repeatedly been described as the punch-bag effect. The effect is not just the simplest and best-known case of substitutability. The complications induced by easy substitutability can in fact be treated as part of the inherent characteristics of the market for a commodity and have been so analysed in this study. The punch-bag effect is different; it arises precisely because commodities are treated in isolation and because the regulations meant for one have unintended effects on others.

The commodity group 'oils and fats' provides the best example of this effect. In itself, it is a complicated interchangeable group comprising tropical and temperature oils, hard and soft ones. The regulation of the market for any one oil is an impossibility. The regulation of the market for all oils is so complex as to be impracticable. The market in oilseeds is of course integrally related to that of oils; so is the market for processed oils, hydrogenated oils and margarine. The series — oilseeds, oils and processed oils — itself provides an example of the problems of access for processed products. The market for oils is also governed by the element of protection provided in importing countries to dairy products, since butter is a competitor of margarine and the edible oils. The protectionist policies for butter and other dairy products are based on considerations of the total return to the farmer in terms not only of these products but also of beef. In another direction, the market for oilseed cake is related to the market for oils since it is a by-product; it is also related to the market for animal feed. The European Economic Community has in the past made its surplus sugar inedible for human consumption and used it as animal feed, thus affecting the market for oilcake. Recently the Community has decided to use skim milk powder as animal feed, thus again reducing the oilcake market. It must be recalled that the skim milk mountain, which necessitates its use as animal feed, is itself a result of the dairy policy referred to earlier. If the market for oilcake diminishes and its price falls, the cost of oils may increase, resulting in competitors of edible oils increasing their share of the market. The vicious circle will revolve with increasing momentum. The reaction on the animal feed market of surplus dairy products or sugar will also be felt by feed grains, which in turn will affect the production pattern of grains, sugar and oilseeds elsewhere in the world. This one example shows how the markets of a wide variety of commodities are inter-connected — oilseeds, oils, oilcake, butter, whole and skim milk powder, sugar, beef and feed grains.

This inter-relationship is not only confined to commodities produced both in developed and developing countries; a similar effect has also been seen in the case of tropical beverages. By adopting the commodity-by-commodity approach, international financial institutions such as the World Bank actively assisted in the production of tea in new areas which could not expand coffee production because of international regulations. The result was that the world tea supply was always in excess of demand and that tea is one of the few commodities to show a secular decline in price over a long period; even the commodity boom did not benefit it much. The effect of regulation of coffee will eventually be felt by cocoa. Faced with the market situations in coffee and tea, a number of countries are diversifying into cocoa, and some will emerge as exporters.

The coffee-tea-cocoa inter-relationship is only one example of the land use problem that has been discussed in the context of the options open to governments to optimise their returns and maximise the earnings of their farmers. Jute and rice, coffee and bananas are two other examples considered. If the highest priority is to be accorded to increasing food production in Bangla Desh, then that country must be compensated for the inevitable loss of exchange earnings that will follow as a consequence of the reduction in jute production. If some Central American countries cannot increase coffee production because of international regulation and if they cannot increase earnings from banana exports because of control by multinational companies, then some means must be found to meet the legitimate objectives of the countries and their farmers. Land use control is a common feature of the agricultural policies of most developed countries, which have the resources to implement them whatever the cost. The cost of the Common Agricultural Policy is illogically enormous and takes 70 per cent of the budget of the Community. But the EEC can afford this extravagance and, willy-nilly, the rest of the world has also been forced to make its contribution by loss of markets, by depressed prices and paying for its dumping. The CAP is the most glaring example of the punch-bag effect. What the Community does in grains, oils and sugar affects all commodity markets. One cannot but conclude that attempts to deal with commodity trade on a commodity-by-commodity basis or on the basis of a restricted geographical area have undesirable effects on other commodities and other areas. They lead to situations in which a success in one product or in one area will automatically and inevitably lead to failures in other products and areas. The flexibility of approach emphasised in other contexts has necessarily to take note of this effect too.

Flexibility in Applying Techniques

A flexible set of solutions is also necessary because of the varying degrees of acceptability of the different techniques of regulation. The acceptability of a technique to different participants is not merely a function of whether the country concerned has the machinery to implement it but also of whether it desires to do so. Centrally planned economies can assure access in terms of absolute quantities: market economy countries can only act indirectly to promote it. A variable levy is easy for the EEC to implement; perhaps less so for countries such as Canada and the United States. Desire to implement a technique for a particular commodity is quite another thing; the United States dislikes quantitative restrictions except when it imposes import quotas on oil or export quotas or soyabeans. Just as importing countries have preferences among techniques, so do the exporting countries. Those with a large domestic consumption or the ability to hold stocks can implement an export quota system successfully. The nature of production also influences ability to impose export or production controls — plantation economies are better able to do so than smallholder ones. The need for an appropriate mix of techniques acceptable to different countries was most clearly seen in the discussion on promoting access to processed and manufactured forms of primary products. The range of possibilities that any one exporting country can undertake processing will be limited; equally, the ability of different importing countries to relax barriers will also be limited. The constraints on exporting countries arise from limitations of natural endowment, technological skills and financial resources. In the importing countries, the limits on liberalisation are determined by the extent of economic loss, the pressure of social factors and the political compulsions of national security.

Reciprocity and Burden Sharing

Among developed countries, negotiations can be undertaken with the prospect of mutually satisfactory trade-offs. Given their vulnerability and lack of bargaining power, developing countries have much less to offer to developed countries in the way of trade-offs. The periphery cannot match increased access for primary products and processed forms with pay-offs of commensurate value in industrial imports. Even if one assumes that stability of markets benefits both importers and exporters, there still remains the important question of resource transfer. It is evident that, in the types of action that have been recommended in this book, a burden devolves on the advanced countries. Which countries can be considered 'advanced' in this context will be discussed in chapter 14.

The burdens of commodity regulation are many. For the exporters, restraint on exports is a burden because it means regulation of production, restraint on incomes of citizens producing or dealing in the commodity and usually provision for them of alternative sources of remuneration. Holding stocks is a more tangible burden, since storage has a quantifiable financial cost. This is sometimes explicitly recognised, as in the case of the higher supply commitment prices in the Sugar Agreement, though generally the cost of holding stocks is considered to be the normal burden borne by any exporter. In particular, the holding of food stocks as insurance against famine and starvation is a contribution to world economic stability. Burdens do not fall equally on all exporters or even in proportion to their share of the market. A differential burden between higher-cost and low-cost producers is always implicit in any commodity regulation, whether the producing country is rich or poor. Countries with a large domestic consumption of an export product are more cushioned against the impact of export restraint than countries with little or no domestic demand. Such differential burdens have to be reckoned in ascertaining the reciprocity that can legitimately be expected.

There are burdens on importers too. Providing access usually involves a sacrifice. If the European Economic Community is to be persuaded to reduce production of sugar and other protected products, the costs incurred must be counted as a contribution to the reciprocity exercise. It may amount to paying somebody not to do something nasty to you — but then protection rackets have always worked in this way. Providing increased access to processed forms also involves a burden. This may arise from loss of revenue due to tariff reduction or may appear as a positive cost to the importing country in adjustment assistance. Harmonisation of synthetic production, if and when it is seriously attempted, also involves a burden. On the assumption that co-ordinating production of synthetics will provide the natural product with a stable and growing market, harmonisation may mean a balance of payments loss to some countries. Participation by importers in control mechanisms may mean imposition of variable levies or at least creation of new administrative or fiscal machinery. It has repeatedly been emphasised that the full co-operation of the main importing countries is essential if the objectives of commodity regulation are to be successfully achieved. Such co-operation can only be bought by giving the importers 'credit' for doing so. In short, there is hardly any area of commodity regulation which does not throw a burden on one participant or the other.

Governments of whatever persuasion are reluctant to adopt policies that have no element of reciprocity built into them; purely unilateral action in any field is almost always impossible. Specifically on the resource transfer question, there is an understandable disinclination on the part of the rich countries to multiply the number of funds to which they can contribute. To add more mechanisms to the bilateral aid programmes and the already numerous multilateral aid agencies makes it more difficult to decide on the equitable sharing of the burden among themselves. Perusal of any report of the Development Assistance Committee of the OECD and its involved discussions on the 'grant element' or the role of private transfers, indicates that the whole argument is about equitable burden sharing. The Oil Facility, the International Agricultural Development Fund, the Prebisch Fund — name any resource transfer mechanism and the argument is always about the fair proportion of contributions.

While negotiations are usually looked on as a bargaining for advantage (pay-offs) to be gained by the parties involved, it is nevertheless essential also to consider them as a means of equalising dissatisfaction. While one party may gain an advantage, the purpose of negotiation is to ensure that the others do not gain what is considered to be an 'unfair' advantage. No one emerges from a negotiation getting all that he has set out to secure. All parties to a negotiation have some dissatisfaction — the gap between what they believe they are entitled to and what they actually get. A successful negotiation is one in which all are equally dissatisfied – in which no one has, *or is seen to have had*, a greater sense of achievement. Reciprocity and sharing of burdens is the opposite side of the coin of equality of dissatisfaction.

Elements of a New Approach

One other concept, referred to in Chapter 1, is the questioning of the legitimacy of the system by some of the participants. The developing countries talk about a *new* international economic order because they see the old order as one which increasingly excludes them from active participation. They also emphasise a new regime for commodity marketing because it is in this area that the adverse effects are most clearly felt. Conversely, the developed countries have very little incentive to change the existing system because, for them, it has had the effect of a steady and sustained increase in the share of the market and in control over the system as a whole. Why should anybody abandon a system that results in a continuous accretion of power to themselves? No wonder Secretary of State Henry Kissinger suggests: 'Let us put aside the sterile debate over whether a new economic order is required.' To him the debate is bound to look sterile – after all, sterility is often seen as a loss of potency, i.e. power. If the debate is felt to be sterile, one course of action is to withdraw from it. In discussing the future roles of UNCTAD, GATT and OECD, Kenneth Dam remarks:

> GATT continues to have the confidence of many, if not most, developed countries. . . With the less developed countries having reached a majority position in the GATT, the situation might change rapidly if they should decide to use the GATT – as they have used the UNCTAD – as an instrument for putting pressure on the developed countries. In that event the developed countries might choose to rely more often on the OECD as the major forum for the resolution of commercial policy issues.[2]

Increasing autarky and making the divisions of the three-part world more impermeable is no way to increase collective economic security. A new approach that will promote interdependence in practical terms must learn the lessons of past experience. In summary, these are:

(i) This is an imperfect world; countries do not always act according to their proclaimed principles. They follow short-term goals and often miss opportunities for improvement. The real world is not a 'free market' world but mostly a distorted, protected, closed one. Governments cannot be forced to participate in regulatory action or negotiate commodity agreements if they have no political or economic interest in doing so.

(ii) The commodity-by-commodity approach has not been successful. This and other rigidities of thought imposed by the Havana Charter must be loosened.

(iii) The limitations of the techniques must be reckoned with; some work some of the time, none of them work all the time, and a few will not work at all. The techniques chosen must be flexible enough to deal with unexpected changes in the environment and be discriminating enough to be acceptable to different participants. The assumption that techniques that work in a stable domestic environment will function equally well in the international arena is false.

(iv) The approach must cover a large variety of commodities in order to avoid the past situation in which action in one commodity or area has adversely affected other commodities or areas.

(v) A global approach that can include all systems of government and that can promote the more efficient use of global resources is to be preferred to piecemeal solutions.

(vi) A fresh global approach must recognise that stability of trading and security of supply of essential raw materials are important to many countries; so are resource transfer and assured earnings to many others. Promotion of processing industries and increased exports of processed products are vital elements. Increased access in general, reduced protectionism and enhanced share of c.i.f. earnings for exporters are all desirable objectives. If, in the process of achieving some of these objectives, distortions and closed markets are reduced and a freer trading system results, so much the better.

(vii) The approach cannot be based on unilateral action by one group of countries; in order for it to be saleable, a concept of reciprocity must be built into it.

(viii) Existing positive political relationships must be used as the basis for building further constructive action.

(ix) And, last, collective economic security depends on decreasing feelings of vulnerability and increasing sensitivity among nations.

Notes

1. See sub-paragraph (a), paragraph 1, 'A. Overall Integrated Programme on Commodities' of Part II 'International Action' of the 'Action Programme'

adopted by the Dakar Conference of Developing Countries on Raw Materials (UNCTAD TD/B/C.1/L.45). The Action Programme is not reproduced in Appendix 2.

2. Kenneth W. Dam, *The GATT: Law and International Economic Organization* (The University of Chicago Press, Chicago, 1970).

13 AFTER UNCTAD IV. . . ?

> For hungry men and women cannot wait for economic discussions or diplomatic meetings; their need is urgent and their hunger rests heavily on the conscience of their fellow-men.
>
> President Kennedy, Alliance for Progress speech

> . . .for the poor of the world are becoming aware both of their poverty and the reasons for it. And as this happens they are becoming angry, and determined upon change.
>
> President Nyerere, Letter to European Socialists

The conclusion that the commodity-by-commodity approach has not been notably successful is not an original one. The redoubtable Keynes even anticipated, as early as 1942, that it *would* not succeed.[1] His three-pronged approach to the organisation of the international economic system after the Second World War involved the creation of three international institutions, one for handling exchange rate problems, one for long-term financing for post-war reconstruction and development and the third for financing commodity stabilisation. The Bretton Woods Conference accepted the first two and created the IMF and the World Bank; the third did not get on to the Conference agenda because of American opposition to interference in commodity markets. The next attempt towards a comprehensive approach was made in GATT in 1956 to negotiate a Special Agreement on Commodity Arrangements. The problem 20 years ago was much simpler than it is today; the objective of commodity arrangements was then merely evening out fluctuations in prices. There were far fewer independent less-developed countries, UNCTAD I had not happened and the resource transfer objective had not become inextricably enmeshed with the stability objective. Producer associations had not displayed any power and producer-consumer parity was the accepted norm. Even so, the GATT attempt failed, again mainly because of the ideological hostility of the United States. The United Kingdom, then the most important importing country, also had reservations; so did Australia for different reasons.[2] After this failure, commodity negotiations in GATT, particularly in agricultural products, floundered on the conflict between the United States and the increasingly important EEC about the means of regulating trade, the former preferring liberalisation and the latter emphasising organisation of markets.

The last major effort at resolving commodity problems on a commodity-by-commodity approach was the series of intensive inter-governmental consultations initiated as a result of Resolution 83 (III) of the third UNCTAD Conference at Santiago in 1972.[3] It is interesting to note that the only dissent on the Resolution came from the United States on the grounds that it gave 'an excessively broad mandate to the UNCTAD Secretariat to call commodity consultations'. The rooted hostility of the United States to any across-the-board negotiations on all commodities is a permanent political reality. The intensive consultations covered 14 commodities or groups of commodities but achieved very little on any one. The Secretary-General of UNCTAD summed up the achievements as 'meagre', since 'the recommendations made were couched, with few exceptions, in such general terms that little, if anything, emerged which could be interpreted as action-oriented, let alone concrete measures'.[4] While the oil crisis, the commodity boom and recession in the developed countries might have contributed to this failure, a fundamental reason was the difference in approach between the developing countries and the developed ones. The poor countries intended the consultations to be negotiations, since in their view they were not likely to get worthwhile results from the Multilateral Trade Negotiations under way in GATT. The rich countries preferred the MTN in their own forum and made it clear that UNCTAD 'consultations' did not mean 'negotiations'. Once again the conflict over forums led to a situation where one party was negotiating while the other was merely 'discussing' to while away the time.

One result of this failure was willingness of most governments (again with the exception of the United States) to try an across-the-board approach. The attempt to tackle commodity problems from an entirely new perspective was initiated by the Secretary-General of UNCTAD, Dr Gamani Corea, under the title 'An Integrated Programme for Commodities'. The Programme is analysed in this chapter in considerable detail because it is the most recent, and on-going, comprehensive set of commodity negotiations. Further, after the debacle of the Sixth Special Session, an impression was created by the developed countries that UNCTAD IV would achieve significant and substantial progress. The negotiations relating to the Programme exemplify almost all the conflicts that have been analysed in this book.

The Evolution of the Integrated Programme

The evolution of the Integrated Programme from its conception to the form in which it finally emerged as Resolution 93 (IV) of the Fourth UNCTAD Conference is in itself a fascinating example of the politics of commodity negotiations. As first conceived, the programme consisted of five major mutually supporting elements: (i) a series of international stocks; (ii) a Common Fund for financing them; (iii) multilateral commitments in trade; (iv) compensatory financing; and (v) expansion in processing in developing countries.[5] In presenting the programme to the eighth session of the UNCTAD Committee on Commodities in February 1975, the Secretariat emphasised stocks as a 'first and major initiative', supported by a generalised financing arrangement. After noting the improvements contemplated in the IMF Compensatory Financing Scheme and the agreement reached between the EEC and the ACP countries on the Stabex scheme, the Secretariat assured the meeting that the remaining two aspects had not been ignored. The Secretary-General specially stressed that

> the proposed integrated programme would be a balanced one; it set out what could be done by producers and consumers together... Adoption of the integrated programme would not mean, in the Secretariat's view, that Government would have to regulate commerce in ways that were impracticable for many important trading countries.[6]

At this point, the approach was balanced and multi-pronged, with the emphasis on the acceptability of the measures to most countries, particularly the important trading nations. As the programme evolved, it lost all three – balance, flexibility and acceptability.

At this session of the Committee, there was general agreement on the approach, though some developed countries were reluctant to consider the details of the financing of the Fund before deciding on the details of the stock proposal. However, a more political approach was enunciated by Algeria:

> The developing countries were determined not only to ensure the effective application of the principles recognized by the United Nations of the *sovereignty* of peoples over their *natural resources* and of their right to exploit these resources, but also to secure fair prices for their exports and to safeguard their revenue in real terms by applying the *fundamental principle of indexation*. In order to

ensure control of their resources they had decided to organize themselves into *associations of producers,* expand the domestic processing of the raw materials which they produced and *establish control over the marketing* of their products. (emphases added)

While ostensibly this was said to be the view of all developing countries, in actual fact it represented only the objectives of OPEC countries — controlling marketing of petroleum products, establishing refining and downstream manufacturing capacity and indexing the price of oil to that of imported manufactures. While the other objectives may have some relevance to some commodities and some developing countries, it has never been established that the so-called fundamental principle of indexation of commodity prices was beneficial to *all* developing countries.

By the time the second round of the Committee's meeting took place in July 1975, the programme had begun to lose some of its main elements. While the five elements were described in February as the 'hard core' (other measures such as increased access to markets and reform of marketing structures were considered to be important but not hard core), the Secretary-General saw the compensatory financing mechanism in July as a 'residual element'. In fact, the Secretariat had concentrated its attention on only three of the elements — stocks, the Common Fund and multilateral commitments. Side by side with the elimination of the others, the Common Fund was made more important; in July, it was seen as a *catalyst* in bringing about arrangements of value to 'individual commodities'.[7] The concept of the Fund having become embedded in the collective consciousness of the '77', their views at this meeting were mainly concerned with means of financing it and the question of distribution of votes. The developed countries, on the other hand, not only reiterated their reservations about the Fund but also expressed a preference for income stabilisation by compensatory financing. Another problem that surfaced at about this time was the fear of some developing countries that the integrated programme might have adverse effects on their balance of payments; the safeguarding of the interests of 'importing developing countries' was therefore added to the objectives of the programme.

When the Committee on Commodities considered the programme again in December 1975, the lines of conflict became clearer. The Secretary-General now expressed the view that the approach embodied in the UNCTAD proposals 'implied the establishment of some kind of regulatory regime to govern world commodity trade'. The stockholding concept, instead of merely being the main element, became one of 'primordial importance', while the 'fund was held to be essential for facilitating the conclusion of international agreements on stocking schemes'. Compensatory financing was pushed even further into the background as 'a supplementary device and in no way a substitute for the direct regulation and strengthening of prices'. He also saw direct indexation as a part of the price determination exercise for individual commodities. Thus, all the mechanisms favoured by the developed countries were rejected, the programme reduced to one element and the objectives elevated to 'global resource management'. In short, the Secretariat had, by this time, adopted the Algerian approach wholesale.

The significant shift from the original set of balanced measures to direct market intervention and a global regime brought a predictable reaction from some developed countries. Whatever their real objections to the programme might have been, countries such as the United States and Germany could not stomach the enunciation of a principle of global restructuring. Not that they actually said so; they produced the usual camouflage arguments about market forces determining resource allocation and price formation, ignoring the fact that in their own policies (such as the Agricultural Assistance Acts or the CAP) these principles had never been recognised. Market organisation did have attractions for some members of the EEC, however; because of different opinions within the Community, the EEC had, in December 1975, no common policy and expressed only a preference for discussing the Fund after examining the stocking requirements of each commodity. Some Nordic countries were prepared to examine the Fund proposal sympathetically. At this stage, there was no uniform position among the rich countries.

Among the poor countries too, some more divergencies (in addition to the problems of indexation and importing developing countries) began to develop. These concerned: (i) commodities to be covered by the Integrated Programme; (ii) the relative importance of the different measures; and (iii) the role of existing international arrangements for different commodities in the future programme. As originally conceived by the Secretariat, the stocking arrangements were intended for ten 'core' commodities; the three tropical beverages (coffee, tea, cocoa) and sugar; three fibres (cotton, jute, sisal); natural rubber; and two metals (copper, tin). This coverage, based on technical considerations of stockability, left out of the programme important perishable commodities such as bananas and meat. The coverage also ignored two other important groups of commodities: (i) cereals, particularly wheat and rice, of significant import interest to many developing countries and export interest to some; and (ii) minerals, such as bauxite and iron ore. Limiting the programme to the core commodities would mean that developing countries not exporting these would not derive any benefit. The six commodities mentioned above, and also wool, were therefore added to the list, bringing it up to 17. Even with these additions, some important commodities (e.g. edible oils) were still outside the programme. Since the additions were clearly commodities not strictly suitable for regulation through the stock mechanism, it became obvious that many developing countries might not get a share of the Common Fund if it was to be used only to finance stocks. An attempt was made to try to get as many commodities as possible into the stocking scheme by suitably rewriting the package of measures for individual commodities.[8] For example, the Secretariat sought to prove, for wheat and wool, that 'internationally held and controlled stocks would have a number of advantages over national stocks'; for rice, 'while there are over-riding reasons for a national stockpiling policy in many countries, a "mobile" international stock has supplementary advantages'. In spite of such contortions, perishable commodities and minerals still remained outside the Fund.

The emphasis on stocking as the 'primordial' element and the consequent de-emphasis of the other measures also led to the fear in some developing countries that their commodities would not be dealt with at all or, at best, only in a superficial fashion. They, therefore, insisted that 'equal importance should be attached to each of the elements of the integrated programme'. The third divergency — on the relationship between the Integrated Programme and existing international arrangements for individual commodities, such as the International Coffee Agreement — arose out of a fear of possible loss of power. The major exporters of coffee, particularly in South America, have in the Coffee Council a power in proportion to their market share; in the integrated programme, voting strength was expected to be based on the share of *total* commodity exports. A dilution of their strength even on coffee matters became a distinct possibility. Every one of these differences of opinion — Algeria's insistence on indexation, India's doubts about the programme's ability to help its commodities, Brazil's fear of losing control over coffee — was based on a legitimate national interest.

The developing countries made an attempt to resolve their differences at the Third Ministerial Meeting of the Group of '77', held in Manila in January and February 1976. Such meetings, to co-ordinate the position of the '77', have been a regular feature since the first in Algiers before UNCTAD II. Like the Algiers Charter and the Lima Declaration and Principles of the Action Programme, the third meeting also adopted a Manila Declaration and Programme of Action. The objectives of the integrated programme, as indicated in the Manila Declaration, once again became a basket of innumerable, often mutually contradictory, objectives. The commodity coverage was expanded by adding manganese, phosphates, timber and vegetable oils (including olive oil and oilseeds); cotton and jute were amplified by adding cotton yarn and jute manufactures. However, wheat and rice were deleted. The difference of opinion on the role of the Common Fund was papered over by defining the purpose of the Fund as 'financing of international commodity stocks or other necessary measures within the framework of commodity agreements'. The resolution of the conflict over the role of existing arrangements was simply postponed; 'the application of any of the measures which may concern existing international arrangements on commodities covered by the integrated programme would be decided by Governments within the commodity organisations concerned'. Since the major exporter of coffee did not want it to be covered by the Integrated Programme but it still figured in the list, nobody knew whether it was in or out. The Manila Declaration recognised that the importing developing countries have a problem and enunciated a new principle, that their interests should be protected 'by appropriate differential and remedial measures'.[9] But there was clearly no agreement on what measures would be appropriate, let alone an agreement on the practicability and extent of the differentials. It is well known that the OPEC countries have steadfastly refused to accept any differential treatment in the price of oil for the least developed and the most seriously affected countries. This principle again was a set of words without any practical utility.

The importance of the Manila Declaration lies not in the methods adopted to compose or sweep under the carpet the divergencies of opinion but in the reiteration of the political unity of approach of the '77'. The preamble to the Declaration emphasises 'the close solidarity of all the developing countries which had made it possible for them to evolve a unified position' and declares 'their firm conviction to make full use of the bargaining power of the developing countries, through joint and united action in the formulation of unified and clearly defined positions'. The objective of this unity was to restructure 'international trade in commodities and [to reshape] the structure of world industrial production and trade'. The approach was clearly to create a New International Economic Order, along the same lines as at the Sixth Special Session of the United Nations, and the words echoed the Dakar Declaration. The premises underlying this approach are that the OPEC countries *can* use their power to change the international economic system and that they *will* use it for the benefit of *all* developing countries, not just themselves and those with whom they share a close sense of political identity.[10]

At UNCTAD IV

The perspective of the Manila Declaration was duly reflected in the document that formed the main paper for discussions on commodities at the Fourth UNCTAD Conference held in Nairobi in May 1976.[11] The Integrated Programme, according to this document, 'introduces an important element of global resource management' and 'would also represent a first step in the international restructuring of commodity sectors'. The restructuring was to correct past dependency relationships 'in the patterns of ownership and control over the commodity trade of developing countries, over the international marketing and distribution of the commodity exports, over their processing and transportation and in important instances over the level of remuneration of the individual producers'. The disadvantage of this approach, however desirable the objectives may be, is that it is counter-productive to proclaim them. If the intention of the developing countries was to *negotiate* with the rich countries towards a decline in the latter's power, the approach was bad strategy; it was a good strategy only if the purpose was to confront them with superior power and force concessions.

By May 1976, the establishment and operation of international stocks had become 'a central feature of the proposals'. The other four measures, which had once been an integral part, were relegated to a subsidiary role under an umbrella of 'other measures' The two major irresoluble conflict items (the impact on developing importing countries and the protection of the purchasing power of developing countries, particularly the concept of indexation) continued to be highlighted. The only new proposal to be placed before the Conference was US Secretary of State Kissinger's suggestion to create an International Resource Bank to promote investment in the development of natural resources by interposing an international institution between host governments and multinational corporations. The proposal was motivated partly by a desire to put forward some positive-sounding suggestion and partly by a fear of continued shortages in world raw materials supply because of decreasing investment in developing countries by multinational companies.

What happened at the Conference can be understood only in the light of this evolution of the Integrated Programme and the concept of the Fund. Many developed countries, particularly the United States, the Federal Republic of Germany, the United Kingdom, and Japan, could neither agree that there was a need for a new international economic order nor that the entire commodity trade needed wholesale restructuring. It was therefore futile to expect them to put money in a six billion dollar fund whose avowed purpose was to change the markets to their disadvantage. Some developed countries were less vehement in their opposition to the Fund; Norway pledged US $25 million; Sweden, Finland and the Netherlands agreed in principle to contribute if others did so. Canada, while not rejecting the concept of the Fund, was reluctant to support it until its usefulness was established. Four developing countries pledged specific contributions (Philippines US $50 million, Yugoslavia 30 million and India and Indonesia 25 million each); 17 other developing countries announced their support of the Fund but did not pledge specific amounts. This group included eight OPEC countries (Saudi Arabia, Kuwait, United Arab Emirates, Algeria, Iran, Iraq, Nigeria and Venezuela). Even the main protagonist of the idea, Algeria, was not willing to specify an amount until it knew what the richer OPEC members such as Saudi Arabia were going to do. The centrally planned countries of Europe, while never opposing the Integrated Programme, had many reservations. In particular, they disagreed with the use of stocks as a central mechanism and were reluctant to contribute to the Common Fund (with the exception of Romania and Yugoslavia). Their preference was for a multilateral contract mechanism, for the obvious reason that this was best suited to their economic system. Only China was unwavering in her support of the developing countries; China, however, made it clear that, though a country in the process of development, her policy was one of self-reliance and her support for the '77' was only for the benefits that they might get, not for itself.

The wide spectrum of views, from specific pledges of contributions to total rejection of the idea, left the final decision ambiguous. The resolution eventually adopted by consensus with one expressed (US) and some unexpressed (Japan, UK, Germany) reservations calls for a 'negotiating conference. . .on a Common Fund. . .no later than March 1977' and for an earlier preparatory meeting to evolve a complete scheme, including financing, operation, management and decision making procedures. The position was similar to that on the intensive consultation resolution at the end of the third Conference; some countries were going to negotiate, some others merely to discuss it, and a few would be dragged into it kicking and screaming. One consequence of the US rejection of the Fund idea was that the Kissinger proposal was also rejected — although by a small majority (33 to 31), most of the countries (44) abstaining.

During the negotiations, all the divergencies within the group of '77' which had been papered over at Manila again surfaced. The principal ones were: (i) Brazil and Colombia did not want coffee to be covered by the Integrated Programme and Cuba had similar reservations about sugar; (ii) Brazil was lukewarm about inclusion of other commodities of interest to it, such as iron ore, sisal and soyabeans; (iii) countries that were not likely to benefit from the stocking proposal, such as India, did not want to over-emphasise the stock financing role of the Common Fund and the under-playing of the other measures; (iv) the OPEC countries had to exercise their power to delete all references that implied that they had an obligation to contribute to the resolution of problems of importing developing countries, especially those affected by the oil price rise;[12] (v) indexation, a mechanism that was likely to benefit only the oil producers and some mineral exporters, was preserved by referring to price arrangements which would take into account 'movements in prices of imported manufactured goods, exchange rates and world inflation', and (vi) the least developed countries, particularly African countries, were unsure of the benefits of the programme to them and unhappy that the compromise resolution was negotiated, possibly to their detriment, by the more advanced developing countries in Asia and Latin America and |OPEC.[13] In the end what emerged as Resolution 93 (IV) (reproduced in Appendix 8) was the usual omnibus document with very little advance on accommodating divergent national interests.

The Common Fund became a symbol of solidarity and the flag under which the poor united to fight the rich. One should not decry the symbol just because it is one. Every symbol is an embodiment of the political perceptions underlying it. The free market principle is also a symbol to many of the rich countries, however much they may disregard it in practice. UNCTAD IV once again demonstrated that the peripheral countries feel deeply their increasing vulnerability which, in turn, leads to frustration and angry demands to change the system itself. Just as naturally, the beneficiaries of the system resist any such attempt. Given the political perceptions and differing economic interests, can the Integrated Programme be negotiated successfully?

Assuming it is negotiated, how effective is it likely to be in resolving commodity problems?

The Stockholding Mechanism

Conflict over ideology apart, the successful negotiation of the Integrated Programme and its future prospects for effective operation depend on the answers to the following questions: (i) are the assumptions on which the Programme and the Fund are based valid?; (ii) are the instruments, as conceived, adequate to achieve the objectives?; (iii) can it be negotiated so as to satisfy a broad spectrum of countries?

Two assumptions form the basis for the Programme and the Fund. A series of internationally financed and internationally controlled stocks is the key element in resolving the problems of 18 commodities and commodity groups. An international fund with very large resources will be the catalyst that will enable a large number of commodity agreements to be concluded.

The analysis in the previous twelve chapters of this book show that commodity conflicts arise for a variety of economic and political reasons. It was also shown, in Chapter 9, that while techniques of regulation are effective within limited circumstances none can be effective for all commodities at all times. This is implicitly recognised, even by UNCTAD, in the paper analysing the measures suitable for individual commodities.[14] This document describes accurately the situation of each commodity and then lists a *series of measures* appropriate to each one, of which only some are identified as crucial, others being supplementary. From UNCTAD's own analysis, it becomes apparent that stockholding as a mechanism is significantly important to a few commodities, is marginally relevant to some others and has no utility in others. Of the 18 commodities in Resolution 93 (IV), the document does not analyse the problem of the edible oil group, since this was added to the list only at the Conference. However, as explained in Chapter 7, the problems of oils and oilseeds are such that the stock mechanism may prove useful only as a supplementary measure in a few cases such as tropical tree oils. Of the remaining 17, the document rules out stocks as a possible measure for the two minerals (iron ore and bauxite) on the grounds of 'cost, multiplicity of classifications of ore and technical problems of location and space'. Manganese ore, an item added to the list at the Conference, will also be considered unfit for the mechanism on similar grounds. Stocks are clearly inappropriate for the two perishable commodities — meat and bananas. No analysis has been made for the other mineral, phosphate rock, which does not seem to have any problems of price, following the sharp price increase after the oil crisis.

For a large number of commodities, the document identifies other measures as being more important than holding stocks. In tea, no stock can be so open ended as to keep on buying in order to maintain prices in a persistent state of over-supply. In jute, the problem is identified as a domestic one in the producing countries of the jute/rice price ratio and of competition from synthetics for jute manufactures. 'The stock required to stabilize. . .would be much smaller if jute policy was co-ordinated with rice policy in producing countries.' The role of stocks in jute and jute manufactures is thus the normal marketing one of assuring supplies to buyers under temporary adverse conditions and cannot be a key element. For sugar, it is said that 'the primary objective of an international stocking policy *could be* in support of a system of multilateral trade commitments'. Before such supporting stocks are needed, a set of multilateral contracts must be negotiated; but no such negotiation is envisaged in the Programme. As mentioned earlier, the document tries to promote international stocks for two commodities, both of which have traditionally been managed by national stocks. Any attempt to internationalise wheat or wool stocks is bound to be totally unacceptable to the major exporters such as the United States, Canada or Australia. As for rice, the document categorically states that the problem 'is basically one of agricultural improvement' and concedes that there are 'over-riding reasons for a national stockpiling policy in many countries'. The neat solution adopted for some uncomfortable commodities which cannot be forced into international stocks is to delete them from the Programme itself!

The problem of sisal lies in the extreme uncertainty about its replacement by synthetics; hence, accurate demand appraisal and corresponding supply management are the crucial elements. All that can be said for a stock policy for sisal is that 'there will be occasions, as in the past, when additional stocks will be valuable'. In the case of natural rubber also there is a similar uncertainty about its future market share, particularly in the light of the increase in the costs of the oil-based raw materials for synthetic production. The document is full of doubts about the measures suitable for rubber. 'As a practical matter, the range of policy instruments. . .appears limited; these would be international stocks, multilateral advance commitments on trade and export or production controls'. Another doubt is that 'the financial viability of the stock operation, if not immediately apparent, should be carefully weighed with the cumulative effect on export earnings'. Cotton is also 'in the category of commodities for which action must be regulated by its relationship to synthetic products'. The cotton market has built into it a large capacity to absorb stocks, the average level being five months' supply. How big does the international stock have to be in order to influence and regulate a market which holds at any time nearly half a year's supply?

There remain but four commodities – coffee, cocoa, copper and tin – for which an international stock mechanism may be said to be an important element for stabilisation. Of these, two have special problems. While a case can be made out for a buffer stock on coffee, provided it is buttressed by effective production controls, 1977 is an inopportune year to think of building up stocks. Prices are at unprecedentedly high levels and world export availability is much less than demand; recovery of Brazilian production and the achievement of an approximate balance between demand and supply cannot be expected for at least a couple of years. In this context, the statement in the document that 'acquisition of stocks to deal with fluctuations around an upward price trend will require pricing provisions that allow some proportion of output to be set aside in relatively good crop seasons over the next few years, taking account of reduced world supply potential' is incomprehensible. What this seems to mean is that when prices are rising stocks should be built up by setting the price range so high that demand is even more drastically curtailed. To buy for stock in times of severe shortage ('reduced world supply potential' is the euphemistic jargon) and drive up prices still higher is not only strange and inequitable to consumers but also against the long-term interests of coffee against competing beverages. In any case, if stocks are acquired 'during an upward price trend' and have to be disposed of when the inevitable fall occurs, how much will the Fund lose? And who will foot the bill? No wonder the major exporters of coffee are reluctant to see it included in the programme.

In copper, the size and cost of stocks that can reasonably be expected to be effective is very large. The document states: 'Simulation of the size of stocks that could perform an effective function. . . produces estimates broadly. . .in the range of 500-800,000 tons. Most of the estimates lie closer to the *upper limit* of the range.' A size of 700,000 to 750,000 tons is not unreasonable when one considers that the LME alone can hold half a million tons, not counting the ability of multinational producers to withhold. Assuming that the stock buying is only at the lowest monthly average price on the LME in the last five years (about 46 ¢ per lb), the acquisition cost will amount to US $700 million; if the stock is held for just 18 months, carrying charges will add another US $120 million. The Secretariat estimates that some commodities may have to be held for as long as three years, in the case of coffee even longer. In fact, the cost of stocking just copper, coffee and sugar will, at a conservative estimate, be 3.5 billion dollars. Considering that total resources are placed at six billion dollars for all 18 commodities and that a part will be required for other measures, there are only two choices — either the 'Common' Fund will become a Fund for just a few commodities or the amounts will be spread so thinly as to be inadequate for any one of them.[15] Finally, one is left with just two commodities. Since the tin buffer stock of 20,000 tons is considered inadequate, the question is one of doubling it with financial contribution from the consuming countries. The Cocoa Agreement of 1973 had a provision for a buffer stock of 250,000 tons but it never came into being because prices during its entire three-year life remained above the ceiling. Since cocoa might move into a state of excess supply, the stock size may need to be augmented.

To summarise, of the 18 commodities in the list, the stock mechanism is suitable for four, of which two already have operating mechanisms and one does not need to be stocked in the near future. The mechanism is unsuitable for five. In the case of fibres, the mechanism can perform a limited role; whether it is useful for timber has not yet been analysed. For the rest, the solutions lie elsewhere. It is difficult to avoid the conclusion that the stock mechanism was first chosen as a saleable proposition and the Integrated Programme then fitted round it.[16]

The second assumption behind the stock and Common Fund proposals is based on the following syllogism: (i) in the past, financing of stocks in commodity agreements has proved difficult because of the lack of resources of the producing countries and non-contribution by importing countries; (ii) stockholding is the essence of all regulatory arrangements; (iii) therefore, if adequate resources are available, stocks can be held and international agreements will be concluded easily.[17] All that need be said about this reasoning is that since the middle statement is untrue, the conclusion is false.

Objectives, Instruments and Institutions

Whether the Integrated Programme proves effective in its operation will also depend on the relationship between the objectives and the chosen instrument. The main objectives included in Resolution 93 (IV) are:

(i) to improve the terms of trade of developing countries and sustain their real incomes taking account of world inflation and changes in the world economic and monetary situations; (ii) to stabilise commodity trade, avoiding excessive price fluctuations; (iii) to achieve prices which are remunerative and just to producers and, at the same time, equitable to consumers;[18] (iv) to improve market access; (v) to improve reliability of supply; (vi) to diversify production in developing countries; (vii) to improve processing in developing countries; (viii) to improve the competitiveness of natural products competing with synthetics; (ix) to harmonise the production of natural products and competing synthetics; (x) to improve market structures and to increase the participation of developing countries in (xi) marketing systems, (xii) distribution systems and (xiii) transport systems. What a lot of objectives to load on to a single 'key' mechanism such as a series of internationally held stocks!

The fact that all these objectives are desirable cannot mean that one mechanism can achieve them all. It can also be argued that it is the fashion in UN resolutions to specify a variety of broad objectives, not all of which are expected to be achieved in the immediate future. Even so, there must be some cognate relationship between objectives and instruments. Precisely because the objectives are desirable ones, the mechanism must be chosen with care so that at least the movement can be in the direction of achieving them. It is a normal tendency to load too many objectives on limited mechanisms with the result that the instrument often becomes incapable of achieving even the original aims for which it was designed. Obviously, the stock mechanism cannot be expected to achieve all or even a significant part of this long list. At best, it can promote stability in a number of commodities; under conditions of stability, other measures have to be taken to achieve all other objectives. It is sad to note that the casualty of the political evolution of the Programme is just these other measures.

The effectiveness of the instrument has to be judged not only in terms of what it includes but also on what it leaves out. The exclusions from the Programme are even more significant than the inclusion of unstockable commodities in the stock mechanism. The two commodity groups responsible for the sharp deterioration in the balance of payments, terms of trade and general economic situation of a very large number of developing countries are oil (petroleum and products) and food. By deleting cereals and scrupulously avoiding all reference to the costs of importing oil, the Programme ignores two areas vital to many poor countries. One main reason for proposing an Integrated

Programme is stated to be 'the inability of existing arrangements to meet the *essential food requirements* of many developing countries'. This requirement was gradually demoted to the point at which it became an item to be mentioned parenthetically in the objectives – 'to diversify production in developing countries, *including* food production'. In the long list of measures (six paragraphs and 14 subsections), there is not one which can be clearly identified as an instrument addressed to the food problem.

It must be assumed that the support of the developing countries for the Programme is based on their conviction that it will be of significant benefit to them. The conviction appears to have been reinforced by some ambiguous statements in the Secretariat's paper on commodities submitted to the Conference. It is necessary to quote paragraphs 48 and 49 (of the section on the impact on developing countries) to understand the fallacies underlying this conviction.

An earlier analysis prepared by the Secretariat of the trading position of individual countries in the years 1970-72 showed that of the 100 developing countries and territories for which detailed trade data were available, 80 were net exporters of a group of principal storable commodities, including those proposed for inclusion in the integrated programme. For 60 of them, the total value of their exports of these commodities was more than three times the corresponding import value.

The conclusion drawn in the very next sentence is: 'Thus, for most developing countries, there should be a net gain from the measures proposed in the integrated programme...' The conclusion does not follow, since the earlier study was a partial one, covering only the ten storable commodities, edible oils, lead and zinc. Even by the time the document was written seven more had been added; the list in Resolution 93 (IV) is quite different. Since no analysis of the number of countries that are net exporters of this final list has been made, the conclusion that most of the developing countries must benefit cannot be expected to follow automatically. Further,

of the 20 countries which were net importers of the commodities proposed for the integrated programme during the period 1970-72, thirteen have relatively high incomes or enjoy relatively fast growth in their export earnings. For the remaining seven countries, the net import position reflected wholly or mainly the fact that they were

deficit countries. The rise in world food prices since 1972 relative to
the prices of other commodities has in all probability resulted in
additional developing countries shifting into deficit in their
commodity trade balances.[19]

Even if one ignores the deterioration since 1972, a number of things
are wrong with this line of reasoning. First, the aggregative concept of
'net exporters' or 'net importers' of a partial list of commodities is
meaningless. Even the assumption that a developing country which is a
net exporter of the limited group will on the whole benefit need not
hold true. The net benefit depends on the country's commodity trade
composition, how much it gains from its export commodities and how
much it loses on imports. The assumption implies that all commodities
in the programme increase by *equal value* (not just by equal
proportionate increase in prices) at *all times*. The second aggregative
concept used is to treat all 102 developing countries as a group and
then maintain that if a large number of them benefit the programme
must be acceptable to all. To imply that high-income developing
countries or those with fast rates of growth of exports can afford to
take losses from the programme is to over-estimate grossly their
commitment to the programme. Why should the countries on the losing
end, even if they are richer than the rest, accept something which is
manifestly to their disadvantage? Third, the numbers game will change
dramatically if oil imports are taken into account. It has been conceded
throughout this book that oil as an energy source is a unique
commodity and not susceptible to the kind of solutions that the
programme envisages for the other commodities. But, in analysing the
impact on importing developing countries, should oil remain excluded?
The objectives of the programme emphasise: (i) the concept of 'real
earnings', taking full account of 'the rate of world inflation' and
'changes in world economic and monetary situation'; and (ii) the
establishment of price ranges which take into account 'movement in
prices of imported manufactured goods and exchange rates'. If the price
of manufactured goods is a relevant consideration, why not the price of
oil, which is equally crucial to development? If oil is the main cause of
the deterioration in balance of payments and terms of trade of the
poorest of the developing countries, it is illogical to attempt to solve it
by attacking other commodities, manufactured goods or whatever —
anything except the cause of the problem. Instruments must bear some
relationship to the causes of the problem.

Inadequate instruments and partial coverage are not the only factors militating against the success of the programme. The key instrument, the Common Fund, may not be negotiable and, if negotiated, may not be successful. It is often said that the Fund will come into being whether the richest of the industrialised countries contribute or not. Raising six billion dollars without US, German or Japanese contributions assumes that the money will be forthcoming from the OPEC countries. While eight OPEC nations have announced their support, not one has pledged a specific amount. They may contribute, but according to the formula of a share proportionate to their share of trade in the listed commodities; since the richest among them export little else but oil, these contributions will be paltry.[20]

It is not irrational to assume that any large contributor will look at the financial viability of the Fund and the commensurate power to control the operation before making commitments. On both these grounds, the proposals appear optimistic. It is assumed that the six billion needed will be raised one third as equity and two thirds as loan. Half the amounts will be needed to set the Fund up, the other half being on call. On the borrowing aspect it is assumed that 'the main operations of the Fund appear a low risk, which should enable the Fund to qualify for a higher rating with potential lenders'. Holding commodity stocks has rarely been considered a 'low risk' investment. Further, if the governments of the developed countries do not contribute, one can at least expect second thoughts before their banks lend money to it. Another difficulty likely to be faced in obtaining contributions is the view that 'the allocation of votes to individual countries needs...to be determined on relevant factors other than subscription to capital'. To ask the man who puts in the money to hand over the power to distribute it to the recipients is to say the least Utopian in the present day world. More complications are added when it is also proposed that countries with low per-capita incomes and/or balance of payments difficulties should pay reduced or nil contributions but that their voting power should not be correspondingly reduced — another admirable but impracticable principle. In the actual negotiation, it is highly unlikely that the payers will reduce their power to call the tune. As usual, the poorest are bound to see that high-minded principles are rarely translated into practice.

The inadequacy of the amounts to tackle effectively the problems of all 18 commodities has been analysed earlier. When can a Fund, designed to support the producers' incomes, work? The experience of the CAP suggests that it can do so only when it is an open-ended tax on the consumers.[21] This is possible within nations, as shown by the income parity concept for farmers' incomes in the United States. It is to some extent even possible in the context of regional economic integration. But there are as yet few indications that it is possible on a global scale.

The effectiveness of the programme also depends on the form and forum in which it is negotiated. The legal form in which the Common Fund will be established is not likely to be difficult; other funds, such as the International Fund for Agricultural Development, have set precedents. The legal Instrument of the Integrated Programme is still the hoary old international commodity agreement. Whether a series of treaties can be negotiated under UNCTAD auspices is also a relevant question. In the twelve years of its existence, UNCTAD has succeeded in negotiating only two new measures; neither is a treaty. The General Scheme of Preferences avoided the legal problem by letting each preference-giving country give effect to it unilaterally. The Code of Conduct for Liner Conferences has yet to be ratified by the requisite number of countries to enable it to come into force; in any case it is a code of conduct and not a treaty with precise obligations. The problem again is one of political perception. While there are good reasons for the evolution of UNCTAD as a skill-support for the poor countries, the consequence has been that the rich view it with suspicion, not to say distrust. Two other reasons why UNCTAD, in spite of its undeniable success in articulating many of the problems of developing countries, has not been able to evolve into a negotiating forum are: (i) that in the absence of a possibility of trade-offs between the inherently unequal developed and developing countries, negotiations cannot even commence; and (ii) that the mode of discussion between groups prevents such a possibility from arising. The group system in UNCTAD ensures that a basket always confronts the lowest common denominator. The '77' adopt a 'basket' approach; every country or regional group puts in it whatever action they believe to be necessary. The result often is that the basket itself contains contradictory proposals. The industrialised countries, on the other hand, attempt to harmonise their position by deleting any proposal which is unacceptable to one set of countries or another; the resulting lowest common denominator is full of holes like a sieve. When the contents of the basket are dumped into the colander, nothing remains; the proposals that do not cancel each other leak through the holes. For the first time, UNCTAD IV saw the expression of openly divergent views among the rich countries; the '77' still cloak their differences under the umbrella of solidarity. Since solidarity is perceived as the main source of their collective bargaining power, the problem is one of how to meet divergent national economic interests without disturbing political solidarity.

Will the Integrated Programme succeed? Given the time, energy and political prestige that has already been vested in it, it cannot be a total failure. On the other hand, given its inherent weaknesses, it cannot hope to achieve even a fraction of its objectives. As is usual in such cases, 'something will happen'. But that something will only be the very minimum. The concessions demanded from the developed countries will not all be given. Only those that are enough to appease a fair number of the poor countries will grudgingly be granted. The optimistic hope that 18 international commodity agreements will be concluded in two years (by the end of 1978) will not be fulfilled. In addition to the existing five, a few more might be negotiated; the United States is unlikely to join many new ones.[22] Some kind of a Fund, probably with less resources, might be created. The impact of the programme on the totality of the commodity problems or on the development problems of the poor countries is unlikely to be significant.

Some More Lessons

If negotiations between sovereign states are to have reasonable expectations of success, there must be an agreement on some fundamental aims, however minimal they may be. The two super-powers, who contend in every area of activity, still engage in talks on limitation of strategic weapons because of a tacit agreement that unbridled arms escalation is not in their national interests in terms of their economies, domestic societies and international political relations. Economic integration in Europe succeeds because of a fundamental agreement on the need to prevent the recurrence of war by increasing economic linkages. GATT succeeds because of two basic agreements among the major trading partners: liberalisation of trade in industrial goods by reduction of tariffs is to be welcomed, and autarkic policies in agriculture are to be condoned. Is there a basic objective in commodity trade that can be shared by all countries? The gap between the desire to restructure world trade and the unwillingness to modify it except to the minimum extent necessary is too wide to constitute an agreement on principle.

Based on the analysis of the economic and political motivations that give rise to commodity conflicts, nine conclusions were drawn at the end of Chapter 12. The UNCTAD Integrated Programme for

Commodities is one worthwhile attempt to tackle a major cause of previous failures, the piecemeal approach. If the programme's likely effectiveness is viewed with pessimism, this is because of its inherent weakness which stems from the over-emphasis on politics rather than economics and on a single mechanism rather than a balanced set of measures. This attempt does however enable one to draw some more conclusions about what is necessary to make a comprehensive approach more successful. First, the importance of facing political realities is reinforced. American opposition to an across-the-board negotiation of international commodity agreements is as much a reality as the direction of OPEC aid or the differences among the developing countries. All are rooted in perceptions of national interest. One cannot also ignore the reality that developed countries have a substantial if not preponderant interest in commodity trade. Second, the political solidarity of the '77' obscures but does not eliminate divergent economic interests. The consequence is the politicisation of the objectives at the risk of foregoing the ability to solve commodity problems. The separation of countries on ideological grounds makes it impossible to commence negotiations. Third, an urgent need is to search for agreement on some fundamental principle that could demarcate the area of negotiation on concrete measures related to specific objectives. Fourth, there is no magic wand to wave which can resolve commodity problems; gradual steps can be taken in a pragmatic fashion. The earlier conclusion that flexibility, balance and acceptability are essential is strengthened by the limitation of a single mechanism approach. Fifth, the choice of instruments, their form and the forum of negotiation are all relevant to the potential effectiveness of any set of measures. Sixth and most important, the enunciation of high-sounding principles is no guarantee that the interests of the poorest among the developing countries will be safeguarded. One needs to search for practical solutions acceptable to the wielders of power; otherwise, the poorest will become the unwitting victims of the preservation of the solidarity of the '77' and the confrontation with the rich.

Notes

1. J.M. Keynes, 'The International Control of Raw Materials', *Journal of International Economics*, 4, 1974, pp.299-315.
2. I am grateful to Shri M.G. Mathur for drawing my attention to the earlier GATT attempts. See also Kenneth W. Dam, *The GATT: Law and International Economic Organisation* (University of Chicago Press, Chicago, 1970), and GATT, *Basic Instruments and Selected Documents, Supplement 3,* 1954,

p.238.
3. Resolution 83 (III) on page 81 and US note of dissent on page 136 of *United Nations Conference on Trade and Development, Third Session,* Santiago de Chile, *Vol.I, Report and Annexes* (UN, New York, 1973).
4. UNCTAD TD/B/C.1/161, 'Intensive Inter-Governmental Consultation in Commodities in connexion with Access to Markets and Pricing Policy — Review of Results', 18 November 1974, pp.4-5.
5. See the documents for Eighth Session (First Part) of the UNCTAD Committee on Commodities, February 1975. TD/B/C.1/166 (Report of the Secretary-General); 166/Supp.1 and Supp.1/Add.1 (Stocks); Supp.2 (Common Fund); Supp.3 (Multilateral Commitments); Supp.4 (Compensatory Financing); and Supp.5 (Processing).
6. UNCTAD TD/B/543 (TD/B/C.1/182), *Report of the Committee on Commodities on its Eighth Session, First Part,* pp.9-10. The quotation on the Algerian point of view in the next paragraph is also from the same document.
7. UNCTAD, TD/B/543(TD/B/C.1/182), *Report of the Committee on Commodities on its Eighth Session, Second Part,* p.44.
8. UNCTAD TD/B/C.1/194, *An Integrated Programme for Commodities — Measures for Individual Commodities, Report by UNCTAD Secretariat,* 1 October 1975.
9. All quotations and references in this and the next paragraph are from *The Manila Declaration and Programme of Action* circulated as an UNCTAD IV Conference Document, TD/195.
10. 'While it is true that by conventional measures of aid, the oil-exporting countries have emerged as relatively generous donors, there is little evidence to suggest that they wish merely to add their resources to the flows already available, or to put the bulk of their resources through the channels already established. Rather, the evidence suggests the reverse, e.g. the heavy concentration of Arab oil-exporters on Islamic countries.' John White, 'Does the United Nations really need a new Structure?', *Populi,* special 3, 1976, pp.23-33.
11. UNCTAD TD/184, *Commodities — Item 8 — Main Policy Issues,* Nairobi, May 1976.
12. The specific point originally found in both the Group B (developed countries) and in the '77' draft but modified under OPEC pressure was the objective 'to take into account the special situation of developing countries which are importers of commodities and raw materials, *including those lacking in natural resources'* (emphasis added). Resolution 93 (IV) contemplates special measures only for the least developed countries; the most seriously affected countries and those lacking in natural resources are meant to be protected only to the extent that the Integrated Programme adversely affects them. In other words, the fact that the MSACs became so only because of the oil price rise must not, in the view of OPEC, be referred to.
13. African reservations were reinforced by the fact that the 'Mount Kenya Group' of ministers which negotiated the Resolution in the usual last day midnight session did not include a minister from any country south of the Sahara, even though Kenya was the host country. Algeria, though geographically on the African continent, was seen as representing OPEC interests.
14. For a commodity-by-commodity analysis see TD/B/C.1/194, *An Integrated Programme for Commodities.*
15. See Alfred Maizels, A New International Strategy on Primary Commodities' in G.K. Helleiner, (ed.) *A World Divided: The Less Developed Countries in the International Economy,* McGill University Perspectives on Development, no.5 (Cambridge University Press, Cambridge, 1976), p.45. Keynes argued

that a minimum stock level, equivalent to at least three months of the value of the trade, would need to be held in the major commodities entering world trade. Maizels calculates that for this level of stocks at 1972 prices US \$7.75 billion would be required for eleven major commodities. The value of trade of the 18 commodities in Resolution 93 (IV) averaged over 1969 to 1971 (i.e. excluding the boom period) was over US \$33 billion. Three months' requirement would therefore need a capital of US \$8.3 billion for acquisition; carrying costs, based on an 18-month holding period, would be another US \$1.4 billion; total US \$9.7 billion! This is a minimum, since questions such as whether three months' stocks are adequate for copper and cotton and whether it is reasonable to assume holding stocks for an average of 18 months for all commodities are answered optimistically.

16. That this was a prior choice can be substantiated by many statements in UNCTAD documents. For example, the mechanism itself was used as an input in selecting the commodities. TD/194 lists a number of criteria relevant to developing countries and adds: 'Finally, there may be considerable merit in action on commodities for which stocks could be a clearly defined element of international action.' This selective criterion naturally produced the ten 'core' commodities. Since these ten were of interest only to a limited number of countries, two had to be deleted and ten new ones added. The result is that the mechanism is now suitable only for a minority of the 18. In this context, John White's observation is relevant: 'The fact is that the middle level staff of the world wide agencies spend a high proportion of their time moulding, bending and twisting their proposals to fit whatever fashion the current strategy dictates.' (See 'International Agencies – The Case for Proliferation' in Helleiner, *A World Divided,* pp.275-93.)

17. While the three statements of the syllogism have been summarised in this author's words, it can be found, described in this precise form, on pages 7 and 9 of TD/184. The originator of the Fund concept says unambiguously: 'If the Fund exists, has sufficient resources and the producers exercise a substantial share of control of its management, it is likely that a large number of agreements will be concluded; if cash is available for buying market surpluses when they threaten to cause major price declines, there will be great incentive to use it, the negotiating details, however important, being likely to be settled quickly under such emergency conditions.' The assumption that commodity conflicts are likely to be resolved more easily under emergency conditions rather than normal stable situations is difficult to swallow.

18. Justice, as a criterion for choosing an appropriate price range, seems to have crept into UNCTAD documents for the first time in this resolution. While no one can quarrel with the concept, it is economically even less quantifiable than equity!

19. UNCTAD, TD/184, p.16.

20. UNCTAD, TD/B/IPC/CF/2, *Consideration of Issues relating to the Establishment and Operation of a Common Fund,* November 1976; viability is discussed in paragraphs 15, 32 and 34, voting in paragraph 16.

21. See, for example, TD/B/C.1/196, *An Integrated Programme for Commodities – a Common Fund for Financing. . .,* p.28: 'In the agricultural policy of the United States, with its long history of commodity stabilization, no specific limits are set on the volume of purchases or on the amounts to be spent on supporting prices of individual commodities. There is an overall budgetary total, however, which, if exceeded, would call for supplementary appropriations; if they are not approved, reduction in support prices across the board would be called for. In the agricultural policy of the European Common Market, the amounts to be spent on individual commodities are specified in

the budget of the Community, by commodity. In the implementation of the budget, however, transfers (*virements*) are made from one commodity appropriation to another at the decision of the Council, in a procedure described as fairly simple and rapid. The experience has shown that transfers have been frequent and large.'

22. Whether the change in the administration in the United States will mean a significant change in long-held attitudes remains to be seen. President Carter, in his address at the United Nations on 17 March 1977, said: 'The United States is willing to consider, with a positive and open attitude, the negotiation of agreements to stabilize commodity prices, including the establishment of a common funding arrangement for financing buffer stocks where they are a part of individual negotiated agreements.' The gap between the Common Fund as envisaged by the '77' and the idea of a fund for buffer stocks in Havana Charter-type agreements is still very wide.

14 ACT! A FRAMEWORK AGREEMENT ON COMMODITY TRADE

> A generation after the General Agreement on Tariffs and Trade, I believe the time has come to balance it with a general agreement on commodities — it is long overdue.
>
> Harold Wilson, Prime Minister of the United Kingdom,
> at the Commonwealth Heads of Government Meeting,
> Kingston, Jamaica, 1 May 1975

> Considering the need to create an international organ to guarantee the effective organization of world trade by adopting a global, integrated approach to all problems...
> The Member States of the Conference of Non-Aligned countries on Raw Materials undertake to work immediately towards the creation of an International Trade Organization.
>
> Resolution 10 of the Conference of Developing Countries
> on Raw Materials, Dakar, Senegal, 8 February 1975

If the UNCTAD attempt to resolve commodity problems with an integrated approach is unlikely to succeed, what else can one do? There are only two choices: the counsel of despair which assumes that these problems are irresoluble and leaves it at that or an attempt to devise another approach which will avoid the causes of failure of past attempts. Any new suggestion must be firmly based on the realisation that commodity conflicts cannot be resolved overnight or even within a few years. In this book a variety of commodity problems have been described and an equal variety of regulatory mechanisms analysed; none of the measures is an instant panacea for any of the problems. One will look in vain for a one-to-one correspondence between politico-economic problems and economic solutions. Hence, the new approach proposed herein concentrates on a *method* of negotiation and a forum in which to do it rather than on a set of specific solutions that can be presumed to be applicable to all commodities and all countries at all times. The lessons of past attempts indicate that any proposal must be comprehensive in its coverage, pragmatic in its philosophy, flexible as regards measures and acceptable to governments in terms of current political realities.

The most important political reality is that there is no commitment to negotiate; there can be no commitment on the basis of the pre-conditions set forth by any of the groups involved in commodity trade. It is no use lamenting that the absence of commitment is a result of 'lack of political will'. The extensive analysis of the constituents of political will in chapter 11 showed that negotiations cannot commence unless and until at least one essential objective of the negotiation is shared by all participants. If one set of participants wants to change the economic system into a new order while the other set is happy with the old order as it is, no common ground can be found. But things are not as clearly black and white as this. In the former set, there are many countries who will agree that a change in the system cannot be brought about quickly or by coercion. Equally, in the other groups there are many who are aware of the shortcomings of the system and some who are even willing to contemplate changes. This grey area cannot be explored so long as countries are automatically pigeon-holed into developed and developing and so forced into unbridgeable positions.

Herein lies a dilemma. Notwithstanding their widely divergent economic interests, over a hundred less industrialised countries have demonstrated political solidarity. The main reason for this solidarity is their perception of vulnerability in the economic system. The conse-quences of their awareness of having become peripheral to the system are their realisation that individually they have little power and that the only power they can hope to have is a collective one. Vulnerability also generates a fear, born of past colonial experience, that attempts are constantly being made to divide them. A new approach that tries to look at the different economic interests of different groups of developing countries will prove counter-productive if it is not accompanied by a reassurance that political solidarity is not threatened. The developed countries also subscribe to a concept of solidarity among themselves; notwithstanding some notable exceptions, so do the centrally planned countries. How does one devise an approach that simultaneously recognises both the political solidarity of each group and the divergent economic interests within each group? In the last chapter, it was seen that a predominantly political approach under-estimates economic divergencies; it is also simplistic to assume that economic conflicts can be de-politicised to the extent that they become soluble by purely economic measures. The middle way, that specifically concerned with exploring the grey area, can only be based on a recogni-tion of economic interests as well as positive political relations between countries in different groups. The first step is to disaggregate the major groups into a number of sub-groups with the aim of identifying potentially positive linkages.

Disaggregation and Re-aggregation

In Chapter 3, the developed countries were classified, on the basis of their economic interest in commodity trade, into four sub-groups: low-cost producers/exporters; high-cost protectionist producers; countries heavily dependent on imports of raw materials; and countries historically important in processing and re-export. Among developing countries, a clear separation already exists between oil exporters and the rest. The former, while still being developing countries, do not have a resource problem and have demonstrated success in regulating the market for their commodity. It cannot also be denied that the oil exporters have acquired the ability to negotiate with the other groups from positions of strength. Their developmental problems of industrialisation and acquisition of technology do not need any new mechanism. Though there are differences in population, surplus wealth and absorptive capacity among the OPEC countries, the qualitative gap between them and the rest of the developing countries is a very wide one. Hence, on both earnings and the need for regulation, the main concern must be with the non-oil exporting developing countries, particularly the poorest and least developed among them.

The non-oil exporting developing countries are numerous, but to disaggregate them is not as formidable a task as might appear at first sight. The disparity in size between the largest and smallest makes it possible to group them say into the very large countries (with a population of over 50 million), the medium size countries (population between 10 and 50 million) and those with less than 10 million population. Nearly three quarters of the developing countries have populations of less than 10 million; about half of these have less than 2 million people. It may therefore be useful to establish a category of countries with very small populations. The large populous countries — India, Brazil, Pakistan, Mexico — have diversified economies and are not dependent on one or two primary commodities for their export earnings. However important coffee may be to Brazil and tea to India for regional and social reasons, the actual dependence of these countries on the 14 main commodities has been progressively declining. With smaller countries, the extent of diversification and the degree of dependence become more important, as the size and correspondingly the domestic market for a variety of goods decrease. Hence, the export pattern — whether diversified, predominantly agricultural or predominantly mineral — and the degree of dependence can be added to size as differentiating criteria. The sub-groups so classified are likely to contain countries more coherent in the kind of problems they face and the type of solutions that can meet the problems. It must however be recognised that in all sub-groups there will be some countries who have a special interest in some commodities by virtue of their being a very large exporter. With this proviso in mind, a classification has been attempted, citing a few examples for each group. No classification can be perfect; Bangla Desh, for example, is difficult to fit into any of the categories. UNCTAD avoids this problem by having a special category of large low-income countries (India, Pakistan and Bangla Desh) and adding Mexico to the group of major fast growing exporters of manufactures. The classification below is only meant to illustrate the point that disaggregation into more coherent groups is possible; the examples do not constitute a comprehensive list.

Classification of non-oil exporting developing countries

Size group A

1. Large, populous countries, with diversified economies, not dependent on one or two primary commodities, significant exporters of
   processed and manufactured products.
   Examples: India, Brazil, Pakistan, Mexico (Brazil has a special
   interest in coffee, India in tea and jute manufactures and Mexico in
   hard fibre manufactures).

Size group B – Countries with more than 10 million population

2. Predominantly agricultural exporters, heavily dependent on one or
   two commodities.
   Examples: Burma, Colombia, Ethiopia, Nepal, Sri Lanka, Sudan,
   Uganda
3. Predominantly agricultural exporters, significant dependence on a
   few commodities.
   Examples: Argentina, Egypt, Kenya, Malaysia, Peru, Philippines,
   Tanzania, Thailand (The special commodity interests are: Malaysia,
   rubber and tin; Argentina, beef; Thailand, rice; Peru, fishmeal;
   Egypt, cotton; Kenya, coffee; Philippines, sugar, copper and timber;
   Tanzania, sisal.)
4. Predominantly mineral exporters, heavy dependence on one or two
   commodities.
   Examples: Chile, Zaire
5. Diversified economy, significant exporter of manufactures.

Example: Republic of Korea

Size group C – Countries with population between 2 and 10 million
6. Agricultural exporters, heavy dependence on one or two commodities.
Examples: Burundi, Cameroon, Chad, Cuba, Dominican Republic, El Salvador, Ghana, Guatemala, Haiti, Laos, Malawi, Niger, Rwanda, Upper Volta.
7. Agricultural exporters, significant dependence on a few commodities.
Examples: Benin, Cambodia, Honduras, Ivory Coast, Nicaragua, Togo, Uruguay, Yemen (A.R.)
8. Mineral exporters, heavy dependence.
Examples: Bolivia, Jamaica, Zambia.

Size group D – Countries with a population of less than 2 million
9. Agricultural exporters, heavy dependence.
Examples: Belize, Costa Rica, Congo, Equatorial Guinea, Fiji, Gambia, Guinea-Bissau, Lesotho, Panama, Sao Tomé/Principe, Seychelles Islands, Swaziland, Tonga
10. Mineral exporters, heavy dependence.
Examples: Liberia, Mauritania

(Note: The special interest has not been indicated in the case of countries heavily dependent on just one or two commodities; the specific dependence may be found in the list in Chapter 3).

It is not unexpected to see that the smaller the country the less diversified it is likely to be and the more dependent on just one or two commodities. In fact, the bulk of the developing countries fall into the last two groups. Many of them will also be numbered among the 'least developed' countries. While they are usually among the worst sufferers from the vagaries of the commodity market and correspondingly the most vulnerable, their resource requirements are likely to be much smaller in magnitude. The complications do increase progressively for other groups. With the largest countries the problems are of a different order of magnitude and obviously require a much greater variety of solutions.

It is not fortuitous that this book started by classifying commodities in Chapter 3 but ends up by classifying countries. This is the result of treating commodity problems not in isolation but in terms of the effects of commodity trade on countries. Singer, one of the celebrated authors of the Singer-Prebisch thesis, has recently re-formulated his views on the distribution of gains from trade and investment.[1] These deal more with the characteristics of *countries* rather than with the characteristics of specific *commodities*.

The country-by-country approach, so far adopted only in considering questions of aid and resource transfer, has an integral relevance to commodity trade. The limited success of the commodity-by-commodity approach has been a result of the failure to place it squarely in the context of the resource transfer problem. If the two could be related to each other, the debate on whether commodity agreements should aim only at stability or have a resource transfer element built into them can be avoided. If the latter objective can be achieved by other techniques, the former can remain the main objective of commodity agreements of the historical pattern.

The second justification for disaggregation is the varying acceptability of techniques of regulation. There is little prospect of a change in the ideological hostility of the United States to commodity agreements on a wide spectrum of commodities, even if the objectives were limited to stability. Being a major producer/exporter of many agricultural products and minerals and holding significant quantities of stockpiles in others, it will always have enough pressure groups working against across-the-board regulation. In spite of aid-weariness, resource transfer is not yet a discarded mechanism; hence, the US preference for compensatory financing schemes and special funds. In the case of the EEC, there are no prospects of a significant change in the structure of the CAP; the three pillars of price support, import levies and export subsidies will remain, though adjustments will be made in the *levels* of the three elements. Obviously, the Community will prefer mechanisms that fit in with this pattern. Relating the sugar import price in the Lomé Agreement to the CAP internal target price is an example. The centrally planned countries have expressed a clear preference for multilateral trade commitments. Within the developing countries, too, there are limitations on acceptability of mechanisms. Production control, for example, is more difficult in countries with a large number of small-holders rather than a few plantations. Only some countries have institutions that can enter into state-to-state bilateral trade contracts. Some countries will find it easier to give assurances on supply than others. Even when the government of a developing country considers a mechanism acceptable, its degree of control over marketing may be circumscribed by multinational company operations, thus making the mechanism difficult to introduce. It is needless to multiply examples. The point is that there are many ways of achieving an objective, but so far little effort has been made to relate the acceptability of measures to the objectives. A rarely posed question is: 'This is what we want to achieve; how do *you* think *you* can do it?'

The third reason for disaggregating is to identify positive political relationships. Chapter 10 of this book was devoted to an analysis of the historical, strategic and political reasons that motivate the choice of beneficiaries from any measure taken in the commodity field. 'Preference' is considered a sin to be avoided in GATT terms; but preferential treatment has always been a feature of commodity trade. Whenever such schemes have operated — the US Sugar Acts, the Commonwealth Sugar Agreement, the Lomé Agreement — they have been of significant benefit to the selected developing countries. It is futile to expect that the rich industrialised countries — or any donor for that matter — will choose measures that will benefit all and sundry. Thus, 'who do *you* want to be the beneficiary?' is also a relevant question to pose.

Disaggregation is not an end in itself; the logic need not be carried to the extreme of treating each country as a sub-group by itself. Advantages can be secured in negotiating both structures and procedures by dealing with groups of countries. By grouping themselves, countries can also acquire additional bargaining power. In their analysis of GATT, Gerard and Victoria Curzon have noted the example of Nordic countries grouping their forces in the Kennedy Round negotiations in order 'to recover the negotiating rights they had lost due to the combination of the six customs territories into a single unit within the EEC'.[2] Another example, cited in Chapter 10, was the manner of negotiation between the EEC and the ACP countries for the Lomé Agreement. Separate negotiations in the smaller groups were subject to the understanding that no sub-group should be left significantly dissatisfied and that as a whole the ACP countries supported the work in every sub-group. Thus the principle of re-aggregation was implicit in the disaggregated negotiations. There is no reason why a similar practice cannot be tried for the developing countries as a whole.

So long as the world is divided politically between developed and developing, any suggestion that seeks to differentiate among the members of the two groups is bound to be viewed with the suspicion that what is really being attempted is division. It is but natural if the developing countries, being more vulnerable, are the more suspicious of the two. Suspecting motivation is nothing new; proposals made by governments are rarely examined in their purely technical aspects. Even if it is unasked, the first question always is 'Why is this government making this particular proposal at this particular time?' Two recent examples will bear out this point. Many in the developed countries have been pointing out that the worst sufferers from the oil price rise have been the non-oil exporting developing countries. While this is eminently true, when somebody like Dr Kissinger says so it becomes suspect — because *his* motivations for saying it are suspect. The charitable view is that the truth needs to be said, if only to make everyone aware of the problems of the poorest countries. The cynical view is that it is yet another exercise in realpolitik; it is after all difficult to believe that there is any great identity of interest or commonality of problems between the richest super-power and the poorest of the poor countries. Similarly, when the Chancellor of the Federal Republic of Germany makes a suggestion that the contribution by the developed countries to the UNCTAD Common Fund should be made conditional on the OPEC countries not raising the price of oil further, this is viewed as an attempt to drive a wedge between OPEC and the rest of the developing world. Since motivations can and will always be questioned, any suggestion of disaggregation must have the concept of re-aggregation built into it from the beginning.

How does one re-aggregate? The example of the negotiations for the Lomé Convention shows that group solidarity can be safeguarded only by using the principle of 'package solution'. While negotiations may cover many areas, many commodities and many different sets of countries, agreement in any one negotiation must be made conditional on an acceptable agreement in all areas under negotiation. No significant commodity or group of countries should be left dissatisfied. The crucial difference between this re-aggregation and the UNCTAD group system is the time when re-aggregation occurs. In UNCTAD, the positions of the two major groups are harmonised first, before they face each other, thus leaving little room for manoeuvre. In the re-aggregation process suggested here, the two groups will negotiate first and the subsequent harmonisation will be related to ensuring that there is no serious disaffection.

The potential for viewing the totality as a package is the means of securing the political solidarity of the '77', the developed and the centrally planned groups. For describing the process of negotiation, disaggregation and re-aggregation are useful concepts. For the package itself to become negotiable, it is essential to add one further element — reciprocity.

Reciprocity and Burden Sharing

Countries do not enter into negotiations seriously unless they perceive that there is a *mutual advantage* in doing so; it must be seen to be a game with potentially positive pay-offs in politico-economic terms for all parties. Because all participants expect to gain, there is also need for *mutual commitments* to preserve the game that makes this possible. Third, the pay-offs must not be seen to be too one-sided; there must be *reciprocity.* Surprising as it may seem, reciprocity is as much a matter of perception as the other two. The experience of GATT has led some to believe that pay-offs in trade liberalisation measures, especially the effects of tariff cuts, are quantifiable. The Curzons have cited examples to show how the same negotiations were presented by different delegations to their own domestic audiences as a victory for their side.[3] In practical terms of achieving success in negotiations, it did not matter whether the actual trade pattern that resulted bore out the claims. It mattered even less that such claims were couched in overall terms and were obtained at the expense of some loss to some domestic groups. The significant point was that both parties perceived reciprocity to have been achieved.

Throughout this book it has been maintained that developing countries have fewer trade-offs to offer to the rich countries in trade negotiations. How does one include reciprocity in such an unbalanced context? This can be done by recognising the distinction between *reciprocity of concessions* and *equality of concessions.* Even in the original GATT there was no clear definition of reciprocity, much less the implication that concessions must be equal in value. In its subsequent evolution, particularly with the addition of Part IV, the principle that developing countries need not offer equal concessions was clearly recognised. Even so, any international understanding to which a country subscribes involves an undertaking of responsibility and, in fact, a surrender of sovereignty and curtailment of freedom of action. Since countries cannot be coerced against their 'political will' to undertake or implement international obligations, they have to be persuaded that it is in their interest to comply and not to evade. Persuasion becomes easier if the extent of the burden is clearly understood. It therefore makes sense to consider the responsibilities and obligations of successful commodity regulation as burdens to be shared in an acceptably reciprocal manner. The burdens of commodity regulation have been summarised in Chapter 12, where their relevance to the equitable sharing of the amounts of resources transferred was also referred to. Comparing the burdens shouldered by exporters and by importers shows that reciprocity between these two economic classes is possible. To what extent is reciprocity possible between the developed and the developing?

The disaggregation of the developing countries clearly brings home the point that some are more advanced than others. While there is a wide gulf between the most developed of the poor countries and the poorest of the industrialised ones, there is also a gulf between the two ends of the spectrum among the developing countries. If the '77' as a whole expect the distribution of gains from future commodity regulation to be more equally distributed in their favour, the same concept must also logically be applied within the poor countries group. It is correctly argued that the surplus wealth of the OPEC countries, all of whom are also developing countries, should be used for improving the lot of their poorer companions. By the same token, the more advanced developing countries owe an obligation to the least developed among them. The fact that high sounding principles in favour of the least developed are not adequately translated into practical action has been stressed time and again. An unambiguous assumption of responsibility by the advanced developing countries to take action within their power and capacity to help the least developed is not only logical but is also essential for the concept of reciprocity. These countries can extract concessions from the rich ones without directly recompensing them if they are able to point out that they in turn are offering concessions to the poorest without recompense. This argument could prove to be a good selling point in some rich countries which face domestic pressures against any concessions to the developing countries. In other words, reciprocity, in a global context, need not be one-to-one.

To summarise, reciprocity does not mean equal concessions, but it must mean that each participant in the negotiation is shouldering a burden that is seen to be commensurate with its abilities. If this comes dangerously close to the old principle of 'each according to his ability', so be it.

A Framework Agreement

Is there a mechanism which is flexible, adopts an overall approach, relates measures to problems, takes into account the disaggregative and re-aggregative concepts, involves a principle of reciprocity and could also provide for periodic re-examination and renegotiation? If we keep in mind the concern for a method of negotiation rather than a set of specific solutions, the only feasible mechanism will be a framework agreement.

The principles of a framework agreement can be set out as follows. Primarily, it has to provide a forum for negotiation. Describing it as a forum implies that it must set the limits of the areas of negotiation. These limits will be defined by the objectives towards which the negotiations are expected to work. The agreement must also contain a catalogue of measures that could be used to achieve the objectives. It must also contain the procedures of negotiation – when and how they will take place and in what legal form the resulting set of solutions will be inscribed. It must provide for a clear description of the obligations and responsibilities that governments undertake as a result of the negotiated set of solutions.

If the set of solutions negotiated under the framework is to operate successfully, it must also provide for the maintenance of the system. Maintenance involves two kinds of problems – the treatment of exceptional cases and the procedures for dealing with violations.

Exceptions, Discipline and Restraint

There is hardly any multilateral agreement which does not contain escape clauses. These can take a variety of forms. *Exceptions* are one means of taking into account particular cases that do not fit into general formulae. GATT, for example, excepts all preferential agreements extant on the day it came into force from the most-favoured-nation principle. Commodity agreements provide for exceptional treatment in initial quotas for particular countries, exemption from some regulations for small exporters and similar measures. *Safeguards* can also be built into agreements. The GATT safeguard provision deals with balance-of-payments. The Multi-Fibre Agreement provides for safeguards if imports threaten particular sectors of local industry. Most countries have safeguard clauses in their GSP regulations. Stabex has the most comprehensive clause of this type. *Waivers* are a third method of dealing with exceptional circumstances arising during the operation of an agreement. These can take the form either of relieving a member from an obligation or of providing an extra benefit not universally applied to all members.

In a framework agreement, it is essential to indicate when the escape clauses may be brought into use. These clauses must perforce be broadly defined because no agreement can anticipate all possible contingencies that might arise during its operation. Too restrictive a definition may well prove self-defeating. If the aggrieved country cannot reasonably use an escape mechanism, it may well go ahead with a violation of the agreement, thus bringing it into disrepute. The GATT of 1947 has been described as an agreement in which 'each rule was accompanied by an exception, and each exception was governed by a procedure, which was intended to prevent the exception from swallowing up the rule'.[4] Escape clauses are substantial matters of negotiation, and it is not possible to lay down precise limits. However well-intentioned and well-drafted they may be, such clauses can never be perfect. Conflicts and disputes are bound to arise in the operation of any agreement.

Three methods of dealing with disputes have been identified by the Curzons — dispute evasion, dispute avoidance and dispute settlement. Nobody can write a rule for dispute evasion; this happens when all participants tacitly agree to condone a violation and prefer not to raise it to a dispute. Dispute avoidance is an essential element of any framework agreement, since dispute settlement in a multilateral forum is a more complicated and often unsuccessful exercise. GATT experience suggests that for effective avoidance two conditions are necessary. First, any participant must have the right to raise any point which it feels is a violation of obligations undertaken adversely affecting its own interests. Second, the other participants, including the alleged violator, must listen to the complaint. 'The right to speak and be listened to is fundamental to GATT's existence.'[5] Once a complaint is heard, GATT allows a period of time for bilateral consultations to achieve a settlement without involving all other contracting parties. A framework agreement on commodity trade must also have similar provisions, though it need not be strictly bilateral. If such first round consultations fail, other procedures must be brought into use. Most international agreements have some provision for a panel of arbitration or adjudication. The International Coffee, Sugar and Cocoa Agreements all provide, in almost identical terminology, for an *ad hoc* panel.[6] GATT, on the other hand, has a choice of two methods: a 'Panel of Conciliation' which has 'the flavour of an international court operating independently, not accountable to specific nations' and somewhat larger 'Working Parties' which include the parties to the dispute. While panels of conciliation can propose acceptable compromise solutions, working parties tend to produce majority and minority opinions and no constructive solutions. In spite of this, there is more recourse to the latter method in GATT; governments are disinclined to accept impartial binding arbitration and prefer political methods of dispute settlement.[7] Consultations and panels are two steps in a set of graded procedures; a series of steps that can prevent every dispute from being blown into a full-scale multilateral conflict is a necessary element in a framework agreement. The existence of such graded procedures will not by itself guarantee that all disputes will be settled. However, the operation of the procedures may well have a restraining effect on the country indulging in or proposing to indulge in a violation of an accepted obligation.

The purpose of restraining governments from unilateral action contrary to the objectives of the agreement is to provide time for it to operate within its rules. If the agreement is successful and benefits do flow by and large as anticipated, the stake of each participant in it increases; so does the opportunity cost of disruption.[8] If, on the other hand, the agreement fails to cope with changing situations or if the benefits are seen by some as being unfairly distributed, the agreement collapses. Sadly, the latter is the case with most commodity agreements. One must therefore conclude that the restraining factor must be given much greater importance in the proposed agreement on commodity trade.

Restraint can be improved by using the following techniques — transparency, notification, scrutiny, surveillance and supervision. Transparency means the acceptance of an obligation by all participants that any action they take which is likely to affect other participants under the agreement will be taken openly and will be notified to all others. Such transparent actions must be subjected to scrutiny by all, and if injury is likely to result to any party the action proposed must be modified, preferably before it is implemented. The implementation must be subjected to surveillance. In short, the actions of governments must be capable of being supervised at all stages. It is important to note that, in a framework agreement, such supervision is not exercised by any supranational body but by all the participants acting collectively. Thus it is still within the area of negotiation and is a part of the political process. Surveillance has in fact been attempted in the Textile Supervisory Body of the Multi-Fibre Agreement. With this precedent, there need not be any resistance to the acceptance of these concepts.

Restraint need not be viewed only with the negative connotation of restricting the freedom of action of sovereign governments. Restraints imposed by international obligations are sometimes welcomed by governments as a means of dealing with domestic pressure groups. Pressures from interested groups for import controls have been resisted on the grounds that they will infringe GATT. Sometimes, international obligations have also been used to sell marginally unwelcome measures. No restraint is of course possible if a government feels strongly about any action because of overwhelming domestic pressure. Within limits, restraint can be of positive use to governments. In commodity trade, its main functions will be to prevent the deterioration of access for raw materials and its improvement for both commodities and processed forms.

The Articles and Rules of ACT

With these various concepts in mind, the articles of ACT can now be described. It will contain a preamble, a set of objectives, a catalogue of measures, procedures for negotiations, negotiating structures, exceptions and safeguards, procedures for consultation, conciliation and dispute settlement, sanctions and the usual legal provisions for acceptance, ratification and the like.

The *preamble* will have to set out the agreement on fundamental principles that can be subscribed to by all participants without any reservations. At this stage in the history of commodity negotiations there are only a few such principles. They will all have to be stated in very broad terms, somewhat along the following lines: (i) Stability in commodity trade is desirable. (ii) Countries heavily dependent on commodity exports face special problems, in particular in relation to their terms of trade, that need corrective action. (iii) Importers of commodities, especially food and fuel importers, have needs that require specific safeguard measures. (iv) Diversification of production and improvements in productivity are to be encouraged. (v) Expansion and diversification of trade of developing countries are also to be encouraged. (vi) Measures need to be taken under ACT to promote and not to retard the developmental process, particularly in assuring predictability of earnings. (vii) The problems of the poorest countries have to be tackled by specific and concrete measures. (viii) All countries, to whichever group they may belong, have a stake in promoting collective economic security. (ix) And, most important, all countries undertake to negotiate in good faith and to act in a manner consistent with the achievement of the objectives. These are the kind of concepts that are normally written into UN and UNCTAD documents as objectives.

The set of *objectives* of a framework agreement must be defined more strictly than these broad generalities, since they must specify the areas of negotiation. It is not essential that the areas should be agreed to by all without reservation. In ACT countries can decline to negotiate on any particular area they disfavour. The more important sectors of negotiation are: restraining protectionist and autarkic tendencies, increasing access for raw materials, improving access for processed and manufactured forms, pricing policy for different commodities, assuring access to supplies, improving reliability of supply, stabilising earnings and providing for predictable growth in export earnings. Though action is less likely, areas such as improving market structures and avoiding unfair or excessive competition from synthetic substitutes will also have to be included.

The catalogue of *measures,* applicable to the different areas of negotiation, has to be exactly that − a catalogue. In the light of the earlier discussion on acceptability, any attempt to make them more than a list will make ACT non-negotiable. It may even be wise to state clearly that the choice of methods to deal with specific problems will be a matter for negotiation, as provided for in the agreement. The catalogue must include all the measures analysed in Chapter 9 as well as any new ones that human ingenuity can think of (e.g. international deficiency payments).

As for *negotiating procedures,* provision has to be made, as in GATT, for periodic 'rounds', when a set of problems will be negotiated in a broad context. The earlier rounds can deal with areas on which there is a broad measure of acceptability − access for raw materials, stabilisation of prices, improvements in the GSP, earnings stabilisation and multilateral contracts. More intractable problems such as harmonisation of synthetic production, the relationship between import purchasing power and export earnings and increasing the developing countries' share in shipping, marketing and distribution may have to be postponed to later rounds at more opportune times. How the 'rounds' could actually be expected to be negotiated is described in the next section.

In the case of *negotiating structures,* the advantage of group negotiation has already been referred to. Apart from the need to preserve group solidarity, negotiations on particular commodities have to be confined to countries interested in them. In commodity trade, two other special cases have also to be taken note of in the framework agreement. The first is existing international commodity agreements. Negotiations under ACT need not and should not rehash negotiations taking place in the appropriate commodity councils. These have to be taken as given facts, and only problems which are not covered by individual councils − such as the effect of commodity regulation in one commodity on another (the punch-bag effect) − will be the responsibility of ACT. By recognising this explicitly, one may hope to allay the fear of some countries that they will lose in ACT the power they already wield in the councils. The second structure that can also be recognised is producer associations. Since a group structure for negotiations is envisaged, there is no reason why a group of producer countries cannot be represented by their own association. At the same time, the universality principle of consumers and producers acting together is safeguarded, since, under ACT, decisions can only be negotiated by all countries acting together. In other words, producer associations will be recognised as negotiating bodies and not as decision-making institutions.

The *exceptions and safeguards* articles will have to be negotiated in the light of the arguments in the previous section, making them neither too restrictive nor so wide as to endanger the agreement itself.

The procedures for *notification, consultation, scrutiny and adjudication* may properly be called the *Rules of ACT*. As in GATT, these will have to be spelt out in considerable detail. The success of the agreement will to a large extent depend on the observance by governments of the consultation procedures. It is |preferable to provide for a variety of graded procedures, even if they will not all be used in practice. A framework agreement, by its very nature, has to survive many changes in circumstances, power structures and bargaining strengths. One cannot anticipate what procedures will prove to be politically acceptable in the years to come. So long as governments accept the obligations to act in a transparent manner, the subsequent dispute settlement must be left as flexible as possible. The guiding principle in drawing up the rules must be to promote conciliation rather than to arraign and convict violators.

The same principle also applies to *sanctions*. Once governments have accepted obligations voluntarily, the aim of supervision is to promote observance. This follows from the fact that a framework agreement does not create a supra-national authority. It is reasonable to assume that nations are not likely to go to war in order to enforce the obligations of a framework agreement on commodity trade. Most commodity agreements contain an 'expulsion' clause; what use is there in expelling a member who is violating an agreement except to encourage it to do so with greater impunity? The only other sanction usually found is denial of voting rights. There is no known case in which either of these drastic punishments has ever been visited on a country. Persuasion, threat of denial of some benefit, actual denial of benefit, threat of imposing a special disadvantage, actual imposition of a disadvantage – a series of such sanctions, short of expulsion or ostracism, can be thought of. What is needed is a graded set of sanctions, since the quality of violations may vary. In a broad-based commodity agreement, there is no need to punish a member on all commodities for a violation in one of them.

A significant omission in the above enumeration of the articles of ACT is *voting powers and procedures.* In a framework agreement, in which the key elements are voluntary acceptance of obligations, consultation and conciliation, it is difficult to see a place for voting on substantive matters. The Havana Charter provision of 'separate two-thirds majorities of producers and consumers' may have meaning in an agreement on a single commodity. In a disaggregated multi-commodity system, there are no clear-cut divisions. Exporters of some commodities may be importers of some others. It is doubtful whether there is need for voting even on procedural non-substantive matters. There are relatively few purely procedural matters; very often a procedural debate only masks a substantive point. Even in procedural cases, a 'consensus' approach may work just as well. By eschewing voting as a decision-making mechanism, a whole lot of controversies (one-country-one-vote? weighted voting? if so, what weights? should the groups have parity? and so on) can all be avoided. If the participating governments are not able to move forward without counting votes, one might as well not have a framework agreement. Assuming that they are able to do so, how will a round of negotiations in ACT work?

The Rounds of ACT

A negotiating round under ACT will have to commence by achieving a consensus that the time is appropriate. The consensus must also include the specific areas on which a particular round will concentrate. There are many ways in which one can project the actual conduct of negotiations. The one suggested here is based on three principles. First, every participating country will both request and offer; it will seek concessions and offer reciprocal concessions, not necessarily to the same party from whom a concession is sought. Second, the starting point of negotiations will be the problems of the small developing countries, particularly the least developed ones. The larger countries with more varied problems will be taken progressively later. Third, all existing agreements, arrangements and systems of relevance to commodity trade will be taken as given facts. The negotiations will exclude all areas which are already dealt with in other forums or which are capable of resolution bilaterally.

To start with, every participant can be asked to table a set of proposals containing its offers and requests. For the developing countries, it might take the form of each country setting out its resource and commodity objectives, what burden it is prepared to undertake and what it seeks in turn from the international community. For example, the proposal might set out first the broad context − the country's total import capability over the next three or five years, its commodity balance sheet (exports and imports), its balance of payments gap. The whole gap can not be filled by trade alone; but it is possible to estimate, as the World Bank frequently does, the amount of aid and private capital inflows and to deduce therefrom the trade gap. The developing country would then indicate how it would prefer to meet this gap − by increasing the volume of exports (tea, coffee, oil-seeds, copper, or whatever), by increasing unit values (as a consequence of price provisions in an existing agreement) or by increasing exports of processed forms (as a result of industrialisation plans). It can then indicate what the country itself is prepared to do to achieve these objectives − agreeing to limit exports, adopting production control or diversification programmes, holding stocks in accordance with a commodity agreement. It can then seek remedies from other countries that would make it possible to realise these objectives − increased access for the raw or processed forms, co-operation from importers in stabilisation if sharp fluctuations are foreseen. Lastly, it can also indicate what it proposes to do to promote the objectives of ACT − guarantee supply, provide access to imports from other developing countries and agree to co-ordinate production of synthetics.

For their part, developed countries' offers might indicate what contribution they are prepared to make to achieve the ACT objectives. These might include quantities earmarked for food aid, stocking of food grains for emergency purposes, reducing protection levels, increasing access for raw materials and processed forms, co-operation in control mechanisms in commodity agreements, price guarantees for imports, reduction in fiscal charges on consumption, contributions to development security funds, .buffer stocks and any similar funds and steps to co-ordinate synthetic production. It is at this stage that countries are offered a choice of mechanisms; each one chooses from the catalogue what is feasible. In return for these offers, they may seek assurances of supply, control of production and exports of some commodities in order to promote stability and assurances about not causing undue injury to declining industries.

The centrally planned countries might indicate what increased access they are willing to provide for products of developing countries, what steps they propose to take to promote consumption of these products and for which commodities they are willing to enter into trade contracts. The long-term contracts might specify the period, the minimum quantities, the optional extra quantities and the pricing formulas. The plans of these countries for imports and exports of commodities will also add a valuable element for projecting the future supply/demand prospects for different commodities.

The obvious next step is to match offers and requests. The disaggregative concept and the selective mix of techniques will make it possible to establish links between problems, countries and solutions. This matching need not be any more complicated than the early skirmishes in any round of GATT. Some facts can be taken as given — if there is an international agreement on a commodity, its prognostications can be fed into the calculations; existing mechanisms such as Stabex and the compensatory financing facility can also be included. Once these comparative lists have been made, the actual negotiations can commence.

It will obviously be easier to start with the problems of the numerous small countries. As mentioned earlier, the commodity and resource problems of the smaller countries are likely to be more manageable in magnitude. The degree of reciprocity required of them will also be less, if there be any at all. Tackling these problems will therefore be easier. It must be emphasised again that not only the developed and centrally planned countries are expected to make concessions, the advanced developing countries are too. If the needs of smaller countries can be taken care of first, the number of countries left in the negotiation will be substantially reduced. Without even bringing in the morality of looking after the weaker countries first, it is more logical, from a negotiating point of view, to deal with the simpler cases first.

By the time the more complicated larger countries are taken up, the patterns of reciprocity will become clearer. If there are countries whose offers and concessions are manifestly inadequate, they will be under pressure to improve them. What one hopes to promote by this means is a competition in improving concessions rather than the current practice of finding the lowest common denominator. One can assume that the richer countries will be keeping a close watch on what each of them is doing and making rough calculations of the resource burdens in order to ensure that no one is being asked to pay more than the fair share.

Eventually, the outlines of a package will become apparent. This will be a set of actions which each government agrees to implement. It will not be a perfect package; no country will be wholly satisfied; nor will it solve all commodity problems in one fell swoop. But if most of them feel that reciprocity has by and large been achieved and can go back to convince their domestic audiences that nothing has been 'given away', a reasonable set of solutions will have emerged.

The imperfect package will not also operate perfectly. Some of the estimates will be proved wrong; some governments will not be able to deliver what they agreed to; some commodity problems will have been left unresolved; and the unexpected will happen in some. But what the first round will do is to provide a standard against which these failures can be evaluated. The whole purpose of a framework agreement is to provide a forum for continuous negotiations. In the next round the failures can be corrected and something more added. In each round one will learn from past errors. The utility of the different consultation and dispute settlement procedures will also have been tested in practice. Re-examination and renegotiation will also enable changes in the situation of any commodity to be taken into account.

ACT, GATT, UNCTAD and Other Institutions

The description of the articles, rules and negotiating procedures of ACT shows its similarities with GATT. This is inevitable since GATT is the only working model of a framework agreement on international trade. But ACT is not a carbon copy; there are also significant differences.

To take the similarities first, both GATT and ACT have a twofold function. They provide a forum for negotiation and a set of rules to be followed. Just as GATT defines agreed rules for the conduct of trade in industrial goods, particularly in the field of tariffs, ACT will define the rules for regulation of commodity trade in the context of the developmental process. The context is given additional importance in ACT because of the lack of diversification, dependence on commodity exports and vulnerability of most developing countries. Both GATT and ACT emphasise the principle of reciprocity. The concept is modified in ACT by extending it to cover reciprocity all along the line of a continuum of countries and by not limiting it to a one-to-one exchange. Both have a negotiating procedure of a set of simultaneous negotiations leading to a package of agreed solutions. Both give importance to dispute-settlement by prescribing a variety of procedures. Learning from the experience of GATT, it is proposed that ACT should stress transparency of governmental actions. Some other concepts of GATT, such as binding (of tariffs), can also be used in a modified form in ACT. Protection levels could be bound; minimum quantities could be guaranteed access; and minimum prices could also be assured by use of variable import levies.

There is, however, one crucial difference between the two. A cardinal principle of GATT is the 'most favoured nation (mfn) clause. The very first article of GATT enshrines the mfn principle thus: 'any advantage, privilege, or immunity granted by any contracting party to any product . . .shall be accorded immediately and unconditionally to the like product. . .of all other contracting parties.' Article II makes it clear that every participant must apply tariff concessions to all contracting parties and not just to the contracting party with which the concession was negotiated. By its very nature, the disaggregated approach in ACT means that the mfn principle cannot be applied. Suiting the technique to the specific commodity and the countries involved prevents ACT from being non-discriminatory. It must be discriminating in the original sense of the word. For example, if the United States negotiates a special quantitative agreement on imports of soluble coffee in order to benefit some Latin American countries, it does not follow that similar quantitative guarantees have to be given to all other coffee exporters; the US can benefit other developing countries by equivalent action in, say, jute manufactures or sisal manufactures. Likewise, if the EEC accords increased access to groundnut products from West Africa, similar access need not be given to the same product from other countries; the Community may offer different concessions, e.g. access for palm products. The idea that any agreement on trade can be discriminating will be unthinkable to those who are blinkered by the rigidities of the Havana Charter. It is necessary to reiterate that ACT will be discriminating and not discriminatory. The concept of selective application arises out of the need to build on the positive aspects of existing political relationships. The EEC cannot be compelled to extend the Stabex stabilisation scheme to all the developing countries. On the other hand, there is no reason why the 46 ACP countries should not continue to enjoy its benefits and, if possible, even to improve on them. So Stabex has to be accommodated into ACT. The GSP is also discriminating in practice; it is beneficial only to those developing countries which export manufactures or are likely to do so with the little encouragement provided by the Scheme.

This distinction between GATT and ACT does raise the question: where does ACT end and GATT begin? The question applies both to products and to countries. In the disaggregated system envisaged here, the countries in the penumbra of the developed world − e.g. Spain, Portugal, Israel − which are neither developing countries (i.e. not members of the '77') nor as developed as the major OECD countries can also be given some concessions to promote their commodity trade. As they develop, they will at some point have to undertake the full rigour of the mfn obligation of GATT. Some of the more advanced developing countries also can reach that position in the course of time. When they will cease to be eligible for concessions under ACT is difficult to decide. The problem is analogous to that of countries electing to be governed by Article VIII of the IMF. At best, ACT can only provide for a possibility of this kind, leaving the actual changes to the political process. There is a similar line-drawing problem concerning commodities. In Chapter 3, difficulties were encountered in defining precisely what is meant by commodities. Further, one of the main areas of negotiation under ACT will be the promotion of trade in processed and manufactured forms. There is bound to be some overlap between ACT and GATT — raw cotton and cotton yarn will be treated as commodities under ACT, but cotton textiles come under the purview of the MFA; hides and skins, leather and even shoe uppers will be considered commodities and processed forms, but leather shoes will be manufactures. Such an overlap is already being experienced; manufactures from developing countries are accorded preferential entry under GSP, an UNCTAD mechanism, but improvements in it are a part of the MTN in the Tokyo Round.

The line drawing question has been raised as an example of the conflicts of relationship that may arise between ACT and existing international institutions. ACT itself will not need to create an organisation or a UN Agency. As a framework agreement, it will have no specific duties in functional areas to implement. It need not have a large secretariat; if a secretariat is required, it need only be a small supporting unit that will arrange the facilities to enable governments to conduct their negotiations. Just as it will accommodate (and not incorporate) international commodity agreements and take into account the IMF compensatory financing facility, so can it take GATT, UNCTAD and FAO as institutions already in position. In particular, there need be no conflict with UNCTAD, which performs the vital role of articulating the aspirations of developing countries in a variety of fields ranging from commodities to transfer of technology and shipping. Indeed, if there is an ACT, UNCTAD can provide valuable technical support to many developing countries, just as OECD does for the industrialised ones. It can even emerge as a powerful negotiator on behalf of the developing countries. FAO will also have a special role to play in ACT. It will continue to be the source of authoritative information on agricultural commodity production and trade. Its Committee on Commodity Problems will continue to provide expert examination. As an implementing agency, it may well be called upon to assist in diversification plans and productivity improvement schemes that may be needed as a consequence of the package of solutions negotiated under ACT. A similar role can also be envisaged for UNIDO in promoting processing and industrialisation in developing countries. In short, ACT will neither be a competitor to existing institutions nor need it duplicate any of the work already being done elsewhere. It is only a forum in which governments can take co-ordinated decisions. So long as the principle of not encroaching on existing organisations is firmly entrenched in its articles, it need not add to the proliferation of agencies. The cost of running it should therefore be modest.

Is ACT Negotiable?

The ACT scheme may well sound too good to be true. Scepticism is a necessary ingredient in judging any proposal about commodity regulation. There are some good reasons for thinking that a framework agreement has better chances than agreements on a wide range of commodities. This cautious optimism is based on the fact that, in designing ACT, political realities are taken fully into account. *First,* the importance countries attach to particular commodities is recognised. Neither the importance of primary commodity exports to the United States, Canada or Australia nor the importance of commodity imports to Japan is under-estimated; the contribution that developed exporting countries make to world food stability as well as the heavy dependence of many developing countries on primary commodity exports are also recognised. *Second,* no government is coerced into doing what it does not voluntarily want to do. Governments are invited to offer only what they can implement; only the sincerity of implementation is made subject to scrutiny by the other parties. In fact, the difficult balance between freedom and regulation is struck by asking governments to specify their own limits of regulation. If some want only minimal regulation, the onus is then on them to think up feasible alternatives. *Third,| all existing commodity agreements, informal arrangements, earnings stabilisation schemes can be taken into account in the 'balance sheet' or 'package set' as negotiations progress. *Fourth,* ACT disaggregates and differentiates. Those who do not have the ability to hang on in times of stress may be helped, but those with adequate resources will not gain an unintended advantage. ACT can differentiate between those who can control production and those who cannot; between those who can impose quantitative measures and those who rely on fiscal mechanisms. *Fifth,* the structure of the markets is not unduly disturbed, except as already provided for in a commodity agreement or as agreed to voluntarily under ACT. Markets may be regulated; synthetic production may be co-ordinated; industrial transfer may take place; closed markets may become more open. All these will be an orderly process of mutually accepted obligations under agreed ground rules. *Sixth,* existing international organisations are guaranteed their role. *Seventh,* there is no need to create another international agency with a large secretariat. *Eighth,* the structure is based on conciliation and not confrontation; dispute settlement is by consultation and not by condemnation and conviction, *Last,* ACT will bring under one umbrella the totality of decisions and obligations of governments. The hope is that if governments understand that the burden has been shared equitably in a spirit of reciprocity, they will be more enthusiastic about shouldering it.

Thus, comprehensiveness, flexibility, reciprocity, absorption of existing linkages and disaggregation have all been built into ACT.

Are there no disadvantages? Critics of this suggestion will no doubt be able to find many; it is difficult for proponents to do so. In any case, the negotiability of ACT as an instrument itself will depend on the reactions to this proposal from the two extreme ends of the spectrum of commodity debate. For the sake of convenience, these may be termed the US Congress and the revolutionaries for a New International Economic Order. Since ACT is envisaged only as a commitment to negotiate, it may be construed to be an 'executive treaty'. If so, it does not require the consent of the US Senate and can be signed by the President of the United States, as happened in the case of GATT. Of course, as in GATT, an Act of Congress may be required before every round of negotiations. That is a bridge one has to cross; the debate before each such Act will help to clarify the areas of negotiation and the extent of American offers. As for the developing countries, it is difficult to estimate the strength of feeling for revolutionary change. It is quite possible that a large number subscribe to it because there is no other alternative. It has also been argued that the revolutionary zeal of even the most radical of countries is only a political stance intended to conserve the support of the developing countries while the confrontation with the developed countries goes on. If there is a way that offers hopes of practical solutions, many governments may well choose to try it in preference to continued confrontation.

Nobody can predict what the commodity world will be like in three, six or ten years from now. If the first one or two rounds succeed reasonably well, a momentum will build up. If they fail, ACT will also be added to all the other failures in commodity regulation. Only one other argument for trying ACT remains. Is there anything better? If there is not, at least let this one be given a try. If the international commodity does not make even this attempt and resigns itself to a continuation of the centrifugal, increasingly autarkic world, the developing world will become increasingly more vulnerable. The frustrations will multiply and the political instability that will follow will be of our own making. Let us hope

> The time for universal peace is near
> Prove this a reasonable day, the three nook'd world
> Shall bear the olive freely.

Antony and Cleopatra, Act IV, Scene 6

Notes

1. H.W. Singer, 'The Distribution of Gains from Trade and Investment – Revisited', *Journal of Development Studies*, 11, 1975, pp.376-82.
2. For the analysis of the operation of GATT, in particular the operation of its Rules, I am greatly indebted to Gerard and Victoria Curzon, 'The Management of Trade Relations in the GATT' in Andrew Shonfield (ed., with Hermia Oliver), *International Economic Relations of the Western World 1959-71*, Vol.I, *Politics and Trade* (Royal Institute of International Affairs, Oxford University Press, London, 1976). For the reference to Nordic countries see p.181.
3. G. and V. Curzon, 'The Management of Trade Relations in the GATT', pp.160-1.
4. G. and V. Curzon, 'The Management of Trade Relations in the GATT', p.152.
5. G. and V. Curzon, 'The Management of Trade Relations in the GATT', p.206.
6. Article 57, International Sugar Agreement 1968 (HMSO, London), Treaty Series 93 (1969); Article 61, International Cocoa Agreement 1972 (HMSO, London) misc. no.5 (1973); Article 58, International Coffee Agreement 1976.
7. G. and V. Curzon, 'The Management of Trade Relations in the GATT', pp.206-7.
8. G. and V. Curzon, 'The Management of Trade Relations in the GATT', p.154.

APPENDIX 1

United Nations Conference on Trade and Employment. Havana, Cuba, 21 November 1947 — 24 March 1948

Final Act and Related Documents
Havana Charter for an International Trade Organisation

Chapter VI. Inter-Governmental Commodity Agreements

Section A — Introductory Considerations

Article 55 — Difficulties relating to Primary Commodities

The Members recognise that the conditions under which some primary commodities are produced, exchanged and consumed are such that international trade in these commodities may be affected by special difficulties such as the tendency towards persistent disequilibrium between production and consumption, the accumulation of burdensome stocks and pronounced fluctuations in prices. These special difficulties may have serious adverse effects on the interests of producers and consumers, as well as widespread repercussions jeopardising the general policy of economic expansion. The Members recognise that such difficulties may, at times, necessitate special treatment of the international trade in such commodities through inter-governmental agreements.

Article 56 — Primary and Related Commodities

1. For the purposes of this Chapter, the term 'primary commodity' means any product of farm, forest or fishery or any mineral, in its natural form or which has undergone such processing as is customarily required to prepare it for marketing in substantial volume in international trade.

2. The term shall also, for the purposes of this Chapter, cover a group of commodities, of which one is a primary commodity as defined in paragraph 1 and the others are commodities which are so closely related, as regards conditions of production or utilisation, to the other commodities in the group, that it is appropriate to deal with them in a single agreement.

3. If, in exceptional circumstances, the Organisation finds that the conditions set forth in Article 62 exist in the case of a commodity which does not fall precisely under paragraphs 1 or 2 of this Article, the Organisation may decide that the provisions of this Chapter, together

with any other requirements it may establish, shall apply to inter-governmental agreements regarding that commodity.

Article 57 – Objectives of Inter-governmental Commodity Agreements

The members recognise that inter-governmental commodity agreements are appropriate for the achievement of the following objectives:

(a) to prevent or alleviate the serious economic difficulties which may arise when adjustments between production and consumption cannot be effected by normal market forces alone as rapidly as the circumstances require;

(b) to provide, during the period which may be necessary, a framework for the consideration and development of measures which have as their purpose economic adjustments designed to promote the expansion of consumption or a shift of resources and man-power out of over-expanded industries into new and productive occupations, including as far as possible in appropriate cases, the development of secondary industries based upon domestic production of primary commodities;

(c) to prevent or moderate pronounced fluctuations in the price of a primary commodity with a view to achieving a reasonable degree of stability on a basis of such prices as are fair to consumers and provide a reasonable return to producers, having regard to the desirability of securing long-term equilibrium between the forces of supply and demand;

(d) to maintain and develop the natural resources of the world and protect them from unnecessary exhaustion;

(e) to provide for the expansion of the production of a primary commodity where this can be accomplished with advantage to consumers and producers, including in appropriate cases the distribution of basic foods at special prices;

(f) to assure the equitable distribution of a primary commodity in short supply.

Section B – Inter-governmental Commodity Agreements in General

Article 58 – Commodity Studies (not reproduced)

Article 59 – Commodity Conferences (not reproduced)

Article 60 – General Principles governing Commodity Agreements (not reproduced)

Article 61 – Types of Agreements

1. For the purposes of this Chapter, there are two types of inter-

governmental commodity agreements:

(a) commodity control agreements as defined in this Article; and

(b) other inter-governmental commodity agreements.

2. Subject to the provisions of paragraph 5, a commodity control agreement is an inter-governmental agreement which involves:

(a) the regulation of production or the quantitative control of exports or imports of a primary commodity and which has the purpose or might have the effect of reducing, or prevent an increase in, the production of, or trade in, that commodity; or

(b) the regulation of prices.

3. The Organisation shall, at the request of a Member, a study group or a commodity conference, decide whether an existing or proposed inter-governmental agreement is a commodity control agreement within the meaning of paragraph 2.

4. (a) Commodity control agreements shall be subject to all the provisions of this Chapter.

(b) Other inter-governmental commodity agreements shall be subject to the provisions of this Chapter other than those of Section C. If, however, the Organisation decides that an agreement which involves the regulation of production or the quantitative control of of exports or imports is not a commodity control agreement within the meaning of paragraph 2, it shall prescribe the provisions of Section C, if any, to which that agreement shall conform.

5. An existing or proposed inter-governmental agreement the purpose of which is to secure the co-ordinated expansion of aggregate world production and consumption of a primary commodity may be treated by the Organisation as not being a commodity control agreement, even though the agreement provides for the future application of price provisions, provided that

(a) at the time the agreement is entered into, a commodity conference finds that the conditions contemplated are in accordance with the provisions of Article 62, and

(b) from the date on which the price provisions become operative, the agreement shall conform to all the provisions of Section C, except that no further finding will be required under Article 62.

6. Members shall enter into any new commodity control agreement only through a conference called in accordance with the provisions of Article 59 and after an appropriate finding has been made under Article 62. If, in an exceptional case, there has been unreasonable delay in the convening or in the proceedings of the study group or of the commodity conference, Members which consider themselves

substantially interested in the production or consumption of, or trade in, a particular primary commodity, may proceed by direct negotiation to the conclusion of an agreement, provided that the situation is one contemplated in Article 62(a) or (b) and that the Agreement conforms to the other provisions of this Chapter.

Section C — Inter-Governmental Commodity Control Agreements

Article 62 — Circumstances governing the use of Commodity Control Agreements

The Members agree that commodity control agreements may be entered into only when a finding has been made through a commodity conference or through the Organisation by consultation and general agreement among Members substantially interested in the commodity, that:

(a) a burdensome surplus of a primary commodity has developed or is expected to develop, which, in the absence of specific governmental action, would cause serious hardship to producers among whom are small producers who account for a substantial portion of the total output, and that these conditions could not be corrected by normal market forces in time to prevent such hardship, because, characteristically in the case of the primary commodity concerned, a substantial reduction in price does not readily lead to a significant increase in consumption or to a significant decrease in production; or

(b) widespread unemployment or under-employment in connection with a primary commodity, arising out of difficulties of the kind referred to in Article 55, has developed or is expected to develop, which, in the absence of specific governmental action, would not be corrected by normal market forces in time to prevent widespread and undue hardship to workers because, characteristically in the case of the industry concerned, a substantial reduction in price does not readily lead to a significant increase in consumption but to a reduction of employment, and because areas in which the commodity is produced in substantial quantity do not afford alternative employment opportunities for the workers involved.

Article 63 — Additional Principles governing Commodity Control Agreements

The Members shall observe the following principles governing the conclusion and operation of commodity control agreements, in addition to those stated in Article 60:

(a) Such agreements shall be designed to assure the availability of supplies adequate at all times for world demand at prices which are in keeping with the provisions of Article 57(c), and, when practicable, shall provide for measures designed to expand world consumption of the commodity.

(b) Under such agreements, participating countries which are mainly interested in imports of the commodity concerned shall, in decisions on substantive matters, have together a number of votes equal to that of those mainly interested in obtaining export markets for the commodity. Any participating country, which is interested in the commodity but which does not fall precisely under either of the above classes, shall have an appropriate voice within such classes.

(c) Such agreements shall make appropriate provision to afford increasing opportunities for satisfying national consumption and world market requirements from sources from which such requirements can be supplied in the most effective and economic manner, due regard being had to the need for preventing serious economic and social dislocation and to the position of producing areas suffering from abnormal disabilities.

(d) Participating countries shall formulate and adopt programmes of internal economic adjustment believed to be adequate to ensure as much progress as practicable within the duration of the agreement towards solution of the commodity problem involved.

Article 64 – Administration of Commodity Control Agreements

1. Each commodity control agreement shall provide for the establishment of a governing body, herein referred to as a Commodity Council, which shall operate in conformity with the provisions of this Article.

2. Each participating country shall be entitled to have one representative on the Commodity Council. The voting power of the representatives shall be determined in conformity with the provisions of Article 63(b).

3. The Organisation shall be entitled to appoint a non-voting representative to each Commodity Council and may invite any competent inter-governmental organisation to nominate a non-voting representative for appointment to a Commodity Council.

4. Each Commodity Council shall appoint a non-voting chairman who, if the Council so requests, may be nominated by the Organisation.

5. The Secretariat of each Commodity Council shall be appointed

by the Council after consultation with the Organisation.

6. Each Commodity Council shall adopt appropriate rules of procedure and regulations regarding its activities. The Organisation may at any time require their amendment if it considers that they are inconsistent with the provisions of this Chapter.

7. Each Commodity Council shall make periodic reports to the Organisation on the operation of the agreement which it administers. It shall also make such special reports as the Organisation may require or as the Council itself considers to be of value to the Organisation.

8. The expenses of a Commodity Council shall be borne by the participating countries.

9. When an agreement is terminated, the Organisation shall take charge of the archives and statistical material of the Commodity Council.

Article 65 – Initial Term, Renewal and Review of Commodity Control Agreements

1. Commodity control agreements shall be concluded for a period of not more than five years. Any renewal of a commodity control agreement, including agreements referred to in paragraph 1 of Article 68, shall be for a period not exceeding five years. The provisions of such renewed agreements shall conform to the provisions of this Chapter.

2. The Organisation shall prepare and publish periodically, at intervals not greater than three years, a review of the operation of each agreement in the light of the principles set forth in this Chapter.

3. Each commodity control agreement shall provide that, if the Organisation finds that its operation has failed substantially to conform to the principles laid down in this Chapter, participating countries shall either revise the agreement to conform to the principles or terminate it.

4. Commodity control agreements shall include provisions relating to withdrawal of any party.

Article 66 – Settlement of Disputes

Each commodity control agreement shall provide that:

(a) any question or difference concerning the interpretation of the provisions of the agreement or arising out of its operation shall be discussed originally by the Commodity Council; and

(b) if the question or difference cannot be resolved by the Council in accordance with the terms of the agreement, it shall be referred by the Council to the Organisation, which shall apply the procedure set forth in Chapter VIII with appropriate adjustments to cover the case of non-Members.

Section D – Miscellaneous Provisions

Article 67 – Relations with Inter-governmental Organisations (not reproduced)

Article 68 – Obligations of Members regarding Existing and Proposed Commodity Agreements (not reproduced)

Article 69 – Territorial Application (not reproduced)

Article 70 – Exceptions to Chapter VI

1. The provisions of this Chapter shall not apply:

(a) to any bilateral inter-governmental agreement relating to the purchase and sale of a commodity falling under Section D of Chapter IV;

(b) to any inter-governmental commodity agreement involving no more than one exporting country and no more than one importing country and not covered by sub-paragraph (a) above; provided that if, upon complaint by a non-participating Member, the Organisation finds that the interests of that Member are seriously prejudiced by the agreement, the agreement shall become subject to such provisions of this Chapter as the Organisation may prescribe;

(c) to those provisions of any inter-governmental commodity agreement which are necessary for the protection of public morals or of human, animal or plant life or health, provided that such agreement is not used to accomplish results inconsistent with the objectives of Chapter V or Chapter VI.

(d) to any inter-governmental agreement relating solely to the conservation of fisheries resources, migratory birds or wild animals, provided that such agreement is not used to accomplish results inconsistent with the objectives of this Chapter or the purpose and objectives set forth in Article 1 and is given full publicity in accordance with the provisions of paragraph 1(e) of Article 60; if the Organisation finds, upon complaint by a non-participating Member, that the interests of that Member are seriously prejudiced by the agreement, the agreement shall become subject to such provisions of this Chapter as the Organisation may prescribe.

2. The provisions of Articles 58 and 59 and of Section C of this Chapter shall not apply to inter-governmental commodity control agreements found by the Organisation to relate solely to the equitable distribution of commodities in short supply.

3. The provisions of Section C of this Chapter shall not apply to commodity control agreements found by the Organisation to relate solely to the conservation of exhaustible natural resources.

APPENDIX 2

Conference of Developing Countries on Raw Materials. Dakar 3-8 February 1975

The Dakar Declaration

The developing countries, meeting in Dakar on 4-8 February on the initiative of the Fourth Summit Conference of Non-Aligned Countries, carried out a detailed analysis of the fundamental problems of raw materials and development in the light of recent trends in international economic relations, and taking into account the decisions of the Sixth Special Session of the United Nations General Assembly on raw materials and development.

They noted the trends in the international economic situation, which was marked by the perpetuation of inequalities in economic relations, imperialist domination, neo-colonialist exploitation and a total lack of solutions to the basic problems of the developing countries.

Determined to pursue together and in unity a joint action to broaden the irreversible process which has been initiated in international economic relations and which has opened the way for the developing countries to put an end to their position of dependence vis-à-vis imperialism;

Convinced that the only way for them to achieve full and complete economic emancipation is to recover and control their natural resources and wealth and the means of economic development in order to secure the economic, social and cultural progress of their peoples;

Decide, in accordance with the principles and objectives of the Declarations and Programmes of Action of the Fourth Summit Conference of Non-Aligned Countries and the Sixth Special Session of the United Nations General Assembly, on the basis of a common course of action, to adopt the following declaration:

1. The present structure of international trade, which had its origins in imperialist and colonialist exploitation, and which has continued in force up to the present day, in most cases through various forms of neo-colonialism, needs to be replaced by a new international economic order based on principles of justice and equity, designed to safeguard the common interests of all peoples, to correct present injustices and to prevent the occurrence of further injustices. The profound crisis now affecting the international economic system has once again demonstrated the breakdown of traditional mechanisms, and with it the

particular *vulnerability of the economies of developing countries*. It cannot be denied that the structure and organisation of world import and export trade operate for the most part to the advantage of developed countries. A powerful weapon which the developing countries can use to change this state of affairs is to defend their natural resources and to grasp the fact (as they are in fact doing) that it is only by combining their forces to strengthen their negotiating power that they will ever succeed in obtaining their rights to just and equitable treatment, something for which our peoples have lived and fought for for centuries. Despite innumerable efforts at international level to tackle the problems which confront developing countries which export primary products, no perceptible progress has in fact been made for several decades in solving any aspect of the primary products problem.

2. According to the views imposed by the industrialised capitalist countries concerning world trade in primary products, the free working of the primary products markets should normally ensure an optimum distribution of the world resources, and the rising trend of demand in the industrialised countries for exports of primary products from developing countries should stimulate the economic growth of this latter group of countries. This would have been the case if favourable conditions had been created, especially with regard to free access to the markets of the developed countries and the marketing of primary products, but the developing countries have, in the performance of this function of suppliers of raw materials to the industrialised countries, run into other obstacles imposed on them.

3. *The framework and organisation of commodity trade,* and especially the marketing and distribution systems for individual commodities prevailing at present, were developed in the nineteenth century by colonial powers and are wholly inadequate today as instruments of economic change and advancement. Under such systems, *transnational corporations control the production* of and trade in many primary commodities, particularly through the exercise of bargaining power against a large number of weak competing sellers in developing countries. World commodity markets experience a *chronic instability* which arises through sudden and substantial shifts in the balance of world supply and demand as well as through excessive speculative activities encouraged by the lack of adequate regulation of these markets.

4. The fact that developing countries have been denied adequate participation in the determination of the international prices of their

export commodities has led to a permanent transfer of real resources from developing to developed countries, because the benefits from the *improvements in productivity* in the production of primary commodities and raw materials *are transferred* to developed consumer countries rather than translated into higher earnings for commodity producers, in marked contrast with what occurs in developed countries where improvements in productivity result in higher profits for those countries. Furthermore the low level of commodity prices has stimulated an *excessive consumption and considerable waste of scarce raw materials in the affluent countries,* resulting in the rapid depletion of non-renewable resources.

5. The repeated MFN tariff reductions in the post-war period which resulted from trade negotiations in the GATT *covered mostly industrial products traded mainly between developed countries.* Moreover efforts towards the liberalisation of international trade tended to ignore non-tariff barriers, which more particularly affect raw or semi-processed primary commodities of export interest to developing countries, and also left unresolved the problem of tariff escalation, which greatly hampers the trade of developing countries.

6. In addition, *developed countries* or groupings of developed countries spend on the *subsidisation of their domestic production* of primary commodities competing with those exported by developing countries a much large amount than that allocated to official development assistance to developing countries. Moreover, they have violated the principles adopted in the framework of the GATT and have failed to meet their obligations under the International Development Strategy with regard to the readjustments of their respective economies. As a result, their *self-sufficiency* ratios for most of these commodities *increased substantially,* and in some cases surpluses became available for *dumping* on third countries' markets, thus reducing the export outlets available to producer developing countries.

7. At the same time considerable research and development efforts were undertaken, in particular by transnational corporations — partly financed out of the excess profits they had made by controlling the exploitation and marketing of the natural resources of the developing countries — and led to the *large-scale production of synthetics and substitutes* which displaced in well-protected markets the natural products by developing countries.

8. The fast growth of developed countries was partly financed through an *international monetary system* tailored to their needs, allowing inflationary trends to affect not only their domestic

economies but also international trade. *Developing countries,* being the
weakest partners in this trade, were those who suffered most from
inflation. Moreover, speculative monetary activities by transnational
corporations contributed significantly to the destabilisation of the
international monetary system. The monetary instability and
devaluation of the early 1970s affected adversely the currency reserves
held by developing countries.

9. The above constraints imposed on the commodity trade of
developing countries have resulted in a *persistent long-term deterioration in their terms of trade,* despite occasional improvements such as
those which occurred at the beginning of the fifties or recently in 1973
and at the beginning of 1974. The sudden increase in commodity prices
which occurred in 1973 and part of 1974, however, was due to
exceptional circumstances and to an increase in demand as a hedge
against inflation and exchange-rate changes rather than to any
conscious international policy. Furthermore, this rise in commodity
prices was uneven among the various commodities, the prices of some
important commodities having actually remained stagnant or decreased
in real terms.

10. Finally, this increase in commodity prices, including oil prices,
followed a long period of deterioration in the terms of trade of the
developing countries.

11. The prices of several major commodities have begun to decline
significantly, leading to a further deterioration in the terms of trade of
developing countries. There is also a real possibility that other
commodities may also experience a decline in prices, given the likelihood that developed countries will take measures to reduce their
imports of many of these commodities as part of their *strategy of
dividing the developing countries.*

12. Ever rising freight rates and the failure by the Liner Conferences
in most cases to grant promotional freight rates in respect of primary
commodities of export interest to the developing countries have further
impeded export promotion, particularly in countries which are landlocked and geographically handicapped.

13. The *high rates of inflation* generated within the economies of the
industrialised developed countries *have been exported* to the economies
of the developing countries by raising their import bills to unbearable
limits. The balance-of-payments difficulties already being experienced
by many developing countries have been seriously aggravated by, *inter
alia,* the *enormous increase in the cost of imports of food, fertilisers,
capital equipment and fuel and in the cost of transport, ocean freight,*

services and insurance, and the implementation of the development plans of developing countries facing such difficulties has been seriously impeded.

In this respect the land-locked developing countries are in a very difficult position, which certainly deserves special attention in view of the special problems with which these countries are confronted.

14. Finally, the potential mineral resources of the sea-bed, the ocean floor and the sub-soil thereof outside the limits of national jurisdiction, the extraction of which might become a reality towards 1985, threaten seriously to reduce the export earnings of developing countries, particularly given the danger that the exploitation of these resources may be undertaken under a regime which will not fully safeguard the interests of the producer developing countries concerned.

15. The fundamental problem remains the same: developing countries still depend on their commodity exports for 75 to 80 per cent of their foreign exchange earnings. The process of their development is still largely dependent upon external factors, i.e. the demand from the developed countries for their export commodities.

16. There is *no price support* at just and remunerative levels in the world market *for primary commodities,* in marked contrast to the systems operating in the domestic markets of the developed countries in favour of their own farmers. Finally, the existing system of organisation of the world food trade has been unable to meet the essential requirements of food-deficient developing countries.

Notes

1. In the above extracts, emphases have been added, in order to indicate the concept dealt with in each paragraph.
2. The Declaration consists of 31 paragraphs, a detailed Action Programme running to 18 typed pages and a number of resolutions on both economic and political subjects.

Source: UNCTAD, TD/B/C.1/L.45, 17 February 1975.

Appendix 3: Direction of Trade of Developed, Developing and Centrally Planned countries (Value in US $ million)

		1955	1960	1965	1970	1971	1972	1973	1974
Developed countries									
	Total	60,960	82,790	126,530	220,950	247,190	296,250	409,290	587,330
From other developed countries	Value	42,150	60,200	95,740	172,460	193,000	230,570	311,960	398,460
	%	69.1	72.7	75.7	78.1	78.1	77.8	76.2	67.8
From developing countries	Value	17,100	19,780	26,110	40,740	45,490	55,960	81,950	166,310
	%	28.1	23.9	20.6	18.4	18.4	18.9	20.0	28.3
From OPEC countries	Value				14,300	18,470	23,010	33,510	95,620
	%				6.5	7.5	7.7	8.2	16.3
From NOEDEC countries	Value				26,440	27,020	32,950	48,440	70,690
	%				12.0	10.9	11.1	11.8	12.0
From centrally planned countries	Value	1,710	2,800	4,680	7,760	8,700	10,120	15,380	22,570
	%	2.8	3.4	3.7	3.5	3.5	3.4	3.8	3.8
Developing countries									
	Total	23,140	29,140	37,580	58,050	65,400	75,100	105,430	171,950
From developed countries	Value	16,730	21,800	26,990	41,910	47,140	53,470	73,720	113,730
	%	72.3	74.8	71.8	72.2	72.1	71.2	69.9	66.1
From other developing countries	Value	5,790	6,100	7,650	10,950	12,940	15,520	22,880	46,600
	%	25.0	20.9	20.4	18.9	19.8	20.7	21.7	27.1
From centrally planned countries	Value	620	1,250	2,940	5,180	5,310	6,110	8,820	11,620
	%	2.6	4.3	7.8	8.9	8.1	8.1	8.4	6.8
Centrally Planned countries									
	Total	8,810	15,000	21,150	31,420	33,860	41,550	55,930	70,650
From developed countries	Value	1,330	2,970	4,990	8,360	8,950	11,860	18,400	26,590
	%	15.1	19.8	23.6	26.6	26.4	28.5	32.9	37.6
From developing countries	Value	580	1,220	2,390	3,150	3,070	3,550	5,140	7,700
	%	6.6	8.1	11.3	10.0	9.1	8.5	9.2	10.9
From other centrally planned countries	Value	6,900	10,820	13,770	19,920	21,830	26,140	32,390	36,350
	%	78.3	72.1	65.1	63.4	64.5	62.9	57.9	51.5

Source: UN *Yearbooks of International Trade Statistics*

Appendix 4: Dependence of developing countries on export of primary commodities 1970-72 average

Commodity	Dependence as percentage of total merchandise export earnings				
	More than 66%	50 to 66%	33 to 49%	20 to 32%	10 to 20%
Bananas		Panama	Ecuador Guadaloupe Honduras Martinique	Costa Rica Cape Verde Tonga	
Bauxite				Jamaica Surinam Somalia	Guyana Haiti
Beef			Uruguay		Argentina Nicaragua Paraguay Chad
Cocoa	Equatorial Guinea Sao Tomé/Principe	Ghana	Togo	Cameroon	Benin Ivory Coast Nigeria
Coffee	Burundi Rwanda	Colombia Ethiopia	El Salvador Guatemala Haiti Ivory Coast Yemen Arab Republic	Brazil Costa Rica Angola Cameroon Central African Republic Equatorial Guinea Kenya Malagasy	Ecuador Honduras Nicaragua Guinea Tanzania Togo Papua New Guinea

Appendix 4 (continued)

Commodity	More than 66%	50 to 66%	33 to 49%	20 to 32%	10 to 20%
Copper	Chile Zaire Zambia	Namibia		Peru	Philippines
Copra	Seychelles Islands Tonga		Comoros		
Cotton		Chad Sudan	Egypt Upper Volta Syria	Nicaragua Central African Republic Mali Uganda Yemen Arab Republic	Philippines El Salvador Guatemala Benin Mozambique Swaziland Afghanistan
Fishmeal				Peru	
Groundnuts Groundnut oil	Gambia		Niger		Mali
Iron ore	Liberia Mauritania			Swaziland	Sierra Leone
Jute			Bangla Desh		
Lead				Namibia	
Maize					Argentina Thailand
Manganese ore				Gabon	
Phosphate rock	Spanish Sahara		Togo		Morocco Jordan

Appendix 4 (continued)

Commodity	More than 66%	50 to 66%	33 to 49%	20 to 32%	10 to 20%
Rice	Nepal	Kampuchea	Burma		Thailand
Rubber				Malaysia	Liberia Indonesia Kampuchea Sri Lanka
Sugar	Cuba Mauritius	Dominican Republic Guadeloupe Fiji	Barbados	Belize Guyana	Jamaica Mozambique Philippines
Tea		Sri Lanka			Kenya Malawi Bangla Desh
Tobacco			Malawi		
Timber non-conifer	Laos	Congo		Gabon Ivory Coast Burma Philippines	Paraguay Indonesia Malaysia
Tin		Bolivia			Rwanda Malaysia
Wheat					Lesotho
Wool				Uruguay	Lesotho
Zinc					Niger

Source: IBRD EC/166.

Note: The percentage dependence is approximate for the reason that the coverage excludes a number of commodities significant in the exports of some countries. For example, the exclusion of diamonds overstates Namibia's dependence on copper; the exclusion of cloves and cashewnuts distorts the dependence percentages of Tanzania. The definition of dependence as a proportion of total merchandise exports also conceals some distortions. Re-exports from coastal countries to landlocked countries tend to reduce the dependence of coastal countries. This is particularly true in cases where some coastal countries with refineries import crude and re-export petroleum products to neighbouring countries.

Appendix 5.1: Steel Purchasing Power of Primary Commodities – Coffee and Bananas against US Steel

Commodity Grade Unit Year	Coffee Santos 4 US $ per bag of 60 kilos	Bananas Central American US $ per 40 lb. case	Steel Hot rolled plates export $ f.o.b.	Terms of Trade Bags of coffee per 100 tons of steel	Terms of Trade Cases of bananas per ton of steel
1948	35.85	2.52	—	—	—
1949	42.07	2.80	—	—	—
1950	66.81	2.92	4.04	6.05	1.38
1951	71.71	2.92	4.22	5.88	1.92
1952	71.44	2.96	4.31	6.03	1.46
1953	76.60	2.96	4.57	5.97	1.54
1954	104.12	3.04	4.69	4.50	1.54
1955	75.54	3.00	4.77	6.31	1.59
1956	76.87	3.04	5.07	6.60	1.67
1957	75.28	3.20	5.45	7.24	1.70
1958	64.03	2.96	5.67	8.86	1.92
1959	48.95	2.64	5.76	11.77	2.18
1960	48.42	2.60	5.75	11.88	2.21
1961	47.63	2.52	5.43	11.40	2.15
1962	44.98	2.40	5.38	11.96	2.24
1963	45.11	3.04	5.44	12.05	1.79
1964	61.78	3.08	5.63	9.11	1.83
1965	59.14	2.88	5.63	9.52	1.95
1966	53.98	2.80	5.63	10.43	2.01
1967	50.01	2.88	5.63	11.26	1.95
1968	49.48	2.76	5.92	11.96	2.14
1969	53.98	2.88	6.42	11.89	2.23
1970	72.24	3.00	6.89	9.54	2.30
1971	59.27	2.56	—	—	—
1972	67.49	2.92	8.15	12.08	2.79
1973	88.51	3.00	8.49	12.58	2.83
1974	90.10	3.34	11.59	12.86	3.47

Source: UN *Monthly Bulletins of Statistics.*

Commodity Grade / Unit	Tea UK North Indian £ per metric ton	Iron ore Liberian $ per ton c.i.f.	Groundnut oil Nigerian $ per metric ton	Steel UK Plates over 3/16 in. export £/m.T.	Steel German Bessemer bars export $ per ton	Tons of tea per 100 tons of steel	Terms of Trade Tons of iron ore per ton of steel	Tons of groundnut oil per 100 tons of steel
1948			438.3					
1949			399.1					
1950			417.5	23.40	54.1			12.96
1951	403		476.2	34.70	66.7	8.61		14.01
1952	330		363.8	46.70	91.7	14.15		25.21
1953	399		385.8	46.50	95.5	11.65		24.75
1954	588	18.02	370.7	36.10	92.1	6.14	5.11	24.84
1955	584	17.25	288.0	40.20	93.3	6.88	5.41	32.40
1956	561	19.29	369.3	51.10	95.7	9.11	4.96	25.91
1957	520	22.17	359.6	57.10	100.2	10.98	4.52	27.86
1958	541	17.26	275.9	47.14	104.3	8.71	6.04	37.80
1959	534	14.28	299.6	41.43	104.3	7.76	7.04	34.81
1960	544	14.42	326.3	41.04	104.3	7.54	7.45	31.96
1961	514	13.30	330.7	40.94	108.2	7.96	8.14	32.72
1962	557	12.16	274.5	40.94	109.5	7.35	9.00	39.89
1963	512	9.94	268.4	40.94	109.5	8.00	11.02	40.80
1964	502	10.18	315.3	42.22	109.5	8.41	10.76	34.73
1965	480	10.03	323.8	42.62	107.3	8.88	10.70	33.14
1966	479	10.07	296.2	42.62	109.3	8.88	10.85	36.90
1967	493	9.65	283.2	42.62	102.0	8.90	10.57	36.02
1968	445	9.20	270.7	42.62	94.5	8.65	10.27	34.91
1969	405	9.23	331.6	42.62	100.5	9.58	10.89	30.31
1970	468	9.94	378.6	49.07	124.9	10.52	12.57	32.99
1971	421	10.86	440.7	56.61	137.1	10.48	12.62	31.11
1972	417	10.53	425.9	59.52	157.4	13.44	14.95	36.99
1973	454	10.80	546.2	65.41	207.9	14.27	19.25	38.06
1974	598	—	1,096.1	90.49	257.3	14.41	—	23.47

Sources: UN *Monthly Bulletins of Statistics*; EUROSTAT *Iron and Steel Yearbooks*

Appendix 6: Trade in Oilseeds, Vegetable oils and oilcake   Exports — 1970 and 1974 (US $ million)

SITC Revised No.	Commodity	1970				1974			
		Total	Developed	Developing	Centrally Planned	Total	Developed	Developing	Centrally Planned
	Oilseeds								
221.1	Groundnuts	216	41	169	6	452	191	242	19
221.2	Copra	170	—	170	—	267	—	267	—
221.3	Palm nuts, kernels	69	—	69	—	139	2	137	—
221.4	Soya beans	1,301	1,221	31	49	4,245	3,546	605	94
221.5	Linseed	70	68	1	1	179	169	5	4
221.6	Cotton seed	32	5	24	3	45	15	27	3
221.7	Castor oil seed	15	—	11	4	31	—	28	3
Ex 221.8	Rape and mustard seed	168	135	24	9	429	423	1	5
Ex 221.8	Sesame seed	53	—	53	—	135	—	134	—
Ex 221.8	Sunflower seed	69	21	2	46	128	101	4	23
	Total oilseeds	2,163	1,491	554	118	6,050	4,447	1,450	151
	Vegetable oils and Soft edible oils								
421.2	Soyabean oil	311	306	5	1	1,083	1,043	34	5
421.3	Cotton seed oil	72	47	17	8	215	182	21	12
421.4	Groundnut oil	146	24	119	3	348	86	251	11
421.5	Olive oil	172	146	26	—	529	283	246	—
421.6	Sunflower oil	201	32	21	148	583	86	2	494
421.7	Rape and mustard oil	52	32	3	17	262	217	2	43
	Total soft oils	954	587	191	177	3,020	1,897	557	565
	Non-soft edible oils								
422.2	Palm oil	201	9	191	—	905	59	845	—
422.3	Coconut oil	189	20	168	—	621	95	526	—
422.4	Palm kernel oil	51	14	37	—	265	52	213	—
	Total non-soft edible oils	441	43	396	—	1,791	206	1,584	—

Appendix 6 (continued)

SITC Revised No.	Commodity	Total	1970 Developed	Developing	Centrally Planned	Total	1974 Developed	Developing	Centrally Planned
	Technical oils								
422.1	Linseed oil	57	20	37	—	195	109	85	1
422.5	Castor oil	50	3	45	2	164	9	154	1
Ex 422.9	Tung oil	17	1	11	5	28	1	16	11
	Total technical oils	124	24	93	7	387	119	255	13
421 + 422	*Vegetable oils*	1,519	654	680	184	5,198	2,222	2,395	578
081.3	*Oilseed cake, meal*								
	Groundnut cake	133	6	127	—	195	16	179	—
	Copra cake	28	3	25	—	65	4	61	—
	Palm kernel cake	17	7	10	—	41	7	32	1
	Soyabean cake	508	460	46	2	1,758	1,448	307	3
	Linseed cake	48	10	38	—	55	21	34	—
	Cotton seed cake	96	5	88	3	154	20	132	2
	Rapeseed cake	15	13	2	—	52	40	12	—
	Sunflower seed cake	39	2	34	2	63	13	50	—
	Other oilseed cake	39	25	14	—	95	67	27	—
	Total oilseed cake, meal	923	531	384	7	2,478	1,636	834	6
	Total oilseeds, oils, oilcake	4,605	2,676	1,618	309	13,726	8,305	4,680	735
			58.1%	35.1%	6.7%		60.5%	34.1%	5.4%

Source: FAO *Trade Yearbook, 1975*

Appendix 7: International Tin Agreements, Price ranges, market price, Buffer stock holding and export quotas in effect

| Period | | Agreement price range | | | London spot price (monthly average) | |
From	To	Floor	Ceiling	Range %	Minimum	Maximum
				£ per long ton		
1 July 1956	22 Mar. 1957	640	880	37.5	770.7	806.1
22 Mar. 1957	12 Jan. 1962	730	880	20.5	718.1	965.2
12 Jan. 1962	4 Dec. 1963	790	965	22.2	852.5	1010.0
4 Dec. 1963	12 Nov. 1964	850	1,000	17.6	1010.0	1586.0
12 Nov. 1964	6 July 1966	1,000	1,200	20.0	1232.5	1531.2
6 July 1966	22 Nov. 1967	1,100	1,400	27.2	1,184.7	1,275.1
22 Nov. 1967	16 Jan. 1968	1,283	1,633	27.3	1273.1	1617.6
16 Jan. 1968	2 Jan. 1970	1,280	1,630	27.3		
				£ per metric ton		
2 Jan. 1970	21 Oct. 1970	1,260	1,605	27.4	1481.4	1629.7
21 Oct. 1970	4 July 1972	1,350	1,650	22.2	1424.5	1554.6
				Malaysian $ per Picul	Penang Market (monthly average)	
4 July 1972	21 Sept. 1973	583	718	23.2	609.8	688.4
21 Sept. 1973	30 May 1974	635	760	19.7	688.4	1302.8
30 May 1974	31 Jan. 1975	850	1,050	23.5	947.9	1300.6
31 Jan. 1975	12 Mar. 1976	900	1,100	22.2	932.7	1003.0
12 Mar. 1976	7 May 1976	950	1,100	15.8	1064.8	1084.7
7 May 1976	—	1,000	1,200	20.0	1144.7	—

Appendix 7 (continued)

Buffer Stocks and quota restrictions

The three periods when the buffer stock held tin and export quotas were also in force were 1957 to 1961, 1968 to 1969 and 1973.

Quarter	Buffer stock holding end of quarter (long tons)	Export quotas (long tons per quarter)
II 1957	3,915	—
III 1957	4,605	—
IV 1957	15,300	27,000
I 1958	22,400	
II 1958	23,300	23,000
III 1958	23,350	
IV 1958	23,325	20,000
I 1959	21,020	
II 1959	13,990	23,000
III 1959	11,150	25,000
IV 1959	10,050	30,000
I 1960	10,030	36,000
II 1960	10,030	
III 1960	10,030	37,500
IV 1960	10,030	
I 1961	10,080	
—		
IV 1968	11,290	42,950
I 1969	11,290	38,000
II 1969	8,450	38,750
III 1969	7,645	39,500
IV 1969	4,590	41,500
—		
I 1973	10,309	34,486
II 1973	9,909	41,970
III 1973	4,665	41,970

Buffer stock holdings

In addition to the periods mentioned above, the buffer stock also had tin in the following periods. The stock started buying in the third quarter of 1962 and held at its highest 3,275 long tons at the end of the first quarter of 1963; all the tin was sold out by the last quarter of that year. The buffer stock again started buying in the first quarter of 1967 and built up to a maximum of 11,290 tons by the third quarter of 1968; at this point export quotas had to be introduced. On the removal of quotas in the last quarter of 1969, the buffer stock started selling and reached a low point of 940 tons in the middle of 1970. It then held small quantities as part of general stabilising operations until the third quarter of 1971 when it began to buy increasing quantities. It held 12,281 tons at the end of 1972 when export quotas were again introduced. On the removal of quotas towards the end of 1973 and the rapid rise in prices during the boom, the buffer stock sold out almost all its tin.

APPENDIX 8

United Nations Conference on Trade and Development
Fourth Session, Nairobi, May 1976

Resolution adopted by the Conference
93 (IV) Integrated Programme for Commodities

The United Nations Conference on Trade and Development

Recalling the Declaration and the Programme of Action on the Establishment of a New International Economic Order as well as the Charter of Economic Rights and Duties of States, which lay down the foundations of the new international economic order, General Assembly resolution 623 (VII) of 21 December 1952 and Conference recommendation A.II.1,

Recalling, in particular, section 1, paragraph 3(a)(iv), of the Programme of Action on the Establishment of a New International Economic Order, relating to the preparation of an overall integrated programme for 'a comprehensive range of commodities of export interest to developing countries',

Recalling also Section I, paragraph 3, of General Assembly resolution 3362 (S-VII) of 16 September 1975, which states, *inter alia,* that 'an important aim of the fourth session of the United Nations Conference on Trade and Development, in addition to work in progress elsewhere, should be to reach decisions on the improvement of market structures in the field of raw materials, and commodities of export interest to the developing countries, including decisions with respect to an integrated programme and the applicability of elements thereof',

Taking note of the work undertaken on commodities in preparation for the fourth session of the Conference, in particular the proposals submitted by the Secretary-General of UNCTAD for an integrated programme for commodities,

Reaffirming the important role of UNCTAD in the field of commodities,

Bearing in mind resolution 16 (VIII) of the Committee on Commodities concerning decisions by the Conference at its fourth session with respect to an integrated programme for commodities, on, *inter alia:*

(a) objectives;
(b) commodities to be covered;
(c) international measures;

(d) follow-up procedures and time-table for the implementation of agreed measures;

Affirming the importance to both producers and consumers, notably the developing countries, of commodity exports for foreign exchange earnings and of commodity imports for welfare and economic development,

Recognizing the need to conduct international trade on the basis of mutual advantage and equitable benefits, taking into account the interests of all States, particularly those of the developing countries,

Recognizing also the need for improved forms of international co-operation in the field of commodities which should promote economic and social development, particularly of the developing countries,

Recognizing further the urgent need for substantial progress in stimulating food production in developing countries and the important bearing of international commodity policies on this aim,

Recalling the proposal in the Manila Declaration and Programme of Action for the establishment of a common fund for the financing of international commodity stocks, co-ordinated national stocks or other necessary measures within the framework of commodity arrangements,

Bearing in mind the view that there might be financial savings in operating a central facility for the purpose of financing buffer stocks,

Taking note of the readiness of a number of countries, expressed prior to and at the fourth session of the Conference, to participate in and financially support a common fund,

Noting that there are differences of views as to the objectives and modalities of a common fund,

Convinced of the need for an overall approach and an integrated programme for commodities which is a programme of global action to improve market structures in international trade in commodities of interest to developing countries, and which is consistent with the interests of all countries, particularly those of the developing countries, and assures a comprehensive view of the various elements involved while respecting the characteristics of individual commodities,

Decides to adopt the following Integrated Programme for Commodities:

I. OBJECTIVES

With a view to improving the terms of trade of developing countries and in order to eliminate the economic imbalance between developed and developing countries, concerted efforts should be made in favour of the developing countries towards expanding and diversifying their trade, improving and diversifying their productive capacity, improving their productivity and increasing their export earnings, with a view to counteracting the adverse effects of inflation, thereby sustaining real incomes. Accordingly the following objectives are agreed:

1. To achieve stable conditions in commodity trade, including avoidance of excessive price fluctuations, at levels which would:
   (a) be remunerative and just to producers and equitable to consumers;
   (b) take account of world inflation and changes in the world economic and monetary situations;
   (c) promote equilibrium between supply and demand within expanding world commodity trade;

2. To improve and sustain the real income of individual developing countries through increased export earnings, and to protect them from fluctuations in export earnings, especially from commodities;

3. To seek to improve market access and reliability of supply for primary products and the processed products thereof, bearing in mind the needs and interests of developing countries;

4. To diversify production in developing countries, including food production, and to expand processing of primary products in developing countries with a view to promoting their industrialization and increasing their export earnings;

5. To improve the competitiveness of, and to encourage research and development on the problems of, natural products competing with synthetics and substitutes, and to consider the harmonization, where appropriate, of the production of synthetics and substitutes in developed countries with the supply of natural products produced in developing countries;

6. To improve market structures in the field of raw materials and commodities of export interest to developing countries;

7. To improve marketing, distribution and transport system for commodity exports of developing countries, including an increase in their participation in these activities and their earnings from them.

II. COMMODITY COVERAGE

The commodity coverage of the Integrated Programme should take into account the interests of developing countries in bananas, bauxite, cocoa, coffee, copper, cotton and cotton yarns, hard fibres and products, iron ore, jute and products, manganese, meat, phosphates, rubber, sugar, tea, tropical timber, tin, and vegetable oils, including olive oil, and oilseeds, among others, it being understood that other products could be included, in accordance with the procedure set out in section IV below.

III. INTERNATIONAL MEASURES OF THE PROGRAMME

1. It is agreed that steps will be taken, as described in section IV, paragraphs 1 to 3 below, towards the negotiation of a common fund.

2. It is also agreed to take the following measures, to be applied singly or in combination, including action in the context of international commodity arrangements between producers and consumers, in the light of the characteristics and problems of each commodity and the special needs of developing countries;

(a) Setting up of international commodity stocking arrangements;

(b) Harmonization of stocking policies and the setting up of co-ordinated national stocks;

(c) Establishment of pricing arrangements, in particular negotiated price ranges, which would be periodically reviewed and appropriately revised, taking into account, *inter alia,* movements in prices of imported manufactured goods, exchange rates, production costs and world inflation, and levels of production and consumption;

(d) Internationally agreed supply management measures, including export quotas and production policies and, where appropriate, multilateral long-term supply and purchase commitments;

(e) Improvement of procedures for information and consultation on market conditions;

(f) Improvement and enlargement of compensatory financing facilities for the stabilization, around a growing trend, of export earnings of developing countries;

(g) Improvement of market access for the primary and processed products of developing countries through multilateral trade measures in the multilateral trade negotiations, improvement of schemes of generalised preferences and their extension beyond the period originally envisaged, and trade promotion measures;

(h) International measures to improve the infrastructure and industrial capacity of developing countries, extending from the production of primary commodities to their processing, transport and marketing, as well as to the production of finished manufactured goods, their transport, distribution and exchange, including the establishment of financial, exchange and other institutions for the remunerative management of trade transactions;

(i) Measures to encourage research and development on the problems of natural products competing with synthetics and consideration of the harmonization where appropriate, of the production of synthetics and substitutes in developed countries with the supply of natural products produced in developing countries;

(j) Consideration of special measures for commodities whose problems cannot be adequately solved by stocking and which experience a persistent price decline.

3. The interests of developing importing countries, particularly the least developed and the most seriously affected among them, and those lacking in natural resources, adversely affected by measures under the Integrated Programme, should be protected by means of appropriate differential and remedial measures within the Programme.

4. Special measures, including exemption from financial contribution, should be taken to accommodate the needs of the least developed countries in the Integrated Programme for Commodities.

5. Efforts on specific measures for reaching arrangements on products, groups of products or sectors which, for various reasons, are not incorporated in the first stage of application of the Integrated Programme should be continued.

6. The application of any of the measures which may concern existing international arrangements on commodities covered by the Integrated Programme would be decided by governments within the commodity organizations concerned.

IV. PROCEDURES AND TIME TABLE

1. The Secretary-General of UNCTAD is requested to convene a negotiating conference open to all members of UNCTAD on a common fund no later than March 1977.

2. The Secretary-General of UNCTAD is further requested to convene preparatory meetings prior to the conference referred to in paragraph 1 above concerning, *inter alia:*

(a)   Elaboration of objectives;

(b)   The financing needs of a common fund and its structure;

(c)   Sources of finance;

(d)   Mode of operations;

(e)   Decision-making and fund management.

3. Member countries are invited to transmit to the Secretary-General of UNCTAD, prior to 30 September 1976, any proposals they may have concerning the above and related issues.

4. The Secretary-General of UNCTAD is further requested to convene, in consultation with international organizations concerned, preparatory meetings for international negotiations on individual products, in the period beginning 1 September 1976. These meetings should complete their work as soon as possible, but not later than February 1978. The task of the preparatory meetings shall be to:

(a) Propose appropriate measures and techniques required to achieve the objectives of the Integrated Programme;

(b) Determine financial requirements resulting from the measures and techniques proposed;

(c) Recommend follow-up action required through the negotiation of commodity agreements, or other measures;

(d) Prepare draft proposals of such agreements for the consideration of governments and for use in commodity negotiating conferences.

5. The Secretary-General of UNCTAD is further requested to convene, as and when required, commodity negotiating conferences as soon as possible after the completion of each preparatory meeting held pursuant to paragraph 4 above. These negotiations should be concluded by the end of 1978.

6. The Secretary-General of UNCTAD is requested to undertake the necessary arrangements for the servicing of the preparatory meetings and the subsequent commodity negotiating conferences, in co-operation with the secretariats of the specialized commodity bodies and other organizations concerned.

7. It is agreed that international negotiations or re-negotiations on individual commodities covered by existing agreements shall be in accordance with appropriate established procedures for the purpose of concluding international arrangements.

8. The Trade and Development Board is instructed to establish an *ad hoc* inter-governmental committee to co-ordinate the preparatory work and the negotiations, to deal with major policy issues that may arise, including commodity coverage, and to co-ordinate the implementation of the measures under the Integrated Programme.

APPENDIX 9

CLASSIFICATION OF COUNTRIES

In this book, the terms developed countries, rich nations and industrialized countries are used interchangeably; the reason for using any one expression is purely stylistic and no special meaning is attached to the usage. Likewise, the terms developing countries, less-developed countries and poor nations are used interchangeably; so are centrally planned economy countries and socialist countries.

Developed countries are those defined by the UN as 'Economic Class I — Developed Market Economies'. These include all countries in Western Europe and the USA, Canada, Japan, Australia, New Zealand, Israel and South Africa.

Centrally planned economy countries are defined by the UN as 'Economic Class III'. In the absence of comprehensive data on Asian socialist countries, the term very often covers only the socialist countries of Eastern Europe and USSR. Though they have centrally planned economies, Yugoslavia and Cuba are usually classified as developing countries.

Developing countries, 'Economic Class II' according to the UN, are all countries except those included in the other two groups. For a list, see UNCTAD *Handbook of International Trade and Development Statistics* (UN Sales No. E/F.72.II.D.3). The total number of countries in the 'Group of '77' ' is about 130. Among these, some special groups exist.

The 13 *OPEC countries* are: Algeria, Ecuador, Gabon, Indonesia, Iran, Iraq, Kuwait, Libya, Nigeria, Qatar, Saudi Arabia, United Arab Emirates and Venezuela. Other major exporters of petroleum (oil exports over 50 per cent of total exports) are: Bahrain, Brunei, Oman and Trinidad and Tobago.

The 28 *Least-Developed Countries* are: in Asia — Afghanistan, Bangla Desh, Bhutan, Lao Peoples Democratic Republic, Maldives, Nepal, Yemen and Democratic Republic of Yemen; in Africa — Benin, Botswana, Burundi, Central African Republic, Chad, Ethiopia, Gambia, Guinea, Lesotho, Malawi, Mali, Niger, Rwanda, Somalia, Sudan, Uganda, Tanzania and Upper Volta; Haiti in the Caribbean and Western Samoa in the Pacific.

The 42 countries *Most Seriously Affected* (MSACs) by the oil price rise are: Afghanistan, Bangla Desh, Benin, Burma, Burundi, Cambodia,

Cameroon, Cape Verde, Central African Republic, Chad, Egypt, El Salvador, Ethiopia, Ghana, Guinea, Guinea-Bissau, Guyana, Haiti, Honduras, India, Ivory Coast, Kenya, Lao Peoples Republic, Lesotho, Madagascar, Mali, Mozambique, Mauritania, Niger, Pakistan, Rwanda, Senegal, Sierra Leone, Somalia, Sri Lanka, Sudan, Tanzania, Uganda, Upper Volta, Yemen, Democratic Republic of Yemen and Western Samoa.

The 46 ACP countries, members of the Lomé Convention are: the 19 members of the Yaoundé Convention, all in Africa (Benin, Burundi, Cameroon, Central African Republic, Chad, Congo, Gabon, Ivory Coast, Madagascar, Mali, Mauritania, Mauritius, Niger, Rwanda, Senegal, Somalia, Togo, Upper Volta and Zaire); 21 countries of the Commonwealth, twelve in Africa (Botswana, Gambia, Ghana, Kenya, Lesotho, Malawi, Nigeria, Sierra Leone, Swaziland, Tanzania, Uganda and Zambia), six in the Caribbean (Bahamas, Barbados, Guyana, Grenada, Jamaica and Trinidad and Tobago) and three in the Pacific (Fiji, Western Samoa and Tonga); and six more African countries (Ethiopia, Liberia, Sudan, Guinea, Equatorial Guinea, and Guinea-Bissau).

APPENDIX 10

A Note On Source Material

Since the bibliographical details of works cited in the text have been given in the notes at the end of each chapter, this essay is about the type of source material consulted in the preparation of this book. While it does not pretend to be a fully-fledged review article, it is an attempt to comment on the availability and utility of data. Material on commodity trade and commodity negotiations is extensive, as one would expect; but material relevant to the perspective adopted in this book is comparatively meagre. The paucity of studies from the point of the poor countries is itself an example of asymmetry; the greater academic and financial resources of the rich nations are, naturally, devoted to a study of *their* problems. Those of developing countries receive attention only if they directly affect a vital interest of the rich nations. The extensive attention paid to coffee as a commodity is only a reflection of the US strategic interest in Latin America. The preoccupation with copper, or chromium or vanadium, is also strategic. The recrudescence of studies on cartelisation is only a reaction to OPEC's success. There are, at best, one or two studies on tea, jute, hard fibres, tropical timber and tropical oils. If this essay gives an impression of covering only European and American sources, this is because these are most abundant. Because of the author's linguistic limitations, all sources are necessarily in English.

BIBLIOGRAPHY

Some useful bibliographies are: *Commodities – A Select Bibliography 1965-1975* (UN – ST/LIB/SER.B/19, December 1975); in Vernon L. Sorenson, *International Trade Policy – Agriculture and Development* (Michigan State University International Business and Economic Studies, 1975); GATT/UNCTAD International Trade Centre, *Bibliography of Trade Press.*

Statistical Data

Statistical material on commodity trade, though voluminous, still has some peculiar lacunae. There is an abundance of up-to-date statistics on quantities traded; value statistics are less comprehensive and timely; this is particularly true of minerals and metals. For renewable commodities, the *FAO Yearbooks (Production Yearbook, Trade Yearbook, and Yearbook of Forestry Products)* are invaluable since they all provide both quantity and value data, for production as well as trade. Apart from the exhaustive coverage, they are also prompt; for example, the *Trade Yearbook* covering the period up to and including 1975 became available early in 1977. In the case of minerals and metals, the only source of value statistics is the *UN Yearbook of International Trade Statistics.* While this is authoritative, it comes out about two years after the last year for which reasonably complete figures are given. The presentation of data is being improved year by year; the 1974 issue had, for the first time, a separate volume giving figures by commodity. In addition, the volume has a matrix showing exports by and imports into the top twenty or so countries for each SITC three-figure group. The 1975 *Yearbook* further shows conveniently, for each group, the share of the market for the top ten countries. The UN *Yearbook* is comprehensive only at the broad level of three-figure groups; break-ups for four-figure sub-groups and five-figure items are given only in a few selected cases. A distinction between the FAO and UN *Yearbooks* is that the former cover world trade and show separate totals for developed, developing and centrally planned countries. The UN publication, on the other hand, only shows market economy trade, i.e. it excludes centrally planned countries; sub-totals for developed and developing countries are given.

For some inexplicable reason, most International Commodity

Councils and Study Groups publish only quantity and price data but no country-wise value figures for exports or imports. Examples are: *World Wheat Statistics* of the International Wheat Council, *Sugar Yearbook* of the International Sugar Council, *Tin Statistics* and *Statistical Bulletin* of the International Tin Council, *Rubber Statistical Bulletin* of the International Rubber Study Group and the *Statistical Monthly* of the International Lead and Zinc Study Group. For price data, two useful publications are the *Commodity Trade and Price Trends* of the World Bank (IBRD – EC/166) and the *UNCTAD Monthly Commodity Price Bulletin*. A *Special Supplement 1960-1974* of the UNCTAD bulletin has complete series of monthly and annual average prices for the 15 year period for 34 commodities. *Metal Statistics* from the Metalgesellschaft Aktiengesellschaft and the *Metal Bulletin Handbook* are comprehensive sources for data concerning all important minerals and metals.

Market conditions and Commodity Negotiations

The relationship between the state of commodity markets and the progress in international commodity negotiations is seen in the quantitative descriptions for agricultural commodities in the FAO annual *Commodity Review and Outlook*. There is nothing similar for minerals or other non-agricultural commodities. The *UNCTAD Commodity Review* and *GATT International Trade,* both annuals, also give descriptions of the trends in international trade. For the years before UNCTAD came into being, see the *Review of International Commodity Problems* (UN, ECOSOC, Interim Co-ordinating Committee for International Commodity Arrangements). *World Commodity Review* (Economist Intelligence Unit) covers current market conditions and the expectations for the immediate future for a variety of commodities.

The conflicts that arise during commodity negotiations are rarely described as they occur, except, to some extent, in the notes in the *Journal of World Trade Law* (see note 4 to chapter 2 on page 51). Apart from items of news interest in the financial press, only the trade press gives some idea of the problems of negotiation and their impact on the market. The main journals are: *Coffee Annual* (George Gordon Paton Co., New York); *World Coffee and Tea,* New York; *Tea Market Report,* weekly (Tea Brokers Association, London); *Cocoa Growers Bulletin,* semi-annual (Cadbury Brothers, UK); *Cocoa Market Report* (Gill and Duffus, London); *International Chocolate Review* (Max Glättli, Zurich); *Sugar y Azucar,* New York; *Australian Sugar Journal,* Brisbane; *Sucrerie Française,* Paris; *The International Sguar Journal,*

High Wycombe, UK; *Edible Nut Market Report* (Gill and Duffus, London); *The Rice Journal,* New Orleans, USA; *Oil World* (Mielke & Co., Hamburg, FRG); *Informations Oleicoles Internationales,* Madrid; *Citrus World,* Winter Haven Fa., USA; *World Tobacco,* London; *Rubber Journal,* Croydon, UK; *Rubber Developments,* Welwyn Garden City, UK; *Rubber Trends* (Economist Intelligence Unit, London); *The Cotton Digest,* Houston, Texas, USA; *World Wood,* Portland, Oregon, USA; *The Jute Bulletin,* Calcutta, India; *The Kenya Sisal Board Bulletin,* Nairobi; *Metal Bulletin,* London; *Metal Trades Journal,* Sydney, Australia; *Japan Iron and Steel Monthly,* Tokyo; *Iron Ore Import (The TEX Report),* Tokyo; and *Tin International,* London.

The publications of the *Commonwealth Secretariat,* in particular the *Tropical Products Quarterly* and the *Hides and Skins Quarterly,* provide material not usually available elsewhere. *Fruit Intelligence, Meat and Dairy Products Bulletin, Wool Intelligence* and *Tobacco Intelligence* are some of the other regular publications of the Secretariat. Among the publications of international organisations on individual commodities may be mentioned; FAO's *Coconut Situation,* the *International Tea Committee Monthly,* the *Cotton Monthly* of the International Cotton Advisory Committee, the *International Rubber Digest* of the IRSG, the *World Wool Digest* of the International Wool Secretariat, *Notes on Tin* from the Tin Council and the *World Wheat Situation* from the Wheat Council.

Problems of Developing Countries

That the understanding of the commodity trade problems of developing countries owes a great deal to Raul Prebisch and Hans Singer has been emphasised in the text. The main papers have been referred to in note 1 to Chapter 4 on page 111. Prebisch's *The Economic Development of Latin America and its Principal Problems* in the American Economic Review (1949-50) and his report to UNCTAD II, *Towards a Global Strategy for Development,* are two other important works. One of the essays in honour of Prebisch, in Luis Eugenio Di Marco (ed.), *International Economics and Development; Essays in Honour of Raul Prebisch* (New York, Academic Press, 1972), contains a clear account of his contributions to political economy.

Two other books which are specially illuminating are Arghiri Emmanuel, *A Study of the Imperialism of Trade* (The Monthly Review Press, New York, 1972) and George Beckford, Persistent Poverty: *Under-development in Plantation Economies in the Third World* (Oxford University Press, London, 1972). Both these have been referred to extensively in the text.

UNCTAD documents, particularly those prepared for the four conferences (Geneva 1964, New Delhi, 1968, Santiago de Chile 1972 and Nairobi 1976) are the best sources of analytical and descriptive material specifically oriented towards the problems of poor nations. Special mention may be made of the following: J.E. Meade, *International Commodity Agreements* and 't Hooft-Velvaars, *The Organization of International Markets for Primary Commodities*, both in volume III of the Proceedings of the first Conference. The Reports by the Secretariat to the third Conference in Volume II of the Proceedings of that Conference and the set of papers on the Integrated Programme (documented in the notes to chapter 13 on pages 313-15) provide valuable recent data.

The following books on the problems of development are also of interest: Harry G. Johnson, *Economic Policies towards Less-developed Countries* (Praeger, New York, 1976) and *United States Policies towards Less-developed Countries* (Brookings Institution, 1967). Roy Harrod and Douglas Hague, *International Trade Theory in a Developing World* (Macmillan, London, 1964); and Gunnar Myrdal, *Economic Theory and Under-Developed Regions* (Methuen, London, 1957).

The International Economic System

The framework suggested by Bergsten, Keohane and Nye is used in this book for analysing commodity conflicts in the systemic context. Repetition of this author's gratitude to these three, as well as to Lawrence Krause and Carlos Diaz-Alejandro, is not superfluous. All those interested in the analysis of the politico-economic system will find the issue of *International Organization,* Volume 29, Winter 1975, a valuable source. Benjamin Cohen's *Imperialism: the Political Economy of Dominance and Dependence* (Basic Books, New York, 1973) is also necessary reading for understanding perceptions and motivations.

The evolution of the post-war economic system has been described in R.N. Gardner, *Sterling-Dollar Diplomacy* (Oxford, Clarendon Press, 1956); W.A. Brown Jr., *The United States and the Restoration of World Trade* (Brookings Institution, 1950) and C. Wilcox, *A Charter for World Trade* (Macmillan, London, 1949). The evolution of the system in the 1960s is well documented in the two volumes, *International Economic Relations of the Western World 1959-1971,* edited by Andrew Shonfield (Oxford University Press, London, 1976). The contribution by Gerard and Victoria Curzon to Volume I has been referred to repeatedly in chapter 14 of this book. 'Western Trade in Agricultural Products' by T.K. Warley, also in Volume I, is also relevant to many of the topics discussed. Gerard Curzon's *Multilateral Commercial Diplomacy* (Michael Joseph, London, 1965) is required reading on GATT, in addition to Kenneth Dam's *The GATT: Law and International Economic Organization* (The University of Chicago Press, Chicago, 1970). The material available on the EEC, particularly the CAP and the Community's enlargement, is quite large. Since only the Community's external policy towards the developing countries has been emphasised in this book, it is unnecessary to list the detailed bibliography on the other aspects. However, mention has to be made of Michael Butterwick and E.N. Rolfe, *Food, Farming and the Common Market* (Oxford University Press, London, 1968).

Instability and Terms of Trade

A list of articles relevant to instability and economic development is given in Commonwealth Economic Paper no.4, *Terms of Trade Policy for Primary Commodities* (Commonwealth Secretariat, London, 1976). A basic work on the subject is, of course, Alasdair Macbean's *Export Instability and Economic Development* (Harvard University Press, Cambridge, Mass., 1960). The UNCTAD paper TD/B/503/Supp.1, *The Indexation of Prices,* lists all earlier studies relating to the concept of protection of import purchasing power of primary producing countries. As mentioned in the text, the controversies over whether the terms of trade of the poor countries are deteriorating and, if they do, whether commodity agreements are a means of correcting this trend, are unending. Three publications by J.A. Pincus are of interest: *Commodity Agreements – Bonanza or Illusion?* (The Rand Corporation, Washington DC, 1967); *Economic Aid and International Cost Sharing* (Johns Hopkins University Press, 1967) and *Trade, Aid and Development* (McGraw-Hill, New York, 1967). Also relevant is Thomas Morrison and Lorenzo Perez, *Export Earnings, Fluctuations and Economic Development* (AID Discussion Paper no.32, 1975).

Market Control and Market Power

Some publications on the bogey of developing countries' 'producer power' have been noted in the text. Some others of interest in this context are: Hugh Corbet, *Raw Materials: Beyond the Rhetoric of Commodity Power* (Trade Policy Research Centre, London, 1975); and *The Potential for Commodity Cartels* (Economist Intelligence Unit, London, 1975). The question has been discussed at length in a number of issues of *Foreign Policy* – 11, 1973, and 14, 1974 – and also in *Foreign Affairs.*

Works on the operation of multinational corporations are by now quite extensive. The starting point can only be Raymond Vernon, *Sovereignty at Bay: The Multinational Spread of U.S. Enterprises* (Basic Books, New York, 1971). For an economic analysis of the efficiency of control mechanisms see C.P. Brown, *Commodity Control* (Oxford University Press, Kuala Lumpur, 1975).

International Commodity Agreements

In addition to J.W.F. Rowe's two books – *Markets and Men* (Cambridge University Press, Cambridge, 1936) and *Primary Commodities in International Trade* (Cambridge University Press, Cambridge, 1965) – others dealing with international commodity agreements in general are: Sir Sydney Caine, *Prices for Primary Products* (Hobart Paper no.24, Institute of Economic Affairs, London); and W.L. Haviland, *International Commodity Agreements* (Private Planning Association, Montreal, 1963). Gerda Blau's *International Commodity Agreements and Policies* (FAO *Monthly Bulletin of Agricultural Economics,* 12, 1963, nos. 9 and 12) is an important work on the subject. So are the two symposia *The Quest for a Stabilization Policy in Primary Products* and *Stabilization and Development of Primary Producing Countries,* edited by Ragnar Nurkse and Hans Singer respectively, both in *Kyklos (The International Review for Social Sciences),* 11, 1958, no.2 and 12, 1959, no.3. The study made by IMF and IBRD together, at the instance of UNCTAD, *The Problem of Stabilization of Primary Products* (1968) is also important.

For brief but useful summaries of the past history of all international commodity agreements see *International Commodity Agreements; a Report by the US International Trade Commission,* Washington DC, 1975. *World Economic Interdependence and Trade in Commodities,* a report presented to the UK Parliament (HMSO, London, Cmnd. 6061, 1975) and the Commonwealth Economic Paper no.4, *Terms of Trade Policy for Primary Commodities* (see above) both provide useful summary data on commodities and agreements.

Individual Commodities

It is not the intention to list here all the articles and books that have appeared on the different commodities. In the light of the comment made earlier on the paucity of material on commodities relevant to developing countries, the brief listing below only highlights some. The articles and notes in the *Journal of World Trade Law,* cited in note 4 to chapter 2 on page 51, will not be repeated here.

UNCTAD has produced two series of Reports on individual commodities. The series *Report on the Problems of the World Market for...* (TD/B/88, 104, 105, 107, etc.) covers products such as phosphates, manganese ore, iron ore and rice. The UNCTAD Permanent Group on Synthetics has produced a series *Review of Problems and Policies for Specific Commodities Facing Competition from Synthetics and Substitutes* (TD/B/C.1/Syn 39, 40, 41, 42, 43, 49, 50 and 51) on rubber, cotton, shellac, hides and skins, jute, hard fibres, oilseeds, etc.

Coffee: a good bibliography of material on coffee appears in Bart Fisher, *The International Coffee Agreement: A Study in Coffee Diplomacy* (Praeger, New York, 1972). See also Paul Streeten and Diane Elson, *Diversification and Development: the Case of Coffee* (Praeger, New York, 1971); V.D. Wickizer, *The World Coffee Economy with Special Reference to Control Schemes* (Stanford University Press, Stanford, 1942) and J.W.F. Rowe, *The World's Coffee* (HMSO, London, 1963). Since there are few articles on the influence of transnational actors on commodity negotiations, particular mention must be made of Stephen Krasner, 'Business-Government Relations: The Case of the International Coffee Agreement, *International Organizations,* 27, 1973, pp.495-516.

Cocoa: T.A. Kofi, 'International Commodity Agreements and Export Earnings: Simulation of the 1968 "Draft" International Cocoa Agreement', *Food Research Institute Studies,* 11, 1972, no.2.

Tea: Goutam Sarkar, *The World Tea Economy* (Oxford University Press, London, 1972); H. Roy, 'Some Observations on a New International Tea Agreement', *Economic Affairs* 17, 1972, no.8; Manmohan Singh, 'The Economics of an International Tea Agreement: A Study of Some Aspects of Stabilization of Commodity Prices', *Indian Economic Journal,* 4, 1970, no.4.

Grains: *The Stabilization of International Trade in Grains* (FAO Commodity Policy Studies no.20, 1970); this contains, in addition to valuable material on trade in grains, an excellent table comparing the provisions of the various Wheat Agreements. Also of interest are two further FAO studies: *The Stabilization of World Trade in Coarse Grains* (no.14, 1963) and *The International Effects of National Grain Policies* (no.8, 1955).

Wheat: *A Reconsideration of the Economics of International Wheat Agreement, 1952* (FAO Commodity Policy Studies no.1); D.R. Olson, 'Wheat Symposium: International Marketing of Wheat', *Canadian Journal of Agricultural Economics,* 18, 1970, no.3.

Rice: D. Ridler and C.A. Yandle, *Changes in Patterns and Policies in the International Trade in Rice,* IMF Staff Papers, 1972; *The Stabilization of the International Trade in Rice* (FAO Commodity Policy Studies no.7, 1955).

Wine: The World Wine Trade and Vine Products Economy (FAO Commodity Bulletin Series no.3).

Oils and fats: Asian and Pacific Coconut Community, *Quarterly Bulletin.*

Rubber: Sir Andrew MacFadyean (ed.), *The International Rubber Regulation Committee: The History of Rubber Regulation 1934-1943* (Allen and Unwin, London, 1944); *A Review of the Prospects for Natural, Synthetic and Reclaimed Rubber,* Special Papers presented to the 17th meeting of the IRSG, Tokyo 1964.

Jute: *Jute and the Synthetics* (IBRD Staff Working Paper, no.171, 1974); *The World Jute Economy* (IBRD Report no.114a-BD, 1973).

Petroleum: What with OPEC and the multinational oil companies, the material available, ranging from the sensational to the academic, is voluminous. A few are: Fuad Rouhani, *A History of OPEC* (Praeger, New York, 1971); Zuhayr Mikdashi, *The Community of Oil Exporting Countries* (Allen and Unwin, London, 1972); Michael Tanzer, *The Political Economy of International Oil and the Underdeveloped Countries* (The Beacon Press, Boston, Mass., 1969); M.A. Adelman, *The World Petroleum Market* (Johns Hopkins University Press, 1972).

Iron ore: *The Economic Aspects of Iron Ore Preparation* (UN, ECE, ST/ECE/Steel/14, 1966); *The Maritime Transport of Iron Ore* (UNCTAD, 1975); *Survey of World Iron Ore Resources* (UN, 1970); *The World Market for Iron Ore* (UN, 1968); *The International Market for Iron Ore: Review and Outlook* (IBRD, Staff Working Paper no.160, 1973); also see *Reports of Annual Conferences,* International Iron and Steel Institute.

Copper: It is unnecessary to list the references since CIPEC periodically publishes a bibliography of all material relevant to this metal.

Tin: Apart from William Fox, *Tin: The Working of a Commodity Agreement* (Mining Journal Books Ltd., London, 1974), an invaluable source book is Yip Yat Hoong, *The Development of the Tin Mining Industry in Malaya* (The University of Malaya Press, Kuala Lumpur, 1969). Notwithstanding its title, the book covers comprehensively all aspects of tin mining, trade and international control. Also see C.D. Rogers, 'Consumer Participation in the International Tin Agreement', *Malayan Economic Review* 14, 1969, no.2 and W. Robertson, 'The Tin Experiment in Commodity Market Stabilization', *Oxford Economic*

Papers, 12, 1960, no.3.

Texts of Resolutions, Agreements, etc.

The UN Resolutions on the New International Economic Order and its related Charter of Economic Rights and Duties of States are readily available in UN documents; so are the resolutions, Final Acts, Reports of Committees etc. of UNCTAD Conferences. GATT publishes a Basic Documents series. Most of the texts of International Commodity Agreements are available in the Treaty Series of HMSO. The main ones are: International Wheat Agreements 1948, 1949, 1953, 1959, 1962 and 1971; International Grains Arrangement 1967; International Sugar Agreements 1953, 1958, 1968; International Coffee Agreements 1962, 1968, 1976; International Olive Oil Agreements 1959, 1963, 1969, 1973; International Tin Agreements 1931, 1934,, 1937, 1942, 1956, 1961, 1966, 1971, 1976; International Cocoa Agreements 1972 and 1976.

In view of the vast amount of material available, no doubt many excellent works have been left out in this brief survey. The apologies of this author are due to all those whose works ought to have been mentioned.

INDEX